The Awakening of Navi Septa

Book Three

The Swarm of Bees

By Linda Williams

CheckPoint
Press

THE AWAKENING OF NAVI SEPTA
BOOK THREE: THE SWARM OF BEES

ISBN-13: 978-1-906628-33-8

PUBLISHED BY CHECKPOINT PRESS, IRELAND

CheckPoint Press
Books With Something to Say..

CHECKPOINT PRESS
DOOAGH
ACHILL ISLAND
WESTPORT
CO. MAYO
REP. OF IRELAND

WWW.CHECKPOINTPRESS.COM

The Awakening of Navi Septa

Book Three

The Swarm of Bees

A Fantasy of Reality

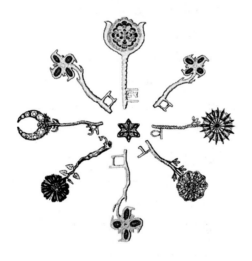

by Linda Williams

This book is dedicated to all seekers of truth,
and to those who have already found what they were seeking.

CONTENTS

Part One - Return to Teletsia

Part Two - Infiltration

Some characters in this book
  Indicates characters we have met in the earlier books

The seven young people of the prophecy
*Raynor Antiquarian
*Tandi Riverside, Raynor's wife
*Asha Herbhealer, married to Robin Markand
*Derwin Herbhealer, Asha's brother
*Conwenna Prospector
*Lee Restorer, Asha's cousin
*Ahren Dairyman

Helpers from the north
*Robin Markand: partisan from Chussan
*Prince Roarke of Vittalia
*King Rajay of Daish Shaktay
*Namoh Hillfarmer: Rajay's friend
*Valya Northwestern: Rajay's friend
*Bonor: Rajay's bodyguard
*Hampen the Tong: naval captain
*Zafan and Dan: sometime pirates and now naval captains
*Merien: son of the Prime Minister to the Emperor of the Ocean

People on the Island of Creations
*Lord Jarwhen
*Lady Mercola: his wife
*Pa Ganoozal: Lord Jarwhen's right hand man
*Ma Ganoozal: his wife

The Teletsians
Lord Coban: the Pearl Lord of Teletsia
*Stellamar: his daughter
*Kitab Antiquarian and Mrs Antiquarian: Raynor's parents
Berny Restorer and *Mrs Restorer: Lee's parents
Mr and *Mrs Herbhealer: Asha and Derwin's parents
*Mr Prospector: Conwenna's father
*Drusilla Prospector: Conwenna's aunt
Wale Fisher and Mrs Fisher: working for the Restorers
Saman and Freddi: failed assassins
Euclip, Rollo, Chariss and Munnir: freed slaves
Mr and *Mrs Riverside and *Gwant and *Mabron: Tandi's family
*Mr and Mrs Dairyman: Ahren's parents
Erin Heber: Duke of Castle Mount
Resistance Group members: the Dyeman family, Fern Innkeeper, Coffius
Coffeeman, Mr, Mrs and Zoey Herder, Sparkly and Borry Diamondcutter,
The Woodseller family, Pat Foodman and Pastow
Professor, Garma and Saray Nalanda from Gyan-on-Sea University
General Woodenton: General, Teletsian army
*Some of the Head Sorcerers: His Supreme Lordship, Head of the Special
Secret Police, Head of the Intelligence Service, Master of Annihilations,
Master of the Spy Birds, Chief Priest for War and Weaponry, et cetera

PROLOGUE

Over five years ago, my younger brother Derwin, my cousin Lee, myself and four other young people – Raynor, Tandi, Ahren and Conwenna, from the country of Teletsia, were chased off to the north of our world on what most sensible people would have called an insane, unachievable journey. Maybe they were right, but sane people are not always the ones to listen to. Hounded by the Sorcerers who ruled Teletsia and wanted us back, dead or alive, we finally made it to our goal, the hidden kingdom of Sasrar. We had a lot of help, without which we would never have even got out of Teletsia, let alone to Sasrar. In this elusively ordinary country we learnt many things, the most valuable being of a subtle, powerful and spiritual nature.

Two years later, Lee, his friend Ahren and I went south to the country of Daish Shaktay, where we helped put the rightful heir, Rajay Ghiry, on the throne. He was, to begin with, a partisan and we joined forces. The boys did the sort of things brave freedom fighters do, while my role was to give inner spiritual awakening.

One of the people in this part of the saga was Robin Markand, from Chussan City, south of Sasrar. He guided us across the desert in the southeast of Chussan so we could find Rajay Ghiry in the first place, and risked his life in doing so, because he was an outlaw at the time. Robin and I met up again in Daish Shaktay, as he played a key role in the war there, and to my surprise he asked me to become his wife, which I naturally did.

Chussan was then governed by a nasty collaboration between the priests, who dominated peoples' minds, and two ruthless brothers, Shaitan and Kaitan, who controlled them politically. Robin, and Lord Albion, the rightful ruler who was then in hiding, made Chussan ungovernable. They and others gave inner awakening to many people there and as a result the predominantly sensible folk of Chussan realised their religion was a con trick and even felt quite ill when they went to the temples. Plus these people did not suddenly have a whole host of problems, as the priests threatened they would, if they stopped bowing down to their ritualistic mumbo-jumbo, and no longer gave these priests a hefty portion of their wages. People were no longer completely addicted to strong drink, because as their awaked subtle systems became more sensitive they no longer desired alcohol. The numerous drink shops lost customers and money, but more so the priests did, because they had the monopoly on growing and distilling it. The economy was in free fall because it relied on taxes from alcohol and money donated to the temples.

All over the country people demanded change. Lamech, the headman of a nomad tribe, raised an army and prepared to march on Chussan City, but Albion asked him and the other groups of Robin's resistance network to wait until the rotten, overripe fruit of the regime was ready to fall; only then would he allow the possibility of war. One summer's day the flying horses took Albion and Robin, along with Raynor and Ahren, to Lamech's army on the plains. Once those animals put their feet on the land of lower Chussan events moved fast, because the horses embodied the power of positive destruction and wherever they put their feet they set this off. In Chussan the flying horses had a good effect on the minds of the people, possibly because this was the country that corresponded to the sixth subtle centre, within us in the brain. By the time Lamech, Albion and the cavalry closed in on Chussan City, the rulers had fled.

The Chussan army and police hadn't been paid for months so lacked enthusiasm to defend the capital and the majority deserted by the time Albion reached town. The rest surrendered and Albion pardoned everyone who had been a part of the former regime provided they admitted their crimes and asked for forgiveness from the families of their victims. Albion emphasised the power of forgiveness as the way forward and many people did nobly forgive those who had given them much grief. Albion offered Robin an important position in the new government, but he said he had other things to do.

'My wife is from Teletsia,' he explained, 'and those people are still groaning in pain from their evil rulers. Now Chussan is free, it's time to go there.'

As in the other two books of this trilogy, I, Asha, am the narrator.

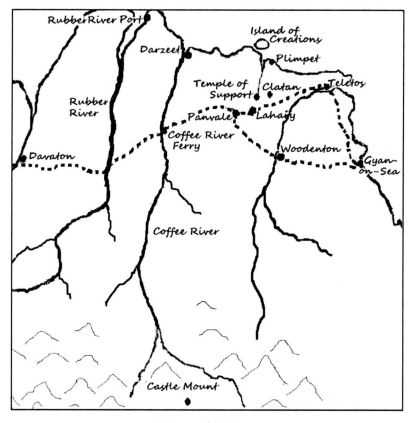

A Map of Teletsia

PART ONE

RETURN TO TELETSIA

CHAPTER 1

THE JEWEL MERCHANT

Robin Markand, alias Ron Jeweller, arrived in the city of Teletos on a Daish Shaktay warship, the *Queen Zulani*. It was a stately galleon with three masts, many sails and a line of cannons on each side. It was the first ship to visit Teletsia from Daish Shaktay since Rajay Ghiry had become king, because until now he had discouraged contact with this inauspicious country.

Teletos, the capital, was built on a number of islands in the estuary of a river, and Robin landed unobtrusively and disappeared into the business quarter, leaving Namoh Hillfarmer, now Lord Santara, to attract attention. Namoh announced he was from King Rajay, on an official mission to buy guns, as Teletsia had the best cannon foundries. With him was Valya, Lord Northwestern, who had come to iron out a few diplomatic problems. These were not the main reasons for the voyage. Robin was, and the other two were just to detract from that.

Robin was finding Teletos uncomfortable. The climate was hot and the vibrations were dire. He had a small lime in his pocket, to absorb some of the subtle heat and pervasive evil, but it didn't do much good, like trying to keep warm in a blizzard with a candle. Except this was the reverse and his body reacted to this ill-fated land by becoming hot and sweaty, in an attempt to throw off the disturbing negativity permeating the place. Robin had put a darkening juice on his face and hands and had dyed his hair black. He was tall and broad shouldered, like many northerners; his features were regular and his eyes brown, nevertheless his disguise wasn't too bad. It wouldn't do if people immediately recognised him as coming from Chussan or Sasrar, because the High Priests, commonly known as Sorcerers, who ruled Teletsia, knew their prophesied downfall had a lot to do with these countries. Robin spent the morning setting up his 'cover'. He deposited his jewels in a reliable bank, made contact with some reputable jewellers, found a good hotel for him and his bodyguard, and they both had lunch. After this he put his feet up for a rest and considered the events that had led up to this moment.

3

The plan had been worked out in Chussan City the previous autumn, when, a few months before, Rajay and some of his friends went there for Albion's coronation. Prince Roarke of Vittalia had brought them up in his flying ship; he had done major modifications on it so it would now go to other countries. It had something to do with the fact that since so many people now had awakened Trees of Life, it was possible to draw on the energy of Mother Earth and Father Sky in a different way.

The day after the coronation Robin and I, Asha, had invited Rajay and the others from Daish Shaktay out for a meal at the best restaurant in town, run by an ex-partisan friend of Robin's. We walked through the streets of the city from the palace, which was set in large grounds. Albion had insisted on some bodyguards accompanying us, but as we strolled along the broad avenues of the city centre we felt safe, because most people recognised us and knew who our guests were.

The locals stood aside for us, greeted us respectfully and many even cheered us, because Robin was famous now, and very popular, and many folk of Chussan knew the stories about Rajay, the brave and gallant young king of Daish Shaktay. We stopped to say a few words to people we knew personally, soon turned up a side street and entered the restaurant, on the ground floor of an old townhouse, at the back of the central courtyard. We sat at a large table that Robin's friend had specially prepared – a crisp white tablecloth, bunches of flowers and the best china – and the table was near the open doors onto the garden, behind which were the high wooded hills that surrounded the city. Rajay asked Robin and me to sit next to him.

'So, Asha, how's life in the mountains?' he began, because we had been living in a cottage near the three astrologers, in the village of Upper Dean.

'Quite a change from Malak Citadel!' I laughed. 'I spent last winter trying to keep warm and helping to reprint the original version of the holy book of Chussan, written by their prophet, who was a simple potter.'

'Tell me more.'

'I worked with a man who has a printing press in the village. He's also a bookbinder and we got a lot of books ready to send down to the plains. Albion has no desire to destroy the religion of Chussan; he just wants everyone to get it right. The priests had changed it so much in order to mesmerise and frighten people so they could dominate them, and make money out of them.

'Anyway, one day I was in the astrologers' library, an enormous room lined from floor to ceiling with books, and was at the shelf where we kept the original of the potter's book. I noticed a small, leather bound volume with the words *Teletsian Prophecy (Chussan version)* embossed on the spine in gold letters. It was in our Chussan dialect, so I took it home to read because the library was freezing. Later Albion came to supper with us, as he often did. He explained that the potter who wrote the sacred book of Chussan, which we were reprinting, and the author of the Teletsian prophecy were the same person. When he'd written the prophecy, he had to leave Teletsia and went to live in Chussan. He worked as a potter to disguise his identity, because he was a learned man and a guardian. In the version of the Teletsian prophecy at the astrologer's house there's a very interesting section called *The Swarm of Bees*.

'It tells how once the world was nearly destroyed by a terrible devil who had a special power: he couldn't be killed by anything on two or four legs. So the Creator made a swarm of bees and told them to go and sting him. They did and the devil died, because there were thousands of them and they had six legs. The bees were reborn again and again, evolving through all the levels of creation. It was foretold that these bees, now people, would search for and find some higher knowledge. Like bees, which are collectively aware of their queen and operate almost like one organism, these people would have one overwhelmingly strong desire – to put the world right when the outlook again looked bad. Maybe we from Teletsia and people like your friends are those same souls.'

'Could be. It's cool on my hands when you say that and the vibrations are flowing strongly,' Rajay replied. 'Any attempt to liberate Teletsia certainly will have to be a group effort; there's no way you seven Teletsians and Robin could do it alone, but we must try something. If the country which corresponds to the first centre of the earth's Tree of Life is not alright, the whole world will suffer.....'

Robin recalled what had happened next in the restaurant. He had heard children's voices and turned to see Raynor's young wife Tandi come through the door. She had five children with her – her twin girls, another small girl and two boys, Robin's sister's children. Tandi saw us with Rajay, smiled, greeted him respectfully and made for a table in the further corner, but the boys had other ideas and ran over to us before she could stop them.

'Hello Uncle Robin! Aunt Tandi is taking us out for a treat!' said Falcon, the elder one.

'That's nice. Go and sit down over there with her. This is Uncle Rajay and we're talking about something important and grown up,' Robin tried to be the authoritative uncle. The boys did not take the hint, and were not going to be put off.

'Wow! Some of Uncle Robin's best bedtime stories are about you!' Falcon went on. His younger brother Eagle just stared shyly, one hand to his mouth, delighted to be so close to his idol but not sure how he was supposed to behave in front of him.

'Sit here with us, all of you,' insisted Rajay.

'Do you know what you're in for?' I ventured.

'I've got to get used to it! I'm a father now, as of last month.' Rajay's wife, Queen Zulani had recently had a son. 'I've had a fair amount of experience in matters of warfare, state and diplomacy, but kids – I'm not so sure of myself there.'

Some time and a number of cakes and frothy milk drinks later, Tandi had been introduced to the visitors from Daish Shaktay. Somehow we managed to keep the children fairly well behaved and went back to the original conversation while they tucked in.

'What brings you to Chussan, Witten?' asked Robin.

'King Albion invited us to the coronation and,' he paused, 'we have the best jewels on the continent in Daish Shaktay, but Chussan used to have the best cutters and setters. If we can find any of the old craftsmen, we could set up some joint trade, to the benefit of both countries.'

'My father has some friends in that business…..'

They talked on, and Witten took a leather pouch out of his pocket, and tipped some stunning uncut stones – diamonds, rubies, sapphires, and also some large pearls, onto the table. The children stared, fascinated, and the two boys, Robin's nephews, stood up to have a closer look. Rajay did not say anything and I could see his attention was elsewhere, possibly on what we had been speaking about earlier. He trusted Witten to look after all the important matters concerning trade and finance in Daish Shaktay – he concentrated on politics and inner subtle wisdom, which for him were intimately connected. He stirred his spiced tea thoughtfully, watching the children as they pored over the priceless jewels.

'What's on your mind?' I asked him, because I knew him well, and was often aware of what his facial expressions meant.

'To cleanse Teletsia, our problem is not only one of power.'

'I don't understand.'

'As I promised, you can have my army and navy and my experience in strategy, if I can come up with anything useful.' This was extraordinarily modest, considering Rajay was one of the most inspired exponents of guerrilla warfare ever. 'I wouldn't lend you my armed forces if it was absolutely hopeless; I'd never send my men to certain death. If it comes to war, it won't be easy though, because the Sorcerers' weapons are better than ours, unfortunately, and their warships more advanced. Also there's some sinister power behind those Sorcerers of Teletsia that we guardians haven't been able to fathom. Nevertheless, there may be ways we can fight them, and you have the flying horses, who'll set off the power of positive destruction if you take them there. We know what they did in Mattanga. Plus with your subtle Sasrar abilities, I doubt the Sorcerers could reduce you to ashes, as they have a habit of doing, I'm told.'

'I hope you're right there.'

'That's not all we'd have to contend with.'

'What else?'

'The Sorcerers have mesmerised and terrified generations of people in Teletsia. As a result, their inner Trees of Life may be so damaged, it might be difficult to awaken them to their own inner joy and peace, and healing powers,' explained Rajay. 'The only way to make them realise they can be free is to give them awakening though, because you can't free people who don't want to be freed. I had the support of nearly everyone in Daish Shaktay, or it would never have worked out.'

Robin joined in our conversation: 'Somehow we're going to have to get into Teletsia secretly and start to awaken people without anyone knowing we're doing it. Then, like here and in Daish Shaktay, the collective awareness will change and everything will improve.'

'But "Who will put the warning bell on the cat?" As the mice said in the children's story,' put in Tandi, while trying, with only limited success, to make the children eat politely, because the wild strawberry tart they were tucking into was too delicious to eat slowly.

'I know,' Falcon piped up.

'Tell me your idea, little one,' Rajay encouraged him.

'See, Uncle Robin is really good at dressing up. My Uncle Robin is a very important freedom fighter. Well he was until we won the war,' said Falcon proudly. 'Whenever he came to see us he looked like someone else. One time he was a shepherd with a beard and another time he was a teacher with a black hat,' Tandi and I looked at each other doubtfully but Rajay indicated to Falcon to go on. 'Sometimes he had grey hair and looked really *old*. If Uncle Witten could give Uncle Robin some of his jewels and if Uncle Robin could make his face a bit brown like Aunt Asha's, he could go to this Tel – what's it called?'

'Teletsia,' I helped him.

'OK, Teletsia,' went on Falcon. 'Uncle Robin could go to Teletsia and sell jewels and no one would know he was from here, because we don't have jewels here much and no one in our country has got a brownish face like Aunt Asha's or yours.'

'Young man, you've hit the nail right on the head,' said Rajay.

CHAPTER 2

MAKING CONTACTS

Robin came out of his reverie, slept for a while and when it was cooler, in the late afternoon, he went out to explore Teletos. He had directions to the bookshop owned by Raynor's father, where my mother Mrs Herbhealer worked, and also had the addresses of Raynor's family house, my parents' apartment and my cousin Lee's family home. He decided to start with the bookshop. He took a boat taxi and after being punted up and down a few canals was put off on one of the many landing stages and told how to find the shop, which was nearby. The door pinged as he went in and between the shelves of books, scrolls and manuscripts a middle-aged man was sitting behind a desk. His brow was furrowed and his expression sad.

'Excuse me,' began Robin, 'I was told you specialise in old manuscripts.'

'Yes sir. Is there anything in particular you are looking for?'

'The one I'm interested in is very rare and I need to discuss it with the owner.'

'That's me, Kitab Antiquarian.' Robin recognised the family likeness.

'Are we alone?'

'Yes, my assistant is not here today.'

'I'm looking for a copy of an ancient prophecy. Someone said it was banned, but that you might have one.'

'If it's banned then I wouldn't have it. I wouldn't carry illegal goods.' A flicker of fear crossed Mr Antiquarian's face.

'I come from a land where we are freer, and we know about this prophecy. It tells of a group of young people who travel from here to our part of the world to gain spiritual powers.'

'I don't know what you're talking about.' Mr Antiquarian was increasingly nervous. This was just the way the Sorcerers would try to catch him out. Although this young man looked pleasant enough, he could still be their informer.

'Mr Antiquarian, I have a letter for you. It's from your son, who's a good friend of mine. Raynor is very well, and is now married to Tandi Riverside, from the farm near Clatan. You're a grandfather because they have twin daughters.' He handed over a letter, written in Raynor's distinctive hand. He felt a tremendous constriction in Mr Antiquarian's heart as he recognised the writing.

'There must be some mistake. Both my sons are dead,' he said sadly. He didn't trust this stranger, who began to see what a terrible country this was. Before this, Robin had only felt it inwardly, on his subtle system.

'Well, forgive me for having bothered you, but he definitely described this shop and... I'll leave the letter. Raynor told me tell you your dog, Nog, also survived and escaped with him.' Robin looked pointedly at Mr Antiquarian. 'I'll drop by again before I leave. I'm here on business for a few days.' He realised he was getting nowhere but felt it might be worth mentioning Nog, who had originally been the Antiquarians' lovable but useless watchdog. The Sorcerers would be unlikely to know that. He wanted Mr Antiquarian to read the letter; it might help him to be less suspicious, because there were references in it to incidents only known to Raynor and his father.

'I'll see what I can do, sir. I can't make any promises though. Good morning.'

Robin left the shop and decided to visit Lee's parents. He hailed a mule cab and gave the driver the address. They clopped through the streets, lined with decaying mansions, decorated, if one could use that word, with hideous gargoyles, and the avenues were lined with shady trees, mostly in need of attention. Every now and again they would cross a bridge onto another of the many islands that made up the city and Robin was eventually dropped off outside the large door of an imposing townhouse, almost a palace. He knocked and was let in by a doorkeeper. Inside was a central courtyard and beyond was a larger yard, through some archways opposite the door he had come in by. Round this second yard were a number of outbuildings and behind was a wharf which gave onto one of the canals.

'Mr Restorer is out at work,' explained the doorman. 'Would you like to talk to his wife?'

'Yes please,' said Robin.

'She's with Mr Prospector, one of the tenants, but if you wait I'll tell her there's a visitor. What name shall I give?'

Robin knew Conwenna's father was a prospector and lived there with his sister. Conwenna was the youngest of our group who had escaped from Teletsia to faraway Sasrar. The problem was, before leaving Teletsia, she had discovered he had been forced to spy on us, for the Sorcerers.

'I'll come back later,' he went on. 'I'm here on business and I need to rent an apartment for a short time.'

'The Restorers own quite a few buildings like this, divided into flats.... Oh – there's Mrs Restorer now.'

Lee's mother also had a sad expression but was as bright as her son when she began talking. Robin told her what he needed and she invited him in.

'I'm from Daish Shaktay,' he improvised, when they were sitting comfortably in her living room. 'I'm a jewel merchant and I need somewhere for my bodyguard and myself - a fairly upmarket place, because my clients are from the wealthier classes.'

'We have one or two flats that might suit you. My husband has just finished converting them,' she began, and offered him a cooling drink.

'Interesting, I met a young chap named Restorer from Teletsia some months back. Looked like you in a way. What was his name?' Robin made as if to wrack his brains. 'Lee, Lee Restorer. Any relation of yours?' He looked at Lee's mother. She put her hand in front of her mouth to stifle a cry.

'Did you say Lee? A young man of maybe twenty?'

'That's right. Mrs Restorer, I have a letter for you from your son, now rising high in the service of King Rajay of Daish Shaktay. You can be very proud of him. Here, read this.' With shaking hands she did so, and then looked in wonder at the stranger.

'And – you're Robin?'

'Yes,' he smiled - that gentle, trusting smile I knew so well.

'And my niece Asha? In the letter Lee says you can tell me about her. Is she - still alive?'

'She's my wife.'

Later Lee's father came in and Robin and Mrs Restorer were still talking.

Robin decided it would be better if he didn't take one of their apartments and continued to live in his hotel. He stayed the night with the Restorers and the next morning they went round to the bookshop. When my mother came in to work Lee's father, my uncle, told her the good news.

'Robin, how is Asha?' asked my mother, with tears in her eyes.

'Fine. You'd hardly recognise her. She's become so beautiful – she's not thin and nervous and dreamy any more, and looks so elegant when she dresses up.' Robin was exagerating about me – but then he is my husband.

'I can't believe this! And Derwin?'

'He's fine too, and he's taller than you – he's strong and stockily built, like Lee. He spent some years in Sasrar, but now he's living with a brilliant young man in the land of Vittalia, who's teaching him to design things you couldn't even imagine – like flying machines, amazing stuff!' Robin paused. He wanted to awaken these people's Trees of Life. That's what he'd come for. 'I don't know how much you know about your prophecy, but the whole point of the young people going to the far northern country of Sasrar was so they could gain spiritual powers to help put this place right.' Everyone was silent and Robin wondered if he had gone too fast. Maybe they were just nervous. It was such an appalling country, with informers and spies everywhere.

'I've been blessed with subtle wisdom, which is why I can judge, quite accurately, whether it's safe to talk openly to you. The powers we learn about in the secret northern country of Sasrar, which is mentioned in your prophecy, are entirely benevolent and I've come here to share them with you. Mr Antiquarian, it was through your son's bravery, helped by Lee and the others, that Asha was able to reach my country of Chussan, near Sasrar. I'd like to give you the most important gift anyone can bestow. If Asha and the others were here, it would be their greatest desire to give this to all of you.'

Robin was shown into a shady back yard with a tall tree in the corner. They sat on the paving stones and he asked them to put their left hand out, palm upward and their right hand on the ground. He told them to request the earth to absorb the negativity of the Sorcerers of Teletsia that was affecting them. He knew some of the more traditional families in this country worshipped the all-pervading power in the form of the Mother Earth, so this made sense to the present company.

'Ask the all-pervading power to awaken your inner Tree of Life,' continued Robin. 'Then you'll become aware of the joy within.' He was quiet for some moments. He put his attention on each person in turn and eased the blocks within their subtle systems. Soon he felt a lightening, a release.

'Put your right hand on your heart and ask, "Am I pure spirit?" Then put it on the top of your head and ask, "Please, all-pervading, compassionate Mother of Creation, awaken my spirit." Now, everyone, put your left hand outwards and your right hand just above your head. Do any of you feel a coolness, or perhaps a warm wind flowing?'

To begin with no one felt anything. Robin knew the strain on the subtle system of living in Teletsia was considerable and would dull their ability to feel the cool vibrations, or even heat, which indicated the subtle system was throwing off impurity. He stood behind my mother and circled his right hand clockwise above her head a few times.

'I feel a breeze flowing above my head!' she said.

'Yes, I do too,' agreed Lee's mother, Mrs Restorer.

'That's the sign that your inner Tree of Life is awakened.'

'The Sorcerers told us that a feeling of heat was a sign of spiritual power,' said Mr Restorer, 'so one can safely assume that's not true.'

'You're right,' added Robin. 'Heat implies friction and some problem, whereas when the subtle power awakens it flows without impediment, so it's cool. The temperature of the spirit is very cold - completely still and orderly, but is the source of all movement.'

He showed them how to sit quietly with their attention on the top of their heads in order to feel peace and joy and inner thoughtless bliss. Then he told them how they could reawaken the connection with this power, this inner state, any time they wanted, by raising their hands up from in front of the base of their abdomen to above the head, and by moving their hands around their body in an arch they could protect themselves from subtle negativity such as the Sorcerers emitted. My mother sent out for some refreshing sherbet drink and they all sat in the yard and enjoyed it, but Mr Antiquarian was uneasy.

'Mr Antiquarian, why don't you trust me?' pleaded Robin. 'I've just risked my life by showing you the first of the powers that will eventually finish the Sorcerers off. If they knew I'd done this, I'd be found dead in one of your canals almost immediately.'

'With respect, how do we know you're not a clever agent of the Sorcerers?' he objected.

'I'm about to show you how to use this awareness to know right from wrong or truth from falsehood and how to resist the Sorcerers' influence over your minds. If I were the Sorcerers' spy, I might put something over you, show you some magic, or hypnotise you, but I wouldn't strengthen your free will and ability to resist them. Now your Tree of Life is awake, you can ask any question you like, or put your attention on any person or situation. If you feel cool breeze on your hands as you do so, you know it or they are in tune with the all powerful and benevolent force of the divine. If something is wrong or someone is evil you'll feel heat on the palms of your hands and tingling on your fingers. Would I tell you that if I worked for the Sorcerers?'

'I apologise, Robin.'

'There's more to show you, but we must be careful. The Sorcerers will soon suspect something, because you're the parents of the young people of the prophecy. My true identity must remain a secret. For the time being I'm Ron Jeweller from Daish Shaktay.'

Robin spent the day with our parents and stayed the night with my mother. My father was away on business; he was a medicinal herb dealer and often out of town. Our flat was not large and Robin was shown into my bedroom. He noticed that my mother had never cleared out my things, even after nearly six years, because she had always had a tiny ray of hope that I would reappear. He asked for a bucket half full of water with some salt in it and soaked his feet in the salty water to draw out some of the darkness of Teletos: the subtle, inner darkness that had eaten into everyone's hearts and minds. After some time he threw the water down the drain and felt better. My mother cooked a tasty meal for Robin and she admitted that she had been having dreams that someone would soon come with news of Derwin and me.

'You're my son too now,' she said. 'I wish I could give you some nice gift, but the Sorcerers make our lives very hard.'

'You've already given me Asha, that's the greatest gift I could ever have. She'll come back soon, but first there's much to be done, and you can help us.'

'You must be so careful what you say. They could even be listening even now.'

'It's all right, in a place like this I check out everything I say on the vibrations. I've been a freedom fighter, and if you get that wrong you don't live to tell the tale. I'm only posing as a jewel dealer. Asha and I have more important things to do with our lives than to spend them getting rich. We have everything we need: a little house in the city and a cottage in the mountains of Chussan, and that's plenty for us.' He did not mention that the house was in the garden of King Albion's palace, a gift from him at the time of his coronation. My mother was increasingly impressed by this courteous young man and delighted that I had such a good husband, but could not help being nervous; in Teletsia people like Robin never escaped the net of the Sorcerers or their Special Secret Police, the Specials, for very long.

'How can I be of help?'

'We need to get into Teletsia and awaken the Trees of Life of large numbers of people and teach them to use their inner powers. Then the collective vibrations of the country will change and the power of the Sorcerers will diminish. We're going to have to do this secretly, because the Sorcerers will do their best to stop us. They know the prophecy too. I, and the seven young people from Teletsia, from Raynor down to Conwenna, have very influential friends these days. We're being lent an army and a navy, as well as other weapons. However, we must first try to free the people here from the influence the Sorcerers have over them. We have to transform your people from within, not destroy them.'

'Raynor's father has a clandestine society of people who are doing research on the prophecy and my brother and sister-in-law, Lee's parents, also have many friends who are trustworthy. But seriously Robin, you might be best to go home to Asha and forget us. These Sorcerers are just too powerful.'

'We're *not* going to leave you to suffer. Your daughter made a vow to try to help this country, and for the last five years her whole life has been a preparation for that, and she's my wife, so I'll support her. In fact that was why she agreed to marry me, because I promised to help her. The power of the vibrations is the strongest force in the universe and we can call on it for help. Another thing, I don't want you to be short of money any more.' Robin handed her a small leather bag with a drawstring tie. My mother opened it and it was full of rubies, sapphires and diamonds. 'There are plenty more where they came from.'

These were from our friend Rajay, who had told Robin to make sure our families were comfortably off from now on. Daish Shaktay was rich, and getting richer by the day, partly because as king, Rajay understood that generosity in the right places created blessings for both him and his people.

'You can't do this.'

'Yes I can. It's only natural to look after my family.'

Robin told my mother he would meet her at the bookshop in some days' time, ostensibly to pick up his purchases. She, meanwhile, would put the word around about the real reason for his visit, and they would take it from there.

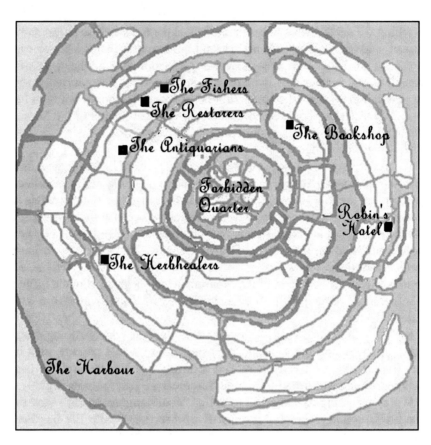

The Fishers

The Restorers

The Bookshop

The Antiquarians

Forbidden
Quarter

Robin's
Hotel

The Herbhealers

The Harbour

Teletos, showing the relevant places

CHAPTER 3

BLINDING LIGHT

Robin returned to his hotel and found his bodyguard Bonor relaxing in their living room, reading. He was short in stature, with close cropped black hair and a medium brown skin, had a fierce expression until he smiled, and was strong and muscular. No one had ever got the better of him in close combat, either with weapons or without.

'Where did you get to? I was expecting you the night before last, but I felt on the vibrations that you were OK,' he said casually. Bonor knew all about the Tree of Life. He was usually Rajay's chief bodyguard.

'I went to see the families and gave them awakening.'

'I assumed you had. I think the Specials might be on to us. There was one here earlier, asking after you.'

'I'll lay a few false trails; some genuine jewel trading. How's Namoh getting on?'

'He says having to deal with the top brass Sorcerers is more painful than his fighting wounds, on a subtle level, and every evening he goes back to the ship feeling nauseous, so has to spend ages clearing his inner Tree of Life of the negativity the Sorcerers emit. He's negotiating to buy guns and spinning it out so as to give you plenty of time. Little do these Sorcerer types suspect that we might use those guns against them one day.'

'Be careful what you say. Walls have ears here. Poor Namoh - rather him than me! What about Valya?'

'He's going through it too. Says these Sorcerers are slimy characters and it's a good thing he can check on vibrations when they're telling lies, which, he says, is almost all the time. He also goes back to the ship at night feeling completely drained. Reckon you've got it easy.'

'So far.'

Two days and quite a few diamond, ruby and sapphire deals later Robin sent Bonor round to the bookshop to see Mr Antiquarian. He told Bonor to bring Robin to his home early the next morning, because there were very few people about then. They set off from their hotel while it was still dark, with a detailed map of Teletos, having left by a servants' entrance. One doubtful looking character tried to follow them but they shook him off after the first mule cab, which dropped them at the fruit and vegetable market, a hive of bustling activity at that hour. They made their way through it, avoiding piles of fruit and vegetables, merchants bargaining with farmers and porters with baskets of produce on their heads, and left by another entrance.

They watched carefully to make sure they were not followed, took three more mule cabs, went a long way round to shake off anyone trailing them and were soon enjoying an early breakfast at the Antiquarians house. Mr Antiquarian had collected together a number of friends who were secretly studying the prophecy and my mother's group consisted of close friends and relations, including the astrologer Mrs Starwise. Robin talked to her as he savoured an aromatic cup of Teletsian coffee.

'Asha told me about you and sends you her best love,' began Robin.

'That's nice of her to remember me. I was worried when they all went off so suddenly - touch and go, that was,' she replied.

'What do your stars tell now?'

'Big changes: war, or maybe inner transformation.'

'Let's hope for the latter, but you've got powerful friends if it has to be war.'

'I've a feeling you know more about life than most people.'

'You're right. I've been blessed in that way.'

'I saw in her stars that if Asha survived the journey north she'd make an excellent marriage and possibly finish up with...' Robin realised she had seen through his best kept secret and indicated with his finger on his lips for her to keep her knowledge to herself.

The Restorer's group included a retired fisherman, Wale Fisher, who offered to ferry Robin around town via the canals. After breakfast the guests gathered round Robin in the part of the garden concealed from prying eyes by high evergreen hedges.

'It's great to meet you all,' he began. 'I know your prophecy says the young people will go to the northern country of Sasrar, gain spiritual powers and then return to overthrow the Sorcerers, but it seems to be working out differently. I'm here in their place to begin with. My wife is Asha and the others are my friends. I've known about these powers since I was a boy and have visited Sasrar many times. Those are my credentials – I hope I pass the test,' Robin paused and an elderly man with white hair came up with tears in his rheumy eyes. He lovingly took Robin's hand in his.

'My son, I never thought I'd live to see this blessed day. We can't thank you enough for risking your life to come and give us what we've been seeking for generations. Before you share this wonderful experience, let's give thanks to our blessed Mother Earth.' Everyone crouched down and put their right hands respectfully on the ground and their left one on their forehead in gratitude. 'And now, show us what you came for.'

'Imagine yeast in bread,' began Robin. 'You don't see it, but it makes the whole loaf rise. It's like that with this new awareness. If a few of you get it, it will affect the whole population, quite spontaneously. The more of you do this and the deeper you go into it, the more powerful this effect will be.'

He gave them their awakening. None of them felt the vibrations straight away, because living in Teletsia had dulled their sensitivity, but their desire to get it and their gratitude to Robin was intense. He and Bonor gave healing vibrations to clear some of the subtle dirt from their Trees of Life, and by the end of the morning most of them had felt something on their hands, all had experienced inner peace and felt a release from the tension and psychological pressure that dominated everyone here. Robin also showed them the bandhans of protection and request, and how to do some of the treatments for clearing their damaged subtle selves, like putting their feet in salty water for a short time each evening and sitting in meditation with some candles at their left side.

He had nearly finished when he felt a constriction in his abdomen. This was the place of the true master, but as he felt discomfort it indicated the opposite, the false teacher. His left thumb began throbbing violently, indicating impure knowledge or sorcery. He looked up and saw some vultures hovering high above the garden. He hid himself under a tree and soon the birds, and the nauseous feeling, went away. He suggested everyone should go indoors and they finished the session in the large hall. Mrs Antiquarian invited Robin and Bonor to stay for lunch after the others had left, and asked for more details about her son Raynor, her grandchildren and the rest of us. Afterwards Wale offered to punt the guests back to their hotel.

'We'll cover you with a tarpaulin so you look like merchandise, if you don't mind,' he suggested. 'There aren't many folk about in the heat of the day so we should be all right.'

'Yes, that's a good idea, but it's not safe to meet here again,' said Robin, 'however, there's one more thing I must show you - the fire ceremony. We need some time together, preferably not on private property, so it won't incriminate anyone if someone sees us who shouldn't. When you've found somewhere, leave a message on our ship, the *Queen Zulani*, with Namoh Hillfarmer or Valya Northwestern.'

Robin and Bonor returned to the hotel without any problem, but that evening a couple of Specials came round to the Antiquarians, demanding the names of the people who had been there that morning. Mrs Antiquarian explained it was their wedding anniversary and they'd had a bit of a do. She apologised for not informing the Specials and offered them some left over celebration cake. She put a gold coin in each of the pieces and they went away after eating the cake and pocketing the coins.

Journal of Warzog, Scribe to the Most High Priests

I, Warzog, scribe to the Lords of Teletsia, do hereby record a special meeting of their Supreme Lordships.

'We must be alert in these uncertain times,' began His Supreme Lordship. 'A spy vulture on a routine flight today came back with some strange information. The Master of the Spy Birds will tell us what happened when he took the spirit out of the bird and made it tell him what it had seen.'

'One of my vultures was hovering over the Antiquarian family's house. It noticed a number of people in the garden and one of them emitted a blinding light - a golden aura. We don't know what this means but we can't be too careful with that family.'

'Let's arrest them. We'd get some sense out of them under torture or by reading their minds,' suggested the Head of the Special Secret Police.

'No,' demanded His Supreme Lordship. 'We'll learn more if we watch them for some time.'

'I don't know if it's connected,' added the Chief Priest for War and Weaponry, 'but I heard something similar yesterday. As you know, there's a Daish Shaktay warship in the harbour. Their Foreign Minister wants to buy back some slaves our slave merchants had captured from there - a few fishermen and artisans. This King Rajay is an odd chap to care about such unimportant people. Secondly, they're negotiating to buy some heavy cannon. Don't worry, I'm only selling them guns we've rejected as unreliable.

'The strange thing is this, the chief Daish Shaktay negotiator for the arms deal is a youngish man who outwardly appears quite normal, but when our Truthsayer went to meet him, he couldn't bear to look at him for long. He too emits a blinding light, but only the most psychically aware High Priests can see this. There was a lesser light coming from Lord Northwestern, the other minister, and even the ordinary sailors have some unseen armour around them. Not only that, the Truthsayer was unable to read their minds.'

'We'll monitor the situation,' ordered His Supreme Lordship. 'I don't trust these Daish Shaktay men. Look what they did to our allies in Mattanga! Total destruction of an entire culture! Make sure a spy vulture follows the Antiquarians, especially if they're involved in any group gathering.'

Two days later, in the early morning, Wale Fisher rowed through the busy harbour to the *Queen Zulani*. He went on board and was shown into the captain's cabin, which Valya and Namoh, now Daish Shaktay ambassadors, shared with Zafan, undercover agent for the Emperor of the Ocean and captain of the ship. They stood up to greet Wale, who was a little taken aback.

'Please sit, Mr Fisher,' began Valya. 'We were waiting for you.'

'Thank you sir, I'll be all right standing,' Wale replied. 'I won't take much of your time. Mr Restorer said to tell you they'll be meeting on an island tomorrow afternoon. I'll take Mr Robin there, because it's some way downriver.'

'Robin feels it would be safer if I came this time,' said Namoh. He had grown and matured in the last couple of years and although still slim had filled out since his partisan days.

'Show it to me on this chart and I'll take Namoh there on one of our launches,' said Zafan. He was tall and heavily built, sported a powerful beard and moustache, but had cut his hair and no longer had a mariner's pigtail.

'As you wish, sir,' said Wale.

'Please sit with us and take some refreshment. In Daish Shaktay we'd never let you leave without having something,' insisted Valya, who, as custom demanded, treated every guest with the same courtesy, regardless of their station in life.

The next day Zafan and Namoh set off looking as if they were going on a picnic, with a hamper of food stowed very visibly in the boat. It contained items for the fire ceremony, hidden under the cold roast chicken, crusty bread and bottles of freshly made lemonade. They also had firewood with them because Namoh didn't want to waste time collecting wood for the ceremonial fire. They sailed down the estuary for some distance then rowed up a smaller river to an island; the same one as where Lee, Raynor and I had made our vow to try to help our country. Here they met the Antiquarians and their friends.

Namoh explained they were going to worship the creator in the form of the fire element, while Zafan prepared it. They would offer various things to the fire, praising this element as the destroyer of negativity and neutralizer of evil forces. Once it was burning merrily, Namoh began saying the qualities of the all pervading power in her form as the Mother Earth. After each name everyone would take a few dried herbs, pieces of scented wood and grains and offer them to the fire. After this was finished, everyone could think of problems and ask the power of the fire to absorb them.

This went on for some time and finally someone said, 'Let the fire destroy that power of the Sorcerers which forces animals and birds to serve them.' At this moment, Namoh felt a constriction in his abdomen and a throbbing on his left thumb. He noticed two vultures flying high above, one wheeled and left and the other swooped down, disorientated.

'Let's say that again,' Namoh requested, and as they did so the second vulture fell into the fire. The smell was awful as it started to burn, so he quickly took it out.

'That wasn't a normal bird,' warned Mr Antiquarian. 'We've been spied on.'

'We've finished now,' said Namoh. 'Let's get out of here.'

Zafan put out the fire, buried the ashes and the remains of the bird and everyone left the island, either walking home via a number of different paths or rowing innocuous pleasure boats down the small river and up the estuary.

Journal of Warzog, Scribe to the Most High Priests

I, Warzog, have this to report concerning another extraordinary meeting of the High Priests.

'What news from those vultures?' asked His Supreme Lordship.

'One returned,' replied the Master of Dead Souls. 'I read its mind and it reported the same light as was seen in the Antiquarians' garden. The other disappeared.'

'It must be the same people,' put in the Head of Psychic Research.

'A Daish Shaktay jewel merchant has been noticed emitting the brightest blinding golden light yet seen. He might be at the bottom of this. Tomorrow, I want some assassins, posing as jewel thieves, to go to his hotel and kill him,' said His Supreme Lordship.

'That man was in his hotel when the vulture saw the light on the island,' noted the Head of the Police.

'I'm sure if we get rid of him this situation will resolve itself. He was absent from his hotel when the first bright light was seen and he might be the one spreading this power. If we do away with him, it will be a warning to the others not to meddle in our country's affairs,' concluded His Supreme Lordship.

Namoh and Zafan returned to the ship and later Valya arrived. He was tall and had a dignified air, and was dressed formally, with a finely embroidered white shirt, a long gold-edged coat and elegant leather boots over silken trousers, so as to impress. After three years of a delightful marriage and with an extremely important position in his country he looked happy and confident, no longer the disowned aristocrat turned partisan.

'So how's the world of diplomacy?' Namoh asked Valya.

'Painful. My Tree of Life is screaming in agony at having to spend so much time with the top Sorcerers, but I've managed to buy back some slaves captured just before Rajay put a stop to all that. It's cost a fortune but it's worth it. I wish we could help the others, taken in earlier times.'

'Once we've freed Teletsia we will.'

'They'll be returned at dawn tomorrow. How did it go on the island?'

'Fine, but something strange happened,' Namoh told him about the vultures.

'It's time we left. We shouldn't push our luck too far.'

'Let's go and get Robin tomorrow morning.'

The next morning Robin was selling jewels in the living room of his hotel suite. Bonor was out of sight in the bedroom, alert and ready for trouble. Robin's first client was a middle-aged woman, who bought three star sapphires and a diamond. He noticed Mrs Antiquarian come in and sit down. While the dowager was counting out her gold coins, Namoh, and Valya, who was now once more able to walk without a limp, came in and sat at the back of the room with Mrs Antiquarian. His friends had swords and Robin knew they would have other weapons as well. However, many well-dressed men wore swords just for show. The dowager left and soon after the door flew open and in rushed three men with stockings over their heads. Two drew knives and the third took out a pistol and pointed it at Robin.

'Give us your jewels!' he demanded. The thugs had not seen Namoh and Valya behind the door. Namoh noticed the first robber had his hand on the trigger, drew a dagger out of his boot and threw it, and it caught the man in the back. He dropped to the floor as his pistol cracked and the bullet somehow caught him in his head as he fell.

Valya pushed Mrs Antiquarian into the bedroom, and Bonor ran in to help drawing his sword. The other two intruders brandished their knives ineffectually. Bonor flipped the weapon of one out his hand, cutting him slightly, and the other knelt on the floor, his hands above his head. Namoh looked at the man he had attacked and what with the knife in his back and his own bullet, he soon breathed his last.

'Are you two working for the Sorcerers?' demanded Valya. 'Or High Priests, if you like it better.' One of the captives tried to run out of the door and Namoh grabbed him.

'Don't kill him too! His vibrations aren't too bad,' cried Robin. He went over to him, put his knife on the thug's neck and continued, 'Are you working for those devils? Or are you armed robbers?'

'Oh, sir, those stinkers sent us to kill you, but now we've failed, they'll kill us!'

'In that case,' went on Robin, removing his knife, 'we may forgive you. Those Sorcerers hypnotise you to do the strangest things.'

'We'll leave you here, trussed up until someone finds you,' said Valya.

'That would be the end for us! Please take us prisoner!'

'That dead one was no friend of ours!' the other spat out, nursing his wounded hand.

'All right,' agreed Robin, 'you can come with us. Bonor, can you bind up his hand?'

'We'll do anything not to have to face the Sorcerers,' begged the first.

'Don't try any tricks on the way back to our ship or we'll kill you,' Valya threatened, and to Robin, 'Namoh and I have finished our business. It's time to go – now!'

'We'll leave by the water gate at the back,' said Robin calmly.

'Our launch is waiting there,' added Valya.

'What about the body?' asked Namoh.

'We'd better put it in the bedroom, and hide that rug – it's covered in blood,' advised Robin. 'Put the clean rug from the bedroom over that bloodstain, then lock the bedroom door and we'll take the key. But hurry.'

Namoh went into the bedroom and told Mrs Antiquarian that someone would contact her group in the next few weeks. They were to give awakening to others but to be careful, as further help was on the way. He warned her about the body, but said on no account to tell anyone and to leave at once. Unfortunately, at that moment a housemaid knocked on the door leading from the passageway.

'Are you all right, Mr Jeweller?' she called nervously. 'I heard a shot.'

'Yes, fine, thanks,' Robin went out. 'I was cleaning my gun and it went off unexpectedly. Take this lady downstairs and see the doorman gets her a mule cab, will you?' He gave the girl a silver piece and packed her and Mrs Antiquarian off.

'That was close,' said Valya, dragging the body into the bedroom and switching the rugs, 'I'm going to check on the women.'

He went along the passage and looked over the banisters, from where he could see Mrs Antiquarian telling the man on the front desk that Mr Jeweller did not want to be disturbed for the rest of the morning. Meanwhile Robin quickly wrote a note for the manager, explaining that the gold he had left in the hotel safe was for his hotel expenses. He didn't say anything about the body, locked the door as they went out, put the 'Don't disturb' sign on it, and the cavalcade left via the back stairs and the servant's entrance.

Wale was waiting at the water gate behind the hotel, as he had brought Mrs Antiquarian in a punt. He showed the Daish Shaktay sailors, in one of the ship's launches, a short cut to the harbour via some narrow canals and some time later the party boarded the *Queen Zulani*. They immediately left the harbour. The current of the river and the wind were with them as they glided down the estuary and away from Teletos. The freed slaves who had joined the ship earlier in the morning were given the best possible treatment and the two failed assassins were locked in the hold.

The hotel maid saw Robin and the others sneak down the back way but didn't stop them; Mr Jeweller tipped well and was a nice young man, and if guests wanted to use the staff exit that was their affair. After they left she went into the room, opened the door with her pass key and saw a bloodstain where Namoh had not quite managed to clear it away. She noticed the bedroom was locked and opened it too, blanched at what she saw, relocked the room, replaced the 'Don't disturb' sign and went off duty at once as it was the end of her shift. The maid who came on next didn't disturb the guests either because of the notice.

The body was only discovered in the evening when some Specials came round to talk to the jewel merchant. Both maids behaved as dumbly as they dared. It was safer that way in Teletos.

Journal of Warzog, Scribe to the Most High Priests of Teletsia

I, Warzog, have this to report concerning another extraordinary meeting of the High Priests.

'What happened to your assassins?' demanded His Supreme Lordship.

'Something went wrong, Your Lordship. One was found murdered in that jewel merchant's hotel room and the other two disappeared, along with the merchant. The Daish Shaktay mission sailed away at the same time,' replied the Head of the Special Secret Police.

'They didn't buy the guns either. I suspect they discovered the ones we were offering were duds. I don't know how, because we tested good ones in front of them,' added the Chief Priest for War and Weaponry.

'In future, we must make sure that the senior priests who can see the blinding light patrol more diligently. Then we can pick out any troublemakers. This light may be connected to a power we cannot control,' continued His Supreme Lordship.

'I'll try and raise a storm to sink their ship,' suggested the Master of Weather Manipulation.

'You'd better, because we must defend the fatherland from these people at all costs,' concluded His Supreme Lordship.

CHAPTER 4

DEBRIEFING FAILED ASSASSINS

The *Queen Zulani* sailed into the open sea, but unfortunately a real grandfather of tempests hit them. The ship was blown way off course, far to the east of the Island of Creations. It should have been an easy trip, but now they were a long way out to sea. Robin, Valya and Namoh, avowed landlubbers, were recovering from the storm and having their first hot meal for three days. They were in Zafan's cabin, which was also his dining room and working space. Down in the hold the failed assassins were suffering horribly from seasickness, but at least it took their minds off their hopeless predicament. By the third day they were feeling better.

'You awake, Freddi?' asked Saman, the other captive. He couldn't see very well in the half darkness of the lockup and was lying in his hammock.

'Yes, and I think the ship has survived the storm. I reckon they'll sell us as slaves, don't you?'

'They may.'

'I pray they don't torture information out of us first,' moaned Freddi, still feeling queasy. 'They didn't look like torturing types, but I've heard awful things about Rajay Ghiry, their king.'

'You've been listening to the Sorcerers' people. I've heard fantastic stories about him, and all his followers too.'

'I hope you're right. I guess this is the end of our researches into the prophecy. It's a pity, because I heard the seven escaped rebels might be coming back soon.'

'I wish we could have contacted that girl who came round and set up our local Resistance Group, and got us going on this prophecy research in the first place.'

'I heard she's from that rich family of pearl dealers, the Pearl Lords, who live up Plimpet way.'

'Let's look on the bright side. We're alive, we're out of Teletsia and from what I've seen of these people, I'd rather be a Daish Shaktay slave than an unwilling assassin, forced to kill for the Sorcerers.' Saman heard footsteps approaching. 'There's someone coming. If they question us, I'm going to tell the truth and I hope it doesn't cost me my life.'

'I agree with you.'

Bonor came into the captain's cabin a little later.

'Is everyone all right?' began Robin.

'We lost a mariner in the storm, washed overboard. He was a friend of mine,' Bonor replied sadly.

'I'm sorry to hear it,' added Valya. 'We must compensate his family.'

'He was a good man and I'll miss him sorely, but it could have been a lot worse. At least we didn't all go to the bottom,' said Zafan, busy at his desk in the corner.

'I've got good news about your captives,' Bonor went on.

'Oh yes?' said Namoh.

'I went to see them and the marines warned, "Remember your bandhan of protection, these lads are quite disturbed." So I made the bandhan and they saw me. I got talking to them and finished up awakening their Trees of Life. Was that all right?'

'Obviously,' replied Valya. 'Rajay didn't lend us this ship to buy guns; that was only a cover. Did they feel anything?'

'To begin with just heat, and they were shaking in fear, at least I think it was fear. The marines and I gave them vibrations and cleared their subtle centres somewhat, and they were fine.'

'That's amazing, considering they were murderers,' said Namoh.

'Would you have a word with them? They've got quite a tale to tell.'

'Zafan, you're the captain, what do you say?' asked Valya.

'Fine by me,' Zafan looked up from his charts. The sailors had spotted some islands and Zafan was trying to figure out where they were.

A little later, washed and cleaned up, the failed assassins were led before their captors by Bonor, who assured them that they were not going to be either tortured or thrown to the sharks. Robin, Valya and Namoh sat at one end of the long table and Zafan was still at his desk. The prisoners knelt in dread and apprehension, despite Bonor's soothing advice.

'Get up,' began Valya. 'This is a Daish Shaktay ship and even our king doesn't allow people to kneel before him. Everyone in our country has the right of appeal, whatever he's done. Sit at the end of the table. We want to talk to you.'

'Yes, sir,' replied the boys nervously.

'You don't strike me as assassins,' Robin sized up the two boys, barely fully grown, with the practised eye of someone who had raised a whole country of partisans. The captives were wide-eyed in terror and Valya, Namoh and Robin, who were relaxed, happy and curious, tried to calm them down.

'Take it easy,' continued Valya. 'We need your help as much as you need ours.' The two Teletsians were surprised - how different these strangers were from the Sorcerers or Specials! Bonor put his hand on Saman's shoulder.

'Just tell Lord Valya what you told me,' he urged. 'You may even have friends in common.' Namoh made a bandhan of request under the table, asking that the Teletsians should speak out and not be afraid. He felt where their inner selves were weak, by putting his attention on each of the boys in turn and checking on his own fingers where their problems were. Each finger corresponded to a particular subtle centre, and so he could help settle their fear.

'What's your name?' asked Robin.

'Saman, my lord.'

'I'm not a lord. My father's an animal dealer. He's the First Lord of Daish Shaktay,' Robin nodded at Valya. He wasn't usually so casual, but wanted to put Saman at ease. Valya, never happy in his nobleman's role, understood this and smiled. He had recently given away nearly all his extensive ancestral lands to his tenants and Rajay had rewarded him for his generosity by making him his Prime Minister.

Saman, less scared now, began his tale.

'Freddi and I are from a small town in the country. At school we were always in trouble and nearly got sent to the Special Clinic, where they do terrible things to children. One day, about five years ago, there was an earthquake in our area. We heard it had been set off by some young rebels who'd messed about with an ancient temple near us. Then a girl called Stellamar visited us and helped us form a group of people who secretly wanted change. She's been doing this all over the country.'

'We need to meet her,' said Robin. On their way down, they had dropped Ahren, Conwenna and me off at the Island of Creations. A launch had taken us to the north side of the island under cover of night, but the Teletsian coast guard was watching the island's port and it had proved impossible to take the ship into harbour, because they had to appear neutral, and the Island was the enemy of Teletsia.

'She told us there was an ancient prophecy about some young people…'

'We know all about your prophecy,' interrupted Robin. 'Go on.'

'No wait,' put in Valya, 'Bonor, go and get some refreshments for these young men. What would you like, some juice, or spiced tea?'

'Whatever you're having, my lord,' said Saman, flabbergasted at this turn of events.

'Continue,' ordered Robin, increasingly interested.

'These young rebels were said to be heading for a magical country where they would get special powers to overthrow these wretched toads we have running our country – the Sorcerers. I hope you're not going to send us back there?'

'Not yet awhile. Tell us more.'

'We heard that a boy from Clatan, the next town to ours, and a girl from a farm near there had disappeared then, although it was all hushed up. We tried to find out more, and also about the prophecy, but about six months ago we were caught by some Specials with some damming information on us.'

Bonor soon returned with the refreshments. They ate and drank without speaking and Namoh, Valya and Robin continued to give healing vibrations to the boys with their attention.

'It's time for some introductions,' Valya broke the silence. 'My name is Valya Northwestern and this is Namoh Hillfarmer. We work for King Rajay of Daish Shaktay. We've just been giving some subtle healing to your damaged Trees of Life, your souls. Do you feel better?'

'Yes,' said Saman, 'As if a great dark cloud has lifted from me.' His friend agreed, between slices of cake.

'I'm Robin Markand. I work for King Albion of Chussan. We didn't come to Teletsia to buy guns and sell jewels; we came to help fulfil your prophecy.' The boys stared in astonishment. It was too good to be true.

'Whatever were you playing at, trying to be assassins?' grinned Namoh. 'You should learn your trade better if you want to have a hope in a million against us. We're seasoned fighters. You're extremely lucky we didn't kill you.'

'I was going to explain that bit, my lord,' said Freddi hesitantly.

'Call me Namoh, but yes, please do.' Namoh, still young enough to be a university student, initially refused to use his new title, Lord Santara. It was a bit of a sticking point between him and Rajay, who said it would give him status as one of his ministers. Namoh insisted he was a farmer and proud of it, and that Namoh Hillfarmer was a good enough name for him in any company. He finally agreed to use his title in public – like the need for smart but unavoidably uncomfortable clothes.

'When the Specials caught us they took us to the Sorcerers in Teletos. We were given the choice of being 'treated', that is having our powers of speech and reason taken from us and being sent to the slave farms, or becoming assassins and killing suspects like you and our former friends. We reckoned the least worst option was assassins and on no account would we actually murder anyone. After some time our excuses for failure wore thin and if we hadn't managed to kill you that was it – the slave farms. You understand why we didn't want you to leave us behind?'

'Most definitely!' said Robin with feeling.

'We can't thank you enough for getting us out of Teletsia,' added Saman. 'We'll do anything in return.'

'Would you like to do what we've been doing in the past?'

'What's that?' asked Freddi.

'Partisans, freedom fighters and more. You can help awaken your benighted country and free it from the curse of the Sorcerers.'

'I can't believe it!' cried Saman. 'We've talked about this for years.'

'And in a few days we'll introduce you to the boy from Clatan who escaped to Sasrar, the northern country. I've just been there myself, learning about the spiritual power,' said Namoh.

'We thought you were going to sell us as slaves!' beamed Saman.

'No way, but we're going to the Island of Creations,' Robin took over. 'We'll have to clear the subtle centres of your Trees of Life before we get there, because if there's too much negativity in them, the protective forces of the island won't allow you to land. If the Sorcerers tried to they'd be fried the moment they set foot on the ground there, or something nasty like that.'

'Can you put us right so fast?' asked Freddi anxiously.

'Oh, yes. We just request the all-pervading power of love to heal you, and you two need that more than anyone,' Robin assured them. 'For us, being partisans isn't all fighting.'

'You're in good hands,' Valya guaranteed. 'I was badly wounded and had lost my will to live, but some of the escaped Teletsians and a friend did this on me, and now I'm completely recovered. Well, the best surgeon in the country operated on me, but it was this extra help that saved me.'

'By the way,' said Namoh to Freddi, 'did the ship's doctor have a look at you?'

'Yes, I'll be fine and.....' he turned to Bonor, standing behind, 'thank you for not hurting me more.'

'I had to disarm you. It's not hard if you know how to use a sword properly, which I'll teach you to do. I'm King Rajay's chief bodyguard and I fully intend to take you boys in hand before you're let loose as partisans. Right now you're a total liability to yourselves and anyone fighting alongside you.' Everyone laughed.

CHAPTER 5

TRAINING PARTISANS

Ahren, Conwenna and I were waiting eagerly, and somewhat nervously, on the Island of Creations for the return of the ship. As soon as it was sighted we hurried to the harbour on the northern coast of the island. We were staying at the home of the guardians Lord Jarwhen and Lady Mercola, an elderly couple full of wisdom and encouragement. We three wanted to go into Teletsia immediately but Robin had absolutely forbidden it. We could probably have got round Valya, Namoh and Zafan, but there were two people we could never hope to persuade against their better judgement: my husband Robin and Rajay, and Rajay had given Valya some stringent instructions.

To my relief I saw Robin, Valya and Namoh hanging over the rails waving at us, along with two young men I did not recognise, but saw from their faces they were Teletsians, with our typically prominent noses and high foreheads. There was also a group of people who looked as if they came from Daish Shaktay - their skins were generally lighter than ours and their noses usually less pronounced. Soon everyone disembarked and we greeted each other. Robin told me about my family and tears of joy came to my eyes to know they were all right, at least so far. The two Teletsians were standing shyly at the end of the gangplank; they had been nervous about leaving the ship, but Robin assured them that it was quite safe to land.

'You've got to be from Teletsia,' said Ahren, going up to them.

'Yes, and you must be Ahren Dairyman!' Saman replied. 'You're famous with the young people of Teletsia, or rather the secretly rebellious ones.'

'News to me! It's great that there *are* some rebellious ones.'

'Oh yes, more than you'd ever imagine,' added Freddi, Saman's friend.

We went back to Lord Jarwhen's mansion some distance away, and Ahren and Saman soon discovered they had some mutual acquaintances. Saman told Ahren that a large number of the young people in Teletsia were now actively trying to discover more about the prophecy and how to fulfil it.

Lord Jarwhen, Lady Mercola and the Ganoozals were in the courtyard to greet us, along with a large peacock called Percy, who lived in the garden and whose job was to squawk loudly whenever anyone came into the yard, to announce their arrival. He made a lot of noise now but no one took any notice of him. They rarely did.

Saman and Freddi had still not quite got over the change in their fortunes, and their reaction at seeing the beautiful house, with its extensive gardens, many wings, the broad courtyard covered with white gravel, and our gracious hosts, was similar to ours when we had first been there some years before - from being outcasts and the scum of Teletsia, like us, they were amazed that they had suddenly become honoured guests.

They went off with the freed slaves, the Ganoozals and Bonor, but not before Ahren and I had warned them about the unforeseen dangers of exploring the many rooms and corridors of the house – mindful of our brush with the prehistoric monsters on our first visit! The rest of us were invited to share a meal with Lord Jarwhen and his wife, and the lunchtime conversation was a debriefing session for their benefit.

'So, that's all we can tell you about our trip to Teletos, but what next?' asked Valya, sampling a mouth-watering dessert after telling his story.

'I'm going to send a message to Stellamar, who lives nearby on the mainland,' replied Lord Jarwhen. 'She and her parents are the guardians of Teletsia, although this is a secret. Stellamar knows what's going on as much as anyone. The family are wealthy pearl dealers, so the Sorcerers let them alone, because the Pearl Lords have threatened to move their business here if they're troubled, and the Sorcerers are terrified of this island. Not only that, if they do decamp here, the Teletsian government would lose the enormous taxes they pay, from the sale of their pearls.'

'And Stellamar's been setting up these Resistance Groups?' asked Robin.

'Yes. It's dangerous, but she's careful, and so far she's got away with it,' said Lord Jarwhen.

'Valya and I felt we should ask Prince Roarke to come here with his flying ship, and obviously Derwin, Asha's brother. We're going to have to get in and out of Teletsia quickly and if possible undetected, and for that, flying craft would be very useful,' Robin went on.

'Absolutely,' replied Lord Jarwhen, 'and we'll see if we can borrow the one from the Emperor of the Ocean. Our grandson is very skilful at handling it.'

'Merien?' I asked.

'That's him,' said Lady Mercola, 'he's also a guardian.' This explained a lot about him I had not previously understood.

'How can we send a message to Prince Roarke?' asked Robin.

'No problem,' Zafan spoke up from the bottom of the table. 'I can communicate with the dolphins and they'll get a message right across the sea in a day. Some of my men are patrolling the north west of the Sea of Illusion, where King Gamsad has his port. They'll pick up the message from the dolphins and have it delivered to Prince Roarke in another day or two. His family have stopped Gamsad's slave trading and we're keeping an eye on things from the seaward side, with the help of the dolphins.'

'Raynor and Tandi, and Lee, are in Daish Shaktay,' said Ahren. 'Raynor is reorganising the Daish Shaktay education system and Lee works for Rajay. Maybe Prince Roarke could collect them on his way down.'

'We're going to need all of you,' said Lord Jarwhen. 'It looks as if the cleansing of Teletsia will be coordinated from here. What about you two?'

'I must go back, but Namoh can stay,' said Valya. 'I'll leave the warship here too, if you've got a boat that could take me to Daish Shaktay.' As Prime Minister, Valya could not be away any longer.

'I recently had an ocean-going yacht built - it's very fast,' said Lord Jarwhen. 'I realised we need some way of crossing the Sea of Illusion. If I'd had it five years ago we could have helped Asha and the others.'

'I should go too,' added Zafan.

'I've heard of Rajay Ghiry's valour, and that you and his other friends helped so much. How did you finally destroy the Mattanga Empire?'

'Ask Robin and Ahren,' replied Valya, and they told him about the flying horses.

'We need them here,' said Lord Jarwhen. 'Any chance?'

'They're waiting for me in Daish Shaktay,' Robin took over. 'They'd try to come here now, alone, if I called them with my key, but I don't think they'd make it across the sea.'

'You go on the yacht too,' said Lord Jarwhen. 'I'll give you a map and you can fly them across the Sea of Illusion from island to island, so they won't have to be in the air for too long at a stretch.'

'I'll be gone some time,' Robin warned me when we were alone. 'I beg you not to be rash. Will you promise me not to go into Teletsia until I get back?'

'If it's necessary to go there to save lives, I must. Don't force me to promise you anything that might stop me helping my country or her people.'

'But you're my wife! You're supposed to at least listen to me.'

'I am listening, but I can't forego my vow to Teletsia.'

'Do you know how much you matter to me, and how much I love you?'

'Yes, and I love you too, but I also love Teletsia and her good people who are suffering so much.'

'I give up,' he said in a resigned tone of voice. 'Oh Asha, I wish you could understand where I'm coming from.'

'I do understand. You also have a Key of Wisdom of Sasrar. You're supposed to have risen above your personal feelings.'

I felt bad saying this, but I couldn't make him a promise I might have to break. I could never lie to Robin. We made up before he left – more or less. The trouble was I had two conflicting vows – one to defer to Robin as my husband and the other to do my best to free my country. It was our first argument since we had been married.

The next day Valya, Robin and the majority of the freed slaves left on Lord Jarwhen's yacht. Because all of them had had their inner awakening they could sail straight across the Sea of Illusion on the current that had carried us. The yacht would get to Daish Shaktay in a fraction of the time it had taken us to cross the sea on our raft.

Four of the ex-slaves stayed back, young men who wanted to topple the regime of the Sorcerers as much as we did – they had suffered so much from it. Soon Bonor and Namoh had an informal military academy going every morning on the front lawn for the new recruits: four freed slaves and two escaped assassins. Ahren joined in, and Conwenna and I watched, apart from the archery; she was very accurate with a bow and arrow. After some days Namoh encouraged them, saying we had a fair to middling guerrilla force, although Bonor was still in despair. We also spent a lot of evenings going round the farms, villages and the port of the Island of Creations doing awakening programmes, and within a week or so everyone on the island knew about the Tree of Life. They were very balanced people in any case, so it was, in many ways, a breeze. We took our recruits with us, so they could learn how to be partisans of truth. Namoh and Ahren spent time with Pa Ganoozal, because they shared his interest in animals - Ahren was plain curious and Namoh was now the Daish Shaktay Agriculture Minister.

One evening, Pa Ganoozal came running into the staff hall, where Conwenna and I were eating supper with our 'Liberation Force.'

'Percy started squawking,' he began. 'Your brother Derwin is here in a flying ship, with Merien in another!'

We went out to the courtyard and there were heartfelt greetings, because it was some time since we had seen each other. Ma Ganoozal came out to see the flying ships, took the newcomers to their rooms and then we sat with them while they ate a late supper.

'How come you arrived together?' asked Ahren.

'We sent messages with the dolphins,' explained Merien, 'and arranged for Derwin to come via the Emperor's Island.'

'Roarke gave me directions so I could island hop to get there,' went on Derwin. 'Having been in Sasrar and learnt about the bandhan of protection, the problems on the islands didn't affect me.'

'No dragons?' I joked, remembering Derwin's near fatal meeting with some on our northern journey.

'No, but we'll have our work cut out for us in Teletsia. Roarke will come soon but he was a bit tied up when the message arrived. He'll go via Daish Shaktay in his big flyer and pick up the others.'

Journal of Warzog, Scribe to the Most High Priests of Teletsia

I, Warzog, scribe to the most illustrious Lords of Teletsia, do hereby record a special meeting of their Lordships.

'Intelligence has reached us,' began His Supreme Lordship, 'that the Daish Shaktay warship we assumed was buying guns and negotiating for the repurchase of some slaves was actually here on a subversive mission, and worst of all was carrying some of the young rebels mentioned in the prophecy. They have been in Sasrar and some of them were with Rajay Ghiry when he overthrew our Mattanga allies, under King Karlvid.'

'This is serious,' said the Head of the Special Secret Police. 'It is probable that the light we saw came from one of them. Do we know where the warship went?'

'It was seen being blown eastwards in the severe storm we had some days back,' replied the Master of the Intelligence Network.

'The Master of Weather Manipulation made sure it was a violent one. Let us hope the ship sank,' said the High Priest of Ports, Naval Matters and Shipping, 'but that won't solve the problem unless all the rebels were on board.'

'Might we get some information out of Mr Antiquarian?' asked the Head of the Special Secret Police.

'Possibly, but I'd rather leave him a little longer before pulling him in, to see if the rebels reveal themselves,' replied the Master of the Intelligence Network.

'You have another week,' concluded His Supreme Lordship.

In the night Stellamar arrived on the Island of Creations secretly, in a fishing boat. The next morning Ma Ganoozal came and asked me to have breakfast with Lord Jarwhen and Lady Mercola on the terrace and we were quite a party. Merien was sitting with Stellamar, and Namoh and Conwenna were with Derwin, who had them gloriously befuddled with his explanations about how flying ships worked. Pa Ganoozal joined us but did not eat with us. He had been up and about since dawn with his animals and Ahren was with him.

'Great to see you, Asha, after so long!' began Stellamar. Her face was thinner than I remembered it and she was taller now, but her hair was long, thick, black and glossy, as it had been before.

'We've all changed somewhat,' said Merien, who to me looked the most unchanged of any of us. He was still wearing seaman's boots and simple clothes even though, as the son of the Prime Minister to the Emperor and a guardian his status was considerable.

'Are you both still rescuing people?' I asked with a smile.

'That's why I'm here,' said Stellamar seriously. 'Our family have informers in Teletos and we received a message yesterday that the Sorcerers may arrest your families, starting with Mr Antiquarian.'

'Did you know one of our people has been there giving them inner awakening?'

'We suspected as much.'

'Go and get Bonor,' interrupted Lord Jarwhen. 'He was in Teletos with Robin – he'll give us the details.' I found Bonor in the garden trying, with limited success, to teach our trainee partisans to shoot straight. He came at once and told Stellamar what he knew.

'How long have we got?' asked Merien.

'Not long. Good thing you two turned up when you did,' Stellamar looked at Merien and Derwin.

'I'll try and rescue Mr Antiquarian,' said Derwin. 'It'll have to be me, because I know where he lives, assuming it's still the same place.'

'It is,' I went on, 'but can you remember your way around Teletos, after all this time?'

'Of course, and no way are you in on this, Asha. I'll go today, and let's hope it's cloudy so as to hide the flyer.'

'I'm coming with you and I'll fix the weather, if needs be,' added Merien. 'What about the other parents?'

'We'll have to try and help them too,' Stellamar said. 'How many people can go in your flying ships?'

'Two: the driver and a passenger,' replied Derwin.

'In that case take me too. By the way, are you aware that some of the Sorcerers see your auras as golden light?'

'No, we weren't,' said Namoh.

'It's an absolute giveaway and the golden aura develops around anyone who's had their awakening, after some time,' explained Stellamar.

'No wonder they looked at me so oddly.'

'If you're a balanced and centred person you don't see this light. You feel it as cool vibrations, but if you've used devious methods to change your consciousness then you may see it. There may come a time when we awakened people will also have this ability, but not at present.'

'How do you manage to conceal yourself when you go around the country?' asked Derwin.

'Oh, it's easy. When you wake up in the morning, you make a bandhan of protection around yourself with the key in your hand. You know how - you make the seven arcs around your subtle system. Then, until the next time you sleep, the Sorcerers can't see the golden light you emit.'

'Why do the evil ones see the light and not us?' Namoh went on.

'When it's daylight, we see the sun, but in the night we see the lesser lights - the moons and stars. The evil ones see the lesser subtle light, and darkness in the form of ghosts, but may not be so at home in the daylight. We live in the daylight and see what is obvious, whereas they don't.'

'I hope your camouflage works,' observed Merien, practical as ever.

'It does. I've used it for years.'

CHAPTER 6

A TRIP TO TELETOS

The Isle of Creations was hot, even in the season of heavy rains, which it was then. The two small flying ships were in a barn near the horse stables and in the afternoon, when most people were having a rest, Conwenna crept into Derwin's ship. It was oval in shape, with one seat for the driver and another behind, and had a roof, hinged at one side. There was a storage space behind the passenger's seat, where Conwenna hid under a rug, and in front of the driver was a steering wheel and a number of knobs and dials. There were also retractable wings.

Conwenna had scarcely concealed herself when she heard Merien, Stellamar and Derwin approaching. Although the sky had been clear in the morning, as was often the case, in the afternoon it clouded over and there would probably be a storm later. Stellamar had a basket of food, which she put in the back of Merien's flyer. I went to see them off but did not think to ask about Conwenna. There were so many things to do on the island and she had a habit of going out without telling anyone, so I left it at that. Soon Ahren, Namoh and I were waving them good-bye and they soared into the cloud cover above.

Merien wanted Derwin or Stellamar to guide them to the island where Namoh had held the fire ceremony. Merien and Stellamar were cousins and had known each other on Master Theon's island some years before. As they were guardians their training there had been even more rigorous than for the other young people. Today they had maps, weapons and their greatest asset - the keys. Lord Jarwhen had some extra Sasrar keys on the Island of Creations – he was a master of the key technology – and lent one to Merien, who was grateful because it had a wider range of powers than his own from the third centre. Merien's ship had been modified; it no longer had hooks and retractable talons, and looked more peaceful. Otherwise it was similar to Derwin's. They flew above the low clouds until evening, and landed near Teletos to stretch their legs in the clearing of a wood. Conwenna struggled out of her cramped hiding place.

'That's why my flyer seemed so loaded! What *are* you doing here?' Derwin looked horrified. Stellamar and Merien did too, as this was most definitely not in the plan.

'I'm sorry to have deceived you,' began Conwenna, 'but you're guardians and if you'd absolutely refused to let me come, I wouldn't have argued with you.'

'I'm tempted to leave you at a farmhouse belonging to some people I can trust near here,' replied Stellamar.

'Ask the vibrations if I should come with you,' Conwenna prayed there would be some coolness.

'Not totally cool,' objected Merien.

'I must try and see my father,' insisted Conwenna, 'just once.'

'My heart tells me you'd better come with us,' Merien continued. 'What do you reckon, Stellamar?'

'I agree. I'll point out the farm where you can hide if you have to. It's one of our network of safe houses.' They flew over the isolated farm and on to the island in the estuary. It was dark by the time they reached there and the clouds hid the moons' light.

'So what's the plan?' asked Merien as he lit a lantern, and Stellamar spread a rug on the ground and laid out the food.

'The priority is to get Mr Antiquarian out,' she began. 'We'll assume he's at home and land both the craft in his back garden. If there are Specials around they'll either be in the street or on the canal watching the gate at the end of the garden, because these old houses all have a water gate behind, and a street in the front.' They sat on the rug to eat a picnic supper.

'That garden is large,' said Derwin as he helped himself to some bread and cheese, 'and stretches back some way. With luck no one will see us.'

'Once at the Antiquarians,' Stellamar went on, 'we have to persuade Mr Antiquarian to leave with Merien in his flying ship, then fly on to Lee's parents, the Restorer's, to warn them, and also your mother, Derwin. On top of that you, Conwenna, want to try this very chancy business of seeing your father. If this works it'll be one of the major miracles of our time.'

'We've got to try,' Derwin continued.

'I'm a realist. I live here.'

They set off again. The dark night was a blessing and they dipped down below the clouds occasionally to see where they were, from the streetlights. Stellamar pointed out the safe house in Teletos city; a small place with a garden giving onto yet another canal, at the end of a street in the Jewellers Quarter. There were never many people walking on the streets at night. The businesses closed at nightfall and if the Sorcerers were short of slaves, or needed people for their sinister experiments, they would sometimes order the Specials to roam around late at night and pick up anyone loitering or sleeping out.

They flew on, hiding in the clouds as far as they could. Even though the flying machines flew almost silently, anyone could raise the alarm if they saw them. Nevertheless, all went well and they landed in the Antiquarian's garden. They had not got another dog since Nog had run away, so the visitors did not have to deal with that problem. Merien and Conwenna waited anxiously with the flying ships in the part of the garden surrounded by tall hedges.

Derwin and Stellamar walked stealthily towards the house. They noticed a light in one of the downstairs windows and crept closer. It was Mr Antiquarian's study and Derwin looked through the window and saw Mr and Mrs Antiquarian working. They had some old manuscripts spread out on the desk and were restoring them, but the most astonishingly fortunate thing was that he could hear the voice of his mother. His heart jumped for joy, but Stellamar put her finger to her mouth, indicating silence.

'There may be other people there,' she whispered. 'Wait!' They listened, but did not hear any other voices. Derwin knocked on the window.

'What was that?' asked Mrs Antiquarian, looking up.

'A cat?' said her husband and went on working. Derwin knocked again, harder. This time Mrs Herbhealer came to the window.

'It can't be! Derwin! Is it really you?' She almost fainted.

'Yes, mum. It's me, your long lost son!' Within seconds Stellamar and Derwin had been let in by the garden door and there was an ecstatic reunion between Derwin and his mother. Stellamar didn't waste a moment.

'Mr Antiquarian, I don't know whether you remember me, but I came to your shop to tell you that Raynor had escaped, five years ago. Now it's your turn. We've got to get you out of here fast, because the Sorcerers' men are about to arrest you. We've also got to get your wife and Mrs Herbhealer out, and the Restorers.'

'I believe you, but however did you get here?' Mr Antiquarian asked. 'Did I forget to lock the canal gate?'

'No,' Derwin reassured him. 'We came in flying machines and you've got to leave in one, like now!' Mr Antiquarian stared wide eyed and Stellamar continued speaking.

'I'm part of the Pearl Lords' family and we have an informer in the Sorcerers' palace, who warned us about the danger you're in. Derwin, take Mr Antiquarian to Merien then come back.'

'But…' objected Mr Antiquarian.

'Your life is in the balance. If the Sorcerers arrest you they'll torture information out of you or hypnotise you, or drug you to make you talk and you'll incriminate many other people. Please, leave now!' With enormous trust in Stellamar, Mr Antiquarian kissed his wife, said goodbye to Mrs Herbhealer and followed Derwin into the garden.

'Pleased to meet you, sir,' Merien began when they reached him. 'Could you get in quickly, because it's going to rain very hard in a few moments.' Sure enough the heavens opened and soaked them all except Conwenna, who was sheltering in the gazebo nearby. Merien and Mr Antiquarian took off and Derwin ran back to the house, this time taking Conwenna too, to the further surprise of the ladies there.

'We've got to figure out what to do with you two,' said Stellamar to Mrs Herbhealer and Mrs Antiquarian. 'Our informer told us that Mr Antiquarian would be arrested first but if he's disappeared the Specials will no doubt come after you. We'll try some alternatives on vibrations. Firstly, is it safe for you others to stay in Teletos?'

'I feel heat and tingling,' said a dripping wet Derwin. Stellamar and the others agreed. 'Robin told us that Wale, who works for my uncle, still has his fishing boat. If he's a fisherman he'll have a pass for sailing out to sea. Perhaps the others could escape like that. Try this one: is it safe for Mrs Herbhealer to go round to her brother Mr Restorer, warn him of what's going on and then raise Wale?'

'That's much better,' smiled Stellamar.

'And Mrs Antiquarian can go too?' asked Derwin.

'Yes, that's also cool,' they all agreed.

'Where does Wale live?' asked Stellamar.

'Near the Restorers, and his boat is moored there. Their apartment block, which was formerly a nobleman's palace, backs onto one of the big canals,' explained Mrs Herbhealer.

'And he'll be there now?'

'Bound to be,' Mrs Herbhealer went on.

'What about my father?' asked Conwenna.

'He's still living there but I'm afraid he's bedridden these days.'

'I want to see him, for a short time.'

'Be careful. His sister Drusilla, your aunt, is with him, and I don't trust her at all.'

Mrs Antiquarian called for the mule cab that always stood in their street at night. The cabby often took Mrs Herbhealer home late, so this was nothing unusual.

'Derwin,' ordered Stellamar, 'you wait here with Conwenna. We need to give the others time to get away with Wale before you go there. As I said, the safe house in the Jewellers Quarter is the meeting place if things go wrong. You can land in the back garden and here are the door keys,' Stellamar gave Derwin two keys. They looked similar to the first centre keys and were on chains. 'Put them round your necks - one for you and one for Conwenna. There're not jewels of power; they merely open doors.'

Conwenna reminded Mrs Herbhealer to make sure they shut up the Restorers' watchdogs, if there were any, so when Derwin arrived at the Restorers with the flyer the dogs wouldn't raise the entire neighbourhood. Conwenna had once been badly bitten and was scared of dogs. Stellamar left for the Restorers with Mrs Herbhealer and Mrs Antiquarian. The two ladies walked out of the Antiquarians' home into the street, – possibly for ever. A figure slouching in the shadows noted them leave and continued watching the house. He had been talking to the previous man on duty when the flyers came in and was hiding from the rain when Merien flew out so had not seen him leave either. As he had only just come on surveillance duty he did not think it strange that an extra person left the house with the two regulars. Meanwhile, unaware of the Special in the street watching the house, Conwenna and Derwin waited nervously in the gazebo.

'Come on, it's time to go,' said Derwin half-heartedly, some time later. 'When we get there, we'll land in the walled garden. Don't be too long. What do I do if you can't get away?'

'I'll be all right.'

'What if you aren't? Get real, Conwenna.'

'Make for the safe house.'

This time the Special watching the Antiquarian's home did see the flying ship. He immediately went back to his headquarters and reported it. His superior suspected he was hallucinating and told him not to take drugs on duty.

When Conwenna and Derwin flew nearer to the Restorers they could see the canal at the back and noticed the fishing boat had gone from its mooring place. Derwin hoped it was because the parents had managed to get away with Wale. It was silent as they landed in the walled garden backing on to the canal. Fruit trees were trained against the walls, and in the night they could smell, but barely see the flowers and herbs which filled the beds. Derwin managed to land on the paved part in the centre and helped Conwenna out of the flyer. He looked imploringly at her as he did so.

'Conwenna, you're my second sister. Please, look after yourself. Take care.'

'I will, but I must try to see dad.'

She crept across the yard she knew so well. After five years, in which time she had grown from a child to a tall, lanky teenager, the whole place seemed so much smaller than she remembered. Her father and maiden aunt lived in the main building on the second floor. The old mansion was built round a courtyard and the night watchman had his room in the front, by the large door that gave onto the street, and was closed for the night,. He did not hear her as she passed noiselessly through the central courtyard and up the broad stone staircase. She was soon at her front door and knocked on it. She heard footsteps and her aunt, Drusilla Prospector, opened it and stood staring at Conwenna, stock still from astonishment. She was a middle aged woman of medium build and height, with pursed lips and frown marks both between her eyebrows and on her forehead. Her nose was beaky, her thin hair was scraped back in a bun and she rarely smiled. Her small, piglike eyes bored through one very uncomfortably.

'It's not possible!' she said finally. 'Is it really you, Conwenna?'

'Of course it's me, Aunt Drusilla. Give me a kiss!' Conwenna walked in and hugged her. She responded like a cold fish. 'Where's dad?'

'He's in bed,' said Drusilla. 'He always is these days. He's ill.' Conwenna's father heard her voice and called feebly from his bedroom, so she ran in and was appalled – he was so pale and wasted. She knelt down by the bed and hugged him and could feel tears flowing down his cheeks.

'I never thought I'd see you again,' he smiled wanly. She sat on the bedside chair and noticed how shabby everything was. Aunt Drusilla came in and sat on another chair, rather primly, but she had always been prim.

'Dad, I can't stay long. How are you?' Conwenna felt fear in his heart, but enormous love as well.

'It's wonderful to see you, my darling, and you're looking so well! Drusilla, go and make some coffee – is that what you'd like?'

'Yes, fine,' said Conwenna, and Drusilla went off. Conwenna held her father's hand and could see the warm, sincere affection for her in his eyes.

'Forgive me, I had to spy for them to save your life,' his breath came in gasps.

'I know dad, but that's all in the past now, and one of the reasons I had to run away.'

'After you disappeared I refused to do it any more.'

'I got to the northern country we were seeking and found something very special – I want to share it with you, right now.' Conwenna gave her father the awakening of his Tree of Life, and after she directed vibrations to his sorely damaged heart centre he felt peace within himself and a slight breeze flowing on his hands.

He explained that when she escaped five years before, the Sorcerers blamed him for letting her escape and forbade him from leaving the city. He could not do any more prospecting and their source of income had dried up. Also, he had recently fallen ill, so now they were living on the charity of the Restorers. Drusilla had taken it all very hard. Conwenna and her father failed to notice that the coffee never appeared; they were so overjoyed to be together again. Then she remembered the time, bid her father goodbye and promised to return. She went into the kitchen, could not find Drusilla, but knew time was short, so left. Conwenna reached the bottom of the stairs and at that moment the night watchman came out of his room to make one of his periodic walks around the compound, noisily banging a stick on a metal tray to scare away snakes, rats, stray dogs or intruders. Conwenna did not recognise him; he was evidently new.

'Who are you?' he asked before she could hide herself. 'How did you get in?'

'I've been with the Prospectors. I'm a relation of theirs and I came by the gate onto the canal – I've got a key. I'm leaving now, that same way.'

'I take it you've got a boat?'

'Yes.'

'Be sure to lock the gate, won't you?'

'Will do.' Conwenna ran to the walled garden, panicking. They had to leave before the watchman found the flying ship. Derwin had heard him talking to Conwenna and powered up the flying ship as she appeared.

'Did you ask the watchman whether our people left?' said Derwin as he helped Conwenna into the craft.

'Not a chance! Let's get out of here. He's gone round the other side of the building and we can leave unseen if we hurry.'

'I'm going to fly down the river to see if we can spot Wale's boat. I want to be sure they've got away, before we go back to the Island of Creations.'

They took off into the dark sky and at the same moment the watchman came across Drusilla at the front of the mansion.

'That young girl who's been with you left just now,' he told Drusilla, who looked momentarily angry, then controlled herself. She went out down the street, met a group of Specials from the local Police Station, and had a few words with them. The watchman assumed they were telling her to go home, because it was well known that they didn't like women being out alone late at night.

Meanwhile, Derwin and Conwenna flew silently down the river. The clouds had cleared and two moons were up, giving some light. Downstream, where the estuary widened they saw, and were seen, by a steam powered coast guard vessel on night patrol. If it reached and questioned Wale's boat there could be trouble. Derwin flew on and spied it some way further down the estuary and as he got nearer saw a school of dolphins bobbing up and down round it. His uncle was on the deck looking at them. He went closer, hovered nearby and shouted across the water.

'Uncle Berny, it's me, Derwin!'

'By the Mother Earth! You people do turn up in the strangest ways! Marvellous to see you! Your mum and aunt are below, hiding in the cabin with that nice young lady – Stellamar.'

'Great! Those dolphins want to tow your boat. They'll pull it very fast if you throw out some ropes. Be careful because there's a coast guard launch behind you and they saw my flyer. Make for the port on the northern shore of the Island of Creations and I'll see you there.'

'OK! Bye for now.'

'Merien must have asked the dolphins to look out for a fishing boat carrying people with good vibrations,' observed Conwenna.

It was morning when Conwenna and Derwin got back to the Island. An exhausted Merien, on his way home, had indeed warned some dolphins to alert their friends in the Teletos estuary, and he had arrived some time before with Mr Antiquarian. Merien and I were sitting on the steps of the front porch and jumped up as we saw Derwin's flyer land. He and Conwenna got out and came over to us.

'Thank goodness you're all right!' I cried.

'I'm dead beat,' said Conwenna. 'Derwin can tell you the story.' She walked purposefully into the house, as if she wanted to be alone.

'What was all that about?' asked Merien.

'Long story. Is she in trouble for coming with us to Teletos?' Derwin replied.

'She was, and so were we, for letting her, but I straightened it out. Lord Jarwhen was more worried than angry though; Conwenna's so young. Did she see her dad?'

'Yes, it was very sad for her,' and he told us everything.

'I'm sorry about your father,' I said to Conwenna when I went to her room.

'It's going to take me some time to get over seeing him like that. Maybe now he's had his awakening he'll get better. He's definitely given up spying for the Sorcerers.'

'I'll help you to ease your sorrow. Let me get you a bucket of salty water to put your feet in, and I'll give you some healing vibrations.'

The next morning the Specials who had been watching the Antiquarians' house sent a search party round but no one was there except the cleaning lady, who explained that her employers had left a note saying they had gone out of town for a few days to see a sick relation. The Specials searched the garden but could not find anything unusual because fortunately the flyers had landed on a paved path so had not left any marks. A report was sent to the Head Sorcerers in the Forbidden Quarter.

Journal of Warzog, Scribe to the Most High Priests of Teletsia

I Warzog, scribe to the most illustrious Lords of Teletsia, do hereby record the gist of a rapidly convened meeting.

There were reports of at least one and probably two flying craft, like great birds with oval bodies and long wings, in the air above the city two nights ago - one leaving the Antiquarian's back garden and the other over the estuary downriver from the city. The Emperor of the Great Ocean has a small flying craft, the Crown Prince of Vittalia has a large one and it is rumoured that he also been making small ones for his favoured followers, so we must treat this as a hostile act and not a figment of people's imaginations, especially as three different people reported seeing them.

The Antiquarians and Restorers, and Mrs Herbhealer, all parents of the escaped rebels, have disappeared, apparently in a fishing boat. What is more serious is that our respected Drusilla Prospector brought some bad news. Conwenna Prospector, one of the escaped rebels, made a brief visit to her father, and then also disappeared, at almost the same time as the flying ships were seen. When we went to question Mr Prospector he was delirious and made no sense at all.

We strongly suspect that all seven rebels are here and that there is some connection between these reports, the blinding light we saw coming from some people recently, and the visit of the Daish Shaktay warship.

CHAPTER 7

THE PROPHECY

The *Queen Zulani* sailed towards Teletos to find Wale's boat, which the dolphins pulled towards the warship. It soon arrived back at the Island with the refugees from Teletos on board, and the fishing boat was now manned by a crew of Daish Shaktay sailors and armed marines, so any coastguard boat from Teletsia would have a hard time opposing the Daish Shaktay warship with the fugitives or the marines on the fishing boat. At the Island there were tremendous welcomes and our parents and relations wanted time with us, and news of those who had not yet arrived from the north. My mother had much praise for Robin and was also very proud of Derwin, who was showing such unforeseen talents.

'I've got to admit your journey to the north has done you all the world of good,' said Mr Antiquarian.

'You haven't seen Raynor yet,' I said to him, and then to Mr Restorer, 'Uncle Berny, you wait until Lee comes, he's a real credit to our family – you always told me our ancestors were in the government.'

'Just don't try to get to better him in a wrestling match,' laughed Namoh, who was strong and wiry but no match for Lee's heavier build. 'He's had me on my back more than once!'

Lady Mercola insisted on a celebration gala for our parents and it was held in the evening, because Lord Jarwhen wanted to give them recognition as representatives of the people in Teletsia who refused to bow down to the Sorcerers. Conwenna and I wore our best gowns. Ma Ganoozal came up and put Conwenna in hers, did her hair and generally fussed over her - the end result was wonderful and when she looked in the mirror she smiled, despite her sadness about her father.

We went into a part of the garden lit with many lamps hung in the tall trees at the edge, there were flowerbeds filled with fragrant flowers and a broad smooth lawn in the centre. The local villagers, the staff from the house, botanical and zoological gardens all came to pay their respects to our parents. There were short speeches, our parents were given garlands of flowers, and we sang and danced until it was time for the feast. These people knew how to have a good time.

That night, Merien flew Stellamar to her home on the mainland and they both returned later with a very important document. The next morning the all-important meeting was in the Great Hall of the mansion. The ceiling was covered in designs of galaxies which moved and glowed, the walls were covered in intricate designs, the floor was of marble tiles, covered with carpets woven in many colours, and we all sat on comfortable chairs of carved and gilded wood, upholstered with regal red leather. The parents were present, also Conwenna, Derwin, Ahren and me, along with Namoh and Zafan. Bonor had been invited, along with the two escaped 'assassins' and the freed slaves. On the dais were the guardians: Lord Jarwhen, Lady Mercola, Stellamar and Merien – and Ma and Pa Ganoozal.

'I've seen Stellamar before,' Saman whispered to me. 'She's the girl who started our Resistance Group.'

I had explained to Saman and Freddi about the guardians, that they were highly evolved souls from another world who had voluntarily come to ours to help us, and that despite her youth Stellamar was a senior guardian. We began the meeting and Lord Jarwhen suggested we made a bandhan of request, asking that we should have the right ideas to be the instruments to solve Teletsia's problems as peacefully as possible.

'Uncle,' said Stellamar to Lord Jarwhen, 'I've brought our copy of the prophecy. My father said we should look at the end part that gives suggestions as to how the Sorcerers might be overthrown. The Antiquarians' copy didn't have this, did it?'

'No,' replied Mr Antiquarian, 'mind you, it's a good thing, because it was taken by the Sorcerers. I always thought it finished too abruptly. It looked as if someone had cut off some pages.'

'Come up to the dais,' said Lord Jarwhen. 'Could you do a quick translation of that bit?' Mr Antiquarian left his seat at the back of the room and went to join the guardians. How proud of him Raynor would have been! He carefully turned the pages of the ancient manuscript and his worried, hopeless expression completely disappeared.

'When the jewel children have journeyed to the top of the tree,' began Mr Antiquarian, *'and have gained some of the fruits of wisdom, they must return to the root, for it is here that the agents of darkness will congregate in large numbers. They will try to prevent the flowers on the Trees of Life from opening, because if enough trees are in bloom, the power of the evil ones will be diminished. These trees will be found all over Teletsia, but especially in the countryside near the Temple of Support and in the southern mountains, beyond the great jungle…'*

I was amazed, because our family originally came from near the Temple of Support and our ancestral lands had been there, before they were confiscated by the Sorcerers when my great-grandfather stood up to them, and been killed as a result. Also this was where Tandi, Ahren and our failed assassins came from.

45

'Our copy of the prophecy came from the mountains in the south,' explained Mr Antiquarian.

'Tell us in detail,' Lord Jarwhen went on.

'My father, Zack Antiquarian, was a specialist in ancient manuscripts. Over fifty years ago, when he was a young man, he heard that the tribal overlord who lived beyond the jungles in those mountains, far from the prying eyes of the Sorcerers, wanted to sell off some of his library. He was old, and wanted money to pass on to his children.

'The Sorcerers tried to destroy all records of the past. Grandpa Zack knew they would also send someone through the jungles and mountains to take anything of interest and that would be the last anyone would hear of it. However, the Sorcerers would not venture forth during Teletsia's violent monsoon season, so my grandfather prayed to the Goddess of our Mother Earth that he could get there first. He set off with two mules, the optimism of youth and little else. My father stubbornly believed that eventually Teletsia would be free of these wretched Sorcerers - and so did the entire clan of mountain dwellers he was visiting.'

'This is a time to share such stories – continue.'

'I remember his diary, and one part went like this:

'What a way to earn a living! Obstinate mules, roads no better than animal paths, blisters on every toe, voracious mosquitoes and most of all this never-ending rain. Today I had to drag those wretched mules up yet another mountain pass, and I saw an enormous boa constrictor on the track in front of me. Soon I'll probably either get eaten by some jungle creature or washed away in the next thunderstorm.' Those of us who remembered Grandpa Zack laughed, because this was typical of the way he talked. He had died eight years before but we knew this story well. Mr Antiquarian continued.

'Eventually Zack arrived at the crumbling castle where the library was housed. He was wet from the most recent rainstorm, filthy dirty and thoroughly fed up with travelling. He hammered on the large gate, a little side door opened and there stood a young woman who was extremely pleased to see him. He was so tired that for some moments they just stared at each other. The caretaker's daughter, like everyone else in the castle, had been expecting an antiquarian book expert. She presumed he would have a long white beard and spectacles, and be ancient and wizardlike. Unexpectedly, here was a bedraggled but handsome young man.

Much later, when they had children and grandchildren and had been happily married for years, they would tell us about this first meeting. Neither of them had been expecting to meet their life partner on that wet evening. What my mother *had* been doing was saying prayers for someone who could be trusted with a vital book, given to her recently by the head of her clan, on his deathbed. It had lain in the castle library time out of mind, entitled 'farming accounts' to disguise its importance. It was one of the last surviving copies of the fabled, rumoured and banned prophecy which foretold the end of the Sorcerers' regime of fear, written by a great seer when they first came to power. He foresaw that a catalyst would come in the form of a group of young people, who would awaken the very soul of the planet to cause dramatic changes.' Mr Antiquarian paused.

'I'd like to go to that castle, where Raynor's family came from,' said Conwenna. 'I could go with Derwin in his flyer. As we're both so young, people won't suspect us as being capable of doing anything important.'

'I'm not going to hold you back,' replied Lord Jarwhen.

'I'll try and contact my father and also Tandi's brothers. Perhaps Merien could take me in his flyer,' Ahren proposed.

My mother mentioned that my father had gone to see some suppliers of medicinal drugs, tribal people in the jungles, between the coastal farming area and the southern mountains, and she knew more or less where he was.

'It's vital to warn Mr Herbhealer not to go back to Teletos,' Lord Jarwhen added.

'Some of you could come and stay with us and start awakening Trees of Life in the Plimpet area,' said Stellamar, 'my family can hide you and I'll introduce you to the Resistance Groups.'

'What about you, Namoh?' suggested Lord Jarwhen.

'I'll go and pretend to be a foreign businessman,' he replied without hesitation.

'I hope no one recognises you as King Rajay's gun dealer. It should be all right, because people from Plimpet don't often go to Teletos,' said Stellamar.

'We'll chance it,' agreed Namoh.

'So, the bees from the swarm that the prophet wrote about are going into action again.' I said. I felt left out, but remembered how vehemently Robin had begged me not to go into Teletsia.

The next day Derwin and Merien serviced their flying ships. Of the two, Derwin's had the longer range. It was powered by the concentrated black dust that the fool's gold broke down into, from the island in the Sea of Illusion. He carried extra fuel on board with him. Merien's was an older model, powered by a combination of mercury and sulphur, and he also carried extra fuel.

Stellamar and Lord Jarwhen prepared fake travel passes and identity documents for everyone. Merien, and Conwenna, now a talented artist, learnt how to do it in case they needed to fabricate more identities when they were in Teletsia, and would take writing materials, a fake seal, and sealing wax with them. The morning before they left, Lord Jarwhen called those who were going into Teletsia to his study and Stellamar was there with him.

'I'm giving you maps of Teletsia,' he began. 'On them are not only the towns, roads and so on, but also the location of the safe houses. To see them you must make a bandhan over the map with your keys and then they'll become visible for some time. We don't want our enemies to find them, if these maps should fall into the wrong hands.'

'The people in the safe houses are all reliable,' continued Stellamar, 'and although they won't expect you to turn up in flying machines, they're used to unexpected visitors. The pass is the four petalled key, so Uncle Jarwhen is lending one to each of you, because your Sasrar keys won't be recognised. Give these people their awakening. I haven't started that yet, as my parents wanted me to wait until at least some of you seven were back.'

'Here are your documents,' said Lord Jarwhen. 'Although they're forged, they should convince any Specials who demand to see your credentials.'

CHAPTER 8

THE SAFE HOUSE

Merien, Ahren, Derwin and Conwenna flew inland through the night. First they saw the line of dunes on the coast, where Raynor had lured the Specials into the quicksand and they picked out the estuary a little to the east. Westwards more open country stretched away into the starlight, and they passed over farmland and villages.

Ahren was the map-reader and he spotted the safe house, or rather farm they were making for. It was some way to the northeast of Clatan, their eventual destination. Merien noticed the dark mass of a wood on the farm and they managed to land the oval shaped ships between the trees in the centre, surrounded by thick undergrowth. It was difficult to get out through the bushes and vines but eventually they managed it, then sat down in a less dense part of the wood and had a snack from the picnic Ma Ganoozal had given them.

'Let's meditate for a bit,' suggested Merien. Conwenna took out a piece of red silk with a golden border and laid it carefully on the ground. On it she put her Sasrar key and the four petalled key, the key of the first subtle centre, that of the land of Teletsia, which Lord Jarwhen had lent her. The others also took off their keys and put them reverently on the silk. They all had Sasrar keys and four petalled ones, and Merien also had his key to the third subtle centre, its petals inlaid with green jewels. It was nearly sunrise and he checked to make sure they were alone. 'Let's pray to Mother Earth that the power in the keys will help us give awakening in Teletsia, to make contact with people who'll help us and that we'll be protected from danger.' As they did they felt a strong cool wind coming from the keys and saw the first rays of the morning sun filter through the branches.

'I think our prayer has been heard,' said Conwenna.

'Let's go,' advised Ahren. 'These people are farmers so they'll be up and about by now.'

They walked over a field and reached a lane leading up to the farm. As they entered the yard they were greeted by a rowdy chorus of watchdogs who bounded to meet them, but quietened down as they got close. Presumably they felt the newcomers were not hostile. Merien was darker skinned than a Teletsian but the other three looked like locals. A man came out of a barn and they went up to him.

'Excuse me,' began Ahren. 'We were looking for Mr Hograr Dyeman.'

'I'm Hograr. How can I help you?' He put the broom he was carrying against the wall.

'We're from Stellamar, and she said if I showed you this you'd help us.' Ahren took out the four petalled key. Hograr was suspicious.

'My friends also have keys, if you want to see them,' and the others also showed him theirs. Hograr was still suspicious.

'You may not believe me, but I'm one of the escaped rebels who went to the north country. I'll hand over my weapons to you and you can do what you want with me.'

'Sir,' began Merien, taking out the map, 'I understand your caution, but let us show you how we found your farm. This map marks all the safe houses in Teletsia. It was given to us by Lord Jarwhen on the Island of Creations.' He made a bandhan over it with his key and the location of the farm appeared on a blank part. Ahren felt fear coming from Hograr's subtle heart centre.

'That's all very fine and magical, and if you are from the Sorcerers, I reckon there isn't much I can do about it,' he conceded.

'If the Sorcerers knew about us we'd be in deep trouble,' added Merien. 'We're here to start the liberation of Teletsia.'

Meanwhile, Conwenna, standing behind Hograr, had been awakening his Tree of Life and directing healing vibrations to his heart centre - moving her hands behind his back and directing healing vibrations to lessen his fear. He began to smile as his heart centre cleared.

'Come in and have breakfast. My wife and children are in the know,' Hograr said, transformed.

'I'm another of the escaped rebels,' admitted Conwenna.

Some farm hands approached and followed Hograr into the farmhouse, a building with a high, pitched roof and small windows in the thick stone walls, to keep off the hot sun. Inside it was decorated with bright wall hangings and carved furniture. The walls were whitewashed and the floors were made of red earthenware tiles, highly polished. Ahren immediately felt at home, because this décor was typical of the country districts where he grew up. He realised he badly wanted to return permanently, if and when their mission was accomplished.

Soon they were all seated around the kitchen table and as some of the farm hands had also come in the visitors kept a low profile. It was a typical family gathering. There were five children: a fully grown boy, two girls of about Conwenna's age, another boy of about ten and a baby, a boisterous little person of about a year. Hograr did not tell the rest of his family who the newcomers were, only that they needed breakfast. They all tucked in and to begin with little talking disturbed the eating.

'We call him our late lamb, but late lion cub would be more appropriate,' Boumi, Hograr's wife laughed as the baby endeavoured to hurl his porridge across the table. Hograr was giving the instructions of the day to the farmhands when the postman arrived. This farm was the end of his round and he often joined the family for a cup of tea and a second breakfast in exchange for the local gossip.

'So, what news today?' said Hograr.

'It's only a rumour, but it's the best thing I ever heard!' replied the postman between mouthfuls of fresh bread, farm butter and honey. 'My mate who delivers to the Specials said the rebel children who set off those earthquakes are back to finish off the Sorcerers.'

'That's too much to hope for,' sighed Boumi, still struggling with the baby.

'No, seriously, one was seen in Teletos last week and the Sorcerers are looking for them. Not that they'll find them.'

'How can you be so sure?' Hograr went on.

'They flew off into another dimension,' continued the postman.

'Have a cup of herbal tea,' Boumi, disbelieving this unlikely tale, put one down in front of him. Conwenna looked at her plate and Derwin prayed hard no one would find the flying ships, or if they did would not realise what they were. 'Be careful of stories like that,' Boumi continued, 'the Specials may have put this out to see what people's reactions are, and then they can arrest anyone who shows delight rather than despair.'

Ahren was interested in the way attitudes had changed in the last five years. Before we left, hardly anyone dared criticise the Sorcerers openly. Now almost everyone was well and truly fed up with them, and not afraid to say so. When we unknowingly activated the Temple of Support before leaving Teletsia, something changed in the vibratory emanations of the very earth herself and this affected the collective awareness of the people. Eventually the farm workers and the postman left and Hograr mentioned that the postman was a member of their Resistance Group. Ahren signalled to Derwin and Merien and they sat together while everyone else cleared away the remains of the meal.

'What do you reckon?' said Ahren quietly.

'They're fine,' whispered Merien. 'We can trust them all. Tell them who you are, give them their awakening and explain why we're here.' Ahren returned to the family.

'My name is Ahren Dairyman.'

'One of the seven?' the eldest boy was amazed and delighted.

'Yes, and I've been to the secret country in the far north to learn how we can oppose the Sorcerers. You've heard the rumours about us and about the prophecy which foretells their doom? I'm not sure we can carry it off, but we're here to try.' Everyone looked at each other and back at Ahren.

'This is going to take a bit of time, and it would be best if you could all join in,' said Conwenna, who was playing with the baby. 'I'm quite good with babies, so why don't I take this little chap into the garden while Ahren talks?' Without waiting for an answer she picked him up and carried him outside, where he took to her at once. Her experience helping with Tandi's twins was paying off.

'It's an honour to meet you,' Boumi beamed. 'We know the stories about you and your friends. My sons and daughters are part of the local Resistance Group. There are others like ours all over the country now, trying to find out about the prophecy and hoping you seven would soon return to help us. The younger generation are quite different from when you left and they're prepared to risk anything for freedom. Are you all here?'

'Only us three at the moment,' said Derwin cautiously. 'Merien's a friend.'

'I need to contact my parents and the family of one of the others,' continued Ahren. 'We've already evacuated our families who live in the city. If we have to hide anyone, can we leave them here for a few days?'

'Of course,' Boumi assured him. 'That's what it means to be a safe house.'

'What do you know about this rumour of the young people's return?' asked Merien.

'The first I heard about it was this morning, from the postman,' replied Hograr. 'You'll have to be very careful, because they're looking all over for you. They still blame you for those earthquakes. Did you, in fact, set them off?'

'I'm not sure,' said Derwin. 'The first one was when the Specials tried to capture us at the Temple of Support. We pinched their horses and escaped.' The four young Dyemans were on the edge of their seats. They could not believe that some of the country's underground folk heroes had walked into their house and eaten breakfast with them, just like that.

'The first thing we have to do,' Ahren came back to the job in hand, 'is to give you the greatest gift we received in the north.' He told them about the Tree of Life, awakened everyone's, demonstrated the two bandhans and explained about the vibrations. Conwenna came back with a much more peaceful baby and declared he had a very strong Tree of Life.

'I think his naughtiness was because he felt what was going on very clearly, on a subtle level, but didn't know how to tell you. He'll be much calmer now.' Boumi looked extremely grateful. 'I'll show you how to clear him. He wants to help but gets affected himself, then hurts inwardly. That's why he's a bit wild.'

Ahren took Hograr aside and admitted that they had come in flying machines, which were hidden in the wood. Hograr told his oldest son, Tom, to go with Ahren to check they were all right, and said that the children would keep an eye on them during the day, while the guests rested.

'I can only see trees and undergrowth,' said Tom, as they reached the wood.

'There – dull grey, oval – about the length of a farm horse.' Ahren pointed at them.

'Oh yes. I see them now, under those bushes. I can't believe they really fly!'

'They fly alright, but not if the Sorcerers come across them and destroy them.'

'We're going to have to hide them better than that.'

Unfortunately, at that moment, one of the younger farm hands came up, very concerned. 'I'm glad you're here. Did you also find those strange contraptions, Tom?'

'Eh, yes.' Tom looked at Ahren for help.

'Look,' Ahren took over, 'they're top secret. They're not to be touched and no one is to say anything about them, even to the local Specials. If anyone does, we're all finished.'

'Don't even tell anyone else on the farm,' added Tom.

'Right you are!' The boy knew about the Specials, the Sorcerers and their awesome powers.

Ahren and Merien wanted to visit Tandi's family that night. They asked Tom if he knew Tandi's brothers, but the Riverside's, Tandi's family, lived a day's horse ride from the Dyemans and he had never heard of them. The founder member of Tom's Resistance Group had met Stellamar once, but had been arrested by the Specials some time ago and the Dyemans suspected he had been 'treated' and sent to a slave farm. In some ways Teletsia had not changed. Merien went out in the evening and made a bandhan of request on his third centre key. Soon the sky clouded over.

'If we aren't back by the day after tomorrow,' Merien said to Derwin as he and Ahren left, 'you and Conwenna go south to the jungles, because you must find your father before the Sorcerers do.'

'Don't try to rescue us if we get into trouble,' Ahren advised. 'If you hear bad news, or none, send word to Stellamar.'

'The vibrations are cool that you'll both be fine,' added Conwenna. What she didn't say was that they weren't so good for the families, but Ahren and Merien would have figured this out for themselves. 'Here are bones to quieten down any watchdogs.' She gave Ahren a bagful. The two young men went to the wood, found the flying ship and flew into the night sky.

Further north, at the port of Plimpet, Namoh, Saman and Freddi were also about to bring some light to the darkness of Teletsia. On the same evening as the flying ships left, they were secretly taken into Teletsia on one of Stellamar's father's fishing boats. It sailed up the estuary and moored at the Pearl Lords' jetty. It was early morning when they arrived and the fishermen were returning after a night's work, but this time it was not only the pick of the catch that they were delivering to their employer before taking the rest to the fish market in Plimpet, but partisans whose Trees of Life were awake and ready to transform the people of the area. Stellamar came to meet them and led them through the gardens to the imposing mansion that was the headquarters of her family's extremely affluent business. At the main entrance were armed sentries holding ferocious dogs on leashes. This was no country retreat.

Saman and Freddi were apprehensive but Namoh was accustomed to the court of Malak Citadel in Daish Shaktay; he had a great deal of respect for

Stellamar's parents, Lord Coban and Lady Artha, and behaved as he would have towards royalty when she introduced them. He was aware that they were not only wealthy and powerful materially but were spiritual guardians in one of the most difficult areas and had managed to retain their dignity and status even though the Sorcerers were their bitter enemies. They also met Lord Olon and his wife. He was Lord Coban's younger brother and ran the pearl business. Their children had left Teletsia, as had Stellamar's brother and sister.

The family were eager for Namoh to give a detailed account of how Rajay Ghiry had won back Daish Shaktay. On the Island of Creations the talk had mostly been about Teletsia, and Namoh would never tell anyone about his part in the Daish Shaktay freedom struggle unless pressed. At lunch and dinner the next day, as he did as asked, it became obvious that he had played a courageous and important role. Saman and Freddi, and also Stellamar, began to see him in a new light. Namoh had a tendency to give credit to others: Rajay and his friends in the stories of Daish Shaktay, Robin when they had gone to Teletos and even when training the boys from Teletsia he made it look as if Bonor was better qualified to teach them about combat than he was. He never mentioned that he was one of Rajay's ministers and had been helping to run the country since returning from Sasrar.

Namoh would pose as a visiting businessman from the city of Mattanga, Saman would be his intermediary and Freddi was given false identity papers to pass him off as an employee of the Pearl Lords from another part of Teletsia. The point of the operation was to contact the locals and awaken their Trees of Life. Namoh and I had taught the two boys from Teletsia the songs which we used for this. Saman was a good singer, Freddi played a stringed instrument quite well and Namoh played the small cymbals and sang very enthusiastically and mostly in tune.

The first group to be given awakening were the pearl fishers. They were invited to the 'Big House' as the Pearl Lords' home was known as, and many fishermen came with their families. They were responsive and enthusiastic, and living and working on the water had purified their subtle systems, so they all had a strong and fulfilling experience. Many had boats, so they could sail Namoh, Saman and Freddi to the villages and small ports up and down the coast.

The three partisans spent some evenings in the houses of headmen, with all the local people collected together. The singers and musicians would enthral everyone, and then give them awakening. Namoh made sure they all knew how to reawaken their Tree of Life, go into a state of thoughtless peace and meditate for a short time each day to re-establish this, and told them how to use the elements to purify their inner selves and make the two bandhans. It was these bandhans, combined with their ever-strengthening contact with the power behind them, which enabled these simple folk to be immune to the hypnotism and black magic of the Sorcerers. Also the overwhelming sense of fear which had formerly dominated so many people living in Teletsia was no longer there, and with this came an even greater desire to be rid of their oppressors of ages.

Initially all went well, and every time the young men reconvened at the Pearl Lords' home, and brought news of more people having been given their awakening, they could feel the heavy negativity and fear of Teletsia lifting as the collective awareness improved.

CHAPTER 9

THE HOMECOMING

On the short flight to the farm of Tandi's family, the Riversides, Merien and Ahren stayed in the clouds, occasionally dipping lower so Ahren could get his bearings. Soon he could direct Merien from his own knowledge of the area rather than the map and they came down in the same thicket by the stream where Ahren had met the rest of us five years before. The light of a moon filtered through the thinning clouds.

'We'll walk from here; it's not far,' advised Ahren.

'You lead,' said Merien. 'Don't forget the dog bones.'

They felt the vibrations on a few things in advance. It was fairly cool to try and contact Gwant and Mabron, Tandi's twin brothers, who were about the same age as Ahren. He had been much closer to the two boys than to Tandi. It was only fate, in the form of their father's insistence on their feeding the poultry and animals that weekend, that had prevented them from being with the rest of us on the trip to the Temple of Support which had been the start of the journey north. The vibrations were less positive for the Riverside parents.

The two visitors approached the farmhouse through the fields, so as to avoid passing the farm workers' cottages. The path they were on, Ahren knew, came out behind the end of the garden. As he opened the gate and stepped into the well-kept flower, herb and vegetable garden the dogs came to greet them noisily. And greet them it was, because two of the three were the same ones that Ahren knew well when he used to come here. Although they barked, after a short while they recognised Ahren and were all over him, especially when he gave them the bones. Soon he heard Mabron's voice.

'The dogs were hollering about something.'

'Better have a look,' said another voice, his brother Gwant. Merien and Ahren hid behind a bushy fruit tree as Mabron approached. He walked up to the dogs, both tucking into their meaty bones, and knelt down, puzzled.

'Mabron, it's me, Ahren!'

Mabron stood up and looked into the darkness. Ahren walked out from behind the tree and they embraced like brothers.

'We thought you were dead!' Mabron began, grinning from ear to ear. 'But it's true, the messages we got!'

'What were those?'

'Come inside and I'll tell you everything. It's great to see you. However did you get here? Are you alone?'

'Whoa! One question at a time! I've got a friend with me. Merien, it's safe to show yourself.' He came out of the shadows into the moons' light. 'Merien – Mabron, Mabron – Merien. Mabron, just don't ask how we got here.'

'OK. Come in, there's only Gwant and me here tonight. Mum and dad are away,' Mabron led them to the farmhouse. Ahren noticed Mabron's vibrations were surprisingly good; Gwant's less so, but Ahren thought nothing of it, because this was Teletsia.

'Have you eaten?' asked Gwant.

'Yes, but we wouldn't say no to some more,' said Ahren.

'Mum left some soup and grilled chicken; there's plenty left over. Have some,' Mabron dished out Mrs Riverside's delicious food and soon they were all seated round the kitchen table.

'So,' began Ahren. 'Where to start? What were these messages?'

'Last week a friend of mine who is part of our Resistance Group was in Teletos,' continued Mabron, handing Ahren some crunchy bread, 'and he met someone who knew you, and he was given an incredible spiritual awakening which could help us withstand the powers of the Sorcerers. Then he returned and gave it to our group. Oh, you don't know about the Resistance Groups, do you?'

'We're learning fast. That was Robin in Teletos - he's Asha's husband. He's from the far north and was here for a short time. We felt you'd had your inner awakening. It's very powerful, isn't it?'

'Yes,' went on Mabron. 'We also learnt about the bandhan and gave one only three or four days ago that you would soon be back too – and imagine – here you are! After five years!'

'So it's spreading fast then?' asked Merien.

'Oh yes, like wildfire with the underground groups, who are mostly young people,' explained Mabron. 'But we have to be so careful, because the Sorcerers' spies are everywhere.'

'By the way,' Ahren put in, 'Tandi married Raynor Antiquarian, and you're both uncles. She carried on the family tradition and had twins, girls of nearly three now.'

'I can't believe it!'

'What about my parents?'

Gwant and Mabron looked at each other.

'Ahren, I'm sorry, but…' Mabron was serious.

'But what?'

'Your dad. He had a flaming row with the Sorcerers last year. You know him. He won't be pushed around by anyone. They took him off.'

'And then?' continued Ahren, mortified.

'They 'treated' him and sent him to work on the Clatan slave farm.'

'That's terrible! Is he still alive?'

'Yes, he's working in the dairy there, but it's considered irreversible, what they do to people. He wouldn't even recognise you now and he can't speak any more.'

Ahren hid his head in his hands for a few moments, then continued speaking, in a shaken voice.

'And mum?'

'She's still in Clatan, running your father's dairy.'

'Do your parents know about the inner awakening?'

'They know Gwant and I are doing something to oppose the Sorcerers, at least dad does. He's told us what we do is our affair and he won't get in our way, but he doesn't want to be involved. You know dad, he's a wealthy farmer and wants to keep it that way. He won't give us away to the Sorcerers, but he won't do anything to offend them either. He's more interested in the amount of money he has in the bank than any freedom struggle.'

'Do you know about the fulfilment of the prophecy?' asked Merien.

'Oh yes, that's central to our Resistance Groups. We try to find out as much as possible,' Mabron replied.

'It's fairly well known that you lot have something to do with it,' added Gwant.

'And how's my mother?' went on Ahren, his head still in his hands.

'She's very depressed,' said Gwant.

'That's not altogether true,' Mabron objected. 'I went to see her a couple of days ago and gave her inner awakening and she felt much better. Especially when I told her that you might come back.'

'Sooner or later, the Sorcerers are going to arrest both of you, your parents and Ahren's mother,' said Merien. 'That's why we've come to find you. We've got to try and rescue Ahren's father. We've also got to get you two and Ahren's mother into hiding and we must make your parents understand their danger.'

'How come dad lost it with the Sorcerers?' Ahren was still brooding over his father's dreadful fate.

'Last year,' replied Mabron, 'there was a rumour that you and Lee were working for a King Rajay, in a country north of the Great Sea. The Sorcerers went to your father and demanded he told them more. He didn't know anything and was extremely rude to them into the bargain. When they accused him of hiding information he shook the pitchfork he was holding at them. They had him for grievous bodily harm even though he only threatened them.'

'So the Sorcerers have mesmerised Mr Dairyman, taken away his power of speech and free will and then forced him to work for them as a slave?' Merien asked.

'Yes. That's what they do,' explained Mabron.

'I want to see my mother,' groaned Ahren. 'Are we both safe here tomorrow?'

'I guess so,' said Mabron. 'We can hide you until my parents return.'

'Is mum still living in the same house?'

'Yes.'

'Who's with her?'

'Your younger sister. She's like my parents – she won't betray you, but she doesn't want to be involved in anything subversive.'

'I'm going to see mum right now.' Ahren turned to Merien. 'You stay here. It doesn't take long to walk to Clatan. I'll take Mabron with me and if I have any problems he'll come back and tell you.'

Soon afterwards they set off for Clatan via the short cut across the fields. All three moons were up and the clouds had disappeared but when they reached the small town it was late and the streets were deserted. Mabron knocked softly on the back door of Mrs Dairyman's house and after some time Ahren's sister Ahria opened it.

'Goodness, Mabron, whatever do you want so late at night?' she moaned sleepily.

'I need to see your mother. It's urgent,' he replied.

'Can't you come at a more civilized time, like tomorrow morning?'

'No, I must see her now. Can you wake her?'

'I suppose so. Come in.' Ahren waited in the yard he knew so well. Soon Mabron reappeared.

'I've told your mum you're here. Your sister's gone back to bed, but wait a little to make sure she's gone to sleep again. I warn you, your mum's in quite a state these days.'

It was a tearful reunion, and Ahren's mother was not holding up well to the latest family tragedy. He failed to convince her that she should leave Clatan and go into hiding. It was well past midnight when they got back to the farm and Merien and Gwant were waiting.

'How was she?' asked Gwant.

'Not great,' replied Ahren sadly.

'We should rest now,' said Merien pointedly, and Ahren understood he was giving an order as a guardian. They were shown to a bedroom.

'Gwant is not all right,' Merien whispered once they were alone. 'I kept him talking while you were gone and meanwhile I was trying to settle his vibrations, but he wasn't responding at all. I know he's an old friend of yours but I wouldn't trust him. Don't tell him anything you don't have to.'

'He was always like that. I'll be careful – thanks for the warning. Do you think we could put my father right, if we could rescue him?'

'One thing I can do, and so can you if I teach you how, is to cure people of this mesmerism.'

'I believe you. I know where the slave farm is, but we've got to figure out how to get him away from there.'

'I've been thinking about that. I'm going to become a slave trader. I'll go back to the Dyemans and make a pass to say that I've come here to buy slaves. I'll be back tomorrow night and we'll go the morning after. You'll have to come too, to identify your father, so find yourself some disguise.'

Merien crept out of the house, found the flyer and returned to the Dyemans. Ahren stayed and the next morning Gwant was not there.

'Where's Gwant?' Ahren asked Mabron, who was in the kitchen eating breakfast.

'He said the cowman wanted some medicine from the pharmacy in Clatan,' explained Mabron. 'He won't be long.' Some time later the cowman came in and Mabron asked him which of the cows were sick.

'None of them. Why?' he replied, puzzled.

Gwant went to the Specials Station in Clatan. Although a part of him wanted Teletsia to change and he had felt the benefits of the awakening of his Tree of Life, the thought of becoming extremely rich for the information he was about to give the Specials was too good to miss. He didn't intend to give away his friends in the Local Resistance Group, but was somewhat jealous of Ahren. His father had given him a stern talk recently about the need to be practical and not bother too much about who was governing the country and how.

He asked to see the Special in charge. His voice was very croaky and he decided he really did need to visit the pharmacy, for himself if not for the cows. He had to wait for some time until the Head Special arrived. Gwant did not want anyone to know he was there, so the Special on duty told him to wait in the cell where treated slaves were put. The longer he waited there the odder he felt and could feel himself being dominated by a force he could not control. His body was hot and sweating and his limbs would not obey him. Eventually a man came and took him to the Head Special.

'So, Gwant Riverside,' he began. 'How can I help you?' Gwant opened his mouth to speak but no words came.

'This is no time for playing games,' barked the Special. 'What have you got to tell me that's so urgent?'

Again Gwant tried to answer, but couldn't, and couldn't even remember what he was doing there, only that it was something about Ahren.

'I haven't got all day,' the Special continued. 'Either tell me what you came for or you'll finish up being genuinely 'treated'. You're certainly behaving as if you've been done.'

Gwant struggled to recall why he had come and grabbed the Special's pen and pad of paper, wanting to write down his valuable information – but couldn't remember it. He realised he had been spontaneously 'treated', and ran out into the street and home. The Special wondered whether to send a patrol out to pick him up, but decided not to bother. The Riversides were good solid supporters of the regime, even though there had been that bad business with the daughter.

Gwant went home, very scared. He still couldn't speak, although he felt less strange once he had left the Specials' Station. Something told him he had to leave home, so he put a few clothes in a back pack. At the time Mabron was out on the farm because he had work to do and Ahren was hiding in the guest room; he didn't want to risk being recognised by the Riverside's staff. Before he left, Gwant managed to write a note which he left on the kitchen table. His handwriting was a scrawl and he couldn't remember how to spell so it came out like this:

Gon to Teltos with Uncl Jo and catel. Gwant

He walked back towards Clatan feeling increasingly dizzy and confused.

Mabron came in from checking on the cows, who all seemed perfectly healthy and were happily grazing in the lush pasture by the river. He saw Gwant's note and couldn't figure out why it was so badly written.

'He's been a bit strange lately,' he told Ahren, 'since the rumours started flying around about you returning. Maybe a trip to town will do him good. Uncle Jo does sometimes need his help when he takes animals to market there.'

Ahren realised Merien had been right about Gwant. Nevertheless he wanted to awaken as many people as possible in the area, so Mabron rounded up a number of his friends and in the early evening they came over. Some of them were old friends of Ahren's and welcomed him with open arms. Ahren did an impromptu awakening session and told those already in the know more about the powers of the Tree of Life. By the end Mabron definitely decided he wanted to make the journey to Sasrar, albeit five years late, but Ahren said the priority was to try and free Teletsia from the Sorcerers.

Merien reappeared in the evening with Tom Dyeman, who would pose as the slave guard. Ahren told Merien about Gwant.

'I hope he doesn't cause us trouble. We must be extra careful, but don't let's change our plans. I've forged a letter of freedom to travel. I'm now a representative of King Gamsad, the slave-trading king. As he's no longer allowed to do this on the mainland, I'm pretending we've moved operations to an island in the Western Ocean and I'm here to buy some samples for him. I've also got a very impressive forged charter from the old rogue,' and Merien produced it. 'Conwenna helped me make that. She's very creative. Looks good, doesn't it?'

Ahren asked Mabron if they could stay one more night. He agreed, saying his parents would not be back until the next day at the earliest.

'We'd better tell you how we've been travelling,' offered Merien. 'I've got a flying ship.'

'You serious?' laughed Mabron. 'They only exist in fairy tales, don't they?'

'My friend is more than he seems,' explained Ahren. 'Think yourself lucky we've got him to help us.' Merien wasn't sure about this remark and frowned at Ahren.

'The flyer is hidden in your far wood. Keep people away from there tomorrow,' Merien warned.

'I'll do my best,' said Mabron. 'No one goes up there much at this time of year because we're letting those meadows rest. I'll find some jobs for the men to do at the other end of the farm.'

'Don't let anyone see it,' reiterated Ahren.

CHAPTER 10

SLAVE TRADERS

The next morning Merien was armed as befitted his trade. Tom looked suitably rough and tough and also had a long knife and a whip. He was a strong, healthy lad so the transformation into slave guard wasn't too difficult. The farm where Ahren's father was working was some way north of Clatan, and Mabron lent them both riding horses. They borrowed a mule for Ahren, who was dressed as a servant and wore a cloak with a hood to hide his face. He had a short beard and moustache these days and had strapped a cushion on his front to simulate a plump tummy. He put some lightening cream on his face and wore dark glasses so as to look like a foreigner from a cooler country. They prayed that after five years, in which time Ahren had grown from a lanky boy to a strong, bearded young man, no one would recognise him under his disguise. They took the road through Clatan and did not attract any unwanted attention from the few people who saw them.

Soon they saw the dismal locked iron gates and high fences around the Sorcerers' slave farm. They explained they were slave traders and were let in. The guard on the gate directed them to the farmstead. It was up a longish track and as they passed, Ahren could see gangs of treated slaves working diligently in the fields, gardens and fruit groves, with ruthless overseers goading them on, but his father was not among them. However, they had been told he was working in the dairy.

The farmstead was arranged around a yard, where there were a number of buildings for animals, slaves and their masters. The 'slave traders' went to another guardhouse, at the entrance to the yard, and after producing their credentials were directed to the office. These farms often bought and sold slaves, and on Merien's forged travel pass was a directive from the Sorcerer's official in Plimpet to give Merien all the help he needed. Ahren looked in horror at the slaves with their glazed eyes and vacant faces, because this was most probably where we would have finished up if we had been caught by the Specials when escaping from Teletsia. Treated slaves were worked to death and usually lasted about seven years. They reached the office, where a farmer was buying a girl for housework. The cruel, oily man in charge was trying to persuade him to take two for the price of one, plus a backhander under the table for himself. Ahren hoped no one had bought his father.

'Good morning, sir, and how may I help you?' oozed the slimy manager, obviously a Sorcerer. Ahren and Merien had put on the bandhan to stop Sorcerers from seeing their golden auras. Merien presented his documents again, the manager glanced at them and was satisfied. He failed to mind read Merien, but if his attention was half elsewhere he couldn't always pry into a mind immediately, so didn't think anything of it.

'My master, King Gamsad, is looking for a new line in slaves,' Merien lied. 'I'd like to take some of your treated specimens on a sale or return basis and try them out for two or three days. If they're as good as I've heard, I'll put in an order for a shipload and we'll take them up to Plimpet, where my boat is waiting.'

'Only too pleased to do business with you, sir. What have you in mind?'

'I'd like to see what you've got and then I'll make my choice, while we look at the different gangs.'

'That's sensible. After all, you want to know what you're getting,' agreed the Sorcerer, wondering how much he could cream off for himself from this lucrative deal.

'I'll need some younger ones and one or two more skilled people. Do they remember their former skills after they have been eh – treated?'

'To a certain extent. My assistant will take you round. You may find our methods quite harsh, but these are people who've committed serious crimes. They're quite docile now though.'

Merien asked to be shown the garden gang first, and Ahren felt deep sadness as he saw these pathetic specimens of humanity. After that Merien wanted to see the group they had noticed pruning vines when they came up the approach road. Only then did Merien say he was interested in some slaves to work in a dairy. Ahren steeled himself as they entered the cowshed and could see lines of cows being milked. His father was not there and they moved on to the actual dairy, where a variety of products were being made: yoghurt, butter and cheese, but there was still no sign of Ahren's father.

'Do you have any other workers in this section?' asked Merien.

'Yes, there are some men taking the milking herd out to the pasture. They are our difficult slaves, such as one who we had to retreat, because he was initially immune to the drugs we give and the rituals we do to mesmerise them,' said the assistant.

Merien asked for a full tour of the fields, plantations and fishponds, and showed a lot of interest in the whole establishment. Then he asked for one more look at the dairy, because he had a special order to buy some slaves who would work in this area. They went again to the milking parlour and Ahren saw a stooping figure cleaning out a cow byre. He immediately recognised his father and was aghast; he looked so aged and showed absolutely no recognition of his son or anything else. Ahren gave the prearranged signal to Merien, who nodded subtly. Merien looked idly at Ahren's dad.

'Right, I've made my choice,' said Merien to the Sorcerer's assistant, once they were out in the yard once more. 'I'd like that pretty young girl of about fourteen, from the vegetable garden - you'd better write these orders down - and there was a very tall chap in the vine gang, and those three in the food store. I'd like to take them away immediately.' He pointed at Ahren's father, struggling out of the cowshed with a load of manure in a barrow.

'What about him?' asked Merien.

'He's the one we had to send back for retreatment.'

'I'll take that one too.'

'Sir, you wouldn't want *him*. He's a headache.'

'That's all the more reason for taking him. If we go into this business we're bound to come up against a few misfits and I'd like to see if we can do anything with the likes of him. These are samples, nothing more. Could I buy some mules or horses for them to ride on? It will slow me down too much if they have to walk.'

'We deliver free of charge up to a day's journey, sir.'

'No, I'm in a hurry: I have other slave farms to visit,' Merien gave the impression that people did what he asked without question.

By the time they returned to the main office, three large mules and a pony, saddled for riding, had been brought to the hitching post where their own animals were waiting. The assistant said they could only spare four animals, but the younger slaves, not yet fully grown, could go two to a mule. Soon the party was wending its way down the farm road, the purchased slaves silent and docile on the mules and pony. Tom rode behind them wielding a whip and looking threatening, and Ahren had a long knife visible for good measure. They had nearly reached the gate onto the road to Clatan, when they saw two Specials and Gwant, who was looking untidy, dirty and distraught, coming towards them. This could ruin everything.

'Cover your face, Ahren,' demanded Merien. 'Get out of Gwant's sight.' The Specials greeted Merien, realising he was from foreign parts, and Gwant looked absolutely blankly at him.

'Good day, sirs,' said Merien. 'I've just bought some samples from your slave farm. It's a brilliant way of resolving problems with undesirables. I'm going to recommend my king does the same thing in our country. I must see if one of your High Priests can visit us and show us how to do this 'treating' business.'

'Who is your king?' said one Special.

'King Gamsad, the renowned slave trader.' Merien looked at Gwant. 'Do you want to sell this one?'

'Our boss told us to bring him here. He was found wandering around Clatan - he's the son of a farmer who lives hereabouts, but somehow he's got himself treated, so this is the place for him.'

'Seems a good strong youth. I'll give you a hundred Telets for him.' Merien knew this was an outrageous price; forty would have been nearer the mark.

The Specials looked at each other. It was too good an offer to miss and they assumed this idiot foreigner did not know the value of treated slaves. If they gave fifty Telets to their boss and split the other fifty between themselves, everyone would be happy. They knew their boss's love of money and how he made a great deal from dubious transactions like this.

'Done, but we don't have any papers for him.'

'I'll deal with that,' said Merien, and they left, having bought Gwant, or a treated slave who was once Gwant. 'I don't know what this is all about. We'll have to take him with us because it'll take time to sort him out.'

Ahren tried talking to him but it was like communicating with a stone wall.

'Leave him be for the time being,' Merien suggested. They put him up behind Ahren on what was Gwant's own saddle horse, an elegant dapple grey mare. The horse recognised its master even if the master didn't recognise his horse.

'The vibrations of that place were agonising!' wailed Ahren.

'At least you didn't have to keep up a conversation with that Sorcerer or his sidekick,' added Merien.

'How did you choose the others?' asked Tom.

'Ahren and I asked the vibrations. You'll learn our methods very soon. Is there a stream near here? We should put our feet in some running water and clear out the subtle negativity we've picked up.'

'Go up there,' Ahren pointed to a grassy track. Shortly afterwards, when they were hidden from the highway, they heard the sound of a Specials' steam-powered car making its way noisily towards the slave farm. Tom and Ahren looked nervously at each other, because Specials usually meant trouble.

'It's important we soak our feet, and if possible get the others to as well,' Merien insisted. 'If we're less affected by bad vibrations we'll be more likely to get away unnoticed.'

They tried to get the slaves to put their feet in the water but they absolutely refused. Ahren attempted to talk to his father but it was useless and Merien took some pieces of fruit out of a basket they had with them, and put his hands over them to give them healing vibrations. He offered them to the slaves, who initially took them but then spat them out. Ahren sighed; the state of his father was crushing his heart.

'They're even worse than I thought,' groaned Merien. 'They're rejecting the fruit because it's got good vibrations which would help them become normal again.'

'I'll lead you back to the Riverside's farm through the fields,' said Ahren. 'It won't take much longer than the road and we'll avoid Clatan. Let's go - it's no good sitting here and waiting for the Specials to find us.'

'I'll take your father on my horse; it'll help him get to know me. He can come to Tom's farm in the flyer.'

Ahren put his bewildered father up behind Merien and they set off once more. In the early afternoon they reached the thicket where they had left the flyer.

'The Riverside parents may have returned. We'll leave their horses and Mabron will find them,' Ahren advised.

'You're right. I'm going to give your father a sedative, because he may be frightened of flying.' Merien mixed some powder from the flyer's medicine kit in a mug of water and gave it to Ahren's father, who by this time was thirsty from riding in the hot sun so drank it without any fuss. 'You'd better keep Gwant's horse.'

While waiting for the sedative to take effect, Ahren and Tom unsaddled the other horse and mule they had borrowed from the Riversides. They let them loose in the nearby field and hid the harness near where they had left the flyer. Under the saddles Merien left a note for Mabron.

We have the uncle of twins. See you shortly.

'That should be clear enough,' said Merien. 'Which way will you go?'

'We'll take the tracks and woodland paths,' replied Ahren.

'You've got five animals between nine of you, so you'll manage somehow.'

'I'm sure we will,' added Tom, 'and where Ahren's local knowledge runs out, hopefully mine will take over.'

'I'll give you the slaves' bills of sale and the forged documents, so if anyone stops you, you'll have some papers. Here's a spare guard's pass – it'll have to do for Gwant. Hope no one tries to speak to him though.' Merien took his key of the third, or ocean area, which had power over the water element, and began chanting softly. Soon clouds started to form and they heard a rumble of thunder. 'Good thing it's the wet season!' he laughed as the rain began to obscure visibility, so he could fly unnoticed. 'See you at the Dyemans' place this evening. Good luck!'

The rain was now coming down like a waterfall. Merien got in his flying ship with Mr Dairyman, who was completely vegetative, and took off into the thunderstorm, leaving the rest of them soaked to the skin. They wended their way through a sodden maize field then along a path through a wood. It was no good trying to explain to the slaves that they were being given a new life; they rode in a dream.

They reached the rivulet, swollen from the storm, which passed through the Riverside's farm. They followed it until it flowed through a gully in a wood and there was barely room between the foaming water and the steep sides for the horses and mules to walk. Suddenly Ahren, in the lead, felt his horse quiver in terror and stop dead. He saw a sight to make anyone's blood run cold. Coiled on the ground with its head raised and hood spread was a snake, the most feared type in the whole of Teletsia – very large, very aggressive and deadly poisonous, with enough venom to kill a hundred people if it felt so inclined. It hissed and its tongue flickered in and out. Everyone froze except for Ahren, who slowly got off his horse, walked forward and felt for his Sasrar key and the four petalled one, which governed this area. He took them off and held them in front of him, swinging them on their chains.

'Brother snake, I have a key to the sacred kingdom of Sasrar and the one of this part of the world. We have come to put this country right, so let us pass. We won't hurt you, and like us, you are a child of Mother Earth.' He went on speaking softly and swinging the keys. The snake swayed and hissed and looked as if it might strike Ahren but then settled down and slithered into the rivulet, which carried him downstream and out of sight.

'That took courage, my friend, a *lot* of courage,' said Tom admiringly.

'The trick is - is to trust the power of the keys,' stuttered Ahren, in shock. 'At one time we used to control tigers using our keys, but I was dead scared then. I should thank our brother snake, because they say dumb creatures feel our fear and react to it, but he didn't.'

'Could he understand what you were saying?'

'Not my words, but the sense. Animals are in tune with the universal unconscious, and once our Tree of Life is awakened, so are we. I was hoping he'd respond to that, and he did.'

'Whatever, we're all still alive, may the Mother Earth be praised. The snake must have been washed out of his hole by the storm. If he'd got you, it would have been the end of you.'

'Don't I know it!' Ahren refrained from telling Tom that he had once been bitten by a similar one, and had escaped death by a hair's breadth. Like Conwenna, Ahren never said more than was necessary. The rain stopped, the hot sun came out, and they went on until late afternoon, taking turns on the animals. After more fields and woods, trying to keep out of sight, they came to a country road.

'I recognise this road. Our farm isn't too far from here. Do you think it's safe to go along it?' Tom asked.

'No, I feel hot and tingling on my fingers when I ask if it's OK,' warned Ahren. 'Is there another way?'

'Yes, we can go through those woods on that hill, but it's further,' Tom pointed across the valley.

'Better to take longer and not get seen.'

They reached the top of the hill and sat down to have a rest, as the sun was setting. Through the trees they saw the road stretching away up the valley and on it was a roadblock manned by Specials. 'That's why the vibrations were so negative. We don't want to get involved with them if we can help it, even if we do have documents saying we're slave traders. Plus the pass for Gwant could let us down, as it's not really valid.'

Some time later their path again led them near the road and once more Ahren tested whether it was safe to ride up it. This time his hands were cool and he felt no tingles on his fingers. They took to the road by the light of the moons and soon reached the Dyeman's farm. As they trotted into the yard Hograr Dyeman came out to meet them, looking very worried.

'Did you all make it here?' he asked, and Ahren smiled. 'Merien arrived some time ago, in the middle of a shocking storm, but before that we had a worrying visit from some Specials. We'll hide the captives in the cellars under the bull pen. I know they're legal purchases but it'll be better if no one knows you're here. Your father is already down there.'

'Can we take my dad into the house with us?' said Ahren to Merien, who came out to greet them.

'There are some things you don't understand about his condition,' Merien explained. 'Believe me, he'll be happier with people he knows and he'll feel safer locked up tonight. Tomorrow we're going to heal them all.'

'If you say so,' conceded Ahren grudgingly. Hograr Dyeman took the freed slaves into the cattle barn and at one end was a pen containing a large, yellowish-brown bull with long horns and a ring in his nose. He looked extremely fierce. The farmer opened the strong metal gate of the pen and went in.

'Move over, Custard,' he said casually, slapping him on the rump, then to the others. 'He's as gentle as a lamb. The way down to the cellars is here,' Custard moved over obligingly and his owner scraped away the straw where he had been standing, to reveal a trapdoor. The bull looked on from the corner of his pen, eating his hay contentedly. He was used to this sort of thing.

Tom and his father pulled up the trap door to reveal some steps. Ahren could see faint light below, coming from a grill which let in the moonlight, and led the captives down. There was a whole living area – food was laid out on a table and Tom showed the slaves a simple washroom and bedrooms. As soon as they were comfortable Tom, Ahren and Hograr replaced the trapdoor and the bull stood over it. Unless one knew Custard was a gentle soul, one would be extremely hesitant to go into his pen, so the slaves were fairly safe.

CHAPTER 11

AHREN'S LAST LESSON

'What a blessing you're back!' cried Conwenna as Ahren and Tom entered the kitchen. Ahren noticed there was something very different about her; her hair was carrot red. He thought it looked awful.

'We had one or two hiccoughs, but we made it,' he said. 'I gather the Specials came here. Who were they after?'

'Me,' replied Conwenna. 'They've got my description. It's serious. I'm sorry about your dad, but remember how Merien helped put Asha right when she was in a dreadful way after being caught on Sir Tootle's Island. I'm sure he can do the same for your father and those other poor boys and girls you brought.'

'Let's hope so.' Ahren sat down, his head in his hands. He was exhausted, both physically and emotionally. It had been a terrible day: not only the shock of seeing his father, but also leading the band to safety and fending off the deadly snake. Boumi brought him a mug of milky tea and a piece of cake to take the edge off his hunger. 'Derwin, Conwenna, give me some healing vibrations,' he asked. After they had done so he felt better. 'What's been going on here?'

'Something very powerful is looking after Conwenna,' began Boumi from the kitchen range, where she was warming up food for the newcomers.

'After you left, the two girls and I decided to have a bit of a beauty parlour,' Conwenna took over.

'We grow dye plants,' went on Lela, the elder daughter, 'and also a plant which colours and conditions the hair very nicely. We persuaded Conwenna to give it a try. The trouble was I forgot to tell her not to leave on it too long. Then the baby started playing up and Conwenna got busy calming him down...'

'What's this got to do with the Specials?' sighed Ahren. He was dead tired.

'Everything,' insisted Conwenna. 'When we finally washed the dye off, my hair was flaming red. That's why I look like one of the tribals from the jungles.'

'I wasn't going to mention it, but you do look pretty odd,' Ahren said cautiously. He knew one had to be careful when making remarks about girls' appearances, especially Conwenna's. She could be prickly.

'It saved her life though,' went on Lela. 'Those Specials were searching for the seven rebels, especially a teenage girl, Conwenna Prospector, with the usual dark hair and green eyes, and they suspected she was in the area, because a flying ship had been seen near here and she was known to travel in one.'

'I was in the garden with the baby. The Specials saw me and asked who I was,' said Conwenna.

'I said, "Oh, she's a tribal girl,"' Boumi took over, '"my nursemaid. With five children and a farm to run, I got her recently to look after the baby. She's brilliant with him and he's such a handful. You know those people from the jungles? That tribe with awful red hair? They make such good nannies. She's a slave and we bought her last month." They went out to question Conwenna, but I got there first and said, "These Specials want to make sure you come from the jungles and have only been with us a about a month," so she got the message.'

'When I was a kid and used to go prospecting with my father,' Conwenna went on, 'we often went to the jungles and I learnt how to say "hello", and one or two other phrases of the tribal's language, which I said. I pretended to be shy, kept my head down so they couldn't see my green Teletsian eyes, and they believed me.'

'Will they come back?' asked Ahren.

'I hope not. Escaped rebels don't usually make good nursemaids,' Conwenna bounced the baby up and down on her knee. 'They searched for the flyer, but luckily Derwin had covered his with a big pile of logs and sticks, and Merien hadn't returned so they didn't find anything, and Hograr hid Derwin under Custard's pen.'

'That's lucky. Now what?' asked Ahren, more to Merien than anyone else.

'Tomorrow we'll try and heal our slaves,' said Merien, 'and for that I need you, and Derwin and Conwenna. Having been in Sasrar, your Trees of Life are strong. That's the most important thing to be done, and if we keep checking on the vibrations we'll have some warning if the Specials come back.'

'There's another way down to the cellars. I'll show it to you in case you need to hide.' Hograr took them into the farm office and on one wall was a bookshelf filled with books on animal welfare, tips for dye plant farmers, farm accounts and the like. He pressed a spring under one of the shelves and the whole thing opened to reveal steps down to a tunnel.

Later, when everyone had gone to bed, Ahren crept downstairs into the office, a candle in his hands. He pressed the hidden spring, the secret entrance opened, he went down to the cellars to where his father lay sleeping and took him in his arms. Ahren was as brave as a lion, but when he held his father tears came into his eyes and as they fell on his father's face he woke up. There was a flicker of recognition.

'Ahren, my son,' he mumbled, 'I knew you'd come for me,' and dropped back asleep. Silently Ahren returned to the bedroom he was sharing with Derwin and Merien. Merien woke up as he tiptoed in.

'Did you go and see your father?' he asked.

'Yes, how did you know?'

'Because you've picked up a bit of his darkness. Come here; let me clear your vibrations. I'd have done the same if it had been my dad down there, but when they start to come out of their trance, mesmerised people can occasionally behave very violently. That's why I want to leave them until daylight tomorrow.' He lit a couple more candles, to clear Ahren's subtle system with. He moved one of them around behind the left side of his back and a lot of black smoke came from it, until Ahren again radiated peaceful joy.

'There, the candle has stopped giving off smoke and your vibrations are alright again.' Merien blew it out and went back to his bed.

'Yes, my sadness has gone. I think dad is going to be all right! For a moment he recognised me!'

'He'll be fine. Stop worrying about him, otherwise I'll do my guardian act and order you to. Not that you'll listen to me,' yawned Merien. He turned over and was soon snoring.

The following morning was wet and windy, but nevertheless a Special rapped on the kitchen door of the Riverside's farm near Clatan and barged in, as was the habit of these people. Mr Riverside was eating breakfast, wondering what had happened to Gwant. Mabron told him that Gwant had left a strange message saying he had gone to town with his Uncle Jo, but Uncle Jo, who lived on the next farm, had dropped round the night before. He had not seen Gwant for days.

'Your boy came to see us the other day, Mr Riverside,' began the Special. 'He couldn't speak and behaved very oddly, as if he'd been treated. Then yesterday he was picked up north of Clatan. Our men took him to the slave farm, because once they're like that, it's permanent. A slave trader from overseas bought him, so you won't see him again.'

Mr Riverside was silent and his wife burst into tears. They thought it was some trick of the Specials, because the Riverside parents knew their sons were involved in subversive activities. Mabron was also silent, but now understood the note from Ahren he had found. He was completely mystified as to how Gwant had got like that.

Over at the Dyemans the weather was cloudy and by mid-morning the rain was coming down in earnest. This was nothing to do with Merien, but only a very intrepid Special like the one at Clatan would venture through that downpour. Merien told Boumi he needed some lemons and asked if she had any caked camphor, used for keeping insects out of stored clothing. She gave him these things and he asked for a metal ladle with a long handle.

Ahren's father was the first to be brought out of the cellars. Merien took him to a room at the back of the house, which gave onto the garden and was not used much. He had Mr Dairyman sit on a stool in the middle of the room and asked the Dyeman family to make sure no one disturbed them.

'Ahren, stand where your father can see you,' ordered Merien. 'It's good he recognised you last night. Derwin and Conwenna, come here and give vibrations from behind. Don't be afraid if he moans. Take off the extra keys that Lord Jarwhen lent you and put them on the table where they can be seen. Oh, and we need a clay pot for the lemons when we've finished with them.'

They did as Merien asked, and Conwenna found a crock for the lemons. Firstly they put a bandhan of protection on themselves, then made a bandhan of request, praying that the all-pervading power, which manifested so strongly through the Mother Earth in Teletsia, would heal the freed slaves.

'I feel very cool on my hands. This is going to work!' said Conwenna. Merien didn't answer, but stood behind Ahren's father and raised his hands up behind and a little away from Mr Dairyman's back, from the base of the backbone to the top of the head. Then he made a bandhan of protection over him. At first it seemed easy. Mr Dairyman awoke out of his trance and recognised his son, and they embraced warmly.

'I thought I saw you last night,' said his father. 'Where am I?' Merien, Derwin and Conwenna went on raising their hands up behind his back to awaken more of the pure energy of his Tree of Life.

'Dad, we've come back to save you and my friends are doing some powerful healing on you.'

Merien, behind, was holding his left thumb and fourth finger, indicating Mr Dairyman was not yet free of the Sorcerers' mesmerising treatment. These fingers were tingling because they corresponded to the subtle centres that were damaged by the Sorcerers' mesmerism.

'Just sit there and don't worry about a thing,' Ahren went on. Merien started chanting and directed his left hand to the subtle centre at the level of the lower abdomen, on the left side. He put a lemon in Mr Dairyman's hand and told him to hold it.

Mr Dairyman again looked blank, sighed and sank back into his former vegetative state. Merien went on chanting and giving vibrations, and indicated for the others to do the same. Ahren held his father's other hand firmly to give him confidence and the hypnotism slowly and surely began to dissolve as the four powerful awakened souls directed vibrations of love and healing towards him. Merien put some lumps of camphor in the ladle and lit them. He moved the ladle with the flaming, fragrant camphor up and down behind Mr Dairyman's back. Very soon Ahren's father looked completely different: relaxed, calm, and the sadness had left his face. Although older and thinner, he again had that carefree twinkle in his eye Ahren remembered so well.

'Ahren,' he cried, 'what on earth is going on?'

'Dad, you're free. The Sorcerers took you and treated you and made you their slave, but now you're normal again.'

'It was an endless nightmare. I couldn't think straight, I had no free will – I couldn't speak, but I'm fine now. And you're back – back to help us get rid of these Specials and Sorcerers and what not for good and all. Oh my boy, it's great to see you!' he hugged his son. Ahren took the lemon from his hand. It was now shrivelled and darker in colour, and he put it in the pot. 'How's your mother? Did they take her too?'

'She's fine, and now you're all right we'll get her to come here.'

'Mr Dairyman, I'm a friend of your son,' Merien took over, 'please, go outside and lie on the ground for some time. The Mother Earth will help in the healing process. We must see to the others who came with you.'

Merien called in Tom and told him he should learn about this, because there would be many other people needing the same sort of help. Merien had him stand back and watch, and dealt with the next two captives in the same way as he had Mr Dairyman. The healing took a bit of time, and the effect of the mesmerism would come and go before leaving completely, as if there was an internal battle going on, but the vibrations flowing through Merien enabled the healing to finally succeed.

Then Merien told Ahren to do the same with the next one, so as to give him some experience as well. Tom Dyeman was shocked, but saw how successful Merien and Ahren were, especially as Merien explained what was happening. The Dyeman parents were called in and Tom and the other young Dyemans kept a lookout at the front of the house. The last two captives were brought in one by one, and Derwin and Conwenna also did as Merien instructed. Soon the formerly mesmerised slaves were normal humans again, even if they were unable to figure out how they had got to the Dyemans. Last Ahren brought in Gwant, who was in the same state as the rest of them had been – silent, torpid and staring vacantly ahead of him.

'You all go out and look after the others. Take that pot of lemons and put them in some running water,' Merien instructed. 'Ahren, stay with me.'

Merien and Ahren started working on Gwant but he did not respond, so after some time Merien decided to leave it for the day and they put him back in the underground hideout, where they put some lemons and chillies in a clay pot under his bed, left him sitting staring into space and went to see the others.

'Maybe the lemons and chillies will draw the negativity out enough for us to have success if we try again tomorrow,' said Ahren. 'In Sasrar we were told they help with really tough cases.'

'Let's hope so,' added Merien. 'There's something very odd going on.'

'Those Specials and Sorcerers do the weirdest things to people. You never know what they'll get up to next with poor innocent souls like Gwant.'

'That's the problem, Ahren. He may not be as innocent as you'd like him to be.'

They joined the rest of the party while Boumi took some food outside. They ate lunch under the trees in the garden, at a table there, because the rain had stopped and everything was clean and sparkling.

'I pretended to be a slave dealer and bought you all,' began Merien, 'but most of all you must thank Ahren, because he was determined to rescue his father, Mr Dairyman, and we bought the rest of you to make it look less obvious.'

'You're not... Ahren Dairyman?' asked one of the freed slaves, a young girl.

'That's me!'

'Treya here and I,' said another, a boy, 'my name is Hyle - were part of the Clatan Young People's Resistance Group, so we know all about you and Tandi Riverside. Did you get to the northern country?'

'Yes, and now we're back to share with you what we learnt there.'

Ahren soon gave all of them, including his father, awakening and told them that Merien, Derwin, Conwenna and he had used this power to nullify the effects of the Sorcerers' 'treatment'. The captives only had a hazy memory of what had happened after they had been treated at the Special Clinic by Sorcerers and been forced to work on the slave farm.

'Ahren has been a partisan and fighter,' Merien went on. 'He's risked his life many times helping one young man regain his kingdom and he also knows a great deal about the powers of the Tree of Life. His last lesson was this morning when he learnt how to clear you of the Sorcerers' evil treatments. We've come to Teletsia with one intention: to break their power. Do you want to help?'

'Naturally,' replied Hyle on behalf of his friends. 'What do you think these Resistance Groups are all about?'

'Excellent,' continued Merien. 'Firstly you must learn how to use the powers of the Tree of Life. Then you've got to awaken as many people as possible. If you do, the vicelike grip the Sorcerers have over your people will grow weaker.'

'Merien,' interrupted Ahren. 'You three leave now and find Derwin's father, but I'm going to stay here. This is my home area and this is where I belong. I'll see to Gwant.'

Merien, Derwin and Conwenna left for the jungles of the south, and Ahren stayed at the Dyeman's farm to train his guerrilla force in spiritual warfare. Before this, however, he had another mission and in the middle of the night he and Tom set off on horses for Clatan. He had two people to visit and the first one was his mother. They reached there shortly before dawn and Ahren told Tom to wait some way out of the small town, hidden in a wood. He approached his house through the back garden and stealthily crept up to the back door. It was locked, but he knew where they always left the spare key so got in undetected. He went up to his mother's room.

'Mum, wake up, it's me, Ahren,' he said, taking her hand as it lay on the pillow.

'What *are* you doing here again? The Specials came asking for you. They suspect you're back. There's one watching the front of the house even now.'

'Mum, I rescued dad and he's all right again.'

'That's not possible.'

'Yes it is. My friend has healed him but you've got to leave here. Get yourself a pass to travel to Teletos and go along the road in that direction, but stop off at the farm where dad is hidden. If you use the pony trap it won't take long, and if anyone asks why you're going there, say they're friends of yours and you're visiting them on the way to Teletos. Can you do that? You must, if you want to get out of this alive.' While he was talking, Ahren was giving his mother vibrations to her left side, the place of the emotions in her Tree of Life, and felt her becoming stronger inwardly. He told her the address of the Dyeman's farm, directions of how to find it and had her repeat it back to him a few times.

'I've got a pass for delivering produce to Teletos.'

'Then go right now. What about Ahria?'

'She's not here; your sister's gone to stay with your cousin Varda. I told her to make herself scarce for the time being. I'll leave a note for the milkmen saying I've gone to Teletos on business.'

'I must go. Love you, mum,' Ahren kissed her on the forehead. He went quietly downstairs, looked through the front window and saw the Special in the village street, then left by the back door, avoiding the milkmen preparing for their morning round, and sneaked out through the garden.

Next they went to the Riverside's farm. Ahren and Tom arrived just after sunrise, and this time hid the horses rather than the flying ship in the thicket. Ahren knew this place well and was able to get near the milking sheds without anyone seeing him. He kept a lookout for Specials and heard Mabron talking to the cowman, who was milking. Luckily the dogs were not around and the cowman was sitting on his milking stool hidden by the cow's flanks, so Ahren was able to attract Mabron's attention without being seen. They both made off into the animals' food store.

'Mabron, you've got to leave here, and fast,' began Ahren. 'I don't know what we're going to do about your father and mother. We've got Gwant...'

'May Mother Earth be praised, but slow down,' said Mabron. 'I've got some serious news for you.'

'What do you mean?'

'Mum and dad came back after that awful storm. Did you get caught in it?'

'Yes, but go on.'

Mabron told Ahren about the visit of the Special and what he had said about Gwant.

'Merien knew he wasn't all right. We could feel that on the vibrations,' Ahren admitted. 'I wonder how he finished up half crazy though.'

'Gwant's had his awakening. Surely that means he's ok, doesn't it?'

'I'm afraid not. Although once we've had our awakening we can know right from wrong, we don't have to follow the advice of the vibrations. We still have free will.'

'This is scary, he might have betrayed our whole Resistance Group.'

'I'll ask on the vibrations,' Ahren put his hands in front of him. 'No, it's all right, he hasn't, but I feel very cool when I ask whether you should go into hiding. There's nationwide search on for us, and if word gets out that you were with me, or if our flyer has been seen here, you're done for. Saddle a horse and leave immediately, with us. Don't even say goodbye to your folks.'

'OK. It's useless trying to get my parents to come with us. Yesterday I told them the Sorcerers may arrest them even if they're innocent, but dad didn't believe me.'

By mid-day, Ahren and Tom, on very tired horses, and Mabron on his, reached the Dyeman's farm. During the long ride Ahren told Mabron that although they had freed Mr Dairyman and the other slaves of their hypnosis, so far they had not been successful with Gwant. Mrs Dairyman also reached the farm safely, having had an uneventful journey in the pony trap. She brought four barrels of butter, a large earthenware crock of yoghurt and some cheeses - most welcome, what with all the extra mouths to feed.

The following day Ahren prayed hard that he would have the inner strength he needed. He explained to Mabron about healing people who had been treated, and they tried again with Gwant. The lemons and chillies had become discoloured and rotten and were thrown in the nearby river, and Gwant was now much more receptive. He looked at them when they came into the room, and tried to speak, even though no words came out. They took him to the garden room again, and had him sit down on the stool so they could start giving him vibrations.

Gwant was going through a waking nightmare. He had come out of his semi-trance state and knew he was on a strange farm, but didn't know how he had got there. He recognised Ahren and his brother Mabron, felt unbelievably guilty for having tried to betray them, and hoped they were not about to kill him. It did not occur to him that firstly they were not absolutely sure he had been trying to betray them, and secondly that they might forgive him even if they did know. He was filled with remorse, but did not know where to run to if he did try to escape, so stayed put.

'Make the bandhan on yourself like I showed you,' began Ahren. 'Then put your hands towards Gwant. What do you feel on your hands and fingers?'

'My hands are hot, especially the left one,' said Mabron. 'Also both little fingers, and my left index finger is quite painful.'

'Yes, that's right,' said Ahren, feeling the same thing. 'If the little fingers are both tingling it means he's scared, because they relate to the heart centre, and when the left index finger tingles or burns it means the person is feeling guilty. That goes with the subtle centre in the throat.'

'At least he's feeling something,' said Mabron, having heard what a complete vegetable he had been the day before. They continued to give vibrations to the different subtle centres, but to no avail.

'Come outside a moment.' They went onto the veranda. 'I think he's aware of us, but he's feeling guilty and that's stopping him getting better. Let's ask this of the vibrations – "Did he try to betray us?"' They both felt coolness flowing on their hands. 'Now this: "Did he say anything important?"' No coolness. '"Is he feeling really bad about having done so?"' Again, coolness. 'OK, let's go back in now.'

'Gwant, you must stop feeling guilty about what you tried to do,' said Ahren firmly. 'One of the most important things we learn in Sasrar is to forgive, because humans always make lots of mistakes. We know you went to the Specials, but you didn't say anything dangerous.' Gwant turned towards Ahren. 'Forget it now. Try to have the courage and the desire to get over this mesmerism. Say to yourself, "I pray to the all pervading power in the form of Mother Earth to let me become all right".' Gwant moved his lips, stood up and looked around him, puzzled.

'I've ruined everything,' he groaned.

'Look, we forgive you,' said Ahren,

'I don't know how you can.'

'I checked on the vibrations that from now on you're going to be true to the cause of Free Teletsia. The vibrations don't lie and you've had a harsh lesson as to what happens to people who try to oppose the freedom quest. No one here knows the whole story and don't you go telling them.'

'As you say.'

'We're going to have to get your vibrations right because we don't want you going all strange on us again. It may take some time, but these folk here will look after you and then we'll take you somewhere safe.'

'Do you really trust me, after the awful thing I tried to do?'

'Yes, I do. Let's drop the subject. Go and lie on the ground under those trees and pray to the Mother Earth, listen to the birds singing and watch the leaves moving in the wind above you.'

Gwant walked outside, rather shakily. He had grown a great deal that morning. They all had, and Ahren began to understand more how they were going to win back Teletsia: with courage, gratitude, faith and complete surrender to the power of the Tree of Life working for them in the strangest ways imaginable.

Later he showed the freed slaves, his mother, Mabron and the Dyeman family more about the powers of the Tree of Life. Ahren asked Hograr to invite his farm workers and their families, and any available members of the local Resistance Group round in the evening for an awakening programme, because all six families who worked for the Dyemans knew this was a safe house and were loyal to Free Teletsia. The two Dyeman girls, Lela and Rintra, were quite musical, so Ahren taught them three or four of the songs which we had used to awaken the Tree of Life.

Tom stood on guard at the end of the lane and Ahren led his first mass awakening programme in his homeland. By the end of it everyone had experienced the cool breeze of the spirit, the inner joy and thoughtless peace, and were dancing and singing in the large front parlour of the farmhouse. Ahren remembered a similar programme that he, Lee and I had conducted at the home of Count Zaminder, for his army and their families three years before. Before they all dispersed, Ahren had everyone do a bandhan of request that the power of the Sorcerers should diminish and that Teletsia might at last be free. The young lad who had found the flying machines got the experience especially well. He was not an active member of the Resistance Group, but now wanted to become one, so Ahren told him the truth about the flyers, which had both left for the south.

CHAPTER 12

INTO THE JUNGLES

Merien, Derwin and Conwenna flew southwest from the Dyeman's farm and by dawn had left the farming areas. They floated over the endless green ocean of jungle with only the occasional river to show them where they were. Villages and towns were few and far between, and the roads, hidden under the overhanging trees, were almost impassable at this time of the year. They came down to rest during the day, the next night flew on and the second morning found the village where Mr Herbhealer was said to be renegotiating his contract for the medicinal drug. The villagers saw the flying ships as they landed. They were primitive and suspicious, and were determined Merien, Derwin and Conwenna were gods from heaven when they walked into the village.

'Hello,' said Conwenna in their language, 'your headman – where is he?' That was about as much as she could say, but it was enough, and a tribesman, clad in a loincloth and a feather necklace, escorted the three of them to the headman with great reverence. He spoke the common Teletsian language and invited them into his small wooden house in the village compound. He realised the visitors were ordinary mortals but treated them with great respect all the same. Merien established that he was a businessman from a far country and the flying ships were the normal way of getting around where he came from, apologising that the tribesman had been deceived.

There was no sign of Mr Herbhealer and Derwin asked if he was out in the jungles, or visiting another village. The headman was full of praise for Derwin's father, calling him a fine, honourable gentleman who brought much prosperity to their simple lives, but he had concluded his business and left. The headman said that in the rainy season the sensible way to travel downstream was by the river and he had taken a boat. He only knew Mr Herbhealer had business somewhere to the west and had left over a week before. Merien said Conwenna was a prophetess who could give his people a very spiritual experience and very soon the entire village had had their inner Trees of Life awakened. They worshipped a deity who had the form of a tree, so it made sense to these innocent folk who lived largely off the produce of the forest trees.

The visitors soon picked up that their hosts heartily disliked the Sorcerers and Specials and made sure that any who came near the village had a hard time. Now and again the villagers mistook them for animals and shot them, and if they came in boats, the local people would sometimes knock holes in them when no one was looking, so they developed leaks and sank. A variety of other disasters befell the authorities of Teletsia, so the tribals were generally left alone.

'Now what?' asked Derwin.

'You two go on to the mountain province,' said Merien. 'I'm going back to the Island of Creations to ask your mother where your father might have gone. There are a thousand places he could be and I can't risk asking people all over Western Teletsia.'

They spent the day with the forest people; in the evening Derwin and Conwenna went south, and Merien flew north over the jungles all night and all day, and reached the cultivated areas at sunset. He was in a hurry, so risked being seen. He stopped near a lonely safe house in a wooded area, hid the flying ship in the trees, went up to the front door and knocked. A woman looked nervously out of a window, so he loosened his shirt and allowed his four-petalled key to be visible around his neck. A man opened the door and Merien fingered his key to attract attention to it, then the stranger relaxed and invited him in, and closed the door behind him.

'Lord Jarwhen and Lady Stellamar sent me,' began Merien.

'Yes, sir, I know what that key means, but we had a rather unpleasant visit yesterday - the Specials came looking for these escaped rebels. My name's Lakriman Woodseller, by the way. And yours, sir?'

'Merien, and I'm from an island in the Sea of Illusion.'

He later gave awakening to the forester and his family, and showed them the bandhans and how to give awakening to others. He slept for a while and left in the middle of the night. Lakriman saw him off and Merien thanked him, and complimented him on the family's good understanding of the subtle knowledge.

'Now awaken everyone you can,' he urged, 'but be careful of the Specials and people who sympathise with them. This is their doom.'

Next morning, having hidden above the clouds most of the way, Merien flew into the yard in front of the mansion on the Island of Creations. I ran to meet him.

'Hello Asha! Where's your mother?' he asked.

'She's gone to stay in a cottage nearby, with the Restorers and Antiquarians.'

'I must talk to her. Your father wasn't at the village in the jungle - he'd left for somewhere in the west of Teletsia. Do you think your mother could help?'

'Maybe. I'll go and get her.' I found her and she spoke to Merien. She said there were three or four places he might be, but that he would be very mistrusting of any stranger and the only way to convince him of his need to escape would be if she herself went with Merien. I absolutely refused to allow her to and the vibrations were not in favour either.

'Merien, I'm going to have to come with you,' I said reluctantly, mindful of Robin's words.

'The vibrations aren't totally cool, but I don't see any alternative.'

'I know Robin didn't want me to go into Teletsia, but you're a guardian and I reckon because of that your advice overrides his.'

'But….,' he looked at me strangely, then continued, 'Robin is your husband. Shouldn't you listen to him?'

'Not when my father's life is at stake.'

'OK, we'll leave this evening and I'll make sure there's a cloud cover to hide my flyer from prying eyes. Can you organise food and so on? You'll need a forged pass; Lord Jarwhen will help you there. I must get some rest. Flying my craft requires absolutely crystal clear attention and I'm dropping on my feet right now.' He bowed slightly, as he probably often did at his home, the court of the Emperor, and took his leave. Occasionally Merien's true nature showed through his carefree exterior.

I found Lord Jarwhen in the newly converted 'Operations Room'. He had a large map of Teletsia on one wall and pins were stuck in various places with coloured flags to indicate who was where. Every morning and evening he would check on the vibrations that everyone was safe. If they were not, he had decided that someone would have to go in and try to help. When I told him that I would have to accompany Merien to rescue my father, he wasn't very happy, but finally agreed.

Meanwhile, Derwin and Conwenna flew over the jungles all night and the next day, and only came down now and again in clearings to rest a little and eat. Eventually they saw high peaks ahead and knew that they were nearing the mountain valley they were seeking. When they arrived, late at night, they left the flying ship hidden near the castle where Raynor's grandfather had come so many years before.

The castle had been marked on the map as a safe house, so they banged on the door of the gatehouse, showed their four petalled keys to the gatekeeper and felt easy about entering. It had changed hands in the last two generations, but like all the people of this province, the new owners valued their independence and despised the Sorcerers. They were taken to comfortable rooms where they could sleep and the next morning met the master of the castle at breakfast. Like Raynor, he had a paler skin than most plains-dwelling Teletsians and was tall and slim.

'Welcome to Castle Mount!' he said, standing up for his guests. 'Are you two of the ones mentioned in the prophecy?' this man believed in getting straight to the point. Derwin and Conwenna greeted him respectfully, and because his vibrations were good, indicating that he could be trusted, Derwin was equally direct.

'Yes, sir, and we're here to share what we learnt in the northern country with you and your people. I'm Derwin Herbhealer and this is Conwenna Prospector.'

'Honoured to meet you. My name is Erin Heber. Actually they call me Duke Heber. I'm a republican at heart and I'll give up the title once we've kicked out the Sorcerers, but in these times a fair amount of authority is needed.'

'Can we call you Uncle Erin?' asked Conwenna.

'Yes, that sounds fine. Now, tell me, however did you get here? It's the most atrocious time of year to travel.'

'We came in a flying ship,' Derwin replied.

'So, the old stories are true! Flying carpets are for real,' Erin rubbed his hands in glee. 'By the way, we've been expecting you for years. Our people made a secret copy of the prophecy, in case the Sorcerers got hold of the original, which I gather they did. Also, when my predecessors sold our copy to Zack Antiquarian, they tore out the last few vital pages and we still have them. They predict that one of the places you'll start your work is here. Did you know that?'

'Yes,' replied Conwenna, 'the Pearl Lords' copy still has that part. That's why we've come.'

'Did you know it also says that when a flame haired girl and a young man come on a flying bird, then the trees will flower and grow tall here?'

'No, we didn't get to that bit,' smiled Conwenna, 'My hair is dyed - it was a mistake.' At this moment Erin's wife came in. She was short and plump, a complete contrast to her tall and lanky husband. She was followed by two girls and three boys, small versions of her and her husband.

'I'm Rasa Heber. I suppose that husband of mine kept you standing talking and didn't even offer you breakfast. Just like a man! Sit down and have something to eat. You must be famished.' This was true, especially of Derwin, who had an appetite like a horse.

Merien and I left the Island of Creations that evening. We had a number of addresses of business contacts, directions to help us locate them, the usual maps of Teletsia with safe houses, and four petalled keys. Much later we landed on a deserted beach. I knew not to talk to Merien when he was flying, but now we were sitting together on the shore.

'Let's give thanks to the Mother Earth,' I said to him. 'This is the first time I've been in my homeland for five years.' So we did, putting one hand first on our foreheads and then on our hearts, and the other on the ground. 'I found the first key in this blessed earth, and that helped us all escape, so I have much to thank her for.'

'You're right. We tend to think of Teletsia as nothing but a problem, but this earth is as sacred as anywhere, probably more so as this first centre land is associated with the earth element.'

'When we were talking about Robin and you were wondering why I don't listen to his advice more, you started to say something, then held back. May I ask you why?'

'Give me that piece of fruit cake from the picnic basket,' I did so and after a few bites he went on, 'I don't want to get between you two. Rather than asking me questions, use the vibrations to figure it out. I'll say this though – you're very blessed to have him as a husband.'

'I know that.'

'I want to sleep for some time. Keep a watch.'

I did as he asked, mostly staring at the waves breaking languidly on the beach. I thought over what Merien had said. I had got no further, but was mightily intrigued. Later I woke him and we took off again. I slept intermittently and gazed at the seacoast passing below, now the clouds had disappeared. We flew on, past a large river mouth, and in the morning landed in some deserted sand dunes near a lonely safe house. We knocked on the door and having established our credentials were given warm hospitality by the people who lived there. They earned their living finding and selling rare sea shells and pearls, which was how they knew Stellamar and her family. I did an awakening programme so Merien could rest some more. I told the family that as they lived on the sea, they should paddle in it every day and request the Father Sea, the water element, to keep them pure and strong inwardly, and it would suck out any negativity that could make them vulnerable to the Sorcerers' tricks.

On the second night we again flew westwards along the coast. After some time we turned inland, floating silently and swiftly above an estuary that became a large river as we travelled south. We checked on vibrations and the coolest place when we asked, 'Where is my father?' was the third address my mother had given us. It was some way up the river in the jungles. My father was after a very beneficial plant that grew there, which had an extraordinary ability to cause malignant tumours to disappear. It was especially effective for children and we called it the Blessed Herb because it had saved so many lives.

CHAPTER 13

REPERCUSSIONS

Later that morning Derwin and Conwenna met Duke Heber's musicians, who were totally in favour of anything which opposed the Sorcerers. Like many creative people, they felt the new consciousness deeply when Derwin gave them awakening. After that, he taught them the songs we used for awakening the Tree of Life and in the evening Conwenna and Derwin led a programme for the people in the castle and the nearby village. It was a tremendous success, especially when he told them to come back the next evening and he would show them how to protect themselves from the black magic of the Sorcerers, who although they did not have a permanent presence at Castle Mount, often visited there.

Two Specials from Woodenton and a Truthsayer, that is a Sorcerer trained to read minds, received an urgent message from the Head Sorcerers in Teletos to look into the report of a flying ship that had been seen in the woodland area near Woodenton. There were a number of people living there but the Woodenton Specials and Sorcerer decided to begin with Lakriman Woodseller, long suspected of subversive activities. His three sons had been given warnings at school for being unresponsive and critical of the sessions in mass hypnosis the Truthsayer conducted.

The upholders of Teletsian law took their steam car and driver and reached the house at dusk, when the whole family was at home. Fortunately the Woodsellers had just had a meditation session, had put on a bandhan of protection and were feeling joyful and mellow. Grandpa's rheumatism was better than it had been for years. They were discussing the pleasant young man who had given them this great gift and then disappeared as mysteriously as he had come.

'Open up, in the name of the Holy Protectors of the State!' shouted one of the Specials, banging on the door and barging in.

'Come in, sir,' said Lakriman's wife, even though the intruders had already swaggered in uninvited.

'We want to know about a flying ship that was seen near here,' demanded the Truthsayer. He stared at Lakriman but could not read his mind and could not figure out whether he was telling the truth when he denied all knowledge of it. The Truthsayer tried the wife, who proved equally unreadable. He had no more success with the sons and the grandfather - a veil was over these country folk who were usually so easy to mind read. There was something suspicious going on, because they were not frightened of him. Then the family dog, a ferocious hound called Grabbem, came bounding in the open door and did what his name implied – he grabbed the leg of the Truthsayer and gave it a crunching bite. He cried out in pain and the Specials turned to kill the dog, but Grabbem ran off into the darkness outside.

The Truthsayer lost his temper and decided to annihilate the whole family, including the dog. He waved his staff in front of them and chanted the words that invariably meant doom for whoever he singled out. This family was going to suffer massively for allowing their dog to bite him so painfully. Unfortunately, chant and wave his magic staff around as much as he could, absolutely nothing happened and after much frantic and futile effort, the grandfather, a little old man with a bent back and a stick of his own, hobbled over to him.

'Young man,' he said croakily, 'do you want to borrow my stick? Maybe whatever you're trying to achieve would work better with mine.' The Sorcerer turned to hit him, but again Grabbem materialised from nowhere and gave the Sorcerer another hefty bite, this time on the hand holding the staff, then darted between the legs of the Specials and disappeared.

'Kill that dog!' the Sorcerer shouted to the Specials as they ran after Grabbem, who was way into the woods by then. 'And you Woodsellers will *not* make a mockery of us,' he threatened. The Sorcerer was completely mystified by his failure to have any effect at all on them and decided to pull them in for interrogation later.

The Specials and Sorcerer left in their steam-powered car and the driver had not come into the house so did not know what had happened. Before they left the wood where the Woodsellers lived a family of jungle elephants appeared and attacked the car and its inhabitants, trampling and crushing the car and killing the passengers. The driver, who had seen them coming, jumped clear and hid until they disappeared, then made his way back to Woodenton and told the grim story. The Specials and Sorcerers there were puzzled; Teletsian elephants were quite small, and were usually shy and retiring. Another Special went to see the Woodsellers and could not find anything wrong with the family. Grabbem was not there; he had been sent to Lakriman's cousins, charcoal burners who lived deeper in the woods. Lakriman had a carrier hawk which was trained to home on the Pearl Lords' house. He sent it with a message tied to its leg:

They cannot annihilate us once we have the long-promised power. After they left us some elephants appeared out of the woodland and destroyed them.

Within days the Woodsellers gave awakening to all the members of their Resistance Group and showed them how to protect themselves.

Journal of Warzog, Scribe to the Most High Priests of Teletsia

Meeting convened by the Head High Priests of Teletsia:

'Flying ships have been spotted east of Clatan, where two of the rebel children came from, and one was seen near Woodenton. We know they are connected with their return, and we have to face the fact that the prophecy may be starting to work out,' began the Head of the Intelligence Service.

'That is not the attitude to take,' demanded the Master of Annihilations. 'Now the young people are back we can finish them off for good and all, and can then stop worrying about this miserable prophecy.'

'Enough!' shouted His Supreme Lordship, banging his staff on the table. 'We will continue our nationwide search.'

'Flying ships have been seen in the area of the Island of Creations and also the Daish Shaktay warship was spotted off that coast,' reported the High Priest of Ports, Naval Matters and Shipping.

'Keep a watch on the comings and goings from there,' ordered His Supreme Lordship. 'And I want any boats going to and from the Pearl Lords' house followed.'

'Do I have your permission to order annihilation of any people who seem suspicious?' asked the Master of Annihilations.

'Obviously. How else are we to crush this threat to our very existence?' commanded His Supreme Lordship. 'However, arrest any who might be the young people themselves and bring them here. They should not be annihilated until we have picked their brains clean of information.'

A week after they reached the mountains, Conwenna had already awakened the Trees of Life of hundreds of people and had taught them how to make use of its blessings. She knew that every Sorcerer and Special in the country was after her, even though there were none at Castle Mount, and felt that if they did a fire ceremony and afterwards among other prayers asked that she should not be found, she might be safe for some time longer. A large number of people were present at it, and Derwin recited the names of the different qualities of the Mother Earth, in the classic tongue. After this Conwenna prayed, on behalf of everyone present, that the evil of the Sorcerers should be destroyed.

At that moment, a large vulture-like bird that had been hovering overhead and flying around the district for the previous two days swooped down near the fire. It gave an almost human scream, then plunged into the forest below the castle as if it had been shot.

Later Conwenna and Derwin were having supper with the Hebers.

'We don't get birds like that vulture round here, so I sent a man out to look for it. He found it dead in the woods,' Erin remarked.

'We heard a similar story in Teletos,' said Derwin.

'The Sorcerers use them to spy on people. It had a message tied to its leg, but it was in cipher, so we don't know what it says.'

'Give me the letter,' asked Derwin. It was brought, and also pen and paper. 'You look at the pattern of the words. It's likely the word 'Conwenna' will be in this message, because somehow the Sorcerers know she's in Teletsia. We'll look for a word which has three of the same letters in the places the 'n's' are.' He scanned the message and soon found one. 'Right – let's substitute the word 'Conwenna',' – which he did. 'Now, let's assume that the whole code takes the letters two earlier in the alphabet – as is the case with that word – and change in those letters throughout the message.'

Derwin soon worked out the meaning. As they suspected, it was from the Sorcerers in Teletos, for a spy in the district:

To: Agent X134, Southern Mountain Province
From: The Head of Psychic Research, Forbidden Quarter, Teletos
You can expect a visit from the long awaited children of the prophecy. We are especially searching for the youngest one, Conwenna Prospector. She may arrive in a flying ship.
If you have any news of her please return a message with this bird. It understands human speech, so tell it what to do. If she appears in your area, watch her and we will send backup. The same goes for the other rebels.

The Sorcerers' spy in Castle Mount village had been away or some days and returned to the news that a strange vulture-like bird had been seen in the area, and had been hovering above the castle when the strangers from the north did some ritual in the yard. He was told it had mysteriously died and its body was up at the castle. He could not believe that there could be any connection between the vulture literally falling out of the sky and the fire ceremony, which he thought was some childish gibberish.

Meanwhile Derwin had written another letter in the same code, also on parchment, and tied it onto the leg of the dead bird. It now read:

To: Agent X134, Southern Mountain Province
From: The Head of Psychic Research, Forbidden Quarter, Teletos
You can expect a visit from an important secret agent, a girl of about fifteen and she has a boy of about the same age with her. When she appears in your area, connect with her and help her. She will make contact with Duke Heber, because we suspect he is fomenting a rebellion. She will pretend to have some important spiritual knowledge to impart.

The man came up to the castle and asked to see the bird, explaining he had made a study of this variety, and was interested to see it. Erin's secretary took him to it and stared out of the window, pretending not to notice when he removed the letter. The spy read it easily as he knew the code well. He asked if he could have a word with the young girl and her friend who were visiting and was shown to the Great Hall, where Duke Heber was sitting with his bodyguards, and Derwin and Conwenna. The Duke was busy with a petitioner and the man took Conwenna aside.

'Are you the one our friends in Teletos sent word about?' the man asked.

'You mean the little plan to put things right?' replied Conwenna.

'Yes, I see we understand each other.'

'Oh, perfectly. Wait there a moment.'

Conwenna glanced at Duke Heber, after which his bodyguards smartly took hold of the spy and put him in the castle dungeons for a long stay in solitary confinement.

Namoh, now working out of the Pearl Lords' mansion, noticed a suspicious boat tailing them when he, Saman and Freddi sailed down the coast to do an awakening programme. They thought they had shaken it off and walked to a village some way inland. Because of the overwhelming response of the villagers in the area around Plimpet, they did the programme in the village square, and the Specials in the boat who had been tailing Namoh and his friends crept up and spied on them, unseen in the darkness. Namoh finished the programme and they were walking back to the riverside jetty in the moons' light when they were ambushed.

'Run! I'll deal with this!' whispered Namoh, and Saman and Freddi hid in the nearby bushes. Namoh removed his Sasrar key from his neck. To the Specials he shouted, 'I'm the one you want! Here's my magic key from Sasrar!' He held it up, put his finger in the indentation in the back and it turned into a fiery golden discus, attracting his ambushers to him.

The key left Namoh's hand to behead the Specials, but before it did, they fired their pistols at him and he dropped like a stone. They had not received the new directive about not killing anyone who might be one of the escaped rebels. In almost no time all the Specials were dead from the key. Saman and Freddi came out of the bushes and felt to see if Namoh was still alive. He was, but his breathing was shallow and blood was flowing from the wounds.

'Quick, let's carry him back to the boat,' cried Freddi.

'Here's his key,' said Saman, finding it near the beheaded Specials, 'put it around his neck. That might help.'

By the time they got back to the Pearl Lords' mansion, Namoh was very weak. Saman jumped out of the boat and ran up to the house for help, and soon someone appeared with a stretcher. Stellamar was not far behind; she had sent for their doctor, who looked after them and all their workers. They took Namoh to the surgery in the house and Lord Coban, himself a great healer, was also there.

'Sir,' began the doctor. 'I must operate, and quickly. We need to make him completely unconscious.'

'Stellamar,' ordered Lord Coban, 'give him vibrations and talk to him, so he knows he's in good hands.' Lord Coban soon found what he needed, a bottle of clear liquid. He took off the stopper and there was a strong smell, then he held it to Namoh's nose and he passed into a coma. 'Those bullets have got to come out and one is dangerously near the backbone. Use his Sasrar key as a magnet and try to draw the bullet out that way.'

Stellamar did as her father suggested and after some time a bullet could be seen below the surface of the skin, in the wound where it had entered. The doctor, amazed, picked it out easily.

'That's the worst one,' he said, relieved, 'now for his shoulder.' Lord Coban held the bottle of anaesthetising liquid nearer to Namoh, but he didn't stir as the doctor dug around, found this bullet and extracted it. Finally the third one was drawn out of his thigh, also with the help of the key, and the operation was complete. 'We can only pray the wounds heal cleanly and don't fester,' concluded the doctor as he swabbed them with herbal disinfectant.

Namoh was moved into the main house and hovered between coma and consciousness for some days. Every time he did come round, either Stellamar or one of his friends was sitting with him, giving him vibrations or just mopping his brow with a damp cloth. Eventually he regained full consciousness but could not move around much - he was brave and positive and healed quickly, but the visits to nearby villages to awaken Trees of Life had to stop, which was a tragedy, because the carrier hawk from the Woodsellers had arrived with the astonishing news that the bandhan of protection could prevent the Sorcerers from reducing people to ashes.

Stellamar came over to the Island of Creations one night via the bar of quicksand and the causeway, on her horse, which could manage the long wade and even longer swim, if the tides were right. She brought Saman and Freddi with her, also on trusty horses. On either side of the causeway, between the mainland and the Island of Creations, were numerous shoals and rocks so the Sorcerers' Coast Guard boats could not easily patrol the area. When the three of them arrived they gave Lord Jarwhen the news, good and bad. The boys left but Stellamar lingered.

'What is it, my dear?' asked Lord Jarwhen.

'It's a pity we guardians are encouraged to only marry other guardians.'

'Not any more. Nowadays we often marry people from here who've had their awakening. Why?'

'Namoh's got good vibrations and we enjoy each other's company. He's sincere and brave, a senior minister in Daish Shaktay and one of Rajay Ghiry's trusted companions. He's a bit too much of a fighter, but he's had to be, and I'm sure he'd calm down in peace time. Only yesterday father asked if I'd like to marry soon.'

'Let's wait a while. The freedom quest is moving onto another level and now is not the time, but he's an excellent young man. I'll mention it to your father. He's probably had the same idea.'

Namoh regarded Stellamar as an angel: a beautiful but very real vision. When he was so ill, he always knew when she was in the room. He could feel her presence even if he didn't hear her enter, and when he opened his eyes and looked at her smiling, glowing face, he immediately felt stronger. He respected and admired her, but never dreamt she would consider him as a husband.

He was a farmer's son, who by good fortune had finished up with an excellent job. It had not yet dawned on him that nowadays he was an important person in his country, as Lord Santara, the Daish Shaktay Minister of Agriculture and a landowner of substance. The fine house and lands that he and his brother Danard had bought with the money Rajay gave them for their part in the Daish Shaktay freedom struggle now belonged to him, since Danard's death. Namoh was an innocent, easy-going soul, and assumed that when he went home it would be about time for Rajay and his friends to help him find a suitable Daish Shaktay girl to marry. Or maybe he would meet someone and ask advice of the others that she would fit in at the court of Malak Citadel, where he spent most of his time. He knew it would work out eventually.

CHAPTER 14

SLAVE FARMS

Back at the Dyemans' farm, Ahren was in the garden talking with Hyle and Treya. They had known Gwant and Mabron before they had been taken and treated. Lela, the elder of the two Dyeman girls, was with them.

'I've got an idea, Ahren,' began Hyle, 'but I want your advice, seeing as you're an experienced partisan.'

'In Daish Shaktay I was only learning. Rajay, who later became the king, always guided us. You know more about this part of the world than me,' said Ahren.

'False modesty! Anyway, you said Merien had us on sale or return from the slave farm. If so, Tom, as the slave guard, could return Treya and me, and say that Merien didn't want us. We can pretend to be still treated and could give awakening and healing to some of the slaves there. What do you say?'

'It's a good idea, but you'd be risking your lives,' said Ahren.

'Haven't you been doing that for years?' asked Treya.

'Yes, but we had a lot of help.' Ahren had told them about the keys and the guardians.

'And you've given *us* a lot of help, like, you've saved our lives,' replied Hyle.

'Alright, but I'll come with you,' said Ahren.

'There's a problem,' said Lela. 'Actually two. Firstly, all treated slaves have a number branded on their arm and secondly you're going to need papers: where you were bought, and where and when you were treated. Some of the farmers round here use slave labour so I know the deal. Treated slaves aren't that popular though, because they occasionally go crazy and attack their owners.'

'Maybe your dad could get hold of some papers,' suggested Ahren. 'And he could put a brand on me. I've had some battle wounds and this will just be one more.'

Hograr reckoned he could manage this, because the owner of the next door farm had tried having slaves, but they had died. He had been sold very sick ones who were sadly about to die in any case, nevertheless, Hograr was certain the farmer still had the documents. This was indeed the case and that evening

Ahren bravely had himself branded with the correct number, indicating he had been treated at a farm a long way from the Clatan one. Boumi gave him a strong pain killer when they branded him, but it was very sore until the burn healed. Tom later told the overseer at the slave farm that they'd rebranded him, as the original one had been obscured by a wound - one of Ahren's fighting scars.

The next day Tom, got up as the guard, drove his three slaves back to the Clatan Slave Farm. He had genuine documents for Hyle and Treya, and spurious ones for Ahren, who was ragged and dirty. Mr and Mrs Dairyman, Gwant and Mabron and the other de-treated slaves stayed with the Dyemans, and Ahren left instructions about looking after Gwant.

Ahren had been disguised a number of times in the past few years. Pretending to be a cabbage like slave who could not speak was certainly a new one, but he enjoyed a challenge. When they reached the slave farm, Ahren hid his keys. He had two: his own Sasrar key and the four petalled one from Lord Jarwhen. As they were going up the lane to the farm he put them both, and also a couple of four petalled ones for Hyle and Treya, in a tree. There was a bird's nest in a hole in the trunk and he hid them under it. The bird returned after Ahren left and happily sat on its eggs once more.

Tom found the overseer and apologised that although his boss was pleased with the other purchases, he would like to return these two as they were too young and would not survive the long sea journey back to Gamsad's island. Tom said his boss had gone to another part of the country to buy more slaves and would soon be back to make a large order. Meanwhile, could he please keep this extra slave (Ahren) until Tom came for him, because they had nowhere to put him, being as the others had already been sent to the coast for shipment overseas. Tom said this extra one was good with cattle and they were welcome to get some labour out of him until he was collected in a few days' time. The officials did not realise Ahren was Merien's servant, because he had disguised himself so heavily when he went there before, and had stayed out of sight as much as possible, so he was taken on as a 'temp'. They were surprisingly lax and didn't bother to search him at all. When Ahren had been there before he had not recognised any of the people working there, so hoped they would not realise he was one of the escaped rebels, the infamous Ahren Dairyman from nearby Clatan.

He was sent to the cowsheds. Hyle and Treya were returned to their former work gangs, Hyle to the vines and Treya to the vegetable patch. Even though they were treated slaves, the other gang members were happy to see them back. The next day Ahren had to take the milk herd to one of the far pastures beyond a wood with two other slaves and retrieved his keys on his way.

Ahren drove the herd out of sight of the lane and the three of them followed. Then he indicated for the boys with him to come and sit under some trees at the edge of a wood while the cows also lay down near them, out of the hot afternoon sun. Ahren began by making a bandhan of protection on himself. The two boys, both about sixteen years old, looked at him with mild interest, as a pet dog might, and Ahren did a bandhan of protection on both of them. He made a bandhan of request on his hand and did the same on both boys' hands, then indicated for them to put their hands on their hearts, while he prayed, 'Please, blessed Mother Earth, let the mesmerism dominating these your children be absorbed in the earth element.'

He took both his keys off and raised his hands up behind the boys' backs, holding the keys. The jewels emitted a healing influence and the boys were docile and passive to begin with, but soon seemed to wake up as if out of a dream. Ahren touched the top of their heads with his Sasrar key - powerful medicine, and he risked setting off a major catharsis, but all went well. Because Hyle and Treya had already been freed from their hypnosis, the power of the collective consciousness made it easier for these two to become themselves again.

'Wherever am I?' one boy looked round in surprise.

'No idea,' said the other. 'I've had the most awful nightmare!'

'Who are you?' the first boy asked Ahren.

'A friend. I've just got rid of the treatment the Sorcerers did on you.'

'What's that jewel in your hand?' asked the other one.

'Speak quietly. I've come to rescue you. If the overseer comes, pretend you can't talk and be very stupid. This is one of the sacred keys of power which will help to free this country from the curse of the Sorcerers and I'm one of the young people who escaped to the north. I want you to each hold a key for a little while, because they will strengthen you.'

Dazed as they were, the boys got up and hugged Ahren in turn. They had both been sent to the Special Clinic for subversive behaviour while still at school and like so many of the young in this area had heard the rumours. Now their minds were clear again they could remember all of them. While they held the keys, Ahren completed the awakening of their Trees of Life and showed them both the two bandhans, to stop the mesmerism overpowering them again. He also kept a watch for the overseer and when he heard him coming they all appeared to be dim-witted slaves.

That evening he saw Hyle in the slaves' eating hall. As if by chance, Ahren sat next to him and slipped him a four petalled key, and indicated he had successfully healed some slaves. They had agreed that if Ahren had any success Hyle and Treya would try as well. Hyle nodded; he knew what to do.

The next day Ahren found more opportunities to free slaves, in the milking parlour in the early morning. He sneaked off during his rest period after lunch, found Treya in the vegetable garden and helped her to free and heal some of her fellow gardeners. He discovered that some of the boys and men in the hut where he was locked at night were also very responsive.

The next afternoon Ahren left the two boys with the cows and when the overseer was asleep he went over to the vineyard where Hyle was working. Hyle's overseer was having a siesta, and Hyle and Ahren managed to exorcise the whole of the vineyard gang. With a little practice Hyle and Treya became more confident to awaken the slaves and exorcise them on their own.

That evening Hyle and Ahren hit on another idea. All the slaves ate together, so Hyle created a diversion to attract the attention of the overseer on guard in the dining hall. Hyle and some of the other healed slaves pretended to have a fight and all set upon each other. They ran out into the yard, leaving Ahren some time to awaken slaves left inside, while the guards rounded up the temporarily berserk ones. He worked fast and risked putting his keys around the necks of some of the slaves for a few moments, as this was one of the most effective ways of clearing a victim. Most of them had been good people, so once they were free of the treatment they responded well, and Ahren usually managed to awaken their Trees of Life. He could not believe how successful they had been.

Hyle and Ahren met in the washhouse on the fourth evening. They made washing noises - splashing water and buckets clanking, to hide the noise of their whispers, because it was Ahren's last night. Hyle and Treya would stay on the farm and try to awaken other slaves and the more that were freed the easier it became, as the individuals responded to the collective purification. The biggest problem would be to stop the exorcised slaves from talking to each other and giving the game away. Ahren promised he would try to get a message as to when to revolt and take over the farm, and said that if it became obvious and easy to take it over anyway, but on no account to risk anyone's lives.

The next morning Tom took Ahren away. He put Ahren on a mule and they trotted off through the fields and woods to his home. Ahren spent the next day recuperating on the Dyeman's farm. It took him a long time to clear his subtle centres, because healing treated slaves was not easy on the Tree of Life and he needed his awakened friends to restore his inner strength and clarity. He wanted to go to another farm and the following day Tom successfully sold Ahren to one some way further east. This time Ahren was going to have to escape by himself.

Five days later, Ahren was hard at work on the second slave farm and had healed about forty slaves. However, on vibrations he knew it was time to leave and return to the Island of Creations. It was night time and he was talking in whispers to one of the healed slaves who had only been treated for a couple of months, before Ahren had freed him on the first night. They were both sleeping in the same hut. Ahren had spent time on the other nights showing him how to free others, and suggested he become the unofficial leader of the secretly freed group. Ahren also told him that when he got a message, or when the time seemed right, to lead the revolt against the overseers. Although Ahren had no idea how to actually bring this next part of his plan to fruition, the vibrations were very cool when he asked if it could work out, so he left it at that for the time being. He was kneeling by his new friend's wooden bunk bed when the door of the hut burst open. In marched two guards and the overseer, who was a Sorcerer.

'Got you!' he cried, and the guards seized Ahren, one to an arm. 'So, you've shaken off your treatment, have you? Heard you speaking, but we'll soon put that right. Guards, bring him to the Treatment Room. We'll redo him tonight. You can hold him down and I'll say the incantations.'

Ahren could do nothing so went along without struggling. They dragged him to a dark, cell-like room in the basement of the administrative building, empty at this time. The Sorcerer lit a lamp and took his staff in his hand. The guards held Ahren firmly so he couldn't get to his Sasrar key hidden under his clothes. The Sorcerer took a lamp and swung it in front of Ahren to hypnotise him and meanwhile started chanting a repetitive dirge. He took some herbs and small bones and put them on a bed of hot coals, and they began to smoulder and give off a smell that dulled the senses. Round the walls were skulls of different animals and Ahren kept his attention on the top of his head, his fortress of inner peace, the place of the thousand petalled flower of the Tree of Life. In a strange way he felt himself watching this awful scene, as if he was not a part of it. After a short while the Sorcerer stopped chanting.

'How are you feeling now?' he asked.

'Fine, sir,' said Ahren, not knowing how he was supposed to react.

'Right, that didn't work – we'll try something stronger,' said the Sorcerer, and Ahren realised he should have pretended not to be able to speak.

Ahren wondered what was coming next: if he started acting as if he was a bit deranged that might work, but then again it might make things worse, in case it would give him away as faking it. He stayed quiet. Then the Sorcerer looked at him angrily and hit him hard with his staff. Ahren did not cry out.

'Let's try the drugs,' said the Sorcerer, and one of the guards went to a cupboard and took out a bottle. The Sorcerer uncorked it and the other guard held Ahren's mouth open while the Sorcerer forced some of the liquid down his throat. He retched, spat it into the guards' faces and something very strange happened. The guards stopped holding him and started behaving as if they were under the influence of some powerful drug. They lay on the ground, rocking backwards and forwards. Ahren wondered whether to make a run for it.

'Damn you, you've got some strange power!' shouted the Sorcerer. 'I can't be bothered with you any longer,' and he started saying the annihilating chants and waving his staff. Ahren prepared to hit him with his bare hands, but hesitated because the Sorcerer, a strong man, could use the staff as a weapon.

'Please don't do that, sir, I mean the annihilating chant,' blurted out Ahren. 'I'm afraid for you.' As he said this, the Sorcerer burst into flames and was instantaneously reduced to ashes, and the guards were in almost as bad trouble. They stared at the ashes in frozen horror, and Ahren, noticing a large club on the table, grabbed it and hit both of them very hard on their heads a few times. The first he knocked out cold before he had time to come to his senses and the second succumbed to Ahren's superior fighting skills after a few moments. He didn't know whether he had killed them or merely knocked them out, but ran out of the room, up the stairs and into the courtyard.

It was night, the building was empty and no one was around. He was now sure that the Sorcerers would not be able to reduce anyone wearing a key to ashes. He wondered if everyone with their Tree of Life awake was also safe, and dropped on one knee, put his left hand to his forehead and his right on the ground, in a gesture of thanks to the divine power in the form of Mother Earth. Even in this demonic place, the earth responded by sending a rush of coolness up onto his hands and face. His confidence returned.

His first priority was to get out of the slave farm, so he hurried to the harness room and took a saddle and bridle, checked he was not being followed and ran to the paddock where some riding horses belonging to the overseers were standing sleepily in the moons' light, out of sight of the farm buildings and slave quarters. He caught a horse, put the saddle and bridle on it and rode it towards the river that formed one of the boundaries at the end of the farm, forced it to enter the water and swim across, then came to the road, having avoided the guard post at the entrance to the farm.

He made for an abandoned hut in a nearby wood. He and Tom had hidden his belongings under some dead leaves that had blown in through the broken door. He found his maps, identity documents and respectable clothes, which enabled him to pass himself off as an innocent traveller. He had arranged with Tom that if he did manage to escape, he would leave him his four petalled key. Ahren had shown Tom the options which went with this one – the authority to ask for help from the earth element and for protection from the Sorcerers, a pass key to the safe houses and the ability to use it to help clear people from the effects of mesmerism. No one wearing a four-petalled key could be mesmerised or annihilated and the aggressor would most probably himself be destroyed. Ahren buried it a little under the earth and covered it with the same leaves that had hidden the maps. He prayed no one else would find it, because the keys were dangerous if they fell into the wrong hands. The horse he had taken was a nondescript brown and he set off northwards at a smart trot, intending to be far away by dawn. The overseers at the slave farms did not expect their slaves to have the wit to steal horses so did not guard them, fortunately.

Ahren rode all night, keeping to the road which, according to the occasional signposts, led eventually to Plimpet, and shortly before sunrise saw a similar looking brown horse to the one he was riding, in a field by the road. He put his worn-out mount into the field and helped himself to the fresh one. He felt bad doing this, but his life was at risk, and he had to get much further away from the slave farm in order to be safe. As he was already some distance from it he reckoned the chances of the first horse being located would be remote, because it had no distinguishing marks or brand. He remembered the name of this farm, Deepal Rose Farm, written on a bar over the lane up to it, memorised the name of the nearest town, and promised himself he would come back and make amends for his theft one day. With his fresh horse he was much nearer the sea by midday and decided to stop at a safe house farm, as both he and the horse were exhausted. Unfortunately, as he rode up the farm track, he heard a Specials' steam car.

He made a bandhan of protection, a bandhan around his body with his key to hide his golden aura, and rode on. The Specials' car came round the corner, frightened his horse, and stopped. Ahren managed to control the animal and was asked to dismount and give his credentials. He presented his fake documents.

'So, you're coming from Teletos, bound for Plimpet,' said the Sorcerer, when he looked at Ahren's travel pass. 'Why are you visiting this farm?'

'I want to rest awhile. I was told these people would be hospitable, by a business contact in the city.'

'Where was your business in Teletos?'

'The Jewellers' Quarter,' lied Ahren. He had never been to Teletos and it was the only area he knew the name of. The Sorcerer suspected something, because Ahren was described as a dealer in animals. He tried to read Ahren's mind, hit a blank wall, became angry and accused him of lying. Ahren responded with a bland smile and something snapped in the Sorcerer.

'Arrest him!' snarled the Sorcerer. 'Take him in for questioning!'

'I'm completely innocent,' pleaded Ahren, 'and I'm only riding round my country on business.' He had forgotten how the Sorcerers expected cringing servility even from free citizens, and this so called Protector of the State was unusually short tempered. He had been told to annihilate anyone who gave trouble, because of the rumoured uprising against their Holinesses the High Priests.

The Sorcerer could not see Ahren's golden aura, so had no idea that he was one of the escaped rebels. He took his staff and began waving it around, stared at Ahren and chanted the spell of annihilation, but Ahren was not even smouldering, let alone turning to ashes. After a few moments the spell rebounded, there was a lightning flash and a puff of smoke and all that remained of the Sorcerer were his golden rings and a heap of burning ashes on the ground.

'Are you.... an agent of... of Their Holinesses?' stammered the Special driving the car.

'You could say so,' replied Ahren.

'Why didn't you tell us?'

'I thought he'd realise. I'm on a secret mission and that information is encoded in my travel pass. He should have understood it, as a High Priest.' Ahren didn't think much, but when he did, he thought fast.

'I'm sorry sir. I apologise deeply for having delayed you,' replied the Special, mortally afraid he was the next to be wiped out.

'That's all right, my man,' Ahren rejoined in a superior tone. 'I accept your apology, but clear up that mess, will you? You'd better not say anything about this for a few days, until I've reported to my superiors, otherwise I'll see that you both get the blame for trying to detain me. Tell your colleagues back at your Police Post that this High Priest,' Ahren pointed to the ashes, 'has been called away on urgent business.' He probably has, thought Ahren, to some very unpleasant part of the netherworld.

Ahren rode on towards the safe house feeling shocked and hollow inside. He had now killed at least two, possibly four people in the last day and he never liked killing people, even Sorcerers. He did not have his four petalled key and when he reached the safe house had to talk his way in without it. He told them that he had been sent by Stellamar, but this did not sway the family, especially as Ahren's anxiety showed and his voice shook. Then he showed the owner his Sasrar key and explained it was a more powerful type and that it had just reduced the Sorcerer who had been bothering them to ashes. The farmer asked if he could see the remains of the Sorcerer, so Ahren took him down the road and although the Specials had left there was still some evil smelling ash on the ground. This convinced the farmer, who told Ahren that the Sorcerer and Specials were searching for a girl of about fifteen called Conwenna Prospector.

He was invited in, given food and then he rested in their hidden room. Ahren asked the farmer to collect together any members he could of their Resistance Group and in the evening he gave awakening to the family and about a dozen young people from round about. He went through the usual routine, his identity slipped out and he was again the renowned hero. He left in the early morning and an easy ride took him to the home of the Pearl Lords near Plimpet soon after midday. He gave his name at the gatehouse and a message was sent to Stellamar. She came to meet him and together they walked up her parents' driveway to safety.

Ahren was appalled to hear that Namoh had been shot. They spent time talking and laughing together, and despite his wounds Namoh was in a good way. Stellamar and her father Lord Coban were adamant that he could not be moved yet but advised Ahren to go over to the Island, so he left the next day, disguised as a stout aunty visiting her family along the coast. He had padded himself, made sure he had shaved very closely, put on a wig that Stellamar had got hold of and practised having a voice which went with a middle aged lady. There was much laughter all round, especially as he rode side-saddle on a fat and docile horse, which befitted his station in life. He borrowed one of the Pearl Lords' men as a bodyguard because Stellamar warned him that there were Specials on the coast road and beaches.

Ahren and the bodyguard took the ferry across the estuary, rode along the road to the west and soon reached a road block, but the disguise held up and they were allowed through. Where the road wound its way through the coastal scrubland they turned into the dunes, Ahren bid the bodyguard farewell and crossed the bar of quicksand using the power of the key, just as the seven of us had done so long ago. By then the sun had set and Ahren swam his horse to the Island of Creations via the causeway, under cover of darkness. The patrols further down the beach did not see him.

Chapter 15

Herb Gatherers

There was no safe house near Davaton, where we hoped to find my father, so Merien landed the craft in the forest before dawn and we hid it as best we could. We both had backpacks, staffs in our hands and had changed into travel stained clothes. We walked down a lightly wooded valley, flowers overhung a fast flowing torrent and it would have been a beautiful walk if our quest had not been so desperate. We reached the village as dawn was breaking and were unfortunately met by some Specials coming off their night shift.

'Your travel passes,' said one.

'Here, sir,' Merien produced them.

'Where are you from?'

'One of the islands in the Western Ocean, but my wife is a Teletsian. We're herb gatherers. We heard there was a wholesaler in the village who'd buy some of our stuff.'

'Yes, there is a chap here. He came to the office to get his pass signed yesterday, but there's some problem and he's in the lockup for questioning.'

'Perhaps we'll be able to see him afterwards.'

'You'll be lucky. He won't be capable of anything much after that. Here are your passes,' he lost interest in us and walked on.

'Merien, you've got to do some quick thinking.'

'What about you? You're just as likely to have a brainwave.'

Together we came up with a couple of possible plans and walked towards the Specials Office. When we got there, the daytime Special had just come on and said he was waiting for a High Priest, in other words a Sorcerer, to come and question Mr Herbhealer, who was in one of the cells. The Special's second in command had gone to fetch the Sorcerer and would be back with him by midday.

'I've got some incredibly valuable and rare healing herbs, and I know Mr Herbhealer,' said Merien. 'Can I talk to him about them?'

'You'll have to wait until the High Priest has seen him,' said the Special. 'You probably won't be allowed to though, because he won't be let free again. Some of his family are on the 'Most Wanted Criminals' list. You know what happens to the relations of people who get themselves in that sort of trouble.'

'Yes. I'm going to have to find a new herb dealer.'

'That's your problem.'

'Sir, these plants really are valuable. They're worth more than twenty Telets a basketful and I know where there are lots more to be found. There's one place a little way out of the village and if I show you where to get them and what they look like, you can make a great deal of money. If I do this, will you let me talk to Mr Herbhealer for a few moments? I need the names of reliable dealers and he'll know them.'

'All right, you show me the herbs and then I'll let you have a word with him.' The Special left the large key ring with his keys on it in the drawer of his desk.

'This way,' and Merien led him out of the village and into the jungle. At first Merien went in front and later I went ahead while he pretended to look at some interesting plant. I talked to the Special to distract his attention. Merien came up behind him and hit him hard enough with a rock to knock him out. Merien was strong and trained in combat, and had a knife to do the job more thoroughly if the rock hadn't worked, which it did. We had some rope in the flying ship, which I fetched, and we tied him up, gagged him and dragged him off the path into the wood.

We ran back to the Special's Station, grabbed the keys and found the lockup, and there was my father, lying in a corner on the floor. Merien tried the keys and finally one worked, by which time my father had woken up. He saw me and I gestured to him to be quiet. Once the iron grid door was open I went in and hugged him.

'Asha, my beloved daughter! How did you find me?'

'Tell you later dad. It's wonderful to see you. Come quickly, but look as if you're walking out, having been released.'

'What's going on?' he was utterly confused.

'Don't ask, Mr Herbhealer, just do as we say,' Merien replied. We walked back to the front of the building and an elderly man came in.

'Where's that wretched Special gone? He ordered me to come at sunrise, and now I'm here and he isn't,' he grumbled.

'Do us a favour and don't say you saw us leave,' Merien begged.

'Don't worry, I won't.'

We set off up the empty street and once out of the village ran up the valley to the hidden flying ship. When we reached it my father was amazed. I explained what was going on while Merien did his storm raising routine and within a remarkably short time thick, low clouds appeared. My father was a slim man of medium height and I am not tall, and was then lightly built, so together we only weighed as much as one tall, heavy man, and the flying ship was designed for two, of any size or weight.

'I can't take you to the Island of Creations, because it uses too much fuel if we overload the flyer and although at a pinch I can fly it more or less with my attention, it's a great strain to do so for a long way,' explained Merien.

As we took off, the rain started to pour down and we flew over the thick clouds, due east. Soon the clouds disappeared and we went on for some time.

This was a very thinly populated part of Teletsia and we landed in an area of jungle. Once on the ground, I gave my father his awakening. Merien was drained and exhausted, and lay flat out on a bed of leaves, resting. My poor father! First he had been arrested, then freed, then seen Merien raise a storm and had finally been bundled into a flying ship. Nevertheless, he got his awakening and was overjoyed we had turned up when we had.

We got out the map and saw we had flown a longish way. We had been navigating partly by compass and partly by landmarks, and worked out we were close to the nearest safe house, which was a waterside inn for people travelling on the large river nearby. There was a ferry here, as the main road from the west of Teletsia to Teletos crossed the river at this point. We could see the inn on a small cliff overlooking the river, below us. We decided to rest and hide for the remainder of the day. Before I lay down under the trees, I put my maps, documents and money in a small bag and hung it around my neck, under my clothing. My backpack, containing clean clothes and food, completed my belongings. We had a sleep, awoke at dusk and ate something from our supplies.

'Merien, I'll hide at this safe house and you take my father to the Island. Come back for me after that,' I said. 'Keep checking on the vibrations and once you feel cool to the question, "Am I safely at the inn?" take off.'

I waved them goodbye, confident that my disguise would hold up, because was I not back in my own country now? I walked down the hill towards the river, glad that with my Sasrar key I didn't need to be afraid of wild animals, being as there were some dangerous ones in these parts. I boarded the ferry across the river, in the company of a number of other travellers, all of whom looked similar to me – ordinary Teletsians doing ordinary Teletsian things. I cautiously approached a rather run-down building, proudly describing itself as 'The Coffee Ferry Inn, First Class Accommodation' and entered the front door. A middle-aged woman was on the front desk and I asked if I could see the proprietor.

'I'm his wife. What can I do for you?' she began. I put my hand on the four petalled key around my neck and placed it outside my clothing. She recognised it and continued. 'Yes, of course. Put that away now, because you don't want the wrong people seeing it. Go down the passage there. It leads to the back, where we live. My daughter will look after you.'

I met her, a girl of about Conwenna's age, and some time later Mr and Mrs Innkeeper joined us. We got talking and soon I awakened their Trees of Life. It turned out that even in this remote area there were pockets of people who wanted change. After this Fern, the daughter, said she would walk me down to some hidden living quarters below the inn, in a series of caves, which could be reached by going along a path through the wood, so we went out of the front door and down the approach road. There were high banks on each side and as we walked I heard the chugging noise of a Specials' steam van. I tried to be confident and continued to walk as if nothing was amiss. The car passed us but then it stopped. Two Specials jumped out, grabbed me and flung me in the back of the van. As they did so, a Sorcerer got out of the front.

'Lock her in and we'll be away to Teletos after we've eaten something. She's one of the dangerous ones, because of her golden aura. Don't touch her. They said we mustn't have more contact with them than is absolutely necessary.'

I realised my fatal mistake. I had forgotten to put on the bandhan to hide my golden aura and the Sorcerer had spotted it. In the back of the van was a bunk bed, a small washroom and some open space where they had thrown me. There were little windows but they were covered with metal bars. I was a luxury class prisoner – cold comfort! On the bright side, they hadn't tied my hands and hadn't stripped me of my keys. I sat on the bed, made every bandhan and key option I could think of except the fiery discus - even the one to call the tigers and flying horses, and waited. Later I heard the Specials and Sorcerer coming back and heard a noise of some wild animal attacking them. Unfortunately the Specials were armed and fought off whatever had come to help me.

'Dangerous part of the country, this,' said one voice.

'Good thing my gun was loaded,' added another.

'Let's get out of here. We'll take turns to drive and should be half way back to Teletos by the morning.' I could hear them stoking the car and off we went. I overheard them saying that a number of these vans were travelling round this area, because our flying ship had been seen. It was my extremely bad luck they had stopped at this inn for dinner on their way home after a fruitless day's searching.

PART TWO

INFILTRATION

CHAPTER 1

ON THE RUN

It was a terrible night because I had to be alert in case the Specials stopped and opened the door. I kept renewing the bandhan for animals, because this was my only chance of escape. I dozed off intermittently and the van trundled on. Periodically the Specials stopped to put more coal in the fire of the machine but did not open the door at the back, and no ferocious beasts came to my aid. In the morning the van stopped once more and again I made the bandhan for the wild animals. Soon after this I heard footsteps approaching and the back was opened.

'Here's some breakfast,' said one of the Specials. I hid by the door, in the corner, silent. 'Where are you?' he demanded and got in. As he did I hit him as hard as I could on the head with an iron bar I had spent most of the night unscrewing and levering off the collapsible bed. He was temporarily stunned.

At the same time I heard the snarling of a large, dangerous creature, the Teletsian tiger. There were two of them and they were attacking the other Special and the Sorcerer. The Special thought he was safe in this less wild part of Teletsia and did not have his gun on him, and the Sorcerer didn't have his staff so they were both vulnerable. I grabbed my backpack, jumped out and made for the cover of the nearby wood, as we were parked in the corner of a large empty yard behind a pile of coal as high as a house. I ran on, to a lane which wound up a hill and when I was well out of sight hid behind a hedge, panting. I heard shouting, stood up and looked through the hedge at the yard below. Some workers there had heard the Sorcerer screaming and the third man had recovered from my blow and staggered out of the truck. The tigers had disappeared and the workers were yelling at their ferocious guard dogs, but before the workers could reach the Specials and Sorcerer, the dogs also set upon them and they were left lying in a mangled heap on the ground. None of my captors were in any state to chase after me or even tell the workers to.

I said a prayer of thanks, but this was only the beginning of my problems. As I was escaping I saw a sign, 'Panvale District Steamcar Refuelling Depot' and at the junction of the main road and the lane I ran up was a signpost on which was written 'Panvale Town - 8', and the lane went to 'Saundar Village - 2'. While sitting behind the hedge I made a bandhan over the map with my keys and the location of the safe houses became visible. I hoped there would be one nearby, but the nearest was a long way east, north of the main road. I made a bandhan of request asking that I might be found by Merien or one of my powerful friends, then made another one for the flying horses, because I knew Robin would soon be arriving from the north with them, and however far away they were they would try to answer my call.

I put on the clothes in my backpack and buried, under some loose stones, the dirty and torn ones I had worn when pretending to be a herb gatherer, because it was no good having a disguise that all the Specials in Western Teletsia were looking for. I took off my battered hat and covered my hair with a long cotton scarf so now looked like a respectable young countrywoman. I had barely finished changing when I heard the clop of horses and the sound of wheels. I checked on the vibrations and felt a welcome coolness as a farm wagon came round the corner of the lane, the driver sitting on the front with a boy.

'Whoa, my beauties!' he reined in the horses. 'Want a lift, lass? I'm going to market in Panvale,' and he indicated for me to climb onto the wagon.

'Yes, please, if that isn't too much trouble.'

'You a stranger around here?' he asked as we set off for the main road.

'Yes, and I need to get to Lahary.'

I looked nervously at the depot as we passed. The Specials' van was still there but the Specials and Sorcerer had been taken away.

'I've got a lot of friends in the market and I'm sure one of them can help you. Some of the farmers sell their produce to stallholders, so they go straight home after delivering it.'

One good thing about the Sorcerers' regime was that it was so draconian it was safe for a young woman like me to travel alone, at least in the daytime. After some time we reached the busy country market. The farmer unloaded the wagon, parked it up a side street and I waited in it while he went to look for a lift. His son stayed with the wagon to make sure the horses didn't wander off. I checked again on the vibrations that I was safe, because if the farmer had gone to the Panvale Specials, I would have been in deep trouble. Again it was cool, and I asked the little boy if he would like to feel really happy inside. I made it like a game, he got his awakening and I showed him the two bandhans, one to keep him safe and one to ask for something. Soon his father returned.

'I've got you a lift some of the way and the wagon is leaving now. I mentioned that you might give money. Is that all right?'

'Yes, fine.' I did have some Teletsian money.

My next lift was a farmer who bred and trained riding ponies, and as we neared his farm I asked if I could buy one, and offered him what I assumed to be a good price, based on what I knew ponies cost five years before. He sold me one and the harness that went with it. It was white and I would have preferred a less noticeable colour, but couldn't exactly say so.

The farmer's wife invited me to lunch with them. I felt her vibrations and they were cool, although I did not trust her husband. I risked giving her awakening when he had gone out to work after the meal and she got it, and I picked up that their relationship was one of convenience, not mutual love and trust. However, that was not my business. I told her my travel pass had been stolen the night before, at the inn where I had stayed, and she agreed to help me out; they had one for going to Lahary on business. She said it would create a problem with her husband when he found it had gone, but that he would be unlikely to make a fuss if I could give her some money for it. I left the farm in the middle of the afternoon, having used all my money on either the pony or the pass. The pass was accompanied by a note, signed by Mrs Horsebreeder, saying I was delivering the pony to its new owners.

All went well and I was soon nearing Lahary, which could be seen in the valley ahead of me. I rounded a corner and there was a road block, right in front of me. On each side of the road were tall trees stretching back some way, with thick bushes and other undergrowth, so there was no chance of escape. Luckily I had previously put on the bandhan to hide my golden aura, because a Sorcerer and two Specials were manning it.

'Halt, in the name of the Holy Protectors of the State!' cried one of the Specials. I stopped and he went on speaking: 'Who are you and what is your business?' I tried my best not to allow my fear to show and at that moment the sun came out from behind a cloud, as if to say, 'Don't worry, the Mother Earth is protecting you.'

'I work for the Horsebreeder family and I have to deliver this pony for them.'

'I know of them,' said one of the Specials. 'They usually have a boy doing that.'

'He's ill, and they've taken me on temporarily,' I lied hopefully. 'Here's my pass, and a note from Mrs Horsebreeder.' I showed it to him.

'She's not the one,' the Sorcerer stared at me and said to the other Special, 'The message said to look out for the light. That's why they wanted me here. There's nothing unusual about her in that way, but I suddenly feel very hot. I want to have a few words with her.' He ordered me to follow him into the shade of a tall tree on the other side of the road and I left the pony with the Specials.

'There's something not right about you,' he complained.

'Sir, I'm a perfectly normal country girl.'

'Then why can't I read your mind?'

'I don't know, Your Honour, but I've nothing to hide.'

'Oh no?' He picked up his staff and poked at my overshirt, exposing my keys. 'Guards, over here! It's her!' he shouted, and turned round to the Specials who were holding my pony.

The Sorcerer started chanting something and I clutched at my Sasrar key. To my utter amazement it rejected my hand and transformed into the fiery discus. I don't know if he wanted to annihilate me or mesmerise me, but I remembered Rajay's words: 'With your Sasrar powers, I doubt the Sorcerers would manage to reduce you to ashes,' and within moments the Sorcerer was beheaded by my key. The Specials saw this and ran away into the trees, terrified. I dashed after the pony they had abandoned, and which was about to make off for its former home and leave me stranded at the scene of the crime, and just managed to catch its trailing rein.

I quickly retrieved my key, which had by now reverted to its usual form and was lying innocuously on the ground, mounted the pony and set off for Lahary as fast as I could. As I rode, it occurred to me that somehow the key knew it had to destroy that Sorcerer. How could a key 'know'? Then I realised that the all pervading power, working through the keys, knows everything.

Fortunately I met no one until I entered the town. I slowed to a steady trot so as not to attract attention and after the fort at the end of the town turned up the lane that led towards the farm which was a safe house, according to my map. I hurried on, always uphill, through four villages, and came to rolling grass-covered downs, the area of the Temple of Support, the sacred stone temple from where we had made our escape five years before.

It was evening and my pony was tiring. There was a fork in the road and I paused, uncertain as to which way to go. As I did so I heard the sound of galloping hooves behind me. Although this was open country, there were brakes of trees here and there, so I quickly hid myself and the pony behind a nearby clump. The light was fading and we could not be seen from the road. I dismounted and held my pony by the bridle, so it did not make any noise. The riders came to a stop. I felt harsh, hot vibrations.

'They said she was riding a white pony,' said a man's voice.

'Which way do you reckon she's gone?' added a second.

'If she's one of the escaped rebels she'll make for the stone circle, and if she's an innocent traveller she'll probably go to the farms up ahead.'

'They were pretty sure she's a rebel. We'll go to the stone circle first, and if she's not there we'll go to the farms tomorrow morning.'

'How far is it?'

'Some way, but we'll make it by midnight.'

'They say those rebels have awesome powers. Do we really want to risk our lives going there? It's creepy enough in daylight, let alone at night.'

'Are you a Protector of the State or what? The reward will be enormous if we can catch her! We'll take the right hand fork.'

They galloped off and I crept out onto the road when all was quiet. Now I knew the way to go I urged my tired pony on and the ground of the whole of this area radiated vibrations, so despite the knowledge that I was being pursued, I felt less scared. Night had fallen when I finally made it to the safe house some time later; this one was in a small village in a dip. I knocked on the door of the largest house, a substantial place with a number of farm buildings behind.

'I'm looking for Mr Herder,' I enquired as a stout, healthy woman opened the door.

'We're three families here, all called Herder. Which Mr Herder would you be looking for, then?' she smiled. I risked allowing my four petalled key to be visible by the light coming from inside the house.

'Come in, dear. We're all in the know here. You can't live so close to the Temple of Support these days and not be! Zoey!' she shouted at her son, a lanky teenager very like Ahren used to be when I first met him. 'Take this young lady's pony. She looks as if she's had a fair ride.'

'The Specials are after me,' I explained nervously. 'They've gone to the Temple, but then they'll come here and look for me.'

'Don't worry, we'll keep a watch. We can hear them coming from a long distance, because it's so quiet up here. Zoey, you know how to hide the pony, don't you?'

'Yes mum.'

'The bootblack is in the cupboard.' She turned to me as Zoey led my pony away. 'Your pony is going to be black and white, piebald, very soon. Even if they do search the stables they won't suspect anything.'

'The Specials will come here tomorrow morning,' I said.

'Can't be too careful.'

The other three children took turns in keeping a lookout while I was given some food. Mr Herder, my host, told me that since the earthquake of five years before, a strange thing had happened. Anyone who even remotely supported the Specials, Sorcerers and their regime had found it impossible to live in this little hamlet. Either they had fallen sick and had to move away, or they had taken a disliking to the area and left. Then a couple of years ago, a young lady, who from their description was obviously Stellamar, dropped in one night, rather as I had, and encouraged them to start an undercover resistance unit. I was amazed at how much she had done in Teletsia and was reminded of the work that Luth had done in Daish Shaktay, where he had set up groups of fighting monks to help in the freedom struggle.

There was still no sign of my pursuers and I was shown to a comfortable bed in the loft. Leading off the room was a secret escape passage which led into the garden if anyone searched for me up there, but the entrance to the ladder up from the lower floor was concealed behind the bed-head of a heavy four poster. Before I went to sleep I again made bandhans on my keys, praying for Merien to find me, or perhaps even the flying horses. I realised that asking for them could give Robin problems if they were the other end of the Sea of Illusion, because they would feel the call and have a hard time responding to it, but nevertheless I had to try, being as so many people were looking for me.

The next morning I stayed in my hidden room and sure enough the Specials arrived early. They demanded to see the stables and were fooled by the bootblacked pony. They did search the house, but not very seriously. When they asked Mr Herder if he had seen me, he replied that one of his shepherds had reported seeing a girl on a white horse riding over the downs in a northerly direction the evening before. Mr Herder warned that she could be far away by now if she had travelled through the night, so the Specials gave up and went back to Lahary.

I asked Mrs Herder to get the members of their Resistance Group together and we did a quick and highly effective awakening programme. Then Zoey told me he had to take a flock of sheep up to the area around the Temple of Support. Our enemies had given me the idea and I realised it would be good to go there with my keys and ask for their power to work with that of the temple to transform Teletsia. After all, extraordinary things had happened when we visited it last time. Mrs Herder dressed me up as a shepherdess and Zoey, one of the Herder's shepherds and I set off, along with a flock of noisy and stupid sheep - and two very competent sheepdogs who knew exactly what they were doing. After a long and tiring day's walking we arrived at the Temple of Support at sunset and camped in the same valley I remembered from years before. Some of the smaller stones had fallen over in the earthquake, and Zoey said no one had dared touch them to put them upright again.

We had some food, and soon Zoey and the shepherd were asleep, but for me the vibrations emitted by the temple were too powerful and I walked up to the four large stones, easily visible by the light of two of the moons. I put both my keys, the Sasrar one and the four petalled one, on the grass in the exact centre of the temple, and made obeisance to the Mother Earth by putting my left hand to my forehead and the right one on the ground. Then I sat with my back against one of the stones and went into a deep meditation. I could feel surges of power radiating out from the temple to the whole country: not an earthquake this time, but on a subtler level, strengthening the good and exposing the evil.

CHAPTER 2

FLIGHT

I must have dropped off to sleep under the menhirs because the next thing I knew was that unique sound, the wings of the flying horses. There were two thumps as they landed on the earth and another thump as their rider dismounted. I could also hear their heavy breathing and knew they were worn out. I stood up, saw Yamun, Tama, and yes, my beloved Robin! In my heart I thanked the benevolent power that had created these wonderful horses, the keys, and everything else that made this moment possible. He ran towards me and embraced me with an intensity that was almost desperate.

'Thank goodness I've found you,' he cried. 'I've been searching for two nights and I don't know how many people have seen the flying horses. I had to spend the day hidden in a thick wood with them. If you'd stayed in one place they could have homed in on your key more easily - but no matter, you're all right!'

'We had to get my father out.'

'I gathered that. Merien wasn't back at the Island of Creations when I left. The horses wanted to come to find you as soon as we arrived, the day before yesterday.' I explained briefly what had happened and how I had finished up here.

'Would you like to come to where we're camping?'

'No, let's stay here awhile. This temple is one of the most sacred spots in the world.'

'This is the third time you've saved me with the help of the horses!'

'Let's hope it's the last!' We both knelt on the ground and gave thanks to the all-pervading power in the form of Mother Earth. Then I became more mundane.

'Food? Something to drink?'

'I have my water bottle, but yes, get me something to eat - I'm starving.'

The horses had wandered off and no doubt found the nearby stream. I picked up my keys and put them around my neck again, and then went to fetch some bread and cheese. Robin was lying on his back sound asleep when I returned. I sat against the menhir and let him be, and the next thing I knew it was much later and he was rousing me. He had seen the food by my side and was tucking in.

'The only good thing about this is that I've had to bring the flying horses here,' he said. 'By putting their feet on this ground they're going to activate further change. The rest of them are at the Island of Creations, but Tama insisted on answering your call, so I followed her on Yamun.'

'Are you angry with me? I completely disobeyed you.'

'I'm never angry with you, just dreadfully worried now and again. Didn't you understand when I tried to warn you? I suspected you'd go into Teletsia when I was away.'

We were silent for a while and looked at the stupendous sight of the menhirs around us. We could feel the effect the horses were having, along with my keys, on the earth and the temple. On this warm night, a tremendous coolness was coming from the centre of the temple, and we both felt the ground shuddering slightly.

'I have something to admit to you,' Robin continued.

'Something good?' It was so magical, sitting under the great standing stones, I couldn't feel worried about anything.

'When I first met you in Chussan, the astrologers and Albion decided I should keep something secret from all of you. When Rajay and Queen Jansy suggested we should get married, it was partly as a result of Rajay's decision to marry Zulani. Before he proposed to her, he was advised in a dream that nowadays it's good if the guardians can marry awakened souls. It's one of the best ways of sharing the wisdom we've gained in the past. I'm a guardian. That's why I was so adamant you should be careful. To some extent I can foresee danger. Do you get it now?'

'Robin, forgive me. Forgive me for all the times I've argued with you – if I'd known I'd never have crossed you.' I now understood what Merien had tried to say to me.

'Please don't stop disagreeing with me! I so enjoy our little tiffs, especially when you get the better of me. I'm only a junior guardian, because this is the first time I've taken my birth on this earth. All the others have been here a number of times and there are many more of us you haven't met, scattered around the world quietly doing what we can to help. The idea is not to force people, but to give advice and set an example. The night Rajay had a dream about young guardians marrying the people of Navi Septa, I had a similar one. He and I talked about it, and Queen Jansy and he advised me to propose to you. I then realised that I had always felt a desire to be with you, but never knew how to express my feelings. However, all this must remain a secret for the time being.

'One thing I do insist is that you go and get your pack, and tell those shepherds that we must leave and they must hide, because my intuition tells me the Specials will come looking for you here again quite soon. The horses have rested long enough, and you're going to have to ride Tama.'

I was overwhelmed by Robin's telling me he was a guardian. I should have guessed, but I was a typical newly married wife who thought her husband absolutely perfect and it did not occur to me he was in many ways deeper, wiser, braver and even more loving than the normal young man. Zoey carried my things up to where Robin was waiting. I introduced them and when Zoey had gone, Robin called the flying horses. They trotted up, we mounted them and they took off. As they gained height I heard the chugging sound of a Specials' steam car coming up the track to the temple. Zoey and the shepherd had left by then; they knew how to hide and how to keep their sheepdogs quiet.

We later landed in the open, empty country between the Temple of Support and the coast, and then again in a large wood, resting for some time on each occasion. Finally we took off on the last leg of a very long and tiring journey for the horses, hiding behind clouds as much as we could. It was late evening when we crossed the narrow straight to the Island of Creations, flying very high so as to be less obvious to any spying Specials on the mainland. When we landed in the yard of Lord Jarwhen's mansion, I noticed Merien's flying ship and knew my father was safe. Percy the peacock screeched his usual welcome and the horses snorted at this strange bird who behaved as if he owned the place.

'Remember not to tell anyone about my being a guardian,' reiterated Robin as we dismounted. 'If our friends know, they'll start behaving differently towards me. Also, when Albion and I checked the vibrations, it was very cool to keep it a secret.'

'Of course I won't say anything, and thank you for saving my life, yet again.'

'For you, any time.' He gave me one of his very special smiles, picked up my bag, slung it on his back and was about to walk towards the front door. 'Stay there and someone will come for you both,' he said as he patted the horses, and at that moment Pa Ganoozal appeared with promises of corn, carrots and other horse delicacies.

Ma Ganoozal knocked on the door of our room the next morning, with breakfast on a tray.

'Glad to see you both back safe and sound,' she began. 'Their Lordships are about to have a meeting in the Operations Room and would like you to be there if you aren't too tired. Asha, your mother and father are coming over from the village to see you. They were so worried – as you can imagine! Merien tried to calm them down, saying Robin would be bound to find you with the flying horses, but they didn't quite understand.'

'Hardly surprising!' I laughed.

We took our meal to the roof terrace outside our room. It looked over the back gardens and I could see the flying horses eating the grass, and also the odd rose or two when they thought no one was looking.

'May I ask you more about being a guardian?'

'Naturally. I wouldn't have told you otherwise,' Robin smiled and I served him, knowing what he liked best.

'How come you - took your birth on this earth?'

'It was a question of desire. Our world is beautiful now, since the greatest of the great ones came to put it to rights, but I heard there were other planets with intelligent life on them. I was partly curious and partly impelled by an unfulfilled longing to help, as others had helped me in the past. I wasn't always confident, happy and reasonably balanced like I am now! I can't explain exactly how I took my birth, but I do know, from the grandmother of Sasrar, that there was a guardian soul here who went wrong and it was necessary to replace her. So I'm the replacement. We all have free will and it's quite possible to go sour. If guardians become evil they can become very evil, because we have quite a lot of subtle power, if we choose to use it.' I looked at Robin, so normal and unassuming. Rajay, Merien and the rest, yes, you never knew what was coming next, but Robin? He hid it very well, as I knew.

'What happened to this fallen guardian?'

'We think she must have been sucked into another realm of creation, but we aren't sure.'

'I hope so.' We ate in silence for a short while, then I went on. 'There's one problem as far as we're concerned.'

'What's that?'

'I'm not sure how our marriage is going to go now. I mean – before I felt more or less your equal, but now I most certainly don't.'

'Because I got my inner awakening in another lifetime, on another world, at another time, it doesn't mean I'm in any way superior to you, only I have less excuse if I do something idiotic. From my side it's a relief to be able to tell you the whole truth. How do you think I've felt, having to conceal that from you, whom I love and respect so much?' I was about to reply, but Robin hadn't finished. 'Before I left Chussan to go to Daish Shaktay two years ago with the flying horses, the astrologers told me that there's a connection between the sixth subtle centre, on the earth the Chussan area, and the first centre, which is Teletsia. They said I would have some important work to do here. So it's perhaps more than a coincidence we finished up getting married.'

'It's a coincidence I'm delighted to go along with!' We both laughed, and made ourselves presentable for the meeting.

Lord Jarwhen saw us walk in and stopped speaking to a number of people sitting with their backs to us, facing the map of Teletsia on the opposite wall.

'Am I thankful to see you, Asha!' he began, and to Robin. 'Where did you find her?'

'The flying horses did, not me. At the Temple of Support, so now two of them have put their hooves there.'

'That explains why we felt such a surge of energy the night before last,' continued Lord Jarwhen.

Some of the other people stood up to greet us and I immediately recognised

Rajay, the King of Daish Shaktay, Prince Roarke of Vittalia, and also Raynor, Tandi and my cousin Lee.

'I'm mighty glad you got here in time, Robin,' Rajay began. 'So, how's my honorary sister?' Rajay greeted me and I felt that bottomless pool of joy which was his heart.

'Safe and sound, thanks to the flying horses and Robin,' I replied. 'What a surprise! We weren't expecting you.'

'No, indeed,' added Robin, 'what happened?'

'After you left,' Rajay explained, 'Roarke turned up with his flying ship. I knew he'd be coming for Lee, and he'd already picked up Raynor and Tandi from the north of my country, where they're setting up Valya's school in the Northwestern's family castle. We felt an extraordinary improvement in the collective vibrations of Teletsia and realised it was time to move fast – plus I did promise to help you here if I can. Let's go on with the meeting now; we'll talk more afterwards.'

We took our seats.

'I've brought a small flyer in the hold of my large one,' Roarke told everyone. 'It could be very useful.'

'If Prince Roarke would take me, I'd like to go into Teletsia,' this was Lee.

'Count me in,' added Raynor, 'but not Tandi, because we have the children here and we're expecting another.'

'I'll do my best,' promised Roarke. 'I have something else for the Teletsian freedom quest. On one of our islands we have a gold mine and I brought quite a few ingots with me.'

'That's a noble gift,' Lord Jarwhen thanked him. 'I need to make some more keys. When I make them, it's possible to create them entirely from the wave frequency and the water in the Keyspond, but it's much easier if I can put lumps of gold in the pond to start with. Anyone doing our work in Teletsia needs a key to the first centre, because they're the pass to the safe houses, and I can imbue them with the basic powers needed for survival. Rajay and Roarke, you would also be advised to have one of the extra Sasrar keys I have here. I know you have the keys to your own areas, but you might as well have the extra help of the Sasrar key.'

'Thanks,' said Rajay. 'In fact, being as my soldiers have all had their awakening I've also brought a large number of silver neck-chains, and enough gold coins for us to melt down and make four petalled keys for any of them who go into Teletsia. That will be the best armour they can have against the Sorcerers, because I don't want *any* of my men reduced to ashes if we can avoid it.'

CHAPTER 3

COUNT CHUHAR

The next morning Rajay was nowhere to be seen and Pa Ganoozal told us he had ridden over to the port where the Daish Shaktay warship was anchored.

'I hope those sailors are up betimes and everything is as it should be,' said Pa Ganoozal. 'The last thing they'll expect is a visit from their king first thing in the morning.'

'Don't worry, Lee and Rajay understand each other by now,' Robin reassured him. 'Lee sent a message yesterday, because he knew Rajay would go and see his men.'

The day after that, the *Wattan Trader*, a cargo ship claiming to be from Mattanga, left the Island of Creations for western Teletsia. Rajay had ordered his sailors to disguise the warship, the *Queen Zulani*. The delicately carved figurehead of the Goddess of Daish Shaktay had been covered up, the guns had been rolled in, the gun ports closed and obscured and the original name repainted. Merien went over to the port and raised a veritable pea-soup of a fog so the ship could get past the Teletsian coast guard boats. It was pulled by the dolphins he called with his third centre key, because there was no wind.

The Coffee River came out into the sea about two days sailing to the west, and this was where the coffee, spices and medicinal plants grown inland were brought downriver to the port on barges. Rajay posed as Count Chuhar, an eccentric nobleman travelling with the ship, a natural scientist interested in collecting strange animals and plants. He had spectacles, a long and curiously curled moustache and a wig which gave him shoulder length hair. Bonor the bodyguard had insisted on going on the ship too, as far as anyone could insist on anything where Rajay was concerned. Also on board were the four freed slaves who had opted to stay back and help with the Teletsian freedom quest.

'I don't know what Queen Zulani would say about this,' Bonor complained to Robin and me before he left. 'I couldn't face any of them back at Malak Citadel if I let His Majesty go off alone with only those few sailors.' Like any self-respecting soldier, he had a dim view of naval personnel. Everyone was sworn to secrecy about Rajay's true identity.

The Wattan Trader

Before he had left Daish Shaktay, as when he was fighting to win back his own country, Rajay had called his closest advisors, his former partisan friends, to him at Malak Citadel, and had given instructions for running the country in case he did not return from Teletsia. When he and Zulani were alone, he spoke to her.

'Will you be alright while I'm gone?' he began.

'Of course. I married a warrior and partisan, and I know what that means,' she replied. 'What do I say to our son Enithar if you don't come back?'

Rajay looked at his beautiful wife, standing on the balcony of their apartment at the top of the fort's main building. Behind her he could see his prosperous country stretching away into the distance. Zulani never abused her position and asked him anything which compromised his role as king, and from his side he gratefully allowed her to rule his heart.

'Where is my boy? I don't see enough of him.'

'He's having his breakfast with the nurse. Please, tell me...' Zulani was not going to be put off.

'We're not an ordinary couple. You're my queen and I'm the king, and we always have to put those roles first. Don't worry, if I could succeed in Mattanga and outwit your father, I'll survive Teletsia and the Sorcerers. And if I don't, when he's old enough to understand, tell Eni I gave my life for freedom, which is why I was born in the first place.'

The Wattan Trader reached the port of Darzeet, where the Coffee River flowed into the sea. Euclip, one of the freed slaves, had been working for a food seller in Teletos, so he posed as a spice and coffee merchant. Rajay sent him to make contact with an exporter who was a relation of Witten the Tong. That evening Turkden the Tong, his brother and their sons accepted the invitation to visit the ship.

After an excellent dinner in the captain's cabin Rajay, alias Count Chuhar, suggested some entertainment for the guests and a group of sailors sang a few songs which helped awaken the Tree of Life. The eccentric count took them through the experience of inner awakening and to humour him the guests went along with it. However, Rajay was as powerful spiritually as he was politically and sure enough Witten's relations proved receptive. Rather to their surprise these hard-bitten businessmen found themselves having a profound and deeply joyful experience. After this Count Chuhar astonished them even more when he told them how to withstand the mind-reading of the Sorcerers, who were always poking their nose into the spice dealers' business and taxing them heavily. The Count also showed them a technique that he called the bandhan of protection, assuring them this would make it impossible for the Sorcerers to reduce them to ashes or mesmerise them if they ever got into bad trouble with their overlords, but this they found hard to believe. Nevertheless, they agreed it would be a great blessing if it worked.

These traders were utterly fed up with being ruled by black magicians, in other words the Sorcerers. Rajay asked them if they knew anyone else who felt the same and they replied, 'The whole business community!' So he asked his guests to bring as many of them as they could the following night, ostensibly for business reasons, should the Sorcerers and Specials in charge of the port ask, but in fact to do a larger awakening programme.

The next morning Euclip, the eldest of the freed saves, presented his (forged) papers to the Port Authority. He rented warehouse space and went through a charade of other activities to connect him to the import/export business. That evening a flotilla of small boats converged on the ship, containing many of the port's leading citizens and their families. *The Wattan Trader* then sailed out of the harbour and into the bay to enjoy the night breeze a little off shore. The real reason was so the singing and dancing on deck could not be heard from the town, because the music would have an adverse effect on the Specials and Sorcerers. The programme was a great success, but then a pleasant looking young man came up to Rajay.

'Count Chuhar,' he began. 'I was on a trading mission to Daish Shaktay last year for my father, who has the biggest coffee agency in town, and I visited Malak Citadel. I discussed business with the Trade Minister, His Excellency Lord Witten and even had an audience with His Majesty King Rajay. If I may say so, you look very like him and your voice is identical.'

'So I'm told,' said Rajay evenly. 'He's my cousin.'

'I see. Do you know anything about this prophecy everyone is talking about? If it's true, then a number of young people, some of whom are rumoured to be working for King Rajay, will.....'

'Oh yes,' interrupted Rajay. 'I know all about that.'

'My name is Coffius Coffeeman, Coff for short. I'm the leader of the Darzeet Young People's Resistance Group and ... forgive me Your Majesty, but I may not be the only one to have seen through your disguise tonight. Nearly everyone here would be totally behind you even if they did recognise you and we're extremely grateful for what you've showed us, but there may be one or two who would tell the Sorcerers and Specials. I suggest you leave as soon as possible.'

'You're right, Coff. I recognised you the moment I saw you. A pleasure to meet you again! We have another place to visit, Rubber River Port. Could you come with us?'

'Yes, and I'll put you in touch with the people you need to contact there. I'll tell my father I'm going to introduce your merchant, Mr eh….Euclip, to our colleagues in the rubber business.'

Soon after this, the trading galleon left for their next assignment. Coff had a comfortable cabin and Rajay invited him to breakfast the following morning. Rajay had been given Coff's name by Lord Jarwhen, but when Euclip asked about him at Darzeet, he was wrongly told he was out of town, buying coffee beans in the mountains. As they sat at breakfast together he soon overcame his awe and they chatted away in a friendly fashion.

'Funny thing happened last week,' said Coff. 'My father sometimes consults an astrologer for advice on his business. We've been having some trouble lately with the coffee exporting, so he sent me to see him. I asked him what was in store for me, businesswise, being as I'm a partner in the company. He said, "Coff, there's nothing whatsoever in your chart about business. You're going to get some great spiritual knowledge." When you gave your awakening programme, it all made sense.'

'I'd never dispute what's in the stars, but it's what we do with their influence that matters,' replied Rajay. 'The main thing is, you're here, and you'll be a great help.'

Later, after Coff had left, Bonor came in.

'The freed slaves would like a word with you, sire. They're good lads,' he began.

'Send them along. I'd like to talk to them.'

The four young men came shyly into the cabin. Being well brought up Daish Shaktay boys, they touched their forehead three times – the traditional way of greeting the king: once for their parents, once for Rajay as the father of the nation and once for the divine creator, the mother and father of everyone. Then they bowed low and pressed their hands together in respectful greeting.

'Sit down and tell me your names,' began Rajay. They did so, and he asked them where in Daish Shaktay they came from, how long they had been slaves and so on. 'Did you send word to your families that you've been freed?'

'Yes, Your Majesty, Lord Valya said he'd do that,' said Euclip, the best educated.

'He'll see to it. What did you want to ask me?'

'It's like this,' said Rollo, younger and more outspoken. 'When we were slaves we realised many of the people of Teletsia are themselves enslaved by the mesmerising powers of the Sorcerers and their fear of the Specials, and now we've been freed, and given this amazing wisdom of the Tree of Life, we'd like to go back there and try to help them. They weren't all evil.'

'Do you really want to risk your lives in a place that's treated you so shabbily?' Rajay admired their enthusiasm, but did not want these boys getting into trouble again.

'Your Majesty,' said Munnir, the third, 'I was too young to fight in your freedom struggle and my companions were captured and sold before it happened, but even though we couldn't help you win back our country, we understand, from Asha and Ahren, that for this world to be all right, *all* the countries have to be free, not only ours. So we'd like to help Teletsia. You're doing just that and as our king you're our example.'

'If you were to barter us for a load of coffee or rubber, we could pretend to be slaves again and could stay in the safe houses and help establish people in the new wisdom. We've learnt about it from Asha,' added Euclip.

'Bonor has been teaching us how to fight, if it comes to that,' said Chariss, the other older one. 'He says we're not too bad.'

'He knows what he's talking about, but you'd be in great danger if you go back into Teletsia,' warned Rajay. 'Did they ever mesmerise any of you from Daish Shaktay and send you to their slave farms?'

'Not that I know of. That was for what they called disturbers of the peace or political dissidents, although they would have if we'd made problems,' replied Euclip.

'The vibrations are cool for you to go,' went on Rajay. 'I make all my decisions on that basis, and you'd be a great asset. There may have to be an armed conflict eventually and you could help the Resistance Groups prepare for that. We have to try to give people courage to stand up to the Sorcerers. The way to do that, as you know, is to give them awakening so they can know good from bad and aren't afraid to stand up for justice.'

'Asha explained all that,' said Chariss.

'Yes, she understands this very clearly. If you want to come home to Daish Shaktay after everything is resolved here, you must visit me at Malak Citadel and I'll see what can be done to get you going in careers. Bonor, go and get some king's travel pass rings and first centre keys, will you?' Bonor, who had been standing behind, nodded and went off.

'How can we thank you, Your Majesty?' said Euclip.

'You don't have to. It's what I do. We all have a job and mine, as king, is to look after you, as citizens of Daish Shaktay. If you're going into Teletsia, you must each have a four petalled key.' Bonor came back and handed a leather bag to Rajay. 'These are on loan from Lord Jarwhen and should eventually be returned to him, if possible.' Rajay showed the boys how to use the keys. 'Also, each take one of these rings, in case we don't meet up again in this country.' He handed all of them a silver ring with a small star sapphire and an inscription on the inner side. 'Show these to the captain of any Daish Shaktay ship and he'll give you a free passage home.'

'Your Majesty, this is incredible!' blurted out Munnir.

'You're doing a very brave thing for a country that isn't even yours. We'll give you bandhans from a distance to help you, but to make sure you're constantly in touch with the all-pervading power you must meditate and clear the inner centres of your Trees of Life every day. Then you'll most likely find yourselves spontaneously doing the right thing at the right time. We're all connected on a subtle level, and as my countrymen you're especially important to me.'

'I don't think we matter that much,' said Euclip.

'I've chosen my ministers because of their bravery in the freedom struggle and you boys show the same tendencies, so you're true citizens of Daish Shaktay. The way we're going to win Teletsia is by planting seeds in people's hearts and minds to help them to change within, and that's what you'll be doing. Now go and talk to Coff and he'll tell you about this area.' They went off chatting excitedly. Rajay felt tremendous love for them - freedom fighters like he had been.

They reached the broad estuary of the Rubber River and gave the port at the seaward end a miss, because Coff said it was full of Sorcerers' supporters. Instead they sailed some way up the river. Coff directed them towards a fair-sized village on the water's edge, where he, the freed slaves and Rajay, again disguised as Count Chuhar, took a small boat to the shore. Coff pretended he was there on business and introduced Euclip to the headman. The others left for the nearby safe house and Resistance Group while Euclip looked at samples of raw rubber and a type of tree bark which was used as a medicine against a serious fever.

Euclip went back to the ship after he had finished his business, but Coff, Rajay and the others stayed the night and gave an awakening programme the next morning, by which time the Resistance Group leader had managed to round up most of his members. Rajay was as inspiring as always and the leader sent a message to the next safe house further upriver, so they could be ready when Rajay and Coff arrived in their ship. Two of the freed slaves, Rollo and Munnir, were bartered for a fair amount of rubber and bark, which was loaded onto the ship. Rajay left gold for the goods, and the 'slaves', now 'owned' by the Resistance Group leader, pretended they had been treated, so if anyone questioned them they wouldn't get any sense out of them.

The following day the Daish Shaktay ship reached a small town. The Resistance Group members there had advertised the awakening programme more openly than Rajay would have liked, and a large number of people came. He wasn't happy about some of them and asked the leader to invite the most trustworthy ones to his house afterwards. They had another programme there and Rajay showed them how to withstand the powers of the Sorcerers, and explained other matters about the freedom quest. He left Charriss, the third freed slave, behind with a small bag of gold for when he needed to leave.

The last safe house was another day's sailing up the river, because the current was against them and even with their oars they could only go slowly. Before they reached there, Rajay was in his cabin alone and Bonor knocked on the door.

'Come in,' said Rajay. 'You look worried. Is there something on your mind?'

'Yes sire, there is,' replied Bonor.

'Tell me.'

'The men heard that you were lucky the Specials didn't arrest you at that last place. There were some spies in the audience. Trouble is, some of the folk there knew we're going to visit this village tonight.'

'I'll only take Coff and Euclip with me. If anything goes wrong, Coff and I will be more likely to get away than a lot of us. He knows the area.'

'Sire, with respect, Her Majesty and Lord Valya asked me to keep an eye on you, so may I come too?'

'I'd rather you didn't.'

'I'd never forgive myself if anything happened to you, in this foreign country…'

'Bonor, surely you understand that if Teletsia isn't all right, our world isn't, because this land is the seat of the first subtle centre on the Tree of Life of the whole planet. My wife understands that, and my part in this, very well. She always respects the vibrations, and the vibrations indicate that only us three should go.'

'But sire, you're the King of Daish Shaktay,' persisted Bonor, thinking of something Valya said to him before he left Malak Citadel: 'His Majesty sometimes forgets he's our king. He can't go risking his neck all the time, like we used to when we were partisans. You make sure he doesn't.'

'It's also my lot,' Rajay reminded him, 'to do my best to help overcome the evil people in other countries who are making the good ones suffer. Trust me. At the least trust the vibrations.'

Bonor apologised, but wasn't convinced.

In the evening Rajay, Euclip and Coff set off in a rowing boat to the safe house. The river was broad, but shallow near the shore so they could not take the large ship to the wharf. When they reached the safe house Rajay explained to the local Resistance Group leader about leaving Euclip behind with them. He thought it was an excellent plan, but felt that if Euclip was posing as a mesmerised slave, he shouldn't come to the awakening programme. The leader asked Rajay and Coff to accompany him to the Rubber Exchange, the largest building in the village, and when they had nearly finished the programme there, he came up to Rajay and Coff. They were at the back of the hall telling some people who were strong vibrationally about the two bandhans and how to resist the Sorcerers.

'Count Chuhar, a group of Specials are outside the hall and they want to speak to you. I fear the worst. I said I'd come and get you,' the leader said anxiously.

'Is there another way out?' asked Rajay.

'Yes, but we'll have to get to the kitchen, where there's a back door. Are you any good at fighting?'

'Yes, and I'm armed, but if I leave some dead or wounded Specials it won't go well for you later on. This is where we make bandhans.' They did so and at that moment two Specials burst in, looked wildly around the room and ran straight past Rajay and Coff.

'Where is he?' shouted one, 'He's got spectacles, a long curled moustache and shoulder length hair.'

'All the men here look like that,' complained the other. 'This is impossible! One of them's got to be him, but which?'

Rajay realised a miracle was happening and took advantage of it. He ducked behind a column, removed his wig and spectacles, and pulled off his false moustache. He picked up a couple of large hats from the nearby chair, rammed one on Coff and another on himself, and also took a couple of cloaks, mentally apologising for having to steal in the interests of the liberation of Teletsia. Everyone was looking at the Specials, who were at the front, assuming Rajay would be on the dais.

'Let's go!' Rajay grinned at Coff. Swathed in cloaks and hats they walked out of the door, politely bidding good night to two more Specials outside. Rajay now looked unmistakably like Rajay Ghiry, the King of Daish Shaktay, but this was the best possible disguise as no one here had ever seen him, and traders often came here from overseas, so his foreign appearance was no problem. Coff looked away as they passed the Specials in case they recognised him, and his hat partly hid his face. They found the kitchen and slipped out of the back door, but noticed more Specials going in the front.

'How are we going to get back to the ship?' gasped Coff, as he and Rajay ran towards the river through the nearby forest.

'I don't know. One thing at a time,' panted Rajay.

'The Specials know we came in the dinghy, and they'll be watching the jetty further down.'

'True enough,' Rajay agreed, and leant against a tree to get his breath back. As yet there was no sound of pursuit. 'We'll try and avoid fighting them. Do as I say.' He blew through his own twelve petalled key. 'If some ferocious wild animals appear, that's because I've called them, and they won't harm us if I've got this key.' At this moment they heard a voice and the baying of a hound.

'That way – the dog has picked up their trail,' someone shouted.

'Quick, up that tree,' Rajay pointed, and just in time they shinned up a large tree with spreading branches going out horizontally, some of which put down roots further away from the main trunk. It was dark and they hid in the thick leaves. They heard a Special's steam car approaching and the hound's baying stopped at the bottom of the tree.

'I reckon they went up here,' said a voice below.

'One of you climb up,' ordered another. 'Take a couple of loaded pistols.' Rajay and Coff crept quietly along one of the long horizontal branches and could not be seen in the darkness. There was a slight wind which set the branches scraping against each other and the leaves rustling, and hid the sound of their crawling. The tracker dog was still snarling but Rajay heard some other animals in the undergrowth.

'Tigers!' yelled one of the Specials. 'Lots of them! It's sorcery – you never get so many together. Back to the steam car!' They shot wildly and retreated. They did not wound any of the animals, who hung back in the face of the gunfire. When the Specials and the Sorcerer with them jumped into their car, the tigers stood in the shadows, out of its lights.

'I'm going to annihilate this whole area unless you surrender and show yourselves,' the Sorcerer shouted. 'Then whatever is living, whether tigers or men, will be reduced to ashes.' He stood up in the car and started chanting and waving his staff - usually a deadly combination.

'Don't be afraid,' whispered Rajay, 'keep your attention on the top of your head, the seat of the all-caring Mother of Creation, and the Sorcerer can't harm you.'

Hardly had he said this when the steam car exploded, killing the people in it, because the more powerful the intended victim the more violently the curse rebounded. One Special, who had been standing nearby, rolled wounded on the ground, screaming in pain and trying to put out the flames burning his clothing.

'Oh god, he must be in agony!' Rajay murmured and looked compassionately at him as he burnt. They waited a short while but there was no other sign of pursuit. 'We've still got to get back to the ship. Any river dolphins here?'

'Yes, but they're rare.'

'We'll go to the river and I'll try to call some.'

They jumped down from the tree and set off through the undergrowth. As they approached the river they heard another Specials' car. This one sounded as if it was making for the jetty where they had left their dinghy. Rajay knelt down by the waterside and blew through his Sasrar key, then put it in the water for a few moments. Soon a dolphin popped its head out. It was puzzled, because Rajay, unlike Merien, did not know its language and could not tell it what he wanted. He pointed to the ship waiting in the deeper water of the wide, sluggish river. Two more dolphins arrived and the first kept turning its head towards its large dorsal fin.

'I think they'll pull us to the ship,' said Coff. 'There are crocodiles in this river, but they won't attack with the dolphins guarding us.'

Rajay kicked off his shoes, jumped into the water and grabbed a dolphin. Coff did the same and off they went, with the third one acting as guard. The dolphins took them across the river to the further side of the ship, they called to the sailors on the deck and a rope ladder was let down. They climbed up and went to Rajay's cabin where they changed into dry clothes, and after some time Dan, the captain, came in.

124

'Sire, Bonor isn't back yet. He went after you in another dingy.'

'I wish he hadn't - the vibrations were so against it We'll have to wait and if necessary rescue him.' At this moment a distraught sailor entered.

'Sire, we picked up Bonor's dinghy drifting in the river,' he began. 'In it was his body. He'd been shot. I'm sorry sire; he insisted on following you.'

'Set sail for the river's mouth immediately,' Rajay ordered curtly. Dan felt his grief and knew he always took it hard when he lost his men, especially those close to him. Dan sent everyone away and consoled Rajay as best he could. Later in the night Bonor was given a river burial and in the darkness no one could see Rajay's anguish. He blamed himself that he had not been firmer with Bonor, but never dreamt he would flagrantly go against both the vibrations and his king's instructions. They made their way downriver fast and the next morning Rajay and Coff ate breakfast together.

'Could you come back to the Island of Creations with us?' Rajay began.

'I'd be honoured,' Coff's face lit up.

'I had a few words with the dolphins,' Dan said, joining them. 'They warned me that the Teletsians have some gunships at the river mouth. I don't know how we're going to get past them.'

'How long will it take us to get there?' Rajay asked.

'With the current in our favour, some time tomorrow afternoon.'

'Maybe the dolphins would pull us and we'd get there faster.'

'There's a few swimming alongside and with their help we could make it by tomorrow morning.'

'We need to be there before daylight. Meanwhile, in case we do have to fight our way out, prepare the cannon and get the ship ready for battle. How many big guns can we man?'

'Four at the most. We don't have many gunners with us.'

'Let's hope we can get out by stealth. Nevertheless, if we have to fight, we will, because I do *not* intend us to get captured by a small flotilla of Teletsian gunboats.'

As they neared the river's mouth Dan asked the river dolphins to find out, from their salt-water cousins, exactly where the Teletsians' ships were waiting, and ask if some sea dolphins could pull the Daish Shaktay ship. It was a sailing ship and the Teletsian ones had a primitive steam engine, so they were at a severe disadvantage.

It was a cloudy night, obscuring the two moons in the sky. In the early morning, well before dawn, they reached the tidal part of the river, which was wide. A number of salt water dolphins met them and ropes were thrown overboard to hold in their mouths. They pulled the ship fast – without them it could never have moved so quickly. Another dolphin appeared and told Dan precisely where the Teletsian ships were waiting so he could avoid them in the darkness. There were four, at intervals across the river. They were going to have to pass fairly close to at least one so Rajay told Dan to run out the guns and be ready to fire.

Dan hoped they had got past unnoticed, but then heard the sound of a ship and a voice ordering him to stop and give his credentials. He didn't, and cried to the dolphins to pull faster. The Teletsian gunship opened fire and some cannon balls hit *The Wattan Trader*, damaging one of the masts badly. It cracked and fell sideways onto the deck, and the sailors on the Teletsian ship could hear this. They assumed they had defeated their foe and as it was a sailing ship would not have moved much by the time they reloaded. However, when they fired again it was well out of range and being pulled towards the open sea. By some enormous confusion another Teletsian ship fired towards where they had heard the Daish Shaktay ship. Somehow the two Teletsian ships began firing on each other; one was badly damaged and the other in flames before they realised their error.

Dan taught Rajay how to thank the dolphins in their language and they pulled the ship back to the Island of Creations. As they neared it more dolphins swam up. They warned Dan that a number of Teletsian ships were blockading the port on the north-eastern side but showed them a creek on the north-western side where they could safely anchor.

Meanwhile hundreds more people now knew how to withstand at least some of the Sorcerers' powers and had the confidence to stand up to them. The four 'slaves' would free many more. Rajay hid his sadness at losing Bonor as well as he could, but his men felt and shared his searing heartache. For Coff Coffeeman a new world had opened and he resolved more than ever to devote his life to the freedom of Teletsia.

CHAPTER 4

FISHERMEN AND ACADEMICS

The day after Rajay left, Roarke, Lee and Raynor decided to visit Gyan-on-Sea, famous for its ancient university that predated the Sorcerers. They would pose as visiting scholars and go in Wale's fishing boat. Roarke stowed his flyer in the open fish hold, covered it with a tarpaulin and they set off round the coast of Teletsia, past Teletos and on southwards.

After a few days they neared the town, and some way north of it, before dawn, Roarke flew the flyer to a safe house on the coast and hid it well. The safe house was a coconut and pepper farm, and he awakened the Trees of Life of the people who lived there. Roarke told them where he had hidden his flyer and asked that if any Specials came, to try and veer them away from it. His request was met with initial disbelief, but when the farmer saw the sleek looking craft he apologised, laughed and agreed to help, and covered it with fallen palm leaves as further camouflage.

Roarke returned to the fishing boat and they sailed on to the quaint old town. He was to be Dr Tarl, an engineer who wanted to do some research on steam cars at the Engineering Department and in return would give a seminar on his theories about the possibility of flying machines. They had taken special care with their clothes so as to look their parts, and Roarke sported a long purple robe with designs of moons, stars and the sun on it. He wore his dark hair quite long – shoulder length - and carried a gold topped walking cane which was reminiscent of a magic wand, so the total effect was suitably unconventional.

Raynor, with spectacles, his hair cut very short, a neat black jacket buttoned up to the neck, dark trousers and shiny black shoes with silver buckles, was Professor Quair, who was interested in Teletsian tribal dialects. Lee, alias Len Shore, was posing as an arrogant Ph.D. student doing an economic study on slave labour, and he wanted to look at the use of slave labour in the nearby armaments factories. He wore a flamboyant multi-coloured shirt over red trousers and sandals on his feet. His disguise was the least in keeping with his character, because since working for Rajay he had become cautious and circumspect and rarely spoke out of turn. A tailor on the Island of Creations had run up their outfits before they left.

Lee and Raynor said their parents had emigrated from Teletsia to the distant land of Mosare, and they all needed to use the resources of the university for a week or so, and had the necessary permission from the Teletsian Academy for Advanced Spiritual Study, in other words the Sorcerer's Academy. Well – faked permission forged by Lord Jarwhen.

They cleared their papers at the Port Authority and asked the Special at Customs and Immigration if he could recommend a good eating house. They listened to his advice, but avoided that one and chose another. The restaurant they visited was marked on their map as a safe house. They had an excellent meal and as they lingered over dessert the proprietor came up.

'Good evening, gentlemen. I take it you're strangers?' he began.

'Yes, we're visiting the university,' Roarke explained and discreetly put the four petalled key on the table.

'Do you need to use us as a safe house?' the proprietor went on in an undertone.

'Not at the moment, but we'd like to ask you a few questions.'

'Come with me. My name is Pat, Pat Foodman. May I know yours, good sirs?' They gave their pseudonyms, went into the back parlour and soon gave awakening to the Foodman family and the staff, because they were all members of a Resistance Group.

'Doctor Tarl, the university is a hotbed of unrest,' said one of the waiters to Roarke. He was a young man who worked there part time while studying. 'My friends and I would do anything to find the young people of the prophecy and help them. The Vice-Chancellor and most of the faculty members are sympathetic towards change, but the Dean of the Economics Department, on the other hand, trained as a Sorcerer. So be careful Mr Shore, if you talk to him.'

'What about the Department of Languages?' asked Raynor, alias Professor Quair.

'No idea, I'm doing Business Studies,' replied the waiter come student, whose name was Pastow.

'We're pretending we're here to do research,' said Lee. 'However, maybe as you're a student, you could arrange a room for us and we'll have an evening of - eh – "folk songs from our respective countries". Dr Tarl and I play instruments and sing, and Professor Quair can sing, and we can awaken the Tree of Life through our music.'

'I can easily fix that,' offered Pastow. 'Come here tomorrow, late afternoon, with your instruments.'

Wale had taken his crew to a quayside coffee shop for the evening and when everyone got back to his boat they compared notes.

'What did you find out, Wale?' enquired Roarke.

'Your Highness, there're all these reports about these "flying carpets", in other words your flying ships. They say there's going to be an invasion of superior beings from outer space who are going to finish off the Sorcerers for good and all.'

'What's the reaction of the Sorcerers to this?' asked Raynor.

'Initially they denied everything - at least that was what we heard in the coffee shop. Now they're scared, so they're tightening up in every direction. Do you really think it's safe to do your programme at the university?'

'It may not be safe, but it's cool on vibrations to try,' maintained Lee.

'That answers the question, doesn't it?' added Roarke. 'Did Lord Jarwhen give you and your boys four petalled keys so you can have access to the safe houses? And maps of the ones nearby, up and down the coast?'

'Yes, Your Highness and he showed us how to use them.'

'You and your boys leave now,' advised Lee. 'Sail up the coast and back to the Island of Creations, stopping at as many safe houses and coastal villages as you can. Give awakening, teach the Resistance Groups the rudiments of the wisdom of the Tree of Life and warn them to prepare for war. Don't take unnecessary risks. The idea is to change the level of consciousness in Teletsia so the ordinary people want us to liberate them and won't be psychologically dominated by the Sorcerers any more.' Wale looked at Roarke for confirmation of Lee's suggestion. He knew Roarke was a guardian and his word would be final.

'I agree with Lee. We don't need you here,' said Roarke.

The next day Wale sailed away. The pseudo-academics moved to a hotel and contacted people at the university in their respective fields. Lee and Raynor were amazed at the changed attitude of the people of Teletsia and realised that most people now wanted to get rid of the Sorcerers. They also now understood that when we had our meeting in Chussan with Rajay, and decided it was time to come back to Teletsia, we were, on a subtle level, because of our awakened collective awareness, merely responding to the desire of many Teletsians.

Roarke arrived at the restaurant first, with his instrument, a cross between a sitar and a guitar, and Lee and Raynor soon joined him. They had left the university earlier and had contacted some of Raynor's relations, who knew all about the prophecy and that both Kitab Antiquarian's sons had disappeared – and why. They had already had their awakening, and were given the address of the restaurant so they could join the Resistance Group. Pastow came in and informed Roarke he had booked the room and invited all his friends. He offered the three honoured visitors an early supper, compliments of the Foodman family.

After eating, the musicians went to the university and were shown into a pleasant room in the Students Union. They arrived early as they wanted to practise and Pastow had got the best room for them, because a friend of his was in charge of allocating them, but this turned out not to have been a good move. There were a lot of student societies and as ill-luck would have it, the

Trainee High Priests Society, in other words young Sorcerers, had been promised this room and then at the last moment put somewhere markedly inferior. Roarke and the others had no idea of this, and began practising the songs which helped activate the Tree of Life.

The Sorcerers' meeting had already started in the next room and they heard the music. Roarke had a voice like molten honey, especially when he sang these powerful songs which awakened the deepest part of people. He also played flawlessly, and when accompanied by Lee and Raynor they were an irresistibly satisfying trio. At least they were to most people, but had the reverse effect on these trainee agents of evil, who after a couple of songs started twitching and shaking, because they could easily hear the music. The longer they listened the worse they got.

Finally one of the trainee Sorcerers went to complain to the Specials who were detailed to keep order in the university, because they suspected these visiting academics. At the same time another of the trainee Sorcerers asked if he could see the leader of the singing group. Roarke went out into the passage while Lee and Raynor went on practising. The trainee asked, between contortions and spasms, if the singers could please stop and if possible get out of the building as they were disturbing the peace. Not wanting to cause trouble, Roarke suggested that the trainee Sorcerers took the good room and his people would go elsewhere.

The musicians were then escorted to a secluded part of the university grounds by one of Pastow's friends, to *The Shrubbery,* an open air theatre. Pastow waited in the entrance hall of the Student's Union and as his friends came in, he redirected them. The programme at *The Shrubbery* was a rousing success and some time later a large number of young people who had received their awakening were still singing and dancing along with Roarke, Lee and Raynor. Pastow put the word around that if any of his friends wanted to know more they should meet later at the eating house where he worked.

The trainee Sorcerer who had complained to the Specials about Roarke and the others had to wait around at the Specials' Office for a long time, but eventually met the officers on duty, who had been sorting out a wild party in one of the men's residences. The trainee produced his pass, showing he was one of the elite and was to be obeyed. The trainee Sorcerer did not know that Roarke and company had decamped to the open air theatre, and informed the Specials that the people in the best room of the Students Union might be spies or subversives and should be arrested immediately and taken into custody for interrogation. He warned that they were probably in disguise but that the Specials should not listen to any excuses and should treat them very firmly.

The trainee then went straight home and did not return to the Students Union, as he felt so ill. The Specials arrested the students in the best room, even though they insisted they were trainee High Priests. The Specials handcuffed them, did not listen to anything they said, put a cover over their heads, kicked and hit them a few times to let them know who was boss and locked them up. A Senior High Priest would arrive the next morning to question them.

It was nearly midnight and Pat Foodman's restaurant was full of eager students, sitting in groups around Raynor, Roarke or Lee, learning more about the Tree of Life.

'Hey, all of you!' Pastow clapped his hands for silence. 'You'll never guess what I just heard. The Specials went into that room we booked in the Students Union and arrested the trainee Sorcerers who had taken it over from us!'

'But how come?' asked one student. 'They have passes to show who they are.'

'That's the whole point. The Specials thought that was Dr Tarl and his friends' disguise. They didn't know the trainees by sight because they were a new group who'd only recently arrived from Teletos.'

'Three cheers for Dr Tarl and his friends!' cried another student, and everyone joined in the rousing shout of praise.

'Nevertheless, you must all go home now, because we don't want the Specials to find you here,' urged Pat Foodman. The students left in a discreet hurry.

'We'll need to stay here tonight,' said Roarke, 'and decide what to do in the morning.' Pat took them down to the cellar where they hid people and Pastow went back to his lodgings.

The next morning Pastow came to the eating house, because a servant from the Vice-Chancellor, Professor Nalanda, had been to see him. The room in the union had been booked in Pastow's name, so the servant told him to take Dr Tarl and the others to meet the professor as soon as possible. Lee checked - the vibrations were very cool to accept the invitation. Pastow knew a maid at their hotel and had asked her a favour. Some Specials were waiting in the lobby for three guests who had not returned the previous night, but no one thought to stop a maid from going into their room. She collected their belongings and gave them to Pastow. Once he had brought their things, Lee, Raynor and Roarke changed into some smart clothes. However, they were armed for the unexpected. They had their keys under their clothing and hidden daggers; if they were walking into a trap they needed to be able to get out of it. Roarke and Lee also took their musical instruments because they heard the Nalanda family loved music and hoped this might be the way to the Nalanda's hearts.

CHAPTER 5

THE NALANDA FAMILY

The Vice-Chancellor had a pleasant house in the grounds of the university near the open-air theatre, so Pastow took Roarke and company there and left them at the garden gate. The servant ushered them into the living room and said Professor Nalanda had been called over to the Ruling Council of the University for an urgent meeting, but wanted the three of them to wait.

'Let's clear the vibrations of this place,' suggested Lee. 'I feel good about this professor, but let's see what we can manage on the subtle level while he's out.' They put their attention on the house and felt on their fingers to see where there were problems. There was a tingling on the fourth finger, especially on the right side. This finger governed the centre in the forehead, and a lot of brainwork went on here, perhaps too much. Otherwise the vibrations were not bad. Then they put their attention on the Vice-Chancellor himself and felt the same constriction in the head, and a tingling on their little fingers.

'He's insecure or afraid about something,' said Raynor. 'Let's give him a bandhan on our hands,' so they wrote his name on their left hands and circled it with their right one. Gradually the tingling went away and they felt coolness all over their hands.

'Pretty good for a successful man of the world in Teletsia,' added Roarke. 'I'm looking forward to meeting him.' However, he did not appear. They waited and waited and at lunch time a young man of about Raynor's age came in with a girl, a bit younger.

'Hello, my name is Garma and this is my sister Saray.'

Lee and Roarke were astonished at how similar to Raynor he looked: tall and slimly built, with the same tousled hair and pale skin, pale for a Teletsian that was. Roarke gave their pseudonyms, and Saray smiled and modestly pressed the palms of her hands together in the gesture of respectful greeting. She was a pretty girl of medium height, trimly built, with the high forehead, slightly aquiline nose and green eyes of so many Teletsians. Her thick, dark brown hair was wavy and tied back casually, and framed her face most attractively. She wore the usual long overshirt and baggy trousers, typical clothing of young people in Teletsia.

'Are you the people who were playing so beautifully last night?' asked Garma.

'Yes, thank you for the compliment,' said Roarke. 'We're not professionals, but that music has a profound effect on some people. I'm glad you liked it.'

'It was - the most extraordinary experience of my life. My father, Saray and I went out for a walk after supper, and we heard you. We didn't want to intrude – the students are so much in awe of dad - but we listened outside the theatre behind the bushes and followed your instructions. We felt the inner peace and joy, and a refreshing breeze flowing over our bodies like a waterfall, even dad, and he's the cynic to beat all cynics.'

'There's much more to show you,' added Lee.

'We realised that. That's why dad asked you over. Where is he, by the way?'

'Your servant said he'd gone to – what did he say? - the Ruling Council of the University had an urgent meeting.'

'He'll turn up eventually. Can I offer you something to drink meanwhile?' asked Saray.

'Thank you, whatever you're having,' said Roarke, alias Dr Tarl.

'Are you studying here?' asked Lee.

'My brother Garma is teaching and I'm studying. We're both in the Music Department. Rather a disappointment to dad, I'm afraid. He's a mathematician,' Saray explained while giving her guests delicious fresh pressed fruit juice.

'Our music must have seemed somewhat amateur to you,' said Lee.

'On the contrary. Whichever of you played the stringed instrument is truly inspired, a great master, and the flute player has a perfect sense of melody,' Garma complimented them. 'The singers had voices like mountain pipes - resonant and lyrical. It was a delight to listen to you, but what attracted us was the effect it had on us. It touched our souls.'

'Or shall we say your Trees of Life?' smiled Roarke. Garma and Saray looked at each other sharply and then at their guests.

'That's why the trainee Sorcerers were so frantic!' cried Saray.

It soon came out that the Nalanda family and many of the teaching staff at the university were part of a secret group that was studying the prophecy. Like the one started by Raynor's father in Teletos, it was so secret that even the local Resistance Groups were unaware of it. Professor Nalanda was related to the Heber family, who owned Castle Mount, which was how he knew about the prophecy. Roarke and the others began telling their hosts more of what they needed to know: the bandhans of protection, how to clear their subtle centres and so on.

Finally Professor Nalanda returned, by which time the others were eating lunch. The guests stood up as he entered, looking anxious. He was also tall, slim, and by the standards of Teletsia, fair skinned, with a shock of grey hair, a goatee beard and an intense expression, but when he smiled it softened.

'Please, sit down. I regret to say I was unavoidably delayed,' he began.

'How impolite of me to have invited you and then to be so late.'

'Dad, our guests know about the prophecy!' Saray exclaimed.

'That doesn't surprise me one bit,' observed the professor.

'Why were you so long? Was old Dean Grumkin rabbiting on as usual?' Garma asked.

'No, much more serious. Give me a glass of water, son. I must get my thoughts together.' The professor drank it down in one gulp, helped himself to some food and began eating hungrily. 'Now, firstly, our guests. You must stay here. As head of the university, I can protect you for some time if you don't leave the campus - at least until we get a directive from Teletos forcing me to give you up. The Sorcerers and Specials suspect you're subversives. You are perhaps aware that some interesting rumours have been going around Teletsia recently.'

'Yes sir, we are,' said Roarke.

'You mean you're subversives, or you're aware of the rumours?' The Vice-Chancellor looked hard at each of them. Lee and Raynor glanced at Roarke. Everyone realised this was an important question and stopped eating.

'Both,' said Roarke.

'I thought so. That's why I called you here. It seems things are finally coming to a head with these dratted Sorcerers.' The professor looked at Raynor. 'You resemble a Teletsian from the mountains, like me.'

'My grandmother came from Castle Mount. My name is Raynor Antiquarian and we've come here to awaken people's Trees of Life.'

'May the Mother Earth be praised that I got you here in time. One of the escaped rebels! And you two?' The professor looked at Lee and Roarke.

'I'm Lee Restorer, another one.'

'I'm a friend,' improvised Roarke.

'Would you meet our Prophecy Study Group this evening? Something happened today that makes it even more important.'

'That's what we came for. What's going on?' asked Roarke.

'The Sorcerers have ordered a national call up. Anyone between the age of eighteen and twenty-five must report to the Enlistment Centre tomorrow. The Sorcerers suspect their regime is under attack. You must have heard this nonsense about an invasion from outer space via flying carpets?'

'Yes, the fisherman who brought us here said it's all the gossip at the port,' said Lee blandly.

The guests spent the afternoon teaching Saray and Garma the songs for awakening the Tree of Life. They picked them up in no time and Saray wrote out the words and music. The Study Group came round in the evening and after receiving their awakening admitted that they had long been making plans for a different method of governing Teletsia. In the room were some of the finest minds in the country and they had been working at this quite fearlessly, every day aware that it might be their last, because the Sorcerers were even harsher on the leaders of society who stood up to them than they were towards the less influential people.

The Nalanda's living room was packed and Raynor did well in front of this formidable gathering. He spoke about Sasrar, how they were trying to free Teletsia and that they were being helped by people who were strong, both politically and spiritually. Everyone was impressed not only by his lucid words but also by the fact that he spoke from the heart, from his own experience. There were a number of younger people in the room who were supposed to enlist the following morning, girls and well as boys. Initially their parents wanted to put them on a ship and get them out of Teletsia that night, because they had the money and contacts to do so.

'If enough of us who've had our Trees of Life awakened enlist,' objected Garma, 'and then refuse to fight, the Sorcerers won't be able to shoot us all for disobeying them.'

'Don't be too sure,' protested Lee. 'You're brave and idealistic but you've never seen war. I have, and it's horrible. People die: sometimes slowly and painfully, and often in large numbers. You can lose your best friends.' He remembered having to take the news to Rajay of the deaths of his friends Varg-Nack and Danard. They were the saddest days of his life.

'Let's take a vote,' Garma went on.

They did so and all the young were determined to enlist and try to subvert the ranks. After the Study Group had left, the professor, Garma and Saray stayed up with their guests, and Saray brought everyone a tisane.

'If I may ask, where is your mother?' Lee asked Saray. They were sitting a little apart from the others.

'Lost to a slave farm, only last year,' she said sadly. 'We'll never see her again. She taught in the Political Studies Department, such as it was, being as the Sorcerers forbade any interesting study of politics. Some students tried to stand up for freedom and were taken off by the Sorcerers – the usual, for the slave farms, but she insisted on a fair trial and defended them. She managed to get them released but then the Sorcerers convicted her, and she was taken off.'

'If we can find her, we might be able to save her and heal her.'

'Do you mean it?'

'Yes, maybe, once we've freed the country. I apologise, I shouldn't have pried into your personal affairs.'

'It's OK. I'm proud to tell anyone about my wonderful mum.' Lee could see tears in Saray's eyes. 'But you see why Garma and I want to enlist and try to sabotage the army.'

'Yes, I do, and believe me, this freedom struggle is unfolding in the most unusual way. Don't raise your hopes too much about your mother, but - you've got some of the most powerful people on earth helping you.'

'The enigmatic Doctor Tarl?'

'You said it, not me. Also the man I work for.'

'Who's he?'

'The King of Daish Shaktay.' Saray's eyes were shining with admiration. 'Believe me, the all-caring divine power has helped us out of worse situations than this,' and he told her about Rajay's imprisonment at Mattanga and their escape.

When Lee heard the tragic story of Saray's mother he opened up to her in a way he would not normally have done to someone he hardly knew, but he wanted to give her courage. He tended to conceal rather than flaunt his past bravery and present position as one of Rajay's senior aides. Quite innocently, within moments Lee became Saray's hero. Although not conventionally handsome, he was fit and strongly built and had an endearing smile. He was also clever and quick-witted, and had led an extraordinarily exciting life for one so young. Saray, an attractive, strong willed and brilliant girl, was utterly entranced.

Since working closely with Rajay at the court of Malak Citadel, a number of ambitious mothers had set their sights on Lee as a prospective son-in-law. Those who could would approach Rajay and he would deflect them to his wife Zulani. She would handle these often single-minded, wealthy and influential ladies tactfully, saying she would talk to Lee when she had a moment, and after the first few never did. On one occasion, Rajay told Lee that Sir Brin Aydriss, one of Rajay's close advisors, had suggested him as an ideal match for his youngest daughter, Coral. Sir Brin and Rajay were possibly aware that Lee and Coral had already decided the same thing. However, Lee had bound himself to his oath to try and free Teletsia, and everything else, including marriage, had to wait. He had to get this over to Saray without hurting her feelings.

'Saray, King Rajay is a master partisan as well as everything else,' Lee explained pointedly. 'He impressed on us time and again that when you're involved in undercover activities you must keep your attention totally and utterly on that. Then you're more likely to survive. Put all personal considerations out of your head until Teletsia is free.' He felt Saray's discomfiture – she realised what he was trying to say. A well brought up Teletsian girl would not openly lose her heart to a stranger, however dashing, in such a short time, and both she and Lee knew this.

'Forgive me,' she almost whispered, acutely embarrassed.

'There's nothing to forgive; you're part of a great family that's got a big future.'

The Nalanda's house was not large, but Garma moved out of his room for Roarke and slept in his father's study, and Lee and Raynor shared their spare room. All three talked together for some time before sleeping and Lee told the others about the professor's wife and how her enslavement had made Saray and Garma even more determined to help liberate Teletsia. Roarke said he was sickened at the way the Sorcerers even treated women, and also that he was very impressed by Saray and Garma.

'With young people of that calibre, I'm amazed the Sorcerers have hung on to power for as long as they have,' he concluded, by way of praise. Then he turned his attention to strategy. 'Lee, you're not going to make it to those armaments factories you wanted to visit. We didn't foresee this call up. We should spend one more day here and then get out of Teletsia.'

'We should give the Nalandas as much help as possible,' said Lee.

'Definitely,' agreed Roarke.

The next morning Pastow came to the back door of the Nalanda's house and asked the housekeeper if he could have a word with the guests. She invited him into the kitchen, where Lee and the others were having breakfast, and they explained to Pastow what was going on. Pastow told them the Specials were watching both the eating house and their hotel.

Raynor told Pastow about the meeting the previous evening and how the sons and daughters of the faculty members' families had all decided to enlist, and why. He suggested Pastow should tell the young members of the Resistance Groups to do the same, in other words enlist and then give awakening to as many people as possible and show people how to protect themselves from the dark powers of the Sorcerers. They should also explain that these so called enemies, invaders or whatever, were going to turn out the Sorcerers and on no account to fight them. Pastow said most of the students and Resistance Group members had already decided to do this, because anyone who refused to enlist would be sent to the coal mines as a treated slave – a death sentence.

Lee gave a four petalled key to Pastow and showed him its powers. Roarke had not slept much the previous night because he had been imbuing the four petalled keys he had brought with him with the fiery discus option, originally a power of his fifth centre key. He was not a hundred per cent sure he had managed it, because he could not test them, but hoped for the best. Lee also gave Pastow a key for Pat Foodman, being as he was the head of this Resistance Group. Finally they bid their friend goodbye and hoped they would soon meet again to celebrate the liberation of Teletsia.

The younger generation all reported to the Enlistment Centre that morning. It was very disorganised but no one could escape once they were in the high-walled compound, and they spent the day sitting around waiting for their marching orders. Saray, Garma and their friends managed to give awakening to many of the reluctant recruits and started making secret plans with some of their closer friends for the subversion of the armed forces.

Many of the university staff had said goodbye to their sons and daughters, possibly for the last time. The university was in turmoil, as all the students had been called up, but in this chaos it was not so obvious that a number of the teaching staff and their families had congregated at the Vice-Chancellor's residence, where Lee and Raynor showed everyone how to clear themselves of mental, emotional and to a certain extent physical problems using the powers of the awakened Tree of Life. Roarke, meanwhile, had been talking to the Vice-Chancellor about the possible political future of Teletsia, and how people like the professor would be vitally important to rebuild the country. Although it was a day of shock and sadness, the vibrations were tremendous and everyone was hopeful that the long awaited change was about to happen.

'How many more four petalled keys have we got?' Raynor asked.

'Quite a few,' Roarke replied. 'Lord Jarwhen gave me a whole pouch full. Why?'

'These folk have access to a lot of places,' said Lee, 'and they might be able to go into the slave farms, and workshops and factories. If we can give them keys they'll be able to resist the powers of the Sorcerers and may be able to free people of the effects of this abominable 'treatment', and from the hypnotism the Sorcerers will try on everyone to get them to fight their war. I've been talking to a lecturer in the Engineering Department. He's been ordered to go and work in the armaments factory I wanted to get into. He says they mesmerise the labourers into believing they're doing a great and patriotic job.'

'Give him a key and tell him to do his best with it,' Roarke suggested. 'I'll find out from Professor Nalanda if any of the others might be made to work in places like that. It would make a big difference if the people making the weapons for the Sorcerers are on our side - a wrong mix in the metal that goes to make a gun or a sword with a defective hilt could count for a great deal in our favour.'

CHAPTER 6

TIME TO DEPART

After a long day of showing academic staff and their families wisdom of a supremely profound and practical nature that they could never have found at their university, Lee, Raynor and Roarke were told by Professor Nalanda that they would have to leave imminently, because the order to arrest them could be back from Teletos at any time. The professor could make out his own travel passes and the story was that he was sending his guests to Teletos for a meeting with their Holinesses the High Priests. If it looked as if the three of them had been duped into visiting the Head Sorcerers, they would be unlikely to be recaptured by the local Specials, or so Professor Nalanda reasoned. Roarke explained that they needed to get to a certain coconut farm up the coast. Initially Professor Nalanda was going to lend them his steam car and driver, but as they needed to leave that night and the driver had gone home Professor Nalanda said he would drive them himself. They left after supper.

'It shouldn't take too long; I know that area,' he explained. They made bandhans of protection and request before leaving and for most of the way all went well. The road went along the side of the sea, and was straight and flat. After that it led through some hills and when they going round a corner there was a deep pothole. The car lurched into it and gave a noisy crack, Professor Nalanda coaxed it to the side and there it stopped.

'Don't worry,' said Roarke cheerfully. 'I'm an engineer and I'm sure we can fix it.' He opened up the works and peered inside by the light of the lantern. He soon found the problem – a small rod had snapped and this was vital to the movement of the car. 'Do you have a tool kit?' he asked.

'Yes, here it is,' the professor produced it, without much conviction. He was happier with his mathematical problems than a malfunctioning steam car.

'Pity, there's nothing in here we can use to cobble it together,' Roarke looked at the tool box. 'A length of strong wire would do. Try that gate there, Lee, the one into that field. Maybe there's some wound round it. We might get lucky.'

They were not.

'See that village on the hill,' Raynor pointed, 'maybe they'll have some.'

'I know a family there,' said the professor, more hopeful now. 'I'll go and get help from them. You three stay here and keep an eye on the steam car,' and he strode purposefully down the road, grey hair streaming out behind him.

Shortly after he had left they heard the sound of tramping feet. The barracks, now to be a training centre for conscripts, was quite close. They could see a long, ragged and undisciplined column of recruits approaching.

'Do we hide?' Lee asked Roarke.

'You keep out of sight when you see any Specials, in case they're looking for the three of us together, but Raynor and I will stay put,' he replied. 'We're not doing anything wrong, and the Specials in charge will be fully occupied keeping the conscripts in line. As they pass, try to give them awakening with your attention. I'm going to risk letting my keys be seen by the boys and girls, but watch out for Specials.'

'I'll show my Sasrar one,' Raynor said. 'Even if it's dangerous, it has such powerful vibrations.'

By now some Specials at the front of the column were passing. They glanced at the steam car and the young men waiting on the side of the road in the moons' light but did not stop. They were in a hurry. As soon as they had gone, they exposed their keys and openly made the gestures of awakening the Tree of Life. They sang some of the songs that went with them as the conscripts marched by and saw them. Raynor wondered how many of them knew about the prophecy and whether the keys meant anything to them on a conscious level. Roarke recognised one student who had been at the awakening programme, then another, and one of the faculty members' sons. Many of them smiled and waved, but none could stop, as periodically a Special marched past. Raynor saw Saray and Garma, and they left the column and came over. A Special followed them.

'What do you think you're doing?' he demanded.

'This is our father's steam car and he's the head of the university,' explained Garma. 'He's hopeless with anything mechanical and we can often help him. Please let us stay a little while.'

'Alright, but you'll be in deep trouble if you don't report to the barracks by midnight.' The Special did not want to get on the wrong side of anyone as important as Professor Nalanda. 'What about you two?' He looked at Roarke and Raynor.

'We're guests of Professor Nalanda, and he's taking us to Teletos for an important conference,' replied Roarke, speaking with the accent of Vittalia.

'Alright then,' and he marched off, leaving Saray and Garma by the steam car.

'Let's make a bandhan that the conscripts don't have to fight a war they're not interested in,' said Raynor, as the column went on and on and finally the tramping died away. He looked down the road and saw the professor in the distance, returning with a posse of young men. 'Did they take your names at the recruitment depot?' He asked Saray and Garma.

'They tried, but it was such chaos, they didn't have much clue,' replied Garma.

'Garma, I'm going to join you. I'll say I'm your cousin from Castle Mount, eager to help the cause of the fatherland and all that rot. Then together we'll subvert the conscripts. It's cool on vibrations, but absolutely no one must know who I really am. You must also warn anyone who thinks I'm Professor Quair.'

'You can trust Saray and me to be discreet. With dad's position, we're used to keeping our mouths shut about certain matters. It would be amazing to have you with us!' cried Garma. 'If I vouch for you the Specials would never realise you aren't genuine and we look so alike no one would realise we aren't related.'

'We may be,' said Raynor. He took Lee and Roarke aside, and although initially they were horrified, when they checked his idea on vibrations it was fairly cool, so they relented.

'The Specials had to stop when they realised who I was,' Professor Nalanda came up panting, holding a roll of wire. 'I asked them why they didn't help you but they just mumbled excuses. Typical! Anyway, I've commandeered some lads from the column. Hello,' he greeted Saray and Garma.

'We thought we'd better stop and help,' said Saray. 'You can drop us at the barracks as you pass.'

Raynor explained his plan to the professor while the others tinkered with the car. It was soon fixed well enough to move again and Roarke thanked the conscripts for their help.

'Anything to be able to get to that dreadful barracks a bit later,' grumbled one boy, 'and it's an honour to help Professor Nalanda. I'm a student, not a soldier in a war I couldn't care less about. What were you doing as we passed, by the way? My friends marching near me felt so cheered up when we saw you making those strange gestures and singing those songs. Plus we noticed those incredible jewels.'

'Awakening you all to the inner joy of your souls, but keep quiet about those jewels; they're very powerful and it's not a power that will help the Sorcerers or Specials,' said Lee, and quickly showed them the bandhans and how to reawaken their Trees of Life.

'Help is on the way, and by the grace of the Mother Earth who protects Teletsia, hopefully none of you are going to come to any harm,' added Roarke.

'The enemy sounds like our salvation, from what I've heard,' said another of the conscripts.

'You boys hop in the back and we'll drop you at your barracks,' said the professor. 'I've got to give the impression I'm on the side of the Sorcerers, but believe me, the inner experience you've had is part of a much more powerful law than the one which rules Teletsia at present.'

So it was that the arch-enemies of the Sorcerers' regime halted innocuously in front of the Sorcerers' barracks. Raynor slipped in with Garma and the conscripts, and no one even bothered to ask his name. When the others neared the coconut farm, Roarke checked the vibrations. They were not cool.

'Professor Nalanda, please leave us here, out of sight of the farmhouse, and we'll make our way onwards alone,' he said.

'There may be some trouble. If we have to fight we have the keys - they're formidable weapons,' explained Lee. 'If anyone asks you, say we escaped and sailed off in our yacht which is moored in the bay down there.'

'I don't see it,' the professor looked at the sea.

'We have a flying ship. I wasn't making it up when I gave that talk on them to your Engineering Department,' admitted Roarke. 'Professor Nalanda, thank you for everything and I hope we meet again when Teletsia is free. I'm Roarke of Vittalia.' The professor bowed low, because he had heard of him.

'Your Highness, what an honour!'

'Don't embarrass me, Professor!' laughed Roarke. 'Maybe I should remain Doctor Tarl. Come on Lee.'

Lee and Roarke collected their belongings and crept nearer to where the flying ship had been hidden. They saw some Specials in the bushes near it, looking at it warily.

'Now what?' Lee was worried, understandably.

'Watch,' whispered Roarke, quite relaxed, taking off his sixteen petalled key.

He began touching each of the petals in a specific order, chanting softly. Slowly the flying ship rose from the ground and hovered silently above the nearby coconut palms. He went on chanting. Initially the flyer moved across the beach towards the sea and the Specials ran after it, over the sand and into the shallow water, away from Roarke and Lee, who were waiting near the road. The Specials got out their guns and Lee noticed with his heart pounding that they were the ones which were programmed to never miss their target. The Specials fired but the shots went amuck. Roarke continued to touch the key and chant, and the flyer suddenly changed direction and darted inland to where he and Lee were standing, and hovered nearby. They jumped in, and with a whoosh! it climbed rapidly and flew north-eastwards over the sea. The Specials fired once more, but again the bullets all missed their target.

'What happened? Why didn't their guns hit us?' asked Lee.

'Those guns are programmed by sorcery, whereas my flyer resonates with the benevolent power of the cosmos. There's a bandhan of protection around us. In my country we worship the all-pervading power in the form of Father Sky and it's by meditating on him that I've been given the inspiration to build these craft. We should give thanks that we're alright.' Roarke sang a simple praise chant as they flew through the night, then spoke again. 'The sky goes on forever and is full of hidden beauty.'

'What do you mean?'

'Take that spyglass; it's extremely powerful. Look at that planet through it,' Roarke pointed to a bright star. Lee did so.

'It's exquisite! Those yellow bands, and the narrow blue ones with white clouds floating over them and those rings around it – each one a different shade, and I can see it has a whole lot of moons too.'

'Have a look at that slight haze below that group of stars.' Roarke pointed to another part of the sky.

'It's the most wonderful spiral galaxy - and the colours!'

'There's much more. Mother Nature is the greatest artist and the whole universe is her canvas. You look, but I'm going to put the flyer on automatic so I can sleep,' and Roarke put his key into the slot. 'I've set the craft to fly to an island off the northeast coast of Teletsia. Wake me up before we get there because it's the home of a ferocious old hermit. He's a friend of my parents but I'd better introduce him to you, because you never know how he'll react when we disturb his serene isolation.'

Lee looked through the spyglass at the distant coastline of Teletsia, then pointed it at the sky and looked in awe at the art gallery of the heavens. When the island came in sight he woke Roarke, who landed the craft on the beach. They unrolled some cotton mats from the flyer and lay down on the sand for some more sleep. Roarke, like all the guardians, was completely detached from material comforts and could sleep anywhere.

Lee was woken by the warming rays of the rising sun. Roarke had disappeared but had left a water bottle and some food. Some time later Lee was sitting in meditation, enjoying the peace and clearing his subtle centres by putting his hands on the sand to ask the earth element to absorb the negativity he had picked up in Teletsia. Then he went down to the sea, and put his feet in the water to clear other aspects of his subtle system. He looked at the sun, still low on the horizon, and said some words of praise for the giver of light and life.

His heart centre was constricted because he was feeling the collective fear of the young people who were forced to enlist, and also the uncertainty of many of the people of Teletsia. He knew that if he cleared his own heart centre it would, to a certain extent, help the awakened people in Teletsia, because they were all connected on a subtle level. He gave a bandhan that the Sorcerers and Specials could be overcome without too much violence, because he would never wish war on his own countrymen.

He heard Roarke approach and walking with him was an ancient hermit, almost bald and wearing a simple garment of woven bark. Lee made humble obeisance to him.

'So, hope for Teletsia at last,' the old man commented, as Lee rose from kneeling before him. 'I was telling Roarke that the Sorcerers use spy albatrosses and they've warned their masters about the navy coming from the north, which I gather is from Daish Shaktay. You must alert Lord Jarwhen that you're being spied on. Who else is on the Island of Creations? '

'There's Rajay Ghiry, King of Daish Shaktay, Merien the son of the Emperor's Prime Minister and,' Roarke paused, 'the new one from the north, and Lord Jarwhen and Lady Mercola. Stellamar comes and goes and all the young people from Teletsia who went to Sasrar are there too.'

'Good. You have my greatest blessings. It will ease my inner pain no end when you've cleared out these vermin, these aberrations of humanity, the Sorcerers - from Teletsia.' He looked at Lee. 'Still, the fact that you young Teletsians had to run away from them to the northern kingdom meant you received spiritual gifts much more easily than I did. You merely went on a long journey and had help from the keys and guardians like Roarke, while I've had to get to the same place through years of arduous penances and introspection, alone on this island.'

'Holy one, why don't you come with us to the Island of Creations?' Lee asked.

'I'm fine here,' a kindly smile came over the old ascetic's face, 'I was only mentioning that we've taken different routes to reach the same place. Keep on with your part in the drama and don't let your head get too big for your body when you come to your destiny. I'll be here to give you sobering advice.'

'Thank you, I will.'

'We must take our leave now,' said Roarke.

'I'd rather talk to two sensible young men like you for a short while, than a crowd of idiots for five years.'

He turned and walked up the beach, and no one would have believed he was an old man, so strong and springy was his stride. That afternoon they returned to the Island of Creations, flying in from the northeast. Lee pondered the words of the old hermit as he watched the sea go by beneath him. He wondered what fate might have in store for him and realised the 'new one from the north', was Robin, meaning he was also a guardian. Lee kept it to himself; he knew the importance of discretion.

When Rajay left for Darzeet and Roarke went to Gyan-on-Sea, Merien went to find Conwenna and Derwin, because when we felt their vibrations there was heat and some tingling on our fingers, indicating problems. Merien stopped at a different safe house to break his journey, where yet another Resistance Group got their awakening. He left a four petalled key and warned them to prepare for an invasion, but told them that at least they would now be immune to attacks of sorcery. He reached the Heber's castle and was warmly welcomed, but was told that Conwenna and Derwin had gone further south into the mountains and had not been seen for some time.

Merien set off to find them and periodically came down at small villages. Often when he stopped he met groups of people who had been given awakening by Conwenna and Derwin, and was told they had left and gone further south. Everywhere the men were preparing for war, so Merien gave out a four petalled key to the leader of each group and told them how to use it. These people had as much reason to want to be rid of the Sorcerers as anyone because they were forced to take a very low price for their coffee when they sold it through the official channels. They could hardly survive on what they made, so risked selling it illegally to private coffee brokers for higher prices. After two days, going from one isolated mountain village to the next, Merien finally located Conwenna sitting in a little square with some girls, and Derwin was with the men in the nearby open air coffee shop.

'Merien, thank goodness you've come!' she cried in relief.

'What's going on?' he asked.

'Derwin will explain,' she continued dryly, and they walked over to him.

'Hello Derwin, you've been up here a long time. How come?'

'You see,' he began defensively, 'we were having such success, flying to all these villages, but one day I realised we were about to run out of fuel. I thought I had another sack in the flyer but then realised I'd left it at the Heber's. So we've been stuck here, because we couldn't leave the flyer behind and go back on mules. We've done a lot of bandhans and finally you came.'

'I felt you needed my help. How much fuel do you have left?'

'A bit, but not enough to get back to Castle Mount and I don't want to get marooned on some mountain.'

'I can fly a ship almost entirely with my attention. You drive mine and I'll fly yours. Take Conwenna, because my attention has to be absolutely perfect to do it and it's easier if I'm alone.'

'Brilliant. So that's sorted. Have some coffee,' and Derwin offered Merien a cup. Although he was now sixteen he still had the total optimism of the very young. All problems could and would be solved very simply. 'This coffee is excellent, home grown, and you can meet the locals. I've told them about you and our other friends, and how Teletsia is soon going to be free. These folk are going to be very helpful if we have to go to war.'

Merien finished up having a meal as well as coffee and realised that these mountain dwellers, like all the others he had met in the previous few days, were very spiritual people who responded well to the awakening of the Tree of Life. No Sorcerer was going to annihilate or mesmerise them any more. They were also intrepid fighters, eager to take on the Sorcerers, especially now they were immune to their sorcery. The next day Derwin, Conwenna and Merien returned to the Heber's castle with both flying ships.

After we returned from the Temple of Support, Robin and I were on the Island of Creations. Robin wanted to take the horses to Teletsia a few more times so they could put their feet on the earth and activate it. The safest time was in the middle of the night and we would set off, he on Yamun and me on Tama, fly over the sea out of sight of land, then turn inland where the coast was uninhabited and deserted. We would land and let the horses roam around while we gave thanks to Mother Earth, made bandhans of request or sat in meditation on the ground. The next evening we would do the same thing in another area. After a few days of this we received a message from Stellamar. The Specials who were posted up and down the coast had begun having strange fits, and shook violently and uncontrollably whenever they were on duty, especially in areas where there were large horses' hoof prints on the ground. Because of this the Teletsian forces could not guard the coast very effectively. This was exactly what Robin had hoped would happen.

Tom Dyeman went to the hut in the wood and found the four petalled key the day after Ahren had been there when he escaped from the slave farm. He took it home and Mabron Riverside, Tandi's brother, who was still staying with the Dyeman's, felt confident to go into a slave farm with the help of the borrowed key to try and free more slaves from the mesmerised state they were in. Ahren had earlier told Tom that it would be all right for Mabron to use it. Hograr Dyeman pretended he had bought Mabron in Teletos. Mabron went through the ordeal of being branded, but as his forged papers said he was a newly treated specimen he didn't have to wait for the burn to heal. Tom delivered him to the only other slave farm in the district with the payment for training him, which was often done with newly treated slaves. That evening Tom went round again, saying he had wanted to leave his slave a change of clothes. He also asked to have a look at him and when he did he slipped the key to Mabron.

Mabron was not as successful as Ahren but did manage to cure about ten slaves with the help of the key. The more people were healed the easier it became, because the collective awareness was changing. He gave them awakening, taught them the two bandhans and told them to awaken others. When Tom came to collect his 'trained' slave some days later, Mabron was much improved and now perfect for simple farm work, so the overseer assured Tom.

At this point Hograr Dyeman decided it was time for the fugitives staying with him to leave, as the Specials had again come round. If it hadn't been for Custard the bull they would have found the trapdoor with Gwant and the Dairymans concealed underneath, because they did an ominously detailed search. Custard was a sensible animal and showed unexpected aggression when the Specials came near his pen; he blew through his nostrils, stamped his foot and looked suitably scary, so they didn't search it. The other freed slaves had returned to their homes and were hiding with their families.

Tom posed as the slave guard and they set off for the coast with mostly forged documents. Mr and Mrs Dairyman and Gwant and Mabron were chained together, and made a point of looking mournful and vacant, in the back of a farm wagon. They started the journey at night and hid at a safe house the next day, the same one as Ahren had visited and where the Sorcerer had incinerated himself. They were periodically stopped by Specials manning road blocks and their documents were checked, and the third time, Tom was given some startling news.

'Your documents are in order,' said the Special, 'but as soon as you've delivered these slaves you must go back home for the call up.'

'I don't understand, sir, can you explain?' asked Tom.

'All young men and women have to enlist and defend the fatherland.'

The next evening they reached the home of the Pearl Lords. Some Specials stopped them outside the main gatehouse, but as their documents were in order and the 'slaves' behaved as treated slaves did, could not find any reason to stop them entering the well-guarded private property.

When the fugitives were safely inside they met Stellamar. Tom asked what the call up was all about but she wasn't sure. The next day she gave healing vibrations to each of the members of the group and checked that the Island of Creations would accept them. They were all fine except Gwant, who still could not get over his guilt at having tried to betray the others. Stellamar suggested he should stay with the Pearl Lords, being as they could easily hide one person in their large establishment. That night the whole party, including Namoh, now well enough to travel, were hidden in crates in the hold of a fishing boat under a cargo of fish, and smelly though it was they had a safe passage to the Island of Creations.

CHAPTER 7

CONWENNA'S NIGHT

Merien left Castle Mount for the Island but told Derwin and Conwenna to stay some time longer as they were doing so well up there. However, when he had left, Conwenna spoke to Derwin.

'I want to see my father once more.'

'You're crazy, half of Teletsia is looking for you. And how are you going to get there?'

'You can take me. If we leave him in Teletos the Sorcerers will eventually kill him. Now he's had his awakening, he might be better physically - his vibrations aren't quite so bad. We might be able to get him out somehow.'

'There are limits to what you can ask of me and that's way beyond it,' insisted Derwin tetchily. These Teletsian girls – they were too much sometimes!

'Then I'll go by myself.'

Derwin didn't believe this but the next day he couldn't find her and was told she had gone to a village on the nearby river which led into the Coffee River. Numerous barges loaded with coffee beans went down it, bound for the coast, especially now the flood waters were subsiding and it was safer to navigate. When Conwenna was not back in the evening, Derwin went to look for her and was told she had left on a barge that morning. He knew he would have to go after her because it was too dangerous not to. He went back to the castle, packed his belongings and apologised to the Hebers, who understood his predicament.

Derwin didn't know how he was going to find Conwenna but gave a bandhan of request. Then he had an inspiration: he remembered that he and Roarke had been experimenting some months before, as they often did, and had figured out how to make his flyer home in on a key – either a Sasrar one or a fifth centre one, which governed the flyers. He tried it and the flyer immediately changed direction, and flew over the jungle, thus cutting off a big bend in the river. Soon he spied Conwenna, by the light of a moon, walking on the deck of a barge moored near a riverside village. He landed the craft nearby.

'What on earth do you think you're doing?' he cried when he boarded the

148

barge.

'I'm going to see my father,' she replied defiantly.

'You'll never make it. You're lucky you haven't been picked up already. There are Sorcerers' spies everywhere.'

'If you won't help, I'll have to make my way as best I can.'

'I can see I'll have to take you. Let's get out of here, at least. Get your stuff and for goodness sake hurry.'

Soon they were airborne and he didn't speak to her for some time as he concentrated on flying over the endless jungle in the balmy night. Finally Conwenna broke the ice.

'I'm sorry, but something tells me I simply have to try to see my dad. It's incredibly cool on vibrations.'

'Get out your map and see if you can find a safe house between here and Teletos.' Derwin was still annoyed and worried.

'There's one near a place called Woodenton. Didn't Merien visit it?'

'Yes,' he was unusually sharp.

'Please don't be like this. We're going to win back Teletsia by allowing the vibrations to guide us, which I am. Don't you see that?'

'You're one of our very special group. We've been through so much together and the others would never forgive me if I don't look after you properly. Men, and even boys at a pinch, are supposed to do the dangerous things, not girls.'

'Really?' Conwenna smiled impishly. 'You haven't had much success with Asha.'

'We've given up with her but we'd hoped you wouldn't turn out so impossible.'

'Would you rather I was a wimp and a coward?'

'No, but I've got to try and stop you, haven't I? Alright, you win this round. See if that river down there is marked on the map and try and figure out if we're anywhere near Woodenton.' Derwin smiled and the tension between them was broken.

So it was that just when Lakriman Woodseller thought his life was coming back to normal, he had another surprise visit. Derwin and Conwenna could not have chosen better because the surviving Woodenton Sorcerers and Specials were horribly scared of the place. The Woodsellers told their guests what had happened when the Specials came to arrest them after Merien's visit, and were destroyed by the elephants. Conwenna and Derwin were pleasantly amazed, and after spending the day with the Woodsellers they set off again under cover of darkness. They then flew towards the safe house farm to the north of Teletos that Stellamar had pointed out to Derwin. Late in the night they landed the flyer in a field of tall maize near the farm and waited for dawn. Soon after sunrise they walked into the farm yard and saw a man carrying a basket of eggs.

'Can I help you?' he asked.

'Yes, we're looking for the farmer who owns this place.'

'That's me, lad.'

'I was told if I showed you this you'd help us,' Derwin produced the four petalled key which Lord Jarwhen had lent him. The farmer put down the basket of eggs, placed his hands in front of him with the palms upwards and checked the vibrations. Rural Teletsia was not what it used to be.

'Yes,' he replied, having felt coolness from Derwin. 'You must be a friend of Lady Stellamar?'

'That's right.'

'Come in. We have breakfast early and I'm sure you'd like to join us. Put your key away though.' They slept for most of the day and in the evening, once it was dark, returned to the flyer.

'I'm not at all keen on taking you into Teletos,' Derwin reiterated. 'It's so unbelievably dangerous, because if the Specials are watching anywhere it's bound to be Uncle Berny's place, where your dad lives. Let's try to raise a cloud cover. We'll both say the words of power and make bandhans over our Sasrar keys like Merien showed us. I hope this works.'

For a short while nothing happened but then the whole sky suddenly clouded over and there was a slash of lightning followed by a crash of thunder. Rain poured down and there was more thunder and lightning.

'Time to go!' cried Derwin through the noise and water. He wondered if their request had been answered too violently and whether it was safe to fly through this tempest, but Conwenna was adamant.

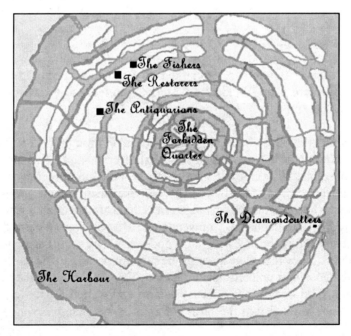

They took off and flew through the blackness to the Restorer's mansion and Derwin had to hover low so he could navigate by the network of dimly lit canals. He landed in the walled garden and the rain was drumming on the roof of the flyer. 'Don't be long. If anyone sees the flyer, I'll take off and make for the safe house in the Jeweller's Quarter. If anything goes wrong we'll try and meet up there.'

'OK, but I've got to do this.'

The rain was such that Conwenna was not met by anyone, and even the dogs had taken cover. She crept across the open area behind the old palace, into the inner courtyard and up the stone stairs to her father's flat on the second floor. So far so good, and the storm was still raging overhead. She rapped the door knocker and no one came. She knocked a second time and Drusilla answered it.

'Hello, you again!' she said, looking at the dripping wet girl. 'Come in and get dry.' Conwenna smiled at her but Drusilla just stared. 'Your father is a little better, go and see him.' Conwenna went into his bedroom and he was sitting up in a chair, and looked much happier than when she had been there before.

'I never thought I'd see you again!' he smiled, and put his arms out for her to give him a hug, which she did.

'Dad, I can't stay long, but I had to come and see how you are.' Conwenna felt fear in his heart but enormous love as well. Drusilla came in behind them.

'It's wonderful to see you again, but - Drusilla, go and make us some tea, will you? And get some dry clothes for Conwenna.' Drusilla took herself off and Conwenna looked at her father.

'I knew you'd respond to the power of the Tree of Life.'

'Yes, I feel more inner peace. But listen - the Specials are after you and they're watching the building. You must leave immediately. I don't know how you're going to get out...'

'Couldn't you come with us? Derwin's here and we've got a flying ship in the walled garden.'

'My goodness! So they do exist! No dear, I can't, because I can't get down the stairs very easily - it would take me ages. The doctor says that even though I've improved since you gave me that – awakening or whatever you called it – there's no hope for me.'

'Dad, there is! You don't know, this can help you recover from almost anything, but you must have faith...' Conwenna talked on but was unable to change her father's mind. Soon she heard the sound of heavy feet on the stone stairs outside the flat.

'You must contact you grandmother,' urged Mr Prospector in a whisper. 'She lives in the old people's home at Twindell, that little town north of here. She may have a secret which could save Teletsia. I had a dream last night.....it all fits...Drusilla...Queen Wasp...'

'She's in here,' Conwenna heard Drusilla say, and to Conwenna's horror three Specials crowded into the bedroom. One came over to her father and gave him a vicious blow on the face which made blood flow from his nose.

'So, thought you'd change sides again, did you?' he sneered.

'Yes. I only spied for your gang to protect my daughter, and never told you anything either true or important,' slurred Conwenna's father painfully. The Special in charge told Drusilla to get out of the room. For a moment the Special's back was turned and Conwenna's father gasped to her, his breathing rattling and faltering, 'Get them, every last stinking one of them, my brave daughter. Now you're back to save this country I can die in peace.'

The chief Special came over to him, pushed Conwenna aside and gave him another hard blow on his head. Conwenna wondered whether to use the fiery discus option of her key, but decided it probably wouldn't work, because her own life was not in danger. She turned to her father and saw that he was slumped in his chair, not moving at all, and his head was at an impossible angle to his neck.

'What have you done?' she cried.

'Miss Drusilla said he didn't have long, so I sent him on his way a bit quicker than he bargained for,' smirked the Special. Conwenna felt for a pulse, but there was none, and his breathing had stopped.

The Special seized her arm. 'And you, little madam, have an appointment with their Holinesses the High Priests who rule Teletsia. They've been waiting for one of you rebels to show yourselves. Oh yes! I'll get a big reward for delivering you to them – alive, unsearched and unharmed.' Conwenna's father lay dead in front of her and she had never felt so shocked, shattered and sad, but this opened an incredible opportunity for her.

'I'll come, you don't have to drag me,' she said pluckily as they pulled her down the stairs and into a waiting horse-drawn van. She was thrown in the back and the door was slammed shut. Conwenna was alone and tears of grief poured from her eyes. She felt the vibrations: surprisingly cool. She had a plan – a one in a million chance. She thought of the bravery of the rest of us and prayed to the Mother Earth who was worshipped in Teletsia, Teletsia as it should be. After some time the van stopped and the door was opened.

'Get out. We walk from here. No wheeled traffic in the palace compound at night.' Conwenna was pushed in front of the three Specials and soon they were at the large, well-guarded gatehouse of the palace of the leading Sorcerers. The Specials showed their passes, and Conwenna was hidden in a large cloak. The guards had no idea who was going in or why. The vibrations were painful but Conwenna walked fast, not wanting to be hit like her father had been.

'The High Priests will have some interesting things in store for you,' sniggered one as they walked. 'Ever been tortured? Now's your chance!' Conwenna didn't respond and concentrated on memorising the layout of the place, to keep her mind off what would happen if her idea didn't work.

One of the Specials went off to alert the Head Sorcerers. The other two told Conwenna to wait in the hallway of the main building, empty at this time of night except for some sentries in the guard room by the front door. After some time the first Special returned.

'We're to take her up to the Interrogation Chamber and wait for Their Supremacies. They'll be along shortly.'

Conwenna was forced up the stairs, along a passage and into a panelled room, the same one as where Mardhang had reported his findings on Raynor to the Head Sorcerers five years before. Conwenna was made to stand alone, in the middle of the room, and Their Supremacies soon filed in and sat behind a heavy wooden table at the end of the chamber.

'Close the door and leave us,' one Sorcerer ordered the Specials. 'Wait downstairs in the guardroom.' There were armed guards outside the closed door but none in the room.

'So, at last we have one of the children of the prophecy,' said the oldest Sorcerer. 'Are you going to talk, or must we use some gentle persuasion? We could keep you in agony for days before we allow you to die, and by then you'll be begging for release. If you tell us what we need to know we'll despatch you painlessly.'

'I will talk,' said Conwenna quietly, her head held high. Her heart was pounding.

'Let me introduce you to the one who'll be in charge of torturing you if you don't answer our questions. Stand up, my good man. It isn't often you get a prisoner like this delivered to you.' Conwenna noticed another Sorcerer stand briefly and stare coldly at her, then sit down again.

'So, you're Conwenna Prospector?' asked the Head of the Secret Police.

'Yes.' She was beginning to feel paralysed with terror. At that moment the door opened, and another Sorcerer came in and hurriedly sat down.

'I'm sorry I'm late, I only just got the summons.'

'That's all right Warzog, you'll have plenty of time to write this up,' said the Head of the Secret Police. 'This is the youngest one. Still extremely dangerous, like a newly hatched cobra, deadly from the moment it leaves the egg. Now, Miss Conwenna, let's start with the jewels of power. Do you have one?'

'Yes. Let me show it to you and then I'll tell you how it works.' Conwenna still had the door key she had been given the first time she went into Teletos. She took it from around her neck, being careful to keep her Sasrar key and the genuine first centre key concealed. She walked towards the table, put the door key down in front of the oldest Sorcerer and then stepped back. He picked it up and they all stared at it in wonder.

This was Conwenna's moment. She felt under her clothing, as if she was readjusting her overshirt where she had taken off the door key, and placed her index finger in the indentation at the back of the Sasrar key, as Robin had showed her. With her other hand she removed the chain from her neck, desperately praying that it would save her life. In an instant the transformation took place, as if the power that activated these keys knew time was perilously short. Lightning fast the discus flew round the room, beheading all the Sorcerers before they even had time to cry for help.

She had done it, or rather the power of the key had.

She was alone in a room, with firmly closed doors, and in front of her lay the rulers of Teletsia in a dead and blood-soaked heap. Conwenna, aged fifteen, shaking with fear and retching at the sight of all the gore, had done what no one had managed to do for over two hundred years. She had successfully challenged the might of the Sorcerers. She had just enough presence of mind to pick up both keys and put them around her neck, then went to the cloak rack by the wall and helped herself to the smallest cloak and wide brimmed hat - the normal street wear of the Sorcerers - put them on and tucked her hair up under the hat.

She took her Sasrar key in her hands and gave thanks to the Mother Earth that she was still alive, then made a bandhan of request that she could somehow escape. She felt marginally less scared - as confident as a young girl could expect to feel when she had been responsible for the death of the rulers of her country. Still shaking with shock, she noticed a small service door in the back corner and opened it slowly and quietly. It led into a pantry and there was a passage back to the main corridor. She crept out into it, and was at the top of the stairs down to the hall below.

The guards outside the main, closed door into the Interrogation Chamber were half asleep and did not react to her, presumably because she looked like a Sorcerer in the unlighted passage. This had been an unexpected meeting, arranged late at night, and the usual staff had gone off duty, so she did not see anyone else until she padded down the dark stairs and saw the guards in the room at the side of the main door into the courtyard. She slipped a little on a rug. One of the guards looked in her direction and she walked on, heart pounding.

'What's that?' another guard looked round.

'I thought I heard something,' said the first one.

'Probably a ghost. This place must be full of them,' added the third with a ghoulish chuckle and put his feet up on the table again.

'No, it's one of Their Supremacies going home,' affirmed the first. 'I don't know which one, but I noticed the hat and cloak.'

Conwenna walked on, petrified. Now where? She paused on the doorstep. She could see across the wide courtyard to the gatehouse. There was a small door open in the closed larger one but a sentry paced back and forth. There had to be another way out. In Teletos every building that backed onto a canal had a water gate, and usually some small boats were tied up nearby. People used them for all manner of things, like going to the markets. She asked a question of the vibrations: 'Left or right out of the door?' and it was cool for left. She set off, trying not to look lost, and walked around the outside wall of the palace. She heard the footsteps of another sentry and dodged into an alcove, but he walked past without noticing her. She saw a perimeter wall and prayed there was a canal on the other side. There were some steps down to a door in this wall, but when she tried it, it was locked. She would have to climb over. She clambered up with the help of a tree growing against it – it was as high as two men - and once on top saw a canal and a row of boats moored to a wharf. She dropped onto the walkway, but then heard a shout in the yard behind.

'Who goes there?' a voice called out.

She ran along the walkway, round a corner and out of sight of the door, but then it came to an end. There was no time to untie a boat and no alternative but to swim. She took off the hat and cloak, threw them into the dirty canal and jumped in after them, pushing them below the surface and behind a moored boat. She swam along the fetid canal some way, turned into another one at right angles to the first, then hid between two boats that were tied up on another walkway, to get her breath back. She heard the sound of a barge approaching, punted by someone who wasn't in a hurry. She dreaded that it was the Sorcerers' people after her, but she had swum quite some way.

'Rubbish, rags and bones – bring 'em out!' cried the boatman.

Conwenna had forgotten about the Teletos Refuse Disposal Service, but horror of horrors, the man was punting towards her. He tied up his boat, climbed onto the wharf and picked up a dustbin. He threw the contents into his barge and was returning the empty bin when he turned and saw Conwenna.

'My goodness me – what on earth are you doing in there?' He grabbed her by the hand and dragged her onto the walkway. Even if he was from the humblest class of people, because rubbish collectors were considered unclean and cursed, he had a kind face.

'Help me! I've got to get away from here.'

'I can see that,' he grinned at the bedraggled girl. 'Do you mind riding in my boat?'

'No, it would be a blessing. The Sorcerers are after me.'

'Well, hop in. Hide under that sacking. Sorry it's dirty, but I do a dirty job. I'll finish my round then drop you off somewhere safer. Where do you want to go?'

'Jeweller's Quarter. Any chance?'

'I'll do my best.'

Two stops later Conwenna heard another boat approaching.

'Did you see anyone in the canal?' demanded an angry voice.

'No, of course not. Only a lunatic would be in this water. It's filthy,' replied the rubbish collector.

'Don't be rude, trash. I'm from Their Supremacies' palace. Someone dressed as a High Priest was seen climbing the back wall but then he disappeared. There's a reward if you have any information.'

'I'm sorry sir, I can't help you.' Conwenna heard the rowing boat going up the canal. 'Reward! The only reward they ever give is to torture more information out of you.'

After what seemed like for ever, punting up and down canals emptying dustbins, the rubbish collector finished his work. 'I take the refuse to the dump on the mainland, but I'll drop you off near the Jeweller's Quarter. You sound like a well-spoken young lady. Shall I get you a mule cab when we get there?'

'Please, if anyone will take me. I'm soaking wet and smelling awful.' Conwenna poked her head out from under the sacking.

'That won't matter as long as you can pay.'

Conwenna had no money on her, because she had left her bag of essentials, including some Teletsian money, in the Restorer's flat, but she was wearing a pair of gold bangles, presents from King Albion for her work in awakening the Trees of Life of many young people in Chussan City. She had been living there with us recently, studying fine art and calligraphy. She also had a gold ring, a gift from Raynor and Tandi – thanks for her help with the twins. The rubbish collector drew up at a wharf in the business district. Conwenna noticed a mule cab standing on a street corner, the driver huddled up asleep. She and the rubbish collector walked over to him across the empty street and he woke up.

'This young lady has had a nasty accident and needs to go to the Jeweller's Quarter,' the rubbish collector explained. 'She took a tumble into the canal. Can you take her?'

'Yes, no problem,' said the cabby. 'I was waiting for her.' The rubbish collector didn't notice this odd remark. Conwenna did but didn't say anything. She was shivering in her wet clothes.

'I don't have any money on me, but take this. You've saved my life,' and she offered a bangle to the rubbish collector, wretchedly poor and clothed in rags.

'It's my pleasure to help someone escape those devils who rule our lives. You don't need to give me anything,' he replied.

'Please, otherwise I'll feel bad. Without you the Sorcerers would have caught me.' Conwenna pressed the valuable gold bangle into his hands.

'If you insist, miss, and I must admit, it will pay for my sons to go to school for a while, then they won't have to follow me in this filthy work.'

'Take it, with my greatest thanks.' Conwenna took its pair off her other wrist and thrust that into his hands too. 'Please, leave me now.' In Teletsia a man of his low standing did not argue with an educated girl like Conwenna.

'You're out late, dearie,' said the cabby cheerily. 'Not safe to be alone on the streets at this time of night. You'd better get in. Where do you want to go?'

'Number 16, Street of the Diamond Cutters, Jewellers Quarter, please.'

'No problem. Close the door well,' and they clopped through the dark streets.

After a short while he dropped her outside the safe house.

CHAPTER 8

HELP FROM THE OLD FOLKS

Meanwhile, Derwin had waited for Conwenna at the Restorers' palace, or rather block of flats. The storm died down but the skies were still cloudy. The flyer was powered up and ready to go at a moment's notice and after a while he heard voices in the yard on the other side of the high wall around the garden.

'We'd better search the grounds, because she must have come with an accomplice. She'll be at the High Priests Palace by now and she'll soon be praying for death. The chap on the water gate said no one had gone out that way, but he wasn't sure if anyone came in earlier, because of the storm.'

Derwin was shattered and felt as if there was a hole where his heart should have been. He took off and flew as fast as possible towards the river. When he was out of sight in the clouds he turned and went in the direction of the Jeweller's Quarter. It took him some time to find the house. Despite the street lights it was very dark and he had to skim low over the buildings, streets and canals, and noticed some people staring at his craft and pointing wildly. He hoped that if they did report him, the Specials would think they were drunk or on drugs or just plain crazy, and not believe them. He landed in the back garden of the safe house but there was barely enough room and he squashed a number of plants and some garden furniture, then got out and made his way towards the door. An elderly man opened it and peered out. He had a neatly trimmed beard, curly grey hair and was short and plump, but what Derwin noticed most were his twinkling eyes and friendly expression.

'Who's there?' he asked.

'I need to use you as a safe house,' begged Derwin desperately, fumbling for the four petalled key round his neck as he came into the circle of lamplight.

'That's our door key,' said the stranger. Derwin produced the right key. 'Alright, come in. Did you come by - shall we say - flying carpet?'

'Yes, but..'

'You'll have to be gone before dawn, because I can't risk having that here in the daytime. Lady Stellamar warned me the Specials are searching everywhere for them.'

'OK, but they've got my friend. Stellamar said if we had problems to come here.'

'Come inside, son. You look dreadful. My name's Sparkly Diamondcutter.'

'I'm Derwin Herbhealer, one of the rebels. It's Conwenna they've got – another one.' Sparkly took him inside and sat him down in the living room. The awfulness of Conwenna's predicament had sunk in and he was nauseous from the dreadfulness of it all.

'Lady Stellamar gave me this awakening last time she was here. She showed me how to ask questions using the power. Why don't you at least ask if your friend is still alive?'

'You're so right, I should have thought of that.'

'Meanwhile, I'll get you a hot drink. Worse things happen at sea, as my old mum used to say.' He pottered off and Derwin asked some questions.

'Is Conwenna still alive?' Very cool indicating, 'Yes'.

'Any chance of rescuing her?' Less cool.

'Any hope that she might escape?' Some coolness.

Sparkly returned to say the kettle would soon be boiling, and sat creakily in the other chair.

'Her vibrations are fairly cool - for some extraordinary reason,' said Derwin.

'Lady Stellamar also told me about this bandhan of request. Let's try it.'

Derwin came to his senses. Here was an old man from the terrible land of Teletsia, telling him, who had been four years in Sasrar, how to use the powers of the Tree of Life. They circled their left hands with their right ones, and the vibrations weren't too dire, although there was a tingling on the small fingers, indicating the heart centre was constricted, signifying fear. Derwin was still in a bad state and Sparkly brought a warm, soothing herbal tisane. They waited anxiously and soon Derwin dropped off to sleep on the daybed in the living room. Some time after this Sparkly shook him gently.

'Wake up, son, a great pressure has lifted from my head, as if something very important has changed. Nevertheless, you must leave now. It's still dark, the clouds have cleared and there are no moons up, so you'll have to risk flying out of the city. If the Specials come here in the morning and find the flying craft, that's the end of you, this safe house and me too. Is there anywhere round here, but out of town, that you can go to?'

'Yes, a farm near Golden Beach, but what about Conwenna?'

'I'll send the members of our Resistance Group out in the morning to try and find out what's happened. We've got some spies in the Forbidden Quarter – cleaning ladies.'

'I'll leave you the address of the farm, and if by any chance you can discover anything about her, send word to me - I'll hide there for a night or two.'

'I wouldn't hold out too much hope, son. I reckon she's done for, even if these vibrations are cool,' added Sparkly sadly. He assumed she had been killed quickly, so was, in a sense, out of trouble.

'There's a woman called Mrs Fisher who worked for the Restorers, where

Conwenna's family live. She might know something, so go and see her. She lives near their place,' suggested Derwin. 'You'd do well to be in contact with her anyway. The address is 7, Nobleman's Road, 2ⁿᵈ Residential Island.'

'I'll go tomorrow.'

Derwin reluctantly took off into the dark sky and Sparkly went to the kitchen to make himself some strong coffee, being as sleep was not an option that night. While he was savouring the coffee he heard someone knocking. He opened the door and there was a girl in soaking wet clothes.

'Are you Conwenna?'

'Yes, how did you know?'

'Derwin was here, but he had to leave. May the Mother Earth be praised that you're safe!'

'Thank goodness he's OK too. Please, have you got any money to pay the cab driver who brought me? I'll make sure you get repaid.'

'Not necessary, but yes, wait a moment.' He went into the kitchen where there was a crock of small coins. 'Give him that – it's a lot, even for this time of night,' and he pressed some silver into her hands.

'Good sir,' Conwenna took it to the cabby, 'do me one favour. Don't tell anyone you brought me here. If you give me your address I'll see you get some more money.'

'You've been very generous already miss, but if you want my address, here's my card. Don't worry, I won't tell those miserable Specials I've seen you. Good night and thank you.' She turned and went into the house, but before shutting the door looked down the street once more, which was straight for some way. There was no sign of the cab. The jeweller took the card the cabby had given her.

'Did you read what was on it?'

'No, what does it say?'

'Mr Guardian Angel, Mother Earth Way, Teletos. You've been brought here by an angel! Whatever have you been up to?'

'Quite a tale! But can I get clean first, before I tell you?'

'You'd better. There's hot water in the kitchen and I'll take a bucketful to the bath house out the back. My granddaughter has a chest of clothes upstairs. The family store stuff here that they don't need right now. Go and help yourself.'

'Thank you, I will.'

Some time later, clean, dry and free of the appalling smell of canal, Conwenna sat in the kitchen with her hands around a hot drink. She gave Sparkly a short version of her adventure and he was utterly astounded. When she had finished, the strain of seeing her father killed, and everything else, was suddenly too much, and she burst into tears and sobbed and sobbed until the kind old man took her in his arms and stroked her head, comforting her as best he could, but nothing could console Conwenna. She was not Lee or Ahren, who had been in war and had seen those close to them die. It had all been more than she could take. Sparkly had put a sleeping draft in the hot drink and gently laid her in the spare room to get some rest. She cried herself to sleep as the draft took effect.

In the early morning the cleaning ladies of the Head Sorcerer's Palace went into the Private Meeting Room by the side entrance, found the bodies of the rulers of Teletsia in a grisly heap and ran out of the room screaming. The Specials who had captured Conwenna and the guards were woken by the noise. They had been snoring in the guardroom downstairs, and the guards outside the door of the Private Meeting Room had also dropped off. All of them, cleaners, guards and Specials, had a short talk and decided to leave quietly and pretend they had seen nothing, because being on the scene of the crime was dangerous and might get them blamed as accomplices. They all found urgent reasons to leave town and disappear, so initially no one had any idea how the leading Sorcerers had been massacred.

When Conwenna woke up Sparkly was pottering around getting ready to start diamond cutting in a small room at the back of the house. A girl about the same age as Conwenna came in to make breakfast. He introduced her as his granddaughter, Sonf, who lived nearby and came in every day and 'did' for him.

'You're going to have to pretend to be a slave so we can get you out of Teletos,' said the old man as they ate breakfast. 'You must be disguised as a boy because the Specials may be searching for a teenage girl. You're thin enough, but we'll have to cut your hair a bit.' He looked at her strange red locks. 'In fact Sonf had better dye it black as well.'

'Fine by me,' agreed Conwenna, who wore her hair short for a girl. Boys often wore their hair almost as long, and she was not happy with her red locks, now fading.

'Also, you're going to have to pretend you've been mesmerised.'

'Anything you say.'

'My grandson Borry, Sonf's brother, will bring you some of his old clothes. He'll pose as your owner and we'll say he's delivering a consignment of diamonds, and you, to a shop in one of the country towns, Twindell. You're a jewel polisher, by the way. With you will be the bodyguard we always use. He's not a member of our Resistance Group so you must play your part convincingly. Luckily I really do have that order of stones ready to go, so it won't look suspicious.'

'Did you say Twindell?' Conwenna recognised the name.

'Yes, is that a problem?'

'Not at all. I need to visit my grandmother, who lives there. My father's last words were that I should try to contact her.'

'I'm sure Borry can help you.'

Later in the morning Borry, the bodyguard and the boy slave left town. Borry, a well-built young man, and the bodyguard were on horses and Conwenna, now unable to talk and behaving in a very servile manner, was riding a mule. She wore a cap and Borry's old clothes and looked remarkably boyish. Sparkly gave them travel documents, necessary for anyone going anywhere in Teletsia. They reached the gatehouse onto the mainland and Conwenna noticed that a young girl of about her age who was ahead of them was asked to go into the Special's office for questioning. Conwenna pretended to be unable to speak at all and kept her head down when Borry showed the Special her pass, which they had borrowed from a neighbour. They were allowed onto the mainland without any delay, but as they went through a small town on their road they were detained at a roadblock, and asked for their passes. When they stopped to eat at a wayside inn no one was talking about the Sorcerers' murders, which meant that so far the story had not become public knowledge.

By early afternoon, after trotting briskly through the country lanes for some distance, they reached Twindell. Borry delivered the diamonds and told the bodyguard to return to Teletos. After he had gone Borry and Conwenna took another road out of town, in the direction of the safe house farm. It led past the old people's home where her grandmother lived, if she was still alive. Borry went in and made enquiries, and was told Mrs Clockmaker was in the garden. Borry pretended he had a message for her and took Conwenna along as if she was his slave in attendance. The granny, in a wheelchair, did not recognise Conwenna to begin with, but did when she spoke, and immediately realised she was in disguise.

'Wheel me behind those trees so we can talk. It's so nice to see you again. They said you'd disappeared years ago.'

'I did, grandma, that's why I'm in disguise.' She gently told her grandmother about her father's death.

'That's tragic, but to be honest, he died to me years ago. He never came to see me except those few times with you,' she said sadly.

Conwenna repeated her father's last words, about the Queen Wasp. Her grandmother asked for more details, so Conwenna explained how she had visited her father and how Drusilla had betrayed her.

'Let's talk alone.' Her grandmother looked at Borry, who tactfully withdrew and kept a lookout. 'I understand now. One day, when Drusilla was a toddler, some of the Chief Sorcerers came to see me. It was all very hush-hush, and they ordered me never to tell anyone. They took out some objects, a bracelet, a ring, a fine silken scarf, a chess piece and a few other things, and put them on the ground. Then they told me to let Drusilla crawl among them and she immediately went to the ring and the chess piece. They nodded knowingly and departed.

'Drusilla was always a difficult child and I soon realised that she had a thoroughly evil character. She was extraordinarily powerful, a ringleader who could dominate anyone round her, in an unpleasant and underhand way. Added to that, my husband, your grandfather, was completely spellbound by that woman who became your step-grandmother, who I think was a female Sorcerer. I never told anyone before, but she threatened to kill both the children if I didn't leave him, and leave them with her and your grandfather. The Sorcerers said if I didn't do this they'd kill the lot of us. I could never figure out why, but did as they ordered. All my life I've been seen as the terrible mother who abandoned her children.

When your father grew up and married, and had you, Drusilla hated your mother, who was such a good influence on your father. I'm sure Drusilla poisoned your mother, because she suddenly died when she was so young and healthy.' The old lady was in tears by now and Conwenna, suppressing hers, apologised for dragging up the past. 'No, my dear, it's good you came. I need to tell someone the truth.'

Conwenna was puzzled by this story and bid her grandmother goodbye, promising to come back if she could. She and Borry changed the mule and horse for two fresh horses at a post house and they rode to the farm as quickly as they could. It was a long way and they reached the farm at dusk. Derwin was sleeping, after having spent most of the day worrying about Conwenna, but the farmer's wife woke him when she saw the strangers approaching up the lane from the road.

'May the Mother Earth be praised!' Derwin cried on seeing them. He rushed to Conwenna and helped her off her horse. 'I have never in my whole life been so happy to see anyone. Who's this?' He turned to Borry.

'Oh, meet Borry Diamondcutter, Resistance Group member! And for my rescue - thank the whole Diamondcutter family, a rubbish collector and a cabby who turned out to be an angel. I've got some very good news, by the way. Somehow, with the help of the keys, something has happened which puts even Asha's wildest escapades in the shade.....'

'Come into this kind farmer's kitchen and tell me everything over a meal. And – sorry I wasn't very nice to you yesterday.'

'That's ok. When you hear my story, you'll understand why your intuition made you panic.'

Derwin, shattered, delighted and sobered by the news, flew Conwenna to the Island that night and Borry made his way discreetly back to Teletos the following day.

Before getting out of Teletos and going into hiding, the Specials who had taken Conwenna to the Forbidden Quarter reported back to their station near the Prospector's flat and warned the other Specials there what had happened the night before. Drusilla Prospector went to see them the next morning and asked for help with the body of her brother, being as the Specials had killed him. The ones on duty denied all knowledge of the murder and cautioned her she might easily be arrested for doing away with him. Drusilla said nothing, but took a mule cab to the Forbidden Quarter.

The night porter at the Restorers' block of flats also received a visit from one of the local Specials. He was told that Drusilla was under suspicion of murder and he would also be taken in as an accomplice if he didn't keep his mouth shut. He was to deny he had seen Conwenna.

Journal of Nishog, Scribe to the Most High Priests of Teletsia

I Nishog, replacement scribe to the most illustrious Lords of Teletsia, do hereby record a rapidly convened meeting of their Lordships concerning the most dire threat to our regime in two centuries. This morning twelve of their Supreme Holinesses and the scribe were found murdered in the Interrogation Chamber. The scribe had not written anything so we have no idea what was going on. A full-scale investigation is under way.

'I hardly know where to begin,' said His Supreme Lordship, the new Head High Priest. 'I have it on good authority that it was Conwenna Prospector who beheaded their Supreme Holinesses when she was captured and taken before them. How could a mere unarmed girl do that? Why hadn't we managed to find her before? She's been on the loose for over a month.' He looked angrily at each man in turn. There was silence. 'Our Police Force is completely useless if they cannot track down one teenage girl, despite having hundreds of people after her all over the country.'

'With respect, Your Supremacy,' interjected the new Head of the Special Secret Police Force, 'if she was not in Teletsia any more then we'd never find her. It seems that the first time she was here she escaped in a flying ship, possibly right out of this space-time dimension.'

'Why did the Master of Annihilations not dispose of her? He can operate from a distance,' His Supreme Lordship demanded.

'He tried to.'

'Why did the Chief Priest for War and Weaponry not blast the flying ship out of the sky?'

'My predecessor only heard about it three days later,' explained the new Chief Priest for War and Weaponry.

'We are wasting time,' added the Head of Psychic Research, who had

survived being beheaded because he was suffering from an epileptic seizure the night the others were killed. 'His Excellency the new Head of the Intelligence Network should bring us up to date. We must know what is going on in order to stamp out the insurgents. We have ruled Teletsia for over two hundred years and there is no reason why we should not go on doing so. Anyone who believes in this piffling prophecy does not deserve a place on our council.'

'It might be wise to accept such a thing exists,' said the new Master of the Intelligence Network. 'Some years back I had a look at it, not that it made any sense.

'Here are some recent reports. One: three weeks ago a slave dealer, purported to be from King Gamsad, bought some slaves from the Clatan Slave Farm, including Mat Dairyman, the father of one of the escaped rebels. The next day Dairyman's wife disappeared from Clatan.

'Two: ten days ago, near Woodenton, some Special Police and a High Priest went to investigate a report of a flying machine. They visited the family of a woodcutter but were killed by a herd of elephants near his house. Only the driver lived to tell the tale.

'Three: two days later our agents located Mr Herbhealer, the father of Asha and Derwin Herbhealer, and he was arrested at Davaton. However he escaped and disappeared. A flying machine was seen in the area. The same day a girl with a golden aura was caught at Coffee River Ferry but she also escaped.

'Four: some flying horses were seen near Coffee Ferry and a man was riding one.

'Are you sure about all this? Whoever heard of horses with wings?' interrupted the new Master of Dead Souls.

'I am merely reading the reports,' countered the Master of the Intelligence Network. 'Five: a girl on a white pony, assumed to be Asha Herbhealer or Conwenna Prospector, murdered a High Priest near Lahary. She beheaded him with a type of discus.

'Six: Last week a priest was found reduced to ashes in the treatment room of a slave farm. His two assistants behaved as if they had been treated.'

'I have information via our spying sea birds that the Daish Shaktay navy is approaching over the Sea of Illusion,' contributed the new

High Priest of Ports, Naval Matters and Shipping. 'Also, these flying craft are coming from the Island of Creations, where we cannot land, or we will be annihilated ourselves. We must continue to blockade that place.'

'Yes,' said the Chief Priest for War and Weaponry, 'but we need to meet the Daish Shaktay navy in the open sea. We have steam-powered boats and much better guns. They won't have a hope against us with their sailing galleons.'

'I agree with you,' said His Supreme Lordship. 'Assuming they are coming to invade us.'

'It's obvious, isn't it? We all know what Rajay Ghiry did to the Mattanga Empire,' added the Master of the Intelligence Network.

'We have placed a number of gunners on the shore near the Island of Creations, so when we see any flying ships coming into our country we can shoot them out of the sky, but our efforts have been hampered by fogs and storms,' continued the Chief Priest for War and Weaponry.

'It is the dry season now so that won't happen any more,' this was His Supreme Lordship. 'We can spare a few ships to continue blockading the port on the Island of Creations.

'Your Honour, 'said the Master of Weather Manipulation, 'I suspect our enemies also have some control over the weather, and are creating these fogs and so on to confuse us.'

'Nonsense,' insisted His Supreme Lordship. 'Only we have that power.'

The Specials who had accused Drusilla of being involved in the murder of her brother were arrested the next day. They were never seen again.

CHAPTER 9

THE STRUGGLE ESCALATES

When Conwenna returned to the Island she was in a state of complete shock. She did not want to talk to anyone, even me. She spent the first day in her room, alone. Stellamar came over from the mainland that night. The morning after she told us how she persuaded one of her father's fishing boats to sail near the coast of the Island, which was being closely watched, and had swum the last part, mostly underwater with the help of a breathing tube. Ma Ganoozal had insisted on a hot bath when she had arrived dripping wet late in the night.

'My dear girl,' chuckled Lord Jarwhen, 'you never cease to amaze me!'

Conwenna appeared at breakfast and everyone wanted to congratulate her, but she ran upstairs and hid in her room again. Lady Mercola and I went up to talk to her. We knocked on her door and she called for us to go inside.

'I'm sorry, I don't know what you must think of me,' she was sitting by the window and looking out at the garden.

'No, we understand perfectly,' replied Lady Mercola. 'Let's give you some vibrations, and then if you want you can tell us about it.' Conwenna soon felt much better and told us her story, including the part about visiting her grandmother. Lady Mercola became very attentive when she heard this, even more so than when Conwenna described the killing of the Sorcerers.

'Would you mind telling that part to my husband and Stellamar?'

'Not at all.'

So it was that a very important meeting took place in Conwenna's room. I was allowed to stay to keep her company, and Mr Antiquarian came in with Lord Jarwhen, but no one else. Stellamar brought in her family's copy of the prophecy, which Mr Antiquarian had been studying.

'Conwenna, I always said you were one of the strongest of you seven,' began Stellamar. 'Now I'm asking you to be that. I hope what we're going to suggest isn't going to shock you too much. Being as you've just pulled off the most explosive deed of the last two hundred years we don't want to keep any secrets from you, in case you can help us further.'

166

'Kitab, would you read us the relevant part of the prophecy?' asked Lord Jarwhen. They had become firm friends.

'Listen to this,' said Mr Antiquarian.

'When the swarm of bees has evolved and the queen bee is the Mother Earth Herself, then it will be time to clean Teletsia. By this time the visitors from afar will be with the members of the swarm and they will mingle with them and help them, in every way. The visitors from the blue and green planet of the star called Sol, or Surya, will come many times, but not all will remain true to their path. One may go sour and become a Queen Wasp. Until she is destroyed the other wasps will regenerate, time after time.

She will take her birth again and again, and her followers will find her, because she will recognise various objects from her previous lifetime when she is shown them as a child.'

'The last words my father said were – Queen Wasp – Drusilla,' Conwenna gasped.

'There you have it,' explained Lord Jarwhen.

'We knew there was a guardian, a woman soul who had gone wrong, but we all thought she had fallen into the vortex and was no longer on this plane of existence,' added Lady Mercola.

'No wonder I always loathed her,' groaned Conwenna.

'Even our spies in the Forbidden Quarter didn't know about her,' said Stellamar. 'The Sorcerers themselves never mentioned her directly, although we did get reports of 'the great one,' 'the ultimate advisor' or 'the hidden one' that we could not understand. The Specials near where she lives have no idea who she really is.'

'When those Sorcerers went to see her as a baby, they showed her some items which she had owned in her past life. When she picked out the ones which had been hers previously, they knew who she was; they were checking that she was the Queen Wasp. She's been at the back of the Sorcerers for lifetimes now. Somehow, we're going to have to finish her off,' Lord Jarwhen declared. 'It's difficult, because if we kill her, her soul will jump into someone else and work through them, or she'll take her birth again. Before she went wrong she studied hypnotism and all that sort of thing. In one of her previous lifetimes as a guardian she was married to the writer of the prophecy, who was also a guardian, so unfortunately she knew more about it than almost anyone. She betrayed him and he had to flee to the north, where he became known as the potter. It's possible that the reason the soul who is now Drusilla went bad was because of her excessive study of the dark arts, and that's why she got caught by the evil forces and became evil.'

'What can we do about her?' I ventured.

'We'll meditate on it,' suggested Lord Jarwhen. 'We'll have to create a situation where her soul is sucked into another realm. If everyone in Teletsia could have their awakening and settle into it, it would work out naturally, because the whole society would reject her, and the vibrational level of the country would completely change.'

'Realistically, that's a long way off,' said Stellamar. 'We guardians don't have all the answers. Our friends who've had their inner awakening are just as likely to come up with a solution.'

Later I told all this to Robin.

'You realise I'm the replacement guardian for Drusilla?' he said.

'I figured as much.'

'There may be a way to destroy her for good and all. Don't tell anyone else about her being the Queen Wasp.' When I tried to question him further he went silent. It was hopeless trying to probe Robin when he was like this and I respected his need to keep some matters from me.

Raynor and Garma were put in a dormitory at the conscript's barracks near Gyan-on-Sea. Some of the boys recognised Garma as the son of Professor Nalanda and one had been at the awakening programme at *The Shrubbery*. He was told not to say anything about Raynor, whom he also recognised. Raynor called himself Norray Nalanda, a cousin of Garma's. Saray was well known in student circles and in the girl's dorm was warmly welcomed by the despondent girls, lying on hard beds waiting for sleep that didn't come. In the uncomfortable dormitories, something happened. Both Saray and Garma had brought small stringed instruments with them and that night sang the songs they had learnt from Roarke, Lee and Raynor. The word got around that another power was afoot, the power of compassion, healing and forgiveness, and one that could protect them from the Sorcerers.

The following morning Raynor and Garma were called before the general in charge of the barracks.

'Have courage,' Raynor reassured Garma, 'the vibrations aren't too bad when I ask if it will be alright.' They entered the general's office and he was sitting at a desk. They stood in front of him, tense and uneasy, and he looked at the names on his list.

'Garma Nalanda. Son of the professor, right?' '

'Yes, sir.'

'You're to be trained as an officer. Any experience with fighting?'

'No, sir.'

'You'll learn soon enough. Norray Nalanda. A cousin of the professor?'

'Yes sir,' said Raynor. 'I'm doing some research work at the university.'

'Can you fight?'

'Yes, sir, I learnt self-defence and combat at home at Castle Mount,' Raynor improvised. He had learnt to fight in Sasrar, where every young man was trained to defend the country.

'You also go on officer training. Now what's this I hear about you doing some psychological stuff on the recruits?'

'I learnt it from a hermit near Castle Mount. It gives courage and helps people fight better.'

'Well, I want to see results, and fast. We may be invaded at any time. You're both responsible for the men under you and if they don't fight adequately, you'll be held accountable. If your mumbo-jumbo helps us defend Teletsia, go for it. But I'm warning you, don't try any funny business or it's the slave farms for both of you.'

'Yes, sir,' replied Raynor and Garma.

As trainee officers they were moved to another hut. This was a mixed blessing: it was more comfortable and they had more privacy – the two of them shared a room so they could give each other vibrations, clear their subtle centres and meditate together, but most of the other trainee officers were sympathetic to the Sorcerers and so their awakening efforts had to stop for the time being. However, they were free in the afternoons and could visit the common room of the girls' quarters, once Garma made it clear Saray was his sister and Raynor her cousin. She brought along some of her friends.

'We heard something has happened in Teletos,' said Saray.

'I heard from the man who cleans our bathrooms that someone murdered the twelve Head Sorcerers,' explained Garma. 'They were found beheaded in the Council Chamber of their palace.'

'They say it was one of the escaped rebels and that they may all be back,' put in a friend of Saray's.

'Some chance of that!' added another girl.

'No, my dad runs the newspaper in Gyan-on-Sea,' went on the first girl, 'and he knows a lot of what's going on, even though he can't print most of it. Apparently, in two different places recently, Sorcerers have been found reduced to ashes.'

'Serves them right,' said Saray vehemently, avoiding Raynor and Garma's eyes. Roarke had given her and Garma four-petalled keys and had shown them how to use them in fiery discus mode.

'That's why there's been this call up,' continued the girl whose father ran the newspaper.

'We must pretend to be model conscripts, but go on showing people how to protect themselves from the Sorcerers and Specials,' advised Raynor, 'I'm absolutely certain that as long as everyone who has had their awakening keeps putting the bandhan of protection on themselves the Sorcerers won't be able to reduce them to ashes, and no one will be able to hypnotise them either.'

'We had a session in mass hypnosis this morning,' said Saray. 'They tried to make us believe the Sorcerers are our friends and protectors and the invaders are going to do all the things to us that the Sorcerers actually do.'

'My dad says we don't even know who the invaders are,' added the newspaper owner's daughter.

'Can't be worse than the rats we've got running our lives now,' commented another girl, and the bell rang for the evening meal.

Within days most of the conscripts in the camp had had their awakening. Many groups of friends made secret vows not to fight, even though the trainees were outwardly docile and compliant. The few who didn't get awakening and who supported the regime could not say anything about something which made you feel joyful and peaceful. Most of the conscripts were not told what would happen if the Sorcerers tried to destroy them, only that the bandhans would keep them safe. Raynor kept his keys safely out of sight round his neck because he knew he was playing a very dangerous game indeed, but meanwhile concentrated on appearing to be a model trainee officer.

Rajay returned to the Island after escaping from the Rubber River and he and Namoh spent some time in the garden of the mansion the next day. They had much to catch up on, even though it had only been three months since Namoh had left Daish Shaktay. Roarke and Lee had also returned the day before, and Robin and I were going to show Roarke the Keyspond. The path that led to it went past where Rajay and his friend were sitting.

'Do you want to see the pond where Lord Jarwhen makes the keys?' asked Robin.

'Not right now,' replied Rajay. 'Come and join us.' We sat on the lawn together, in the shade of a tall, spreading tree. 'I was telling Namoh about his cousin Ariani. You remember her, Asha? The girl who was captured by Scorpius Offlen and imprisoned in Tiger's Head Fort, when Danard captured it and won us Daish Shaktay?'

'Yes, she's a great girl,' I said.

'We finally managed to persuade my friend Ekan to get married. Ariani's parents were trying to get *her* to marry, and eventually she admitted she'd set her heart on Ekan, because they'd met a few times. It was so right, on vibrations and in every other way. When I told him, to begin with he didn't want to, as he felt he might be a burden.'

'But his health is all right now, isn't it?' asked Namoh.

'More or less,' said Rajay. 'Anyway, they got married last month, and I hope you don't mind, I suggested they live on your manor farm and keep an eye on it for you while you're away.'

'Good idea, and I'm happy for them both.'

'There was another thing,' went on Rajay. 'Roarke, could you, Namoh and I have a word in private?' Robin and I tactfully took ourselves off.

'How's *your* health?' Rajay asked Namoh.

'Never better, thanks to the skill of Lord Coban and the excellent nursing of Stellamar.'

'I'm glad. I heard it was touch and go. Roarke, you know about the fiery discus option of the keys. I thought that once someone had called on that, he or she was invulnerable?'

'Not exactly. It's just that the keys are so quick, they kill anyone threatening the bearer of the key before the attackers have a chance,' explained Roarke.

'So what went wrong?' continued Rajay.

'When I was lying wounded,' said Namoh. 'I remembered that the keys are only to be used for defence, not attack. I had a lot of aggression in me at that moment and a strong desire to kill the Specials who were after us.'

'You've understood your mistake,' Roarke smiled kindly. 'Even if you're a warrior, you must be detached. Otherwise you set off the law of karma, that is, every action has an equal and opposite reaction. You've been to Sasrar, and I'm sure that your level of awareness is such that you are nearly always rooted in that inner peace, stillness and – how shall I say? Balance?'

'Yes, that's how I feel most of the time these days. It's incredible unless you actually live it,' said Namoh.

'You must fight to kill only when it's vibrationally right to do so, and must be detached and free of hatred. Isn't that what Rajay told you years ago?'

'Yes.'

'And for a split second you lost that detachment, when you activated the fiery discus option that night?'

'You're right.'

'For your own safety only use the key for defence. If you're on the attack, use conventional methods. The fiery discus option is designed to save your life and if people get themselves killed, they've well and truly asked for it by trying to kill you. We guardians can stretch things a bit but you might be safer not to. I hope I haven't offended you,' concluded Roarke.

'I'm grateful for your advice.'

CHAPTER 10

SHEEP

It was over two months since Robin, Valya and Namoh had first set foot in Teletsia, ostensibly to sell jewels, negotiate for slaves and buy guns, and it was over a month since Ahren, Derwin and Conwenna had gone into the rural areas with Merien. By now everyone except Raynor was safely back on the Island of Creations. Tandi had been remarkably detached and philosophical when Lee told her that Raynor had joined the Teletsian army but was less confident when we talked alone later. On the same day that Roarke and Rajay gave advice to Namoh, Robin and I also had an important conversation with Rajay. We were sitting in the gazebo by the Keyspond.

'Tell me about the Temple of Support,' Rajay began.

'It's beautiful,' I explained, 'rolling hills, great stones in the centre and smaller ones spiralling round the edge. It's deserted except for flocks of sheep and a few shepherds. If only we could get there to do a fire ceremony, I'm sure it would set off some tremendous changes. The trouble is it'll be watched now the Sorcerers know we're back.'

'A lot of sheep?' asked Rajay.

'Yes,' I replied. 'We should do a ceremony on Midsummer's Day, less than a week from now. That place is very tied in with the equinoxes, and mid-summer and mid-winter's days.'

'We need to move fast,' Robin looked at Rajay.

'Sheep,' repeated Rajay.

They were up to something.

They gave me the names of the people they wanted to meet, so we returned to the house and I rounded everyone up. We went to Rajay's room, a large one as befitted his status. He and Robin were already there, sitting in front of a map of the area near the Temple of Support. Rajay was introduced to Saman and Freddi, the failed assassins, and Tom Dyeman, the farmer's son - these boys had previously been too much in awe to actually talk to him. Roarke, Merien, Ahren and Derwin were also present.

'Robin, you're in charge of this one,' said Rajay pointedly, and together they laid their plans.

172

Some time before midnight the three small flyers, parked in the front courtyard, were ready to leave for the south. We assumed Roarke would be flying his, and he asked Ahren and Robin to get in. Then Rajay appeared and climbed in the driving seat.

'I'm coming too, and if anyone asks, my name is – um – how about Ray Horsetrader? I've been that before,' he grinned.

'I didn't know you could fly these,' Robin was impressed.

'I can't,' replied Rajay. 'Roarke has put it on automatic. With my borrowed Sasrar key in this slot it flies on its own, but it will follow Derwin's ship. So we're in his hands.'

'He's got a better grasp of all this than anyone except Roarke. You'll be quite safe,' added Merien.

'I've got to bring a lot of other people in the big ship,' said Roarke.

Derwin flew his nippy flyer and his passenger was Tom. Merien had Namoh and Freddi squashed in the back of his machine and the extra weight meant he was going to have to keep it airborne with his attention, because the fuel and aerodynamics were not sufficient. Freddi came from a family of farmers so went in preference to Saman, whose people were businessmen.

There were some Teletsian ships blockading the port and a large contingent of Specials with guns on the coast, well back from the beaches, because they found they could not go on the sands without having violent fits. They were again confused by a thick fog which came up over the whole area shortly before the flyers left. Lord Jarwhen and the other guardians had together done their best to call on the elements to hide the young men going in to Teletsia that night, and as the flyers flew almost silently they managed to get past the Teletsian guns on the shore with no trouble. It was the middle of the night, so by the time the Sorcerer who was in charge of clearing away these tiresome fogs had been roused, the three flyers were well inland.

The partisans reached their destination, the safe house of the Herder family, shortly before dawn. They reduced height, came in low, skimmed over the open grassland and left the flyers over the hill to the north of the farms, in a thicket of thorn bushes. Robin, who had already met Zoey Herder, went on ahead. He knocked on the door and a sleepy Mrs Herder, clad in a nightgown and shawl, opened it. He showed her his four petalled key.

'Hello, - another one!' she began brightly. 'Come in. Are you alone?'

'Eh - no. There are eight of us,' said Robin cautiously.

'The more the merrier. Is Asha with you?'

'No. This is a different type of operation. She's my wife, and thank you for hiding her.'

Soon they were all in the farm kitchen, being refreshed with a drink of creamy milk. Zoey appeared, rubbing his eyes with sleep. Mrs Herder suggested the visitors should go to the safe room for some rest but Robin wanted to talk to Zoey right away.

'Zoey, we need your help,' asked Robin when they were alone. 'It's a very important mission.'

'Just say the word!' Zoey had all the enthusiasm of a fourteen year old boy.

'We need to do a ceremony up at the Temple of Support. Have you been there recently?'

'Yes, yesterday, to check on our flock. There are a whole lot of Specials and a platoon of conscripts, to guard the place against these suspected invaders from outer space. Have they gone doolally as well as everything else?'

'Could be. How many is a whole lot?'

'About forty. They've posted themselves all-round the temple and their camp is some way away, on the track up to it. They had guns and changed shifts periodically.'

'What's the story with your local Resistance Group?'

'They've mostly been called up. It's only people like me, who are under age, who are still around. The others decided to go to the call up but swore not to fight. The joke is they'll be some of the ones helping to guard the temple.'

'Excellent.' Robin hadn't thought of this. 'How many boys who can fight can you get hold of?'

'Well,' Zoey was counting on his fingers, 'my three cousins, they're sixteen and seventeen, and a shepherd's son. He's only fifteen but he's a big strong chap. I can bring you about ten of us and we're all country lads so we know how to look after ourselves. We've got plenty of machetes, and bows and arrows, and catapults, and dad's got a gun he uses for shooting deer and so on – I'm pretty accurate with that.'

'Zoey, you're about to become a freedom fighter. OK?'

'And half! I was so angry when my older sister had to go off to be a nurse, "to look after the brave Specials who might get wounded saving the fatherland." I told her to finish 'em off good and proper if she had the chance. When do we start?' Zoey spoke in a rush and excitedly. Robin was touched by his innocent zeal and prayed nothing tragic would happen to him.

'Go and fetch your friends and we'll meet at breakfast. Can you leave a note for your mother to wake us?'

'No problem.'

'We've got a great deal to arrange tomorrow. I want to see the shepherds of as many flocks as possible and their owners as well, but only if they're in favour of the freedom quest. What's the general feeling around here?'

'Everyone I know would be a resistance fighter if they had the chance, especially since Asha was here and gave us inner awakening. We all have so much more courage now and we're not afraid of the Sorcerers or Specials any more.'

'I'm glad she helped you. Also – we need to be disguised to look like shepherds. Here, I've got something for you.' Robin took a four petalled key out of his jacket pocket. 'Wear it so no one can see it. It's a key to the first subtle centre, and on the Mother Earth its place is the Temple of Support.'

'You don't say?'

'Yes. It might save your life. It's not an ornament. Can you also get the shepherds here by breakfast time?'

'Will do, Captain!' Zoey gave a salute as he went out of the door.

Robin smiled and went to sleep. What seemed like no time later, Mrs Herder brought hot spiced tea to her snoring guests, mostly lying on the floor in the hidden room.

'Robin,' she called out, trying to locate him. 'My husband is waiting to see you and Zoey has brought you five shepherds, eleven young men, my two cousins who own the other farms here - and their sheepdogs. They're all in the front parlour except the dogs – I don't allow working animals in the house. They're sitting in a row outside.'

Zoey came up with another tray of mugs of tea and sat with the young men as they drank it. Namoh was chuckling, because there was an old Daish Shaktay folk song that sounded similar to what Mrs Herder had been saying, and had a chorus – 'And a granny with the baby on her knee,' which came at the end of every verse, when you added more farm personnel. He explained the joke, after which Rajay and he gave an impromptu rendering, adding the sheepdogs for good measure.

'Are you also from Daish Shaktay?' Zoey asked Rajay.

'Yes, and I grew up partly in the countryside, so I know the old rhymes,' he replied, while the others suppressed grins. Zoey picked up something and shyly kept quiet after that. There was no way anyone could tell him he was talking to the king. They all sat in meditation for a short while and then gave bandhans, praying that the operation would be a success. Afterwards Derwin went to check on the flying ships and Zoey's younger brother helped him hide them with covers and some hay to make them look like hayricks. The others went to meet the locals in the large front room of the farmhouse.

Robin introduced himself and the other partisans, using pseudonyms where necessary, and explained the plan. Lord Jarwhen had given him a bag of Teletsian gold coins, Telets, and he offered this to the farmers as down payment, in case the operation lost them some of their flocks. However, none of the three Mr Herders would hear of it and said it was their contribution to the freedom struggle.

It took most of the day to get everything organized and the following morning six flocks of sheep, about two thousand animals, along with almost everyone else who would be a part of the operation, set off on foot for the Temple of Support dressed as shepherds. Derwin, Rajay and Merien had gone on ahead in the night. They took the flyers closer to the temple and left them hidden some distance away, then mingled with the shepherd already up there and explained what was afoot.

The first flock reached the temple in the late afternoon and with it were three shepherds: one genuine with his two dogs, one a young member of the Resistance Cell, and Zoey. They had come with some ponies loaded up with panniers, ostensibly full of food, clothes and bedding, but actually containing firewood for the ceremonial fire.

They approached the temple from the hill on the other side of the valley and track, and saw what they at first thought were the Specials in groups of four or five, lounging around the perimeter of the temple menhirs, and looking bored. As the shepherds went closer they saw that there was generally only one Special and the other guards were conscripts. The sheep were driven closer to the temple and Zoey recognized one of the boys in the first group. Zoey went up to his friend, and asked who else was there. Neither the Specials nor the majority of the conscripts had wanted to go near the Temple of Support – no one had forgotten that the devastating earthquakes of five years before had started there. When Zoey was told the names of the people he realised that they included almost all his Resistance Group. They knew the Temple of Support was very auspicious, powerful and holy, so to everyone else's amazement at the Recruitment Training Centre they had volunteered to come here. As they all had awakened Trees of Life they felt great when near it, whereas anyone who was not positive, especially the Specials, felt weak, ill and uncomfortable.

Zoey asked what time the guard changed and was told that the night shift came on at nightfall, which was quite late as it was midsummer, and went off in the early morning, at dawn. He then left the temple area, and went to talk to the shepherds of two other flocks that had come up from the Herders, and the shepherd of the one that had been there for some weeks. The flocks were all concealed over the hill, being kept in order by the sheepdogs. Slowly more and more sheep arrived, and later Ahren and Zoey went down to where the Specials and conscripts had their camp. It was lax and disorganized, because the conscripts had only been called up the week before, and it takes more than a week to turn reluctant civilians into soldiers. Zoey saw a friend sitting with another boy who was a member of their Resistance Group, cleaning a primitive and inefficient looking gun.

'Psst, Jo,' hissed Zoey, dressed as a shepherd and holding a shepherd's crook. 'Come here!' Jo and his friend went over and stood behind a thorn bush. 'How's the army?'

'Appalling. Thank your lucky stars you're too young,' said Jo.

'When are you going on duty?'

'At sunset, why?'

'We've got a plan. We've got to capture, or if necessary kill all the Specials. Something very important is going to happen tonight at the temple. You've got to put the word around for our friends to *attack* the Specials, not defend them, when the fighting starts. We've got some experienced partisans hidden under the flocks of sheep we're bringing up. How can our people tell who are the Specials?'

'Oh, they wear a hat, but they don't always wear it. We conscripts wear berets.'

'If you value your lives wear your berets when you go on duty tonight. Can you make sure your friends do this?'

'Yes, of course. This is an answer to the collective bandhan we gave when they first sent us up here!' Jo was one of the boys who had been at my awakening programme when I had been at the Herders.

All went well until near sunset, when one of the Specials came and ordered a shepherd to move away from the temple, because his flock had been slowly grazing its way closer to it.

'But sir, it's traditional for the shepherds to celebrate the Midsummer Festival here,' pleaded Ahren, also posing as a shepherd.

'Do as you're told!' commanded the Special.

'Yes sir,' Ahren replied humbly, and he and the genuine shepherd began driving the sheep towards the Specials' camp.

'Not that way, idiots!'

They started driving the sheep down the approach road instead.

Robin knew they had until shortly before dawn to dispose of the Specials, because that was when the others were expected to arrive from the Island of Creations. The flying horses were to leave there at dusk, under the protection of a fog or storm and the flying ships would come later via a different route – out to sea and then inland further to the west or east, whichever was safer, according to the indication of the vibrations. Robin wanted to attack the people guarding the temple as late as possible because the watchers would be sleepier and less vigilant.

The Specials had given up trying to chase away the sheep that were swarming everywhere. Their brief was to guard the temple against invaders, not flocks of sheep. Most of the Specials felt extremely uncomfortable at the Temple of Support and didn't believe in this nonsense about raiders from outer space, plus no one with any sense would want to come to this deserted and accursed spot, they reasoned. As more and more flocks of sheep arrived it looked as if it was going to be well nigh impossible to clear them away in any event; the shepherds seemed so determined to do their inane rituals, so the Specials left them to it.

Teletsian sheep are tall, leggy and not very woolly. When the moons are up they often feed at night and sleep in the heat of the day. A crawling man can easily hide in a flock of them if they are grazing close to each other, and the sheep dogs herded them very efficiently so they were tightly packed. Soon after midnight Robin, Zoey and one of Zoey's cousins were crawling along with one of the flocks of sheep, and the shepherd was behind, driving it towards the first group of guards. Slowly the sheep nibbled their way closer to the guards, who were sitting on the grass in the moons' light. The shepherd placed himself between this group and the next one along, further round the perimeter.

The Special in charge had his back to the sheep, having tried rather ineffectually to shoo them away. There was one conscript in this group who was a part of the Resistance Group and he signalled to Zoey, indicating that one of the others was an ally. That left three men to dispose of. Robin clubbed the Special from behind. He went down like a falling stone and then Robin, Zoey and Zoey's cousin grabbed the other two in a vice-like grip, holding knives to their throats and pulling them to the ground so they were concealed under the sheep.

'Silence, and you live,' whispered Robin to the first.

'But sir, you've just freed us from the Specials. Now I can run away from here! Please don't kill me when it looks like I can escape. I've had enough of this stupid call up!' the captive whispered back.

'Check on vibrations if it's safe to let him go,' Robin ordered Zoey.

'Yes, it's cool,' said Zoey, with his hands out. Robin didn't have to use his hands to feel vibrations and had already come to the same conclusion.

'We've come to free Teletsia,' explained Robin. 'No time to tell you the details,' and the sheep pressed around them. The dogs were doing an excellent job keeping them bunched up over their captives.

'Please set me free too,' the other conscript cried, as a knife held by Zoey's cousin tickled his throat.

'He's lying,' said Robin. 'Shocking vibrations. Are you at the Sorcerer's Academy?' he asked the boy.

'Yes, I mean no,' he replied, and Robin gave him a crack on the head from behind. He knew exactly how hard to hit him to knock him out and he also dropped like a stone. The unconscious guards were bound, gagged and propped up facing away from the next group.

A similar scene was going on at the other side of the temple. Here was another flock, with Ahren and Zoey's other two cousins lurking under the animals. This group of guards was easier, because all of them were members of the local Resistance Group except the Special in charge, and they themselves helped knock him out when Ahren rose out of the flocks behind him. They said the Special was incredibly cruel and had already threatened to have them treated and sent to the slave farms for insubordination.

Derwin, Tom and the shepherd's son, and Freddi, Merien and another of Zoey's relations tackled different groups simultaneously and in the same way. These first four groups guarding the temple were all successfully neutralized without any of the Specials, or conscripts loyal to them, raising the alarm. But there were three more groups and it took time to get to them. They could not press the sheep to move too fast if it was to look as if they were naturally making their way over the plain, eating grass as they went. Namoh and his three farm boys crept towards the fifth group of guards, which consisted of a Special and two others, and managed to drop the conscripts - useless characters, so they were knocked out, tied up and gagged. The Special put up a fight, so Namoh knifed him fatally. He had no pity for these types, some of whom had nearly killed him.

Rajay and some more of Zoey's friends crept up behind another group. Unfortunately the sheep were not so closely packed here and the dogs were in another part of this flock. The few sheep covering Rajay and his boys parted when they were very close to their quarry, and worse, the Special in charge looked around at the wrong moment. Lightning quick, Rajay brought the Special down and knifed him in the neck. Luckily the others in this group were standing a little apart behind one of the large stones of the temple and were not immediately aware of what was going on.

Rajay had assessed which, if any, had reasonable vibrations. One was not too bad so he left him and grabbed the other two, smashing their heads together. As they were reeling from this he threw one on the ground in a strangling wrench and pinned him down. Within seconds he had his long knife at the man's neck, telling him to remain silent if he wanted to live. He tried to fight so Rajay knifed him too. The boys had by this time dealt with the other one; he surrendered and was tied and gagged.

The fourth member of this group stood looking on dazed and extremely grateful that this veritable tiger of a fighter who had sprung out of nowhere had spared him. This conscript was not a member of the Resistance Group, but was friendly with them and had had his awakening, which accounted for his better vibrations. He certainly had no love for the Specials and thoroughly resented the call-up.

'We're not going to hurt you,' said Rajay to this last boy. 'We know whose side you're on, but keep quiet and don't give us away or you'll be in serious trouble, because there're more of us fighters hidden in the sheep.'

'Sir, you're heaven sent,' said the boy. 'Are you the saviours from outer space?'

'No, get real! But we're here to free your country,' laughed Rajay. 'Look as if you're still manning your post, if you want to help.'

There was one more group and Robin and his crawling companions neared them. Regrettably, as they did, a large snake in the grass distracted both dogs and sheep. The sheep darted away and in doing so exposed the partisans just as the members of the guard's group looked at the cause of the sudden movement. The snake darted off somewhere, more frightened than either sheep or people, but the damage was done.

Robin had his knife out, and so did Zoey but this guard-group could see they were up to no good, from the Special's point of view. The other partisans, Namoh, Rajay, Merien and the rest were too far away to be of any help, and were hiding in the sheep. Robin made for the Special, who shouted loudly as Robin struggled with him. None of the conscripts in this group were friends of Zoey or indeed friendly at all. Robin was overpowering the Special, but it was taking time and the other three, Zoey and his young cousins, were no match for the older conscripts. Robin shouted to Rajay, who was nearby, but as Rajay and his helpers crawled to Robin's aid the sheep got in the way so they lost vital moments. Robin had been wounded in the arm and was bleeding quite heavily, but worse the Special was hollering for help and one of his boys had run off in the direction of the camp.

'Hide in the sheep!' Robin shouted to Zoey and his cousins. 'We'll handle this!' The boys didn't hide, but they were not trained in combat and things were looking bad for Robin. The sheep were in complete confusion, running every which way, but at this moment Rajay and Zoey's other cousins arrived. This Special and his faithful conscripts were fighting to kill, so the partisans fought back in as deadly a fashion. Now the odds were against the defenders of the Sorcerers' Teletsia and they didn't have a hope. Soon all three of them lay dead at Robin's feet but that was only the beginning of the problems, because by now the conscript who had run away had reached the camp.

Plan B!' shouted Robin, clutching his wounded arm. The shepherds within earshot starting whistling commands to their dogs and a stampede of sheep started. Sheep, sheep and more sheep were herded in a mad mass towards the Specials' camp. Nevertheless some of the Specials there managed to get at their guns, and tried to locate the partisans among the sheep, and some of them had guns specially treated by the Sorcerers never to miss. Shots rang out and some sheep fell dead or wounded. Sheepdogs darted here and there, and one of them was hit, yelping horribly. However, strangely, some of the bullets, which had been aimed at specific people such as Rajay, not only missed him but one or two of the Specials themselves fell, wounded by bullets from somewhere. Something else was happening too - most of the conscripts were turning against the Specials.

Far above the chaos the flying horses came into view, earlier than expected. Some of the Specials in the camp took a shot at them, then, seeing they were too high, mostly decided they'd had enough of the Temple of Support and its notorious reputation. They ran down the track, avoiding the sheep as best they could, but after running through the flocks they began bleating like sheep themselves and some even dropped down on all fours.

The power of positive destruction, working through the Mother Earth at the temple, had done to these Specials what they had done to so many others and they now behaved like sheep themselves. It was most unwise to try any form of aggression on the flying horses, especially near the Temple of Support. The rest of the Specials who were coming up to the temple now began firing guns at the sheep, hoping to expose the partisans.

'Fiery discus!' shouted Rajay, lying hidden among some sheep.

'Go for it,' agreed Robin. 'There's no alternative. Pray the keys only kill those Specials who are shooting at us.' Derwin crawled up to Robin through the sheep and Rajay was already taking off his borrowed Sasrar key and putting his index finger in the back to allow it to convert into the lethal discus. He risked standing up above the cover of the sheep to set it off, and as he did a shot rang out in his direction and caught a nearby sheep. 'Rajay, be careful, we can't afford to lose you, of all of us,' cried Robin, from the ground.

'OK, these days I have to be more cautious,' grinned Rajay as he crouched down and a particularly energetic sheep jumped over both of them.

'Robin, are you all right?' called out Derwin, crawling up to him through the sheep. 'You're wounded!'

'It's not too bad,' Robin held his arm to staunch the bleeding. 'Help me take off my Sasrar key, and put yours in fiery discus option. Quickly! The Specials' guns won't miss for long, bandhan or no bandhan.'

Within seconds two more keys were set to fiery discus, their owners hidden amongst the sheep, and they went flying through the air. Ahren, at the other side of the temple, saw the golden discs streaking away and knew it was all up for the Specials. The keys would kill anyone who had aggressive tendencies towards their bearers, but not at random, so did not kill those who had run away, or the innocent conscripts.

'Let me see that wound,' insisted Rajay.

'Not now,' replied Robin, 'and don't tell Asha when she arrives or she might panic.'

One recruit, a trainee Sorcerer, had been sleeping some way apart from the rest of the camp, because he was addicted to a certain drug and had crept away into the bushes to have his fix earlier in the night. When he heard the commotion he came out of his drugged haze, took one look at the disorder and corpses and made off on foot at a smart pace. Unlike the Specials, who were now either dead or behaving like sheep, he intended to go for reinforcements and the nearest ones were in a village some distance away. Off he went, hallucinating and staggering, to save the fatherland for the Sorcerers. Great would be his reward and fast would be his promotion, and he could only thank the idiots who had let themselves get killed or driven mad in the little valley, for the chance they had given him. Callous, selfish ambition was the hallmark of all Sorcerers and this one was no exception.

CHAPTER 11

THE POWER OF MOTHER EARTH

The dazed recruits appeared from the bushes where they had been hiding. Some had been actively fighting their commanding officers while others had no idea what had happened, except that somehow all the Specials, and one or two of the conscripts who were well 'in' with them, were either dead or had run away and become like sheep. Rajay and Namoh walked over to the camp, knowing they were safe with the survivors, and Zoey, Tom and Freddi soon joined them. One conscript who knew Zoey came up to him. He was part of his Resistance Group and had had his awakening.

'What happened?' he cried in horror.

'Liberation army - meet Ray and Namoh,' and Zoey introduced them. 'They're partisans from Daish Shaktay and they've come to sort out our country for us, along with a lot of others.'

'Fantastic! It had to start here at the Temple of Support!' said Zoey's friend.

'Your first job, if you don't mind, is to bury the bodies,' ordered Namoh, who had taken command now Robin was out of things.

'Is there a doctor here?' Rajay asked.

'Yes, that's me,' another young man came towards them.

'We've got a man wounded in the arm. Can you come and look at him?'

'My pleasure,' he replied. Rajay took him to Robin, who was in pain but was trying to conceal it. Soon he was bandaged up and helped to the temple. While he was being treated, the dead Specials were tipped into the camp refuse holes by the rebellious conscripts. They had previously been ordered to dig these by the same people who were now being put into them. After the Specials had been buried the earth was replaced and those in charge of this grisly operation put their left hands to their heads and their right ones on the ground, and apologised to the Mother Earth for putting such inauspicious bodies under Her ground. It was better than having them lying around while they did the ceremony. There were a few prisoners and these were tied up and left in the camp, so eventually someone would find them.

Next, Namoh instructed the shepherds to take their flocks of sheep to the north of the temple and to spread them out along the shallow valley wherein lay the track which led to the nearest proper road. If any reinforcements arrived, they would most probably come that way and would have an unbelievably frustrating time trying to get through nearly two thousand sheep. Then he ordered reliable groups of young men, loyal to the new Free Teletsia, to position themselves round the temple at regular intervals, in case any Specials should appear from other parts of the plain.

The flying horses and their riders flew on further than the temple and hovered at a great height until everything had quietened down. Then they circled downwards and landed outside the temple. Conwenna and Lee were riding theirs, and Stellamar was on mine. Lord Jarwhen and Lord Coban rode the other two, and Stellamar's uncle Lord Olon rode Robin's. Guardians could all ride the flying horses, but even so the horses preferred their owners to give permission first, which everyone had. They dismounted, and the animals, who had the power of setting off positive destruction in an area, were now where the first subtle centre on Mother Earth resonated most strongly with the primordial cosmic Tree of Life.

It was already getting light when the large flying ship appeared and landed behind the temple. A number of people including me piled out and quickly took our places on the ground, near the four great menhirs in the middle of the smaller stones. Merien, Derwin and some of Zoey's friends had laid out the wood, decorated the area where the fire was to be lit with flowers and prepared the other items – a tub of clarified butter, some fruits, a coconut and some small containers of fragrant dried woods, rice, spices and herbs to offer.

Lord Coban, the senior guardian of Teletsia, asked us to begin by making the bandhan of protection, and a still calm replaced the recent frenzy. After that we all humbly asked the Mother Earth to accept our praise and thanksgiving. Lord Coban called those of us who had travelled to Sasrar from this very place to come to the front. He explained that Tandi, Namoh and I would have to stand in for a Sasrar guardian, as we had all spent time up there. Then he called for a guardian from each of the other areas, those connected with the second to sixth subtle centres of the Tree of Life on the planetary level. Stellamar, Pa Ganoozal, Lord Jarwhen, Merien, Rajay and Roarke took their seats.

'Come on Robin,' said Lord Coban. 'You come for Chussan.' Robin was wearing a cloak against the chill of dawn and I did not notice he had been wounded.

As the sun rose we lit the fire and asked for blessings from all the elements, especially fire and earth. Lord Coban recited a number of qualities of Mother Earth, and each time one was said those of us in the front threw some herbs and other offerings into the flames. Strangely enough, every time we did this, I felt a wave of coolness emanate from the hot fire. After this we asked the fire to burn any subtle negativity stopping the cleansing of Teletsia. To finish, Lord Coban asked Lee to play the melody on his flute and the rest of us seven sang the poem to the Mother Earth, which Raynor had first sung there five years ago. I will quote a few lines:

'Wreathed in an endless garment of white clouds, you hide your vast equanimity,

With your changing moods and seasons, you reveal your tender fragility.

You know to perfection your part, in the dance of the planets and stars,

When we learn how we travel with you, then perhaps we'll come to know ours.

How carefully, how delicately, you slowly form your great creation,

With man as the crest-jewel, mirror of all evolution,

So let us worship and respect you, and accept all your variety,

At a moment in time when mankind could in spirit be one.'

We all knelt in worship of Mother Earth, our foreheads on the ground. Then we sat in meditation soaking up the vibrations, wave after wave of loving energy flowing into and between our hearts and we also experienced a sign from Mother Nature herself. Around the temple and from the menhirs themselves where they had been roosting, songbirds rose up simultaneously and sang a loud and melodious chorus of praise, hovering above the plain.

Suddenly we heard a commotion down the valley on the track - shouting and abuse – evidently someone had got a message to the nearest Specials Post and reinforcements were arriving.

'Roarke, get everyone you can out of here in your large flyer,' shouted Robin. 'The sheep will hold up the Specials for a little while. Take the friendly conscripts and the Resistance Group boys to the Herders, and we'll rearrange everyone there.' He turned to me, 'Asha, you come with me on Yamun.'

Almost everyone jumped up, ran towards Roarke's large flyer and managed to fit in. Within moments the temple was deserted. Derwin and Merien ran off to their craft and Roarke's small one, taking passengers with them. Robin loaded all the flying horses up with two people. They had the power of levitation so the extra weight was no problem. He called someone to put me up behind him on Yamun and I noticed his wound.

'Don't worry about me,' he said sharply, 'we've got to leave.' When we were in the air I could feel he was very unsteady. At one point he seemed to be about to fall off, and I held him upright.

184

Immediately we left the ground the power of positive destruction started manifesting and we could see wave after wave of earthquake radiated outwards from the Temple of Support, as the red earth rippled and shuddered. The Specials coming up the track never got past the sheep because a vast chasm opened up and swallowed them. The shepherds were frightened but unhurt and when the roars and rumblings moved out to the rest of the country; all that was visible in the area was the temple, the countryside and thousands of very confused sheep being rounded up by the shepherds and their dogs. There were scars where the earth had swallowed the remains of the Specials' camp and their reinforcements.

The flying ships and flying horses soon reached the Herders' farms, and we all landed over the hill and out of sight of the hamlet. Lee and Ahren crept down to the houses to check there were no Specials around, but there were none, so the rest of us followed, and we were quite a crowd. The farming folk were up milking the cows and Zoey went into his house.

'Hi mum,' he called, 'I'm back, and I've got a lot of people with me needing breakfast.'

'Mrs Herder,' I asked as she came to the door and greeted me, 'can we hide some people here?'

'Yes, of course. How many?'

'About twenty-five, but not for long.' These were the conscripts from the Temple of Support, who intended to return to their homes and raise the local people in case of an armed struggle, and Coff Coffeeman, who had come to the Island with Rajay, wanted to go home to Darzeet - he would travel by country roads to western Teletsia then get a ride downriver from Coffee Ferry, as he knew many of the barge owners. He had a pass which enabled him to travel widely on business and once home he would prepare his Resistance Group in Darzeet for war.

The other Herder families helped feed everyone. They had no idea of the dramatic events at the Temple of Support, because the earthquake had not affected their hamlet in the least. They had felt a slight tremble, but minor earth tremors were common in the area so they didn't think anything of it. I was worried that Robin was not well enough to ride, but didn't want to say anything after his earlier remark to me, so sat down in the farmyard with my plate of food: bread, butter and honey with a cup of coffee, and made some bandhans on my hand. Rajay, who had been thanking the conscripts for their support, noticed and came over.

'What's the problem?' he asked.

'It's Robin. He's very unsteady on Yamun. I'm afraid he'll fall off while he's flying. Trouble is, he won't listen when I try to tell him.'

'Let me deal with this. That's what honorary brothers are for.'

Sure enough Robin did listen to Rajay and he agreed to go in Roarke's flying ship with me. A little later I thanked Zoey's mother for all her hospitality.

'That's nothing. I wish we could do more. Our food was very simple.'

'Mrs Herder, this morning you've opened your home to a king, a prince and some other very important people. They all thought your breakfast was just the thing.'

'The partisans?'

'Yes!' I laughed. 'Oh – and you can keep that pony I left here last time I came. I have a flying horse.'

Mrs Herder's mouth dropped open in surprise, but at that moment someone came up and asked her something, so our conversation was finished.

When we were in Roarke's large flyer, going home, Robin apologised to me. We both knew there were moments when we came second to each other and there were more important priorities. Nevertheless, I didn't want him falling off Yamun when we were in the air and was very grateful to Rajay for making him see sense.

Although we were aware that a strong earthquake had occurred in the area of the Temple of Support, from the height that we flew at we did not have much idea of what had happened in the rest of Teletsia.

CHAPTER 12

ULTIMATUM

The following evening Lord Jarwhen called us to the Operations Room. 'Reports are coming in by carrier hawk from safe houses all over the country,' he began.

He read us the notes, which had been hastily penned and tied to the legs of messenger birds trained to fly to the Island of Creations. The earthquake was many times more devastating than the one five years before, when we had run away from Teletsia. Many Sorcerers had been killed. Throughout Teletsia catastrophic things happened: on the Clatan Slave Farm, all the houses and buildings where the Sorcerers, mesmerisers and overseers lived and worked were reduced to rubble, and many of their occupants were buried. Strangely enough, all the slaves were unharmed and many escaped. Some returned to their homes, completely normal and somehow no longer under the influence of the Sorcerers' treatments. The local Specials had other problems so let them be. This also happened on two other slave farms in the same district. Specials' stations, offices and homes throughout the country were destroyed and no one could understand how the blind force of an earth tremor could have been so discriminating as to where it did damage, and who was killed.

Worst of all was the Forbidden Quarter in Teletos, right in the centre of the island city. The administrative offices of the Sorcerers were there and most of them had houses in that part of town. Few servants lived there and out of the working day almost the only people in the quarter were either Sorcerers or Specials guarding them. Shortly after dawn on Midsummer Day the entire Forbidden Quarter sank into the water, so only the highest towers could be seen above water level. Rather than resembling half an onion to anyone flying over it, the city with its canals now looked more like a doughnut with a hole in the middle, and the hole was filled with cleansing water.

An unusually high wave had washed over the platoons of Specials guarding the beaches and trying to stop flying ships entering or leaving the Island of Creations. It only flooded Teletsia, not the Island of Creations, because the shore on the Island sloped up steeply in most places. It had also caught most of the gunboats blockading the Island, and had neatly deposited them in some

Teletsian fields.

When the Sorcerers came to question the shepherds who had been up at the Temple of Support they could not read their minds, because they had all had their awakening. The shepherds insisted they had merely performed their annual Midsummer Ritual, and it was not their fault if some powerful beings appeared from outer space and all manner of odd things happened that morning. The prisoners who had been tied up and left in the camp could not be found. The Mother Earth had taken them back into herself; she was not as forgiving as the humans who inhabited her.

'So, what next?' asked Lord Jarwhen.

'Let's send the surviving Sorcerers an ultimatum: surrender or be destroyed,' Lee proposed.

'The dolphins have reported that the Daish Shaktay navy is approaching and the troop ships are behind them,' added Merien, 'and the other good piece of news is that the Emperor will give the Sorcerers and any Specials that surrender an island in the Sea of Illusion. It's an agreeable place, but it's a time/space warp area, so once on it they won't be able to leave, at least not in this realm of creation. They don't need to know that though.'

'Is that honest?' Lee was uncertain.

'It's fair enough,' replied Roarke.

'Lee, you know how to write this type of letter, to the Sorcerers,' said Rajay.

'I'll take it,' offered Merien. 'Lee and Ahren should come with me - also Derwin, but not Asha or Conwenna, because it might turn violent.' I agreed. I'd learnt my lesson by now.

'I'll come too,' said Roarke.

'Namoh, you go for Daish Shaktay,' suggested Rajay, 'and Robin, you for Chussan.'

'I'm not important enough,' replied Robin. 'Jewel merchants can't give ultimatums on behalf of their rulers.'

'But your disguise has worn off by now and they wouldn't recognise you,' I added.

'We could pretend the Daish Shaktay navy is doing manoeuvres in the Sea of Illusion,' contributed Ahren. 'We could say we've heard of all the awful things that are happening to the Sorcerers and that the forces of nature may completely destroy them if they don't leave Teletsia. It will seem we are helping them by asking them to leave.'

'You're very optimistic, but anything is worth a try,' said Rajay hopefully.

After this Rajay took Robin and me into the garden and we sat under our favourite tree.

'Robin, I've got a message for you from Albion. I was going to wait until we'd finished here, but I'd better tell you now, because you're going to Teletos as an ambassador. When things are resolved here Albion needs you. The Prime Minister who was elected isn't working out. He doesn't use his vibrations to make decisions and doesn't listen to Albion's sane advice when things inevitably go wrong. The people have unanimously decided they want a different Prime Minister, and an overwhelming majority are determined it should be you. Congratulations!' Rajay beamed at him and then turned to me. 'So until such time as Albion marries, you're the First Lady of Chussan. No more unpredictable escapades!'

I didn't know what to say, so instead I also congratulated Robin, delighted that at last he had got the recognition he deserved. Rajay went back to the house, leaving us alone. Robin put his hand on his forehead and sighed.

'Is your arm hurting?' I asked, because his other arm was in a sling.

'Not especially. My heart is.' I looked at him searchingly and he returned my gaze. 'Again I'm going to have to be less than sincere with you.'

'What do you mean?'

'When we married I promised we'd live wherever was best for both of us, and as you're one of these children of the prophecy you may be needed here, but if Albion needs me I'll have to go back. If you want to stay here for a year or two, or even longer, I'll understand.'

'Robin, you're not serious! I couldn't imagine my life without you at the centre of it. You've been honoured with the top job in Chussan and I'm unbelievably proud of you - but I'm not sure I'll be much good as your First Lady.'

'You'll do fine. Plus I'll need your support if I'm going to carry this off in any way successfully.'

Lee spent the rest of the morning composing the letter to the Sorcerers. It finally came out like this:

To: Their Holinesses the Protectors of the State of Teletsia

From: Representatives of countries of the Central Area of Navi Septa.

Your Holinesses,

We the undersigned are at present in the Great Sea on joint naval manoeuvres and it has come to our ears that there is a grave problem in Teletsia. We have heard that the Mother Earth is unwilling to support your regime any longer and is destroying large numbers of you, along with your property and land.

This being so, the Emperor of the Sea has graciously offered all of you asylum on an island to the west of his realm, to be yours in perpetuity. It is suggested that you, along with any members of your Special Secret Police, should make your way to the island as soon as possible on your naval ships, and once there you will be safe. We promise not to impede the passage of these ships in any way, provided they do not attack us.

We advise that you take up our offer soon, to avoid further calamity to yourselves and your police force.

Signed:

Lee Restorer, Ahren Dairyman and Derwin Herbhealer, on behalf of the people of Teletsia

Merien Vizier, Ambassador of the Emperor of the Great Sea

Namoh, Lord Santara, Ambassador of Daish Shaktay

Prince Roarke, Ambassador of Vittalia

Robin Markand, Ambassador of Chussan

'We've certainly told them who's here and what we're up to,' noted Ahren. He was not very happy about putting his name on the letter. 'I'm not into politics; I'd rather do the undercover stuff, but I'll go if you need me to.'

'It's time they realized the prophecy is well on the way to being fulfilled,' added Lee. 'However, we have to do the decent thing and offer them a way out.'

'It's a good idea to send Namoh,' Lord Jarwhen observed. 'Rajay definitely shouldn't go, because he's a crowned king, not an ambassador.'

At the barracks outside Gyan-on-Sea, Raynor was certain the earthquake was something to do with the freedom struggle. As elsewhere, it had been extremely selective. All the conscripts, including him and Garma were out on endurance training and were camping, so were shaken but unhurt. It utterly destroyed the buildings where the Specials lived and damaged the others quite badly. A number of Specials had been killed, along with some trainee officers who had got out of the field course and were in the barracks when the earthquake struck. Raynor and Garma got promotions, because of the lack of personnel to fill the more senior officers' posts.

They were given extra instruction, including being let into the secret of how the guns which rarely missed their target worked. As Raynor suspected there was sorcery involved. The guns were specially treated by a Sorcerer and it only worked for a day or two, and then wore off. When they were given the guns to practice on, Raynor noticed his had horrible vibrations. He cleared it by putting one hand to the gun and the other to the earth, saying some cleansing words of power he had learnt in Sasrar, and asked the earth element to take the negativity. However, when he practiced, his gun did not have the never-miss option any more, and missed the target. Luckily Raynor was an accurate marksman, so when he reloaded it, he made sure it hit its target, due to his skill rather than sorcery, so the instructor was puzzled but satisfied. These guns took a long time to reload and many people used a bow and arrow or catapult if they were in a hurry.

Raynor shared his suspicions about the earthquake with Garma and they listened to the rumours flying around: the invaders from outer space could arrive at any moment, the seven rebels were returning with armies and invincible weapons; it was all nonsense, or maybe a plot of the Sorcerers to frighten everyone and make them easier to control – and so on.

Back at the Island of Creations, the next day the Daish Shaktay warship *The Queen Zulani*, no longer disguised as *The Wattan Trader*, prepared to sail to Teletos with the ambassadors. The harbour of the Island was again blockaded by Teletsian war ships, but Merien and Roarke made an official request to allow the Daish Shaktay ship to pass out to Teletos with diplomatic immunity, in order to ask for a truce and terms. They did not say exactly what the terms were, but after a fair amount of bribe money had changed hands the admiral in charge of the Teletsian ships agreed to let them through.

Soon the ship sailed up the estuary towards Teletos. It was flying the flags of all the countries represented and also the white flag of peace and parley. As they approached the town they saw a large number of Teletsian warships in the harbour. Their ship anchored out in the broad river away from the town and waited. All the delegates wore their best clothes and looked important, especially Roarke and Merien, and everyone put on bandhans to protect themselves and to hide their glowing golden auras. A small boatload of harbour police approached and asked them their business.

'Please, good sirs, come on board,' offered Dan, the captain. 'I have here some ambassadors from various countries who have heard the plight of Teletsia and want to offer help.'

'Your ambassadors can come with us,' agreed the Sorcerer in charge of the harbour master's delegation. Roarke, Merien, Robin, Namoh, Lee, Derwin and Ahren got into their launch and followed the harbour master's. It was evening and Teletos looked beautiful from the water, even though it did not feel beautiful vibrationally, and everyone going in was praying that this would not be a one-way trip. They were silent as they sailed into the labyrinth of canals and Lee soon realised they were going in the direction of the palace his father had converted into flats.

'This was my home,' he murmured to the others when they disembarked at his family's private wharf, 'it's typical that the Sorcerers should have taken over this building as their new headquarters.'

'Don't worry Lee,' whispered Roarke, 'you're going to take over the whole country quite soon.'

As they crossed the courtyard Lee assumed all the former tenants had been turned out, but noticed Conwenna's aunt, Drusilla Prospector, peeping from her window on the second floor. They were led into what had formerly been the main reception room. Lee's father had rented it out to a practice of upmarket doctors; now it held the best the Sorcerers could do in the way of a government. Most of the twelve Sorcerers present were either young and just out of the Academy, or very old and decrepit; Sorcerers did sometimes retire and went to live in opulent retirement homes. One of these had survived destruction and its residents had been called back to office. As the ambassadors walked into the room the Sorcerers began shaking and shuddering uncontrollably.

'We represent a number of countries from this area of the world,' began Roarke. 'We would like to make you an offer which might solve your problems.' One Sorcerer, an ancient cove who could hardly even speak, indicated that he was in charge. Merien presented the proposal to him and his aide opened it and read it out. When he had finished the old Sorcerer looked angrily at Merien.

'D – do y – you really th - think we're going to leave our homeland, young m - man?' he stammered.

'Who are you, anyway?' demanded another, with a violent jerk of his head.

'I'm the son of the Emperor's Prime Minister. His Excellency only wants to help you,' replied Merien politely.

'And what if we refuse your ever-so-kind offer?' inquired a third sarcastically, unable to control his whole body from twitching.

'I would strongly suspect that your situation might become even more untenable,' Robin stated.

'Not half s - so unten… Guards, arrest these men. We'll get the t - truth out of them, then make an example of them!' stuttered the very ancient Sorcerer.

'Peaceful delegation!' snorted a young one, bloated with newly-bestowed power. 'I know who you are,' he pointed rudely at Lee. 'I recognise you from school. And you other Teletsians, your names are well known. You're those rebels who ran away to the north and started all this trouble five years ago. Come on guards, if you won't arrest them, kill them! What's keeping you?' The guards were hesitant to obey, because they had heard what had happened when Conwenna was taken before the Sorcerers.

'Arrest them!' shouted the young Sorcerer again, 'or you'll be reduced to ashes as well as them!' But it was too late; the guards' momentary hesitation had given the ambassadors time to activate their keys in fiery discus mode. In his heart, as he released his key Roarke asked that the Specials should not be killed, as they had initially refused to obey the Sorcerers' orders. The keys flew to their victims and as the first Sorcerer was beheaded the Specials guarding them took to their heels and ran out of the door and down the stairs, scared witless and braying like donkeys. The keys may have spared their lives, but the power of positive destruction, innocently unleashed by the flying horses at the Temple of Support, had created another fate for the Specials. Just as so many of them had condemned thousands of innocent people to the slave farms to be treated and mesmerised, so now increasing numbers found themselves in equally bad trouble. The Sorcerers lay in a gory, headless heap.

'How do we get out of here?' Robin asked as they picked up their keys from among the carnage. 'These people will be back to get us.'

'There's a secret exit – follow me,' Lee went to the corner of the room and pushed aside a table that was up against the wall. Behind was wooden paneling and he pressed a carved flower on one of the panels. A little door flew open, revealing some stone steps. The Sorcerers had not discovered this but Lee had known about it from childhood. Ahren had by this time closed and bolted the main door of the large room and they could hear the Specials braying and growling as they tried to explain to the guards downstairs what had happened. Lee pushed everyone through the door in the panel, on their hands and knees because it was small, and closed it behind him. They found themselves in a normal sized passage with steps leading down to the ground level and heard the guards breaking down the main door into the big room. He hoped they wouldn't realise the table had been moved, but with luck, even if they did they would not be able to open the secret door. The steps in front of them ended at another door that opened onto a deserted part of the back yard. Ahead was a wall with a gate in it and beyond was the canal. They hurried through the gate onto a pathway between the wall and the canal.

'Close it behind you!' Lee cried. Roarke was last and he heard a cry from a Special, across the yard. Robin and Namoh came back, swords drawn.

'We'll hold the door,' shouted Robin. 'The rest of you fetch the launch and pick us up!'

'I'll have my key ready in discus mode,' said Roarke.

Derwin ran along the embankment and waved at the Daish Shaktay marines waiting on the launch at the main quayside. Merien knelt near the water, whistled though his key and within seconds a dolphin, which had been tracking the boat since they left the warship, surfaced. Merien indicated for it to pull the launch fast to where the others were holding the door against the Specials. The dolphin grabbed a rope and helped by the oars of the sailors the launch soon neared the gate.

The Specials had by now opened it. First they had tried to use their guns which never missed, but the bullets flew all over the place, so they drew their swords. There was a violent fight going on, with Robin, Roarke and Namoh holding the gateway. As the launch came close enough to jump on it, Roarke, who was trying to avoid using it, threw his key at the crowd of Specials. They saw it coming and tried to run away but the key caught them and one by one they met the usual fate of being beheaded. Roarke had no time to retrieve his key, turned away and jumped on the launch. By now three more dolphins had appeared in the dank waters of the canal, and the launch made off in double quick time towards the harbour.

The ambassadors hid under a tarpaulin and the some of the sailors sat on them with their feet on it too. In Teletsia it was extremely bad manners to put your feet on anyone, so no one would have suspected there were people, and important people at that, underneath.

'If anyone questions you, say you left us at the Sorcerers' Palace,' said Merien from under one of the marines, who was trying not to hurt him, knowing he was sitting on the Prime Minister's son. Lee, peeping out from a corner of the tarpaulin, directed the sailors, and when they left the canals and reached the harbour, the harbour master's guards were waiting for them. The dolphins disappeared and the sailors rowed as well as they could with their valuable cargo hidden beneath their feet.

'Our orders are that the Daish Shaktay warship is to be treated as a hostile craft,' warned the Special in charge of the harbour master's boat. 'You have until midnight to surrender, otherwise she'll be sunk by the Teletsian navy. Where are those so-called ambassadors?'

'They're at the palace. We were told to go back for them later,' improvised the Daish Shaktay officer.

'Don't bother,' replied the Special. 'They'll have been annihilated by now. If you want to save your skins I suggest your people surrender immediately.'

'I'll relay the message,' shouted the Daish Shaktay officer, and went on rowing across the harbour. When they reached the ship the ambassadors crept on board as unobtrusively as they could in the moons' light.

'I left my fifth centre key in your back yard,' Roarke mentioned as they walked along the deck.

'I doubt anyone will dare touch it, even if they find it. How are we going to get out of this one?' Lee asked as they entered Dan's cabin.

'First we do the two bandhans and then we pray for inspiration,' Merien suggested. They did this, and Robin came up with an idea.

'There's something Albion and I did when we were in a tight spot in Chussan. As you know, the quality of our sixth centre is transformation into that which is subtler, so Albion and I made a bandhan of request on our keys that we would become so transformed that no one could see us, and for a short time it worked.

'This invisibility option is from the sixth centre key, but some of us have Sasrar keys, which also have that power. All the Daish Shaktay officers, and also the sailors and marines have had their inner awakening. Everyone on board must make a bandhan of request that we can make the whole ship invisible long enough to get past the Teletsian navy, which is lying out in the river and will try to prevent us from passing them.'

'It's very cool on vibrations,' asserted Merien, and the others agreed. 'Meanwhile I'll go down to the water level and call some dolphins. We'll need them to pull us downriver fast.'

'The invisibility idea is a slim chance,' admitted Robin, 'but unless anyone has a better idea we'll have to try it.'

'With your permission,' asked Dan, 'I'll have the gun crews in place as well. It's night now and with the dolphins to pull us and a bit of luck, we could possibly fight our way out. The Teletsian navy will never expect us to try, and the dolphins will pull us much more quickly than we could move otherwise.

None of their ships are on battle alert; I looked through my spyglass just now and checked. They reckon they've already defeated us.'

'Whatever you think best,' concluded Roarke.

The ambassadors sat in deep meditation and prayed that they would escape. The whole ship was still and it felt as if some great power was focusing attention on it. They made the bandhan on the keys, and all the seamen and marines were asked to be in meditation. At first it seemed that nothing had happened, and in any case the ship would always stay visible to those actually on it, but then they noticed some people on shore pointing in their direction, looking agitated and fearful, as they peered at the ship by the light of one moon.

'That ship looks as if it isn't really there, it's like – transparent,' cried one man nervously as their small boat passed by, 'almost as if it could disappear any moment.'

'Let's get away from here,' said another.

Merien ordered ropes to be thrown to the dolphins just under the surface, occasionally coming up for air. A Specials' launch came towards them and Merien, hanging over the rail, heard them talking.

'Where's the Daish Shaktay galleon?' asked the captain of the launch. 'Did our warships already sink it?'

'Isn't that it?' replied the Sorcerer with him, pointing at the Daish Shaktay ship.

'There's nothing there, sir,' insisted the captain, staring straight at it.

'There is, you idiot,' snarled the Sorcerer. 'It's turned into a ghost ship! Ayee!' Unfortunately the invisibility option had its limits and blocking out a whole ship with everyone on board had stretched it too far. 'I'm going to send it back to the realm it came from. Guns won't have any effect. Our enemies have come from another dimension.' At this the Sorcerer stood up in the launch with his staff and began the gestures and incantation for the ship's removal from this realm of creation, or if it was material for reducing it to ashes. Unfortunately for the Sorcerer his attention was fixed on the ghost that was Merien, hanging over the rail giving instructions to the dolphins.

Within seconds the Sorcerer was himself smoldering. Soon he was a heap of ashes on the deck and the Teletsian harbour guards were mortally afraid. They turned their launch round and headed for the quayside. At this moment the dolphins started pulling the Daish Shaktay ship, because there was virtually no wind, and it slipped quietly downriver through the Teletsian navy. Fortunately, invisibility did not work on dolphins, so they could see the ropes thrown at them.

PART THREE

WAR

CHAPTER 1

AN UNEVEN SEA BATTLE

The *Queen Zulani* sailed out to sea, moving fast despite the lack of wind. A whole school of dolphins leapt in and out of the water in their enthusiasm to help Merien. After directing them in their language, he came into the captain's cabin, where the others were enjoying a late dinner with Dan.

'I reckon we've declared war,' commented Roarke.

'I'd say the Sorcerers have declared war on at least four countries, including the supporters of Free Teletsia. That's assuming they can get a government together to oppose us,' added Robin.

'They will,' groaned Lee. 'These Sorcerers are like mosquitoes – everywhere, and you can be sure they'll force their army and navy into battle.'

'I've sent word to Zafan and the Daish Shaktay navy via the dolphins, telling them what's happened,' said Merien.

'The Sorcerers will also send messages, via the light signalling,' warned Lee. 'I doubt we'll be able to get back into the harbour at the Island.'

'No problem,' said Dan. 'I need to be with our navy.'

The next day the dolphins reported to Merien that there were not many ships blockading the harbour, but nevertheless, Dan didn't want to risk it, so passed the Island out of sight of land, and when they were some way to the north, the flyers, which had been stowed on the ship, took those who didn't need to be with the navy, such as Robin, to the Island by night. The dolphins kept a lookout for Teletsian Coast Guards and gave the all-clear before the flyers left the warship.

I was relieved that our ambassadors had returned safely, even if the mission had not been successful. Not that we seriously expected it would be, but now we had an excuse for invasion. However, it wasn't going to be easy, because first we had to get the Daish Shaktay forces past the powerful Teletsian navy. Even before our warship reached the north shore of the Island, Merien received a message from the dolphins that the Teletsian navy was sailing out to sea.

Later, when the ship was some way north of the Island, Merien asked to be put in a dinghy and pulled along behind the ship so as to talk further with the sea creatures. Afterwards he came back to Dan and Lee in the captain's cabin.

'I must make some plans with Zafan,' said Merien. 'The Daish Shaktay navy is quite close. I'll land my flyer on his deck.' Soon Lee and Merien were sitting with him in the captain's cabin of the flagship, the *Daish Shaktay Queen*. Zafan greeted them with his usual enthusiasm and then they talked strategy.

'How long have we got?' he asked.

'Not long. They know you're here, because they use birds as spies. You can expect to meet the Teletsian navy tomorrow morning,' replied Merien. 'The whales have promised to help. They'll be here around midnight. Before they go into action we must get the Teletsians to fire one volley – even one shot will be enough and then we can't be accused of being the aggressors. The power of the Emperor will only protect us for defence, and so will the whales, who work for him.'

'Let's put an empty ship out in front as a decoy,' suggested Lee. 'We can afford to lose one ship to save the lives of the Daish Shaktay men.'

'Good idea,' Zafan agreed, 'we'll dress up some barrels and spars in old clothes to look like sailors.'

No one had much sleep that night and some time later two decoy ships were in place with a lot of counterfeit sailors on their decks. They didn't move, but they looked fairly realistic. Later the great whales arrived – at least thirty or forty, bobbing up and down and listening to Merien's instructions, while the phosphorescence on the waves where they broke the surface gleamed and danced in the night light. The Daish Shaktay navy was arranged in a fan formation and the first few were in a line, one ship behind the other; first were the two dummy ships and behind was Zafan commanding the *Daish Shaktay Queen*, a gracious sailing galleon with a row of cannon on each side.

Proceedings of the War Council

I Malvog, replacement scribe to the most illustrious Lords of Teletsia, do hereby record a rapidly convened meeting of the new Lordships.

Yet again the treacherous rebels have murdered twelve of their Supreme Holinesses the High Priests, two guards and the scribe, when they and certain foreigners came on a supposedly peaceful diplomatic mission. We have been forced to declare war and our navy is sailing north to meet the one from Daish Shaktay

These invaders have some form of sorcery, otherwise they would never have managed to escape from Teletos harbour, but we are confident that our navy will defeat theirs when it comes to the defence of our fatherland.

The next morning, soon after dawn, the Teletsian navy was spotted on the horizon by the lookout in the crow's nest of the *Daish Shaktay Queen*. Behind was the *Queen Zulani* with Merien and Dan, the captain, and on the ship behind that was Lee, with Captain Hampen the Tong, a naval officer formerly from the land of Tong, who had been rescued by Zafan when he captured the Mattanga fleet at Port Volcan two years before. Behind these three the Daish Shaktay ships fanned out, ready to meet the enemy, knowing they were facing a technologically superior foe. There was a fresh wind from the north, and although the Sorcerers on the Teletsian ships tried to quell it, the breeze blew strongly and white flecks of foam showed on the waves. Everyone in the Daish Shaktay navy made the two bandhans, each man was ready at his post, and they waited in silence.

Slowly the Teletsian navy drew within range of the decoy ships, which were being kept in place by dolphins, holding ropes under the surface, but the Teletsians did not open fire. What had gone wrong? The enemy navy kept coming, spread out in a long line, ten ships wide and four deep. Zafan, looking with his spy glass, realised with horror that they had seen through the decoy ships and were not attacking them. The Teletsian navy was bearing down on his ship, the *Daish Shaktay Queen*. Soon they were within range and worst of all were broadsides on. The Teletsians opened fire and three cannon balls holed it badly at the water line, so it began listing as it filled with water. Zafan's men retaliated, but the Teletsians blasted his ship again and it was sinking fast. Virtually everyone except the captain jumped overboard. Now the Teletsians were in range of the second and third Daish Shaktay ships, and attacked them too. A ball caught some gunpowder in Dan's ship, with Merien on it. There was an explosion and many people on deck were thrown into the sea as the *Queen Zulani* began to go down, taking Merien's precious flyer with it.

Lee and Hampen's ship was also under fire and irrevocably damaged. Here people had time to launch the lifeboats, but the battle would soon be lost – the Teletsians were completely in charge. As he jumped into a lifeboat Lee thought he saw Merien struggling in the water but everything was too chaotic to be sure. A spar fell on Lee's lifeboat, tipped it up and everyone fell in the water. Mariners screamed for help among the flotsam and still the cannon fire kept coming from the Teletsians. The Daish Shaktay ships fought back as best they could and the dolphins pulled them rapidly into position, but they were outclassed in every way. It looked hopeless.

Then it happened. The secret weapon came into play. There was a flurry of white water, a slash of enormous fins, a rolling of bodies in the churning waves and four of the leading Teletsian ships rose out of the water in the middle of a volley. Pushing them up from below were many whales, all surfacing underneath the ships at exactly the same moment. They had been swimming under the surface, tracking the Sorcerers' navy. Their combined strength lifted the ships right out of the sea and then the whales sank down to one side of the ships, which fell sideways as they hit the water and were badly damaged. By this time the whales had submerged and the ships tipped over and foundered. These ships had more metal in them than the Daish Shaktay ones, so sank all the faster.

The sailors in the other Daish Shaktay ships shouted for joy as the next five Teletsian ships met the same fate. Underneath each of them, vast whales surfaced in synchrony, lifting them way out of the water, then they would dive out of sight. One of these ships actually snapped in two, so sank like a stone as it hit the water again. Now the enemy ships further back were also under attack. Some of the Teletsian gun crews on the ships tried to aim their cannons below the water line, but met a different fate as the giant narwhals, with vast tusks, stabbed into the hulls of the ships from underneath, then the long writhing tentacles of giant squids pulled them down.

At random, so the Teletsian ships did not know where to aim their guns, ship after ship was heaved out of the sea by the vast whales, tipped over and left to sink. To these huge creatures the ships were like child's toys. When about two thirds of the Teletsian warships had disappeared beneath the waves, the sea was full of debris and sailors were hanging on to wreckage and crying for help. The remaining ships ran up the white flag of surrender.

Each ship had a Sorcerer on board, supposedly to annihilate any survivors of what they assumed would be an easy victory, and some huge whales appeared and attacked them when they fell into the water. Somehow they knew which the Sorcerers were. The Daish Shaktay mariners and the ordinary Teletsian sailors in the sea were unharmed, and many were supported and pushed towards floating debris by dolphins.

The Daish Shaktay sailors lowered launches to collect up their colleagues and also the Teletsian sailors. Lee was taken on board a ship, and Dan and Hampen, wet but unhurt, but neither Zafan nor Merien could be found. A doctor staunched Lee's arm, which was bleeding heavily, and bound it up. His back had also been badly bruised by a falling spar, but he had no intention of giving up the fight yet.

'We'll take an escort of marines,' he ordered, 'and board all the Teletsian ships in turn. Imprison the sailors and replace their crews with our men, but each enemy ship has at least one Sorcerer on board and I don't trust them at all.'

'Lee, you're wounded,' objected Dan.

'We're in the middle of a battle, in case you hadn't noticed. Carry me to the launch. You'll need my Sasrar key and me to deal with these Sorcerers.' He told the boarding parties to be extra careful to put on a bandhan of protection as they climbed onto the deck of the first Teletsian ship. Lee was carried up onto the deck and put on a stretcher, along with the marines and replacement crews, and the result could have been foreseen.

The Sorcerer came forward to offer surrender but as he approached Lee, Hampen and Dan he tried to reduce them to ashes. Predictably, he himself met this fate as the curse rebounded on him. On almost every ship the same thing happened. It was a long job but finally they finished it. Lee eventually succumbed to his wounds and passed out from pain and exhaustion. His final order was that the captured ships should make for the port of the Island of Creations.

The doctor on one of the ships looked again at Lee's arm and back. Nothing was broken but he needed attention, including a strong sleeping draft to knock him out for some time. When he came round he was back at Lord Jarwhen's mansion, in the sick bay. Lying in the next bed was a bandaged Merien, happy to see Lee conscious.

'How did you get here?' asked Lee, still groggy.

'I was found on the beach. The dolphins supported me and pushed me into the shallows and nearly got washed ashore themselves.' He did not say that next to him was found the body of Zafan. It had been a great victory, but a number of sailors including Zafan had lost their lives.

The troop ships were called from further out to sea, where they had been waiting behind the warships. The captains of all the Daish Shaktay ships and the chief officers on the troop ships were welcomed into the home of Lord Jarwhen, and the sailors and troops were invited into the homes of the islanders. Zafan received a fitting memorial service and a sad message was sent via the dolphins to his relations: his parents on the Emperor's Island, Zafeena his sister in Daish Shaktay, Theon the Master Mariner and Mazdan on their island in the middle of the Sea of Illusion.

'You lost your flying ship,' said Lee to Merien when they were both sitting in the garden a day or two later, convalescing.

'Not to worry,' replied Merien. 'Roarke has promised me a more up-to-date model; he and Derwin have made some major modifications recently. That cousin of yours is quite something as an engineer and inventor, Roarke tells me.'

'I'm glad someone in our family is good at that sort of thing. It's way beyond Asha and me.'

'You have other talents.'

'Like surviving sea battles, but I'm going to miss Zafan terribly.'

CHAPTER 2

FIND HIM!

Soon after the ambassadors had escaped, a woman crept out of the shadows of the yard at the Restorers' palace. She picked up the fallen key belonging to Roarke after the ambassadors had escaped from the Sorcerers' new headquarters in Teletos. She did not touch it but put it in a silken cloth. Long had she wanted to get her hands on one of those keys! It was Drusilla Prospector, who had been watching from her window. She had been expelled from the order of guardians before the others had made the keys, but she still possessed much sinister power and this key would help her use it.

When she was watching the fight she did not know who were guardians because for some reason none of them had golden auras, as she would have expected. She could no longer feel the warm and cool vibrations, so could not test out whether they were powerful spiritually, but realized at least one of them had to be, to wield the key. As she also knew about the prophecy, she had been making plans to avert it. She could imbue people with the evil powers of the Sorcerers, and reckoned if she had one key she could figure out how they worked, and could make some similar, but negatively charged ones for her own use. She wasn't beaten yet: the Queen Wasp could easily regenerate her swarm of lesser wasps and continue to govern Teletsia through the Sorcerers, as she had done for lifetimes.

Drusilla went over to the main building, where the carnage of the evening was being cleared up. She appeared to be a trembling little-old-lady, watching in terror as the medical people collected the body parts. When she tried to get the details of the disaster from the Specials who had been on duty at the time, they could only moan incoherently or make animal noises, as if they were treated slaves. On the table she noticed a letter, spattered with blood. It was from the ambassadors, who, against all codes of diplomacy had murdered the High Priests – that was what would be what would be made public. She picked up the letter and read it. She did not expect to see the names of the female rebels but immediately wondered why Raynor Antiquarian was missing. She suspected all seven were back.

Since her brother, Conwenna's father, had been killed, Drusilla had made the Prospector's flat in the Restorers' mansion more to her liking. She now had a room where she could do black magic, and late that night called for her most helpful spy birds and questioned them. The disembodied souls of humans had been forced into them, so they had human intelligence locked into a bird's body.

'If Raynor Antiquarian is in Teletsia, tell me,' she ordered. The birds cawed.

'Is he with the Pearl Lords?' No sound.

'Is he at Castle Mount?' Silence. Then Drusilla had an inspiration, because she knew he was academically inclined.

'Is he at the university at Gyan-on-Sea?' slight cawing.

'Should I order an extensive search in that area?' The vultures flapped their wings and cawed loudly.

'Find him!' she ordered them. They took off from the roof and flew south.

Derwin told Conwenna he had seen Drusilla at the Restorers' place, now the Sorcerers' headquarters. The next evening, after a harrowing day spent nursing the wounded and attending the cremation of the dead from the naval battle, Conwenna went to see Lord Jarwhen in his study.

'Uncle, can I have a word?' she began.

He had been healing people with vibrations all day and had just finished clearing his own subtle system by putting his feet in a bowl of salty water. A servant took it away and he was relaxing with a book, some poems in praise of Mother Earth written by a famous Teletsian poet many centuries past.

'Come in, my dear. Find a chair that's not covered in papers,' he said with a kindly smile.

'When a Sorcerer tries to annihilate someone with a key and then gets annihilated himself, where does his soul go?' she began.

'To another time/space matrix.'

'Do you think my aunt can annihilate people?'

'Most definitely; she probably taught the Sorcerers that trick in the first place.'

'So the way to permanently fix her would be to get her to try to annihilate someone with a key?'

'I think she'd know if a person had one. Remember, she's been a guardian and may still have the heightened sensitivity we all have. But it's a thought. You're a bright girl, as well as a brave one.' Lord Jarwhen looked at Conwenna intently. She was not the first person to come to him with a similar idea.

Down near Gyan-on-Sea reports were coming in about the naval disaster. Raynor and Garma were called to an officer's meeting in the general's quarters. His name was General Woodenton, because his family came from that area.

'Right, men, at ease,' he began. 'Close the door. What I say here does not leave this room, and anyone disobeying this order will be demoted and possibly sent to the slave farms. A report will be prepared for circulation to the rank and file.'

Raynor and Garma glanced at each other. Obviously something else dramatic had happened. The General itemised all the disasters, much to the delight of Raynor and Garma, who tried to look shocked, but neither of them were very talented actors. Raynor could figure out who was responsible for what, to a certain extent. Throughout the meeting he gave the general vibrations with his attention and was extremely surprised to feel that he was responding. General Woodenton came to the end of his report and Raynor tried to look worried and attentive.

'Almost the entire Teletsian navy has been either sunk or captured, the High Priests on the ships reduced to ashes and the sailors made prisoners in their own boats. The Daish Shaktay navy overpowered our vastly superior one with some immensely damaging secret weapons. They also have a number of troopships with them.

'This regiment will be moved to the outskirts of Teletos to protect the city, as it is assumed the invasion will come there, so be ready to leave at noon tomorrow. Thank you gentlemen, that is all.' As they left the general ordered Raynor and Garma to stay behind and spoke to them further when they were alone.

'I noticed your faces during my report and I've long suspected you two. If you value your lives you'll do the following: first you will demonstrate to me this psychological power you've given to some of the conscripts and then we have other matters to discuss.'

Raynor had never given awakening to anyone under these circumstances, but when he asked on his hands, 'Should I try?' the cool vibrations were definitely flowing. He thought of Tandi and the twins, and realised sadly he would probably never see them again. He never foresaw this would be the way he would incriminate himself but began showing the general how to awaken the Tree of Life. Amazingly, after initially feeling heat pouring out of him, the general experienced inner peace and stillness, and a cool breeze flowing on his hands.

'Is that all?' he demanded.

'Yes sir, that's all we do on the first occasion,' Raynor had no intention of teaching him the two bandhans, because then he would know how the conscripts and awakened souls all over the country were able to withstand the Sorcerers. He continued speaking, giving an abbreviated version of the truth. 'This will give you courage, and you can go into that state of inner peace whenever you sit quietly and put your attention on the top of your head.'

'I certainly need that, at this point in time,' replied the general with a new openness. A change had come over him, and his face had softened and lost its harshness. Garma, sitting behind, was making bandhans of request like he didn't know was possible. Their lives hung on the edge of a cliff, because although Raynor had said as little as possible it was blindingly obvious this was not something that helped the Sorcerers dominate and terrify people. Suddenly the general put his head in his hands. 'It's no good, I've tried to trick you, catch you out.'

'Please, sir, stop,' cried Raynor. 'I know I'm being insubordinate, but please ask Garma to leave the room. This is between you and me, and he is not involved.'

'Go! It's all going to end soon anyway,' moaned the general. Garma stood up to leave and the general turned to Raynor. 'I know who exactly who you are and....'

'Sir please, wait until he has gone,' said Raynor firmly, knowing full well this was absolutely *not* the way one addressed one's commanding officer. The untidy scene became less so when Garma left. General Woodenton motioned to Raynor to sit down. 'I apologise for my rudeness,' Raynor went on, 'but whatever you do to me, I wouldn't want that fate for him.'

'Raynor Antiquarian, like all your friends, you're an exceptionally brave and honourable young man. I was told by my spies that you were not who you said you were some days back, and that you were originally posing as Professor Quair, a visitor from some far off land. Then we received descriptions of you seven and were warned you might be in Teletsia.' Raynor prayed for deliverance, and strangely did not feel terror but rather a calm stillness in his heart. General Woodenton went on, 'Now we're alone we can get down to basics. I didn't give the full story at the officers' meeting. I'm committed to defending my country but I'm fully aware that I've chosen the wrong side. I too went to the Sorcerers' Academy – we all know its popular name – because I wanted to serve my homeland – but unlike you I didn't have the good fortune to find the prophecy and follow its instructions. I was disgusted at what I saw there and left the academy to join the regular army, and now look where it's got me! I've got to lead a lot of reluctant conscripts and a few loyal officers against a foe we cannot defeat, because the very forces of nature are ranged against us. Do you know what the secret weapon was?'

'I have no idea, sir.'

'Whales! And they sank almost half our navy! Do you know how many theoretically invulnerable High Priests have been killed by your people recently?'

'No sir.'

'Twelve in the Forbidden Quarter, thanks to Conwenna Prospector, the youngest of your group, then another twelve at the new headquarters in Teletos, and nearly sixty either killed or drowned at sea. I dread to think what will happen when your land forces invade. After the earthquake and the sinking of the Forbidden Quarter, which was somehow connected with a ritual your people are suspected to have done at the Clatan stone circle, nearly three hundred more were lost. There aren't many left now. Tell me, young man, what am I to do?'

'I'm sure if you surrender our people will show leniency. Forgiveness is one of the cornerstones of our philosophy.'

'If I suggest that to my superiors they'll mesmerise or annihilate me.'

'I think not, sir. I'll show you how to avoid that fate.'

'Impossible. I've just received a top secret message that you're known to be in this area. The new High Priests want to see you, alive, unharmed and unsearched, but with your hands securely tied behind your back.'

'Then you'd better deliver me.' From what Raynor had heard, he gathered that some of us had used the fiery discus option of the keys to finish off a number of the Sorcerers. He hoped to try to do the same and even if they did kill him he could do away with a few of them first. However, General Woodenton had a completely different agenda.

'I'm going to offer you a deal, and am relying on your sincerity and honesty to stand by it,' he begged.

'I'll do what I can to save all of us. Our intention is to transform people, not to kill them unless there's absolutely no alternative.'

'I believe you, although that's not what the propaganda says. If you'll grant me amnesty when your people are in power I'll get you out of here, because only I know who you are. If you go to Teletos you'll be dead, or worse. Their Holinesses won't get caught again like they were by Miss Conwenna or your ambassadors.'

'I'll accept your offer. I can't absolutely promise you immunity from our armed forces but I'll do my best. However, I want my friend Garma to come with me and I want you to send his sister Saray home.'

'I'll agree to that. I'll give you a pass for the Woodenton district. There's a major search on for you around here, so I'll pretend I want you to take some information to the Specials in Woodenton. You'll be taken in a steam car and they'll leave you at my family estate. What you do then is up to you. You and Garma Nalanda leave immediately.'

Raynor thanked the general from the bottom of his heart and went back to his room, where Garma was waiting on tenterhooks. He explained the situation, but unknown to them a large bird, Drusilla's vulture, was hovering outside the room where they were talking. It heard every word and immediately flew back to Teletos.

They left the barracks under cover of night. Drusilla's other vulture was spying on them and followed their steam car all the way to Woodenton. It noticed when Raynor and Garma were dropped at the Woodenton's luxurious mansion, set in extensive pleasure grounds, the following evening and returned to Drusilla in Teletos as fast as it could fly.

Raynor presented his credentials to the Woodenton's gate keeper and explained he had to go into Woodenton the next morning to deliver some documents to the local Specials Office, but General Woodenton had suggested they spent the night with his family. They were taken to the gracious country seat, introduced to Lady Woodenton and Raynor gave her a letter from her husband. The sons and daughter had been conscripted and were not there. Raynor felt her vibrations – not very good – and decided it was too risky to give her awakening. They ate supper and were afterwards shown into a comfortable room, where they were left alone.

'There's a safe house somewhere round here belonging to a family of woodcutters,' began Raynor.

'How are we going to find it?' asked Garma.

'Look on my map.' Raynor spread it out on his bed.

'I don't see anything.'

'Watch!' Raynor made a bandhan over the map with his Sasrar key, the location of the safe house appeared for a short time and they plotted their route. Gradually it faded away. 'In the letter to his wife the general said she should lend us a couple of horses. We'll take up the offer and go tomorrow morning.'

'Don't you think we should leave now?'

'If we do we won't have any horses and furthermore it will look very suspicious.'

The first vulture had reached Drusilla's roof terrace earlier that day.

'Did you find him?' there was a caw from the vulture.

'Is he at Gyan-on-Sea?' no caws, and so on.

After some time Drusilla discovered they were going to the Woodenton's estate. Then she sent this vulture out again, to Woodenton.

In the late evening a light signal was picked up by the Woodenton Specials. The order came from the very top and said a Class One Traitor was with the family of General Woodenton at Woodenton Park, and was to be detained and delivered to the High Priests at Teletos as soon as possible. After the disaster with Lakriman Woodseller, the Woodenton Specials were not totally enthusiastic about this and decided to leave everything until the following morning, when their boss would be in.

Later two spy vultures landed on the front porch of the Specials Office and were very agitated about something, but the night shift Specials were tired and lazy, and could not be bothered to raise the local Truthsayer, who could communicate with them. At dawn the day shift Specials came on duty and when they learnt about the message from the light signal, sent a patrol out to Woodenton Park without waiting for their boss to arrive. *They* didn't want to get into trouble for having let a Class One Traitor slip through their fingers.

At Woodenton Park, Raynor and Garma ate breakfast as early as they could, hurried out to the stables and found two horses waiting, ready saddled for them. Raynor was about to mount up when a servant came out and asked if he could go back to the house for a moment. Garma waited and waited, and eventually asked the servant where he was.

'Oh, some people turned up in a steam car from the Specials Office in Woodenton and insisted he went with them. Lady Woodenton knew you had to deliver some information to them so she called Raynor. Didn't anyone come and get you?'

'No, but it's all right,' Garma tried to look casual, 'we arranged to meet up in town. I'll lead his horse.' He mounted and left by the main gate but turned left towards the nearby woodlands, not right in the direction of the town. Once out of sight he broke into a gallop, dragging the second horse with him. When he was well away from the country estate he dismounted, changed out of his uniform and left the extra horse in a field.

Chapter 3

Preparations

'We've got the advantage but we must move fast,' began Rajay, as we sat in the Operations Room in Lord Jarwhen's home on the Island, the day after the sea battle. 'We now have nearly five thousand Daish Shaktay fighters here.'

'We also have partisans all over the country,' put in Stellamar, 'but the problem will be to contact them.'

'I have some hawks which will home onto the safe houses,' Lord Jarwhen mentioned, 'but it won't be easy for the partisans to find the main army.'

'Erin Heber's men are waiting for our call, at Castle Mount,' said Derwin, 'and Roarke and I could alert a lot of groups in our flyers.'

'I've already sent a message to Vittalia, via the dolphins, to send another small flyer for Merien, if he's well enough to pilot it,' added Roarke.

Rajay stood up, took a piece of writing charcoal and went over to one of the wall maps.

'If you were going to invade a country, where would you go for?' he asked.

'Teletos, the capital,' said Lee.

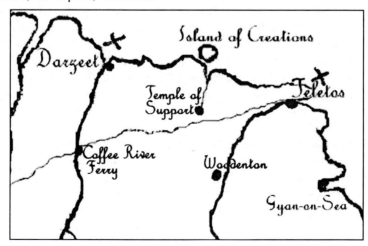

'Exactly,' continued Rajay. 'Now, we know the Sorcerers have large sea birds, albatrosses, spying for them, so they can figure out the position of our shipping. They know I've sent you some troop ships full of soldiers, so we'll send these ships, minus the soldiers, in the direction of the Teletos estuary. They'll stop and wait here,' he made a cross on the map off the east coast of Teletsia.

'Meanwhile, we'll get down to the real business of invading Teletsia, from here.' Rajay put a cross near Darzeet, 'Is that doable?'

'It's your navy and they're your men,' said Lee.

'I take it we're all in favour?' Rajay looked at everyone. 'Fine, then we'll go for it.'

The following morning Pa Ganoozal announced that about three hundred men from the Island had offered to dress as Daish Shaktay soldiers and marines, and go on the troop ships to make the fake invasion force look more genuine. They were to be kitted out in the brown and green uniform of the Daish Shaktay army, and the neat brown and blue of the navy. These ships left the following morning, accompanied by some warships bristling with guns and a number of large whales making themselves very obvious, in case any boat from Teletsia should contemplate attacking them.

Roarke and Derwin set off in their flyers to raise the Resistance Groups and partisans. Roarke went to the ones on the eastern shore to tell them to start destroying the Specials in the towns and villages, if they could, and to be alert and ready. He gave everyone their awakening who had not already had it, distributed a number of four petalled keys and showed the leaders how to use them for protection and defence. There were some violent storms on the east coast in the next day or two – very localised and not long lasting, but they enabled Roarke to get to where he wanted without being seen. He had a fistful of fake travel documents in case he was stopped by any Specials and hoped he would be able to hide the flyer, because they could not afford to lose another. In the event he was all right because he did not stop anywhere for long.

Derwin flew first to the family on the lonely stretch of coast near Darzeet that Merien and Asha had visited, and then turned inland. He stopped at two safe houses and told the local partisans what was happening, gave awakening to two more large groups of people and left a four petalled key with the leader of each one. He only took off for the Woodenton area, on his way to Castle Mount, after nightfall.

It was evening when Garma finally reached the Woodseller's home. He got lost twice and found the place as the sun was setting. He was not stopped by any roadblocks, fortunately, because his travel pass was for Woodenton, not the woodland areas around it. He saw one roadblock but managed to avoid it by taking to the fields and persuading his horse to leap a wide boundary stream.

Lakriman Woodseller was by now quite accustomed to freedom fighters dropping in unexpectedly, and at least this one did not come in a flying machine. As long as they showed the four petalled key that was good enough for him. He hid Garma's horse in a woodshed, after which Mrs Woodseller gave him supper and showed him to the hidden room in their attic. He immediately fell asleep but in the middle of the night woke up when someone crept into the other bed. He could see, by the light of a candle, a boy making a bandhan of protection over himself.

'Who are you?' asked Garma.

'I was going to ask the same thing,' replied Derwin.

'I'm a friend of Raynor Antiquarian,' and the whole story came out.

'This is incredibly serious, but I don't know what to do. I've absolutely got to get a message to Castle Mount, where Duke Heber and his men are waiting for the word to join us. As it is I'm taking a major risk by flying in daylight, because if I get caught and don't deliver the message we could be in deep trouble. The army we're bringing from Daish Shaktay and the total number of partisans are not large, compared to the Teletsian Sorcerers' troops.'

'Did you say fly? Have you got one of those flying machines Raynor told me about?'

'Yes, why?'

'Because if so, we could try to rescue him right now. He might still be in Woodenton and together we'd have a chance. I've got a gun and a sword, and a four petalled key which will protect me from annihilation, and can pass myself off as an army officer. Do you have any weapons – and one of those Sasrar keys?'

'Yes I do. Man, I'm tired! But give me some vibrations and I'll make it, if it means we can rescue Raynor.'

Soon after this Derwin and Garma landed in a copse near Woodenton and Derwin hid the flyer as best he could. Garma was an officer on leave, Derwin was posing as his friend and they were enquiring about his lost horse they had been looking for all night. They walked into the Specials Post having made every bandhan they could, but the Specials on duty were not on the front desk. Derwin could hear them talking in a back room.

'….Raynor Antiquarian, no less,' said one, 'he should be in Teletos by now. Their Holinesses are getting quite frantic, what with the Forbidden Quarter drowned and two groups of Head High Priests murdered.'

'There are plenty more to take over,' added the other Special. 'They'll get a lot of information out of this Raynor chap. There won't be much left of him, mentally or physically, by the time they're done with him.' Derwin and Garma had heard as much as was necessary. They crept out and flew back to the Woodsellers, reached there as the sun was rising, landed in the hilly woodland and hoped they had not been spotted.

'Derwin, you go to Castle Mount. I'll get to the Pearl Lords as fast as I can and tell them about Raynor.'

'It's cool on my hands when you say that.'

Derwin gave Garma his pouch of gold Telets so he could change horses frequently and travel more quickly. They said goodbye, hoped to meet again somewhere and Garma galloped north on the Woodenton's horse. After he had gone Derwin explained everything to Lakriman Woodseller. Lakriman said he would contact all the people he knew who opposed the Sorcerers' regime and assured Derwin that the young and able bodied would now actively start to attack the Specials and Sorcerers. Derwin had some sleep then flew south.

On the same day, Dan, now commanding a number of ships from the Daish Shaktay navy, left the Island of Creations and sailed north. The next day the lookout on the *Prince Enithar,* named after Rajay's son, espied a flying ship approaching at great speed. It landed on the deck and two people got out – Merien and a tall girl with thick dark hair and a fair skin. They were shown into the Captain's cabin.

'Merien, what are you doing here?' Robin began. 'You're supposed to be off sick. And how did you get here?'

'Get a few guardians together giving vibrations and it's amazing how quickly I got better!' he grinned. 'This is Marimba, Roarke's sister. She's brought me a new flyer and it's much better than the other!'

'A pleasure to meet you,' said Rajay, indicating for her to sit down.

'And you too,' replied Marimba, with a radiant smile to match Rajay's own. 'I couldn't make it to your coronation, because my parents needed me to do some delicate diplomatic work.'

'Roarke told me, but how come you brought the flyer? I thought you lived in the countryside?'

'I do, but that doesn't mean I can't pilot flyers. It runs in the family – plus the key does nearly all of it. I've also brought you something else.' The sailor who had shown them in put a large bag on the table. Out of it Marimba took

a coconut, dried and polished, with a silver rim and small holes in the shell.

'Whatever is this?' asked Rajay.

'It's something my father has perfected recently,' explained Marimba. 'You can talk to anyone else who has one, regardless of where they are on the earth. You tap a specific code on the top, then hold it to your ear and whoever you're contacting can hear you and respond. Or you say their name, once you've tapped in the right code and they'll hear you if they're near their nut. Very useful if you need to communicate during military operations.'

She showed them that each coconut had a specific 'tune' or rhythm and this was written around the circumference. She also explained that they needed to be put in the sunlight regularly to renew the power which enabled them to make contact with other nuts.

'You Vittalia guardians are incredible!' Rajay exclaimed. 'Still, you are from the subtle centre that governs communications and the ether element. Just when we're in dire need of something like this! I remember something similar on the world we came from. How can we thank you?'

'By freeing Teletsia, then all of us with awakened Trees of Life will be in less pain! I've brought – let's see – there are twelve here. I've got another sack of them back at the Island.'

'How did you get here so soon?'

'This new flyer is very fast, and I put it on automatic for most of the way, so I could get some sleep.'

'I wish we could get some coconuts to Derwin, because it's the mountain people we need to be in touch with more than anyone.'

'I intend to do that,' put in Merien. 'I'll drop Marimba back on the Island, and then try to find Derwin and Erin Heber.'

Raynor's hands were tied behind him when he was captured at the Woodenton's and he was thrown into the back of the steam car. A guard was with him at all times and eventually they reached Teletos. 'What a homecoming!' he thought grimly as they crossed the bridge from the mainland. He remembered when they had last been there and his dog Nog had found them on their way to the Temple of Support, over five years before.

Later, Raynor was forced to get out and immediately recognised the yard of Lee's family home. He was marched up the stairs to the Prospectors' apartment and pushed into a small dark room with appalling vibrations. He felt hands grope around his neck and remove his keys.

Eventually someone came in and unlocked his handcuffs, relieving the stiff agony of his arms. In front of him was a middle aged woman and he also recognised her – Drusilla Prospector. Raynor, like most people, did not find Drusilla a particularly amiable woman, but he always tried to find some good in everyone and almost always forgave people their shortcomings.

'Hello Raynor. It's been a long time. They wanted to crack open your mind straight away but I persuaded them not to. Would you like to wash and change?'

'Yes, but what are you doing here?' said Raynor. 'It looks as though this place had been taken over by the Sorcerers.'

'It has, but they allow me to stay. You're quite safe with me though, for the time being.'

CHAPTER 4

DARZEET

Journal of Malvog, Replacement Scribe to Their Holinesses

I, Malvog, replacement scribe to Their Holinesses the Protectors of the State, do hereby report an Emergency Meeting in the mansion of the Restorer family, now taken over by the state for the defence of the realm.

'The Daish Shaktay troop ships are approaching Teletos,' began the new Head of the Special Secret Police, 'and a report has just reached us of a force from Castle Mount coming north via Coffee River.'

'Some of the Daish Shaktay warships are sailing away northwards,' added the High Priest of Ports, Naval Matters and Shipping.

'These traitors from Castle Mount will probably leave the river at the Coffee River Ferry,' said the Head of the Special Secret Police Force. 'The Darzeet Regiment is being sent there to destroy them.'

'We should be able to counter the attackers with our never-miss guns. What can their primitive guns and bows and arrows do against our superior fire power?' insisted the Chief Priest for War and Weaponry.

'We've got a problem,' continued the Master of the Intelligence Network. 'In a number of areas the conscripts can't be mesmerised and we can't read their minds. They say they're eager to defend the homeland but there's something wrong.'

'Easy solution to that one,' continued the new Head of the Special Secret Police. 'Put them in the front of the armies and they will be the first to suffer from the onslaught of the enemy.'

'We must destroy the invading armies with our subtle powers. This is how we have controlled Teletsia for generations,' asserted the Master of Annihilations.

'How come so many of the High Priests have themselves finished up heaps of ashes recently?' objected the Chief Priest for War and Weaponry.

'That problem will soon be resolved. The Great One now has some of the magic keys and she will soon learn how to combat this alien sorcery,' concluded the Master of Annihilations.

Some way out to sea the navy was transformed. The spick and span warships now looked like run down traders manned by slovenly sailors. The guns had been rolled in, the gun ports closed and disguised, some of the sails had holes in them, the decks were untidy and vulgar women were wandering about talking and laughing with the men, something which would never be allowed in the Daish Shaktay navy. Other sailors were lying around periodically swigging from bottles and still others were smoking something, which from their behaviour would appear to be a powerful drug.

They were all, including the women, sailors dressed up and issued with the necessary equipment. There was great amusement when they were told those were their orders, straight from His Majesty. The ships were flying the flags of Tong in the east, Subersk in the north and Equitoria near the equator in the west, and these craft were a threat to no one except themselves. It would be a miracle if any of them got home in one piece. The many soldiers on board hid beneath the decks.

The Daish Shaktay fleet, thus disguised, turned round and neared the coast of Teletsia. Some large white seabirds appeared and briefly hovered near the ships, luckily after the sailors had completed the transformation. They reported back to their controlling Sorcerers that the Daish Shaktay navy had sailed out of the area but a convoy of merchant ships was approaching.

Saman, the failed assassin whose family were businessmen, had often gone to Darzeet with his father on business, and knew the whereabouts of the safe houses in that area, each with Resistance Group members only too eager to go to war against the Sorcerers. A small force of about a hundred veterans of Rajay's own freedom struggle landed on a deserted beach to the east of Darzeet in the middle of the night, dropped off by launches from the disguised naval ships. Saman and Ahren were in charge, and everyone was dressed to look like Teletsian country people. They had two contact-coconuts, one for Saman and another for Ahren, and their job was to mobilise the Resistance Groups, gather information about the Teletsian forces, destroy as many Sorcerers and Specials as they could, and make their way to the Temple of Support. They had also to set up supply lines and ask farmers sympathetic to the freedom struggle to be prepared to sell food when the army invaded.

'I'll be in touch with you via the coconuts,' said Rajay to Ahren as they bid each other goodbye.

A number of sailors in the Daish Shaktay navy had been galley slaves and were from far off countries. When Zafan had captured the Mattangan navy from Port Volcan they had opted to stay and work for Daish Shaktay rather than make their way across the world to lands they had not seen for years. Some were tall men from the north with broad shoulders, blond hair and beards, some were short in stature and black skinned and others came from Tong, famous for its clever businessmen and the homeland of the brilliant Daish Shaktay Finance Minister, Lord Witten of Rivers Mouth Port. Like him they had dark brown skins and narrow eyes, round smiling faces and spoke the common speech with a curious sing-song accent. They were ideal for the plan Rajay had for capturing Darzeet, the largest town in northern Teletsia.

The *Spicy Coffee*, initially a warship called *Lucky Escape*, and now disguised as a trading barque, was the first of these ships to put in at Darzeet. She was flying the flag of Tong – a red sun on a blue background, and the sun was portrayed as a round smiling face with narrow eyes, like the people of Tong. The vessel sailed into the harbour past the fort, which was built high on the headland at its entrance. No one thought to stop a trader about to bring some much needed business to Teletsia, especially as it was the season when many barges were coming down the river from the highlands further south, laden with sacks of coffee beans, raw rubber and the valuable bark which cured the most dreaded tropical fever when made into a medicine.

The captain of the *Spicy Coffee* was Hampen the Tong, whose original ship had been sunk in the naval battle. Rajay was sharing the captain's cabin with him and discovered that his father had been an admiral in Tong. He had followed his father into the Tong navy but had been captured in the first action he fought in and subsequently sold as a slave to Mattanga. He had been noticed and promoted within weeks of joining the Daish Shaktay navy, because he was brave and intelligent, tireless in the performance of his duty, an excellent mariner and also a very spiritual person who made all his decisions with the help of the vibrations.

Hampen, pretending to be a businessman from Tong, had letters of introduction to Mr Coffeeman, the largest coffee trader in town. He presented his credentials (forged) and was most put out when the Special at the Port Authority warned that Coffeeman's eldest son was a known rebel, wanted by the authorities, and hadn't been seen for weeks. Hampen questioned the Special closely – was it advisable to do business with a man whose son was suspect? The Special replied that the father was considered reliable, by which he meant that he paid his taxes and necessary bribes, and Hampen was alright with him, as long as he did not get involved with the son. The Special directed Hampen to the Coffeeman mansion on the waterfront. Hampen knew that Coff's father, though not a member of a Resistance Group, was sympathetic to his son's political ideals and once in the privacy of Mr Coffeeman's office, Hampen asked if Coff was there.

'Yes, he's waiting for you. He noticed His Majesty on the deck of your ship.' He led Hampen to a room in the attic where Coff was standing looking out of the window at *The Spicy Coffee,* moored by the quayside not far away. Hampen showed Coff his four petalled key and told him to come to the ship, where Rajay was waiting for him. Soon afterwards Hampen left with a tall veiled woman, her face mostly covered and only her eyes visible, carrying a basket of medicinal herbs.

'Good to see you, Coff,' Rajay welcomed the veiled woman into the captain's cabin. 'Glad you made it home all right.'

'It helps to have friends who are Coffee River barge owners,' explained Coff, taking off the veil.

'The Daish Shaktay navy is lying off the coast, disguised as a convoy of run-down trading vessels. We intend to enter the harbour and attack the fort, those buildings containing people hostile to free Teletsia, and the Specials' Offices. We need you to do a few things for us. Firstly, is there any chance of putting the guards and lookouts at the fort out of action? Secondly, you must warn anyone you know who is against the Sorcerers to put white sheets out of their windows when we start attacking, so we don't bombard their homes, and thirdly, can you round up as many resistance fighters as possible? A number of our men have booked into the Harbour Hotel, posing as merchants, and they're here to help you fight the Specials.'

'Your Highness, I can try, because I'm the coordinator of the Resistance Groups in Darzeet, but there's a strong garrison in the fort and a lot of them are conscripts, many of whom don't want to fight. Some are our partisans but they felt it better to obey the call up. If you reduce the fort to rubble you're going to kill many of them, but if you don't capture it the garrison will blast your ships to smithereens, and you won't be able to take the town, because as you can see, the fort overlooks the harbour.'

'How many in the fort are on our side?'

'About three hundred, but about twice as many will either support the Sorcerers or remain neutral.'

'Coff, give me some time. I'll meditate and pray for inspiration.'

'I know I'm not a tenth as powerful as you spiritually, but I'll join you.'

'Don't say that - your vibrations are excellent now, and you're just as likely to have a good idea.' They sat in silent bliss but no inspiration came.

'Call Robin and Namoh,' said Rajay. They were in the Officers' Cabin playing chess. Robin was faring badly and was happy to escape his inevitable defeat by answering Rajay's summons.

'What would happen if we could get our people to a safe distance and then someone on the inside blew up the arsenal, which is in the cellars below the fort?' asked Coff.

'Do you have any idea how large the blast would be?' said Robin. 'You'd destroy half the town too.'

'Maybe not,' continued Coff. 'We have a man working for the light signallers and he received a message from Teletos last week to move most of the troops from here down to Coffee River Ferry. They went some days ago and took a great deal of ammunition and weapons from the fort.'

'Interesting,' observed Rajay.

'I'll pretend to be a visiting dignitary,' suggested Robin, 'and try to get into the fort, then we'll see what can be done. We'll dye my hair blond and I'll pretend to be Prince Hal of Subersk, where these fair-haired chaps on board come from. Prince Hal is a guardian and I'm sure he wouldn't mind my impersonating him. I'll blow up that fort, if anyone can.'

'If you say so,' Rajay rubbed the fourth finger on his right hand, which corresponded to the ego.

'Perhaps that was a little arrogant. Let's say I'll give it my best try.'

'We're all in the hands of fate, my friend.'

Rajay gave Coff a coconut and told him to let them know how things were developing. He returned home veiled, cloaked and carrying his basket.

'That was vital information Coff gave us,' said Robin. 'Hampen had better buy some coffee, because this is going to take a day or two to set up and we don't want our enemies getting suspicious about us.'

'Yes, and we must get word to Erin Heber about those troops at Coffee River Ferry,' Rajay tapped in the rhythm on his coconut to raise Merien, wherever he was.

'Merien, is that you?' began Rajay when he heard his voice.

'Yes, how's it going?'

'Alright so far. Where are you?'

'Looking for Derwin and Erin - I'm flying down the Coffee River. They're getting close to the end of the jungles and Erin's force is on coffee barges, I'm told. Trouble is there are so many barges going down the river right now, and I can't locate Erin's, so far. I've been seen in a stack of places asking their whereabouts.'

'You've got to find them before they get to Coffee River Ferry. There's a large force of Teletsian troops there.'

'I'll do my utmost. I stopped at the Woodseller's safe house and I've got bad news. Derwin and a friend of Raynor's had been there and Raynor has been captured and taken to Teletos. I contacted the people on the Island...'
The connection was cut. Merien had forgotten to recharge his coconut by putting it in the sunlight. Rajay took a deep breath; he had been about to tell Merien to contact Roarke for instructions on how to use his keys to find Derwin. He put his attention on Raynor and felt fear. He sighed, but had to go on contacting people and the next was Ahren, somewhere in the countryside fairly nearby.

'How are you getting on?' Rajay asked.

'Excellent. We haven't been seen by any patrols or roadblocks and I now have over two hundred partisans with me. Saman has collected up another hundred or so; I'm in touch with him on the coconut. These nuts make all the difference! Also, there'll be no problem with food – the safe house owners have already stockpiled plenty of supplies. They've offered us horses, and the partisans have their own, but they're difficult to hide and can't go through the woods, so at present we're moving on foot, mostly.'

Rajay explained about the troops waiting at Coffee Ferry then closed the connection by tapping on the bottom of the nut. This was a totally new way of fighting a war, but there were still many difficulties. He put his coconut to recharge in the afternoon sun, shining in through the stern window.

CHAPTER 5

SOME GOOD LUCK

Merien was getting desperate. He had flown to Castle Mount, where he had discovered that Derwin had arrived before him and left with Erin Heber and the army, in barges. The next day Merien asked the owners of nine strings of barges if they had any idea where Duke Heber and the army were. The barge owners were all supporters of Erin and the answer was always the same – 'They're further downstream.' Merien was chased by tribals when he picked up his flyer from its hiding place one time and later was nearly bitten by a snake when he inadvertently stood on its tail in the jungle. Fortunately he was wearing his knee high leather sea boots so was unharmed. He was also shot at by some Specials.

In the evening he spied a convoy of barges moored on the riverbank, perilously near Coffee River Ferry. He had a Sasrar key and his own third centre key, but he was weak and exhausted as he had not fully recovered his strength. He landed his flyer in a jungle clearing, staggered to the river and called through his third centre key. After a short while a river dolphin popped its head out of the water and Merien asked whether it had seen the soldiers in barges. The dolphin didn't understand the word soldiers, but replied that it had seen a great number of men get off the barges carrying metal sticks. It said a girl on a boat had met them. Dolphins, like humans, liked to gossip, and those from further downstream had sent a message saying there were many more men with metal sticks near the ferry.

Merien made his way back to the flyer and saw some men looking at it. In the dusk he could not see if they wore the Specials' uniform, so he melted into the trees and felt their vibrations – quite good - then approached slowly.

'Hello,' said one, a tribal with red hair and a squat body. 'We're from the local Resistance Group. I've seen one of these before – they fly, don't they?'

'Yes.'

'Are you one of these aliens from another dimension who are going to help us get rid of the Sorcerers?'

Merien didn't know whether he was joking, or very intuitive, but answered as best he could. 'Um – I'm definitely part of part of your freedom struggle, and right now I'm looking for Duke Heber and his force.'

'They got a message from a girl who came up from Coffee Ferry Inn. She warned them to leave the river because there's a big force of Sorcerers' men there.'

'Thank god! Where have they gone?'

'That way,' he nodded eastwards. 'They're making for some place beyond Panvale so I drew them a map and showed them the jungle paths. There was a boy with them in one of these flying things. He had it stowed on a barge, but flew off towards the north.'

'When did the soldiers leave?'

'About midday, why?'

'I must contact the duke.'

'I told him to make for a hilltop that used to be a fort. You'll see it if you're up in the air, because it's rocky and bare of trees. Good place for them to spend the night.'

'Thanks for your help.' Merien's heart was at rest for the first time in days. He got in his flyer, took off in the direction of the fort and soon saw campfires. He landed, a man recognised him and he was taken to Duke Heber's tent. Erin was enjoying every moment of his journey to war.

'Come in, Merien. Supper?'

'Yes, that would be most welcome. Who warned you to leave the river?'

'A girl called Fern Innkeeper, from Coffee Ferry Inn. It's a safe house - did you know?'

'Yes, I did.'

A soldier brought in some trays of meat, bread, fruit and nuts.

'Here's the food. Simple, but it will do.'

'Thanks, I'm starving. Where's Derwin gone?'

'Back to the Island. He told me to make for the Temple of Support and left a big bag of four-petalled keys for my men.'

'I've also got something very useful for you.'

'What's that?'

'A coconut,' and Merien took it out of his shoulder bag.

'Whatever's that for?' Erin was most amused.

'I'll show you. You won't believe it until we try it out.' They called Rajay, who reminded Merien to charge up his nut. Erin was astounded but realised its value straight away.

The next morning, Erin told Merien the route he intended to take to the Temple of Support. He would hide in the jungles as much as possible and try to take out the Specials and Sorcerers in the small towns and villages on the way. Merien left to find Fern Innkeeper. He flew downstream and landed some distance from the inn. Then he put a pack on his back so as to look like a traveller, walked to the inn and found it full of officers.

'Hello, can I help you?' asked Mrs Innkeeper, on the front desk. Merien took his four petalled key from under his shirt, making sure no officers saw it, although Mrs Innkeeper did and understood. 'Follow me, sir,' she said and led him down a passage. 'Fern, this gentleman's for you,' she shouted.

A girl of about Conwenna's age appeared. She had the usual slightly aquiline nose and green eyes of so many Teletsians but her dark brown hair had a rusty tinge, indicating that there were some tribal people in her ancestry. She showed Merien into their living room.

'Miss Innkeeper, you've just saved many people's lives. You're a heroine.'

'Really? Who knows? Not too many people, I hope,' she replied tersely. Merien explained about the plan to get as many armed partisans as possible to the Temple of Support, and asked how she knew about Erin Heber. She said the coffee bargemen had told her he and his army were coming down the river and it didn't take much intelligence to figure out that meeting a Sorcerers' regiment wasn't going to help them any.

'I have a request for you. Fairly soon these troops are going to realise that Duke Heber has slipped past them and then they'll follow him. If we know where the Sorcerer's troops are we could ambush them rather than having them ambush him.'

'I'll do my best,' Fern was less bristly now, 'but how do I get the information to you?'

'That's why I came to see you.'

Merien gave her a coconut and showed her how to use it. After that he left, mission accomplished, and made his way back to the navy north of Darzeet.

Derwin returned to the Island, where he met Marimba. She gave him some coconuts and he set off again to deliver them. First he flew to the safe house farm near Teletos. He crept warily towards the farm late at night and the barking of the dogs brought out the sleepy farmer.

'Hello,' he said, 'you mustn't stay long. The Specials have come round so many times recently, because your flyer was seen near here last time you came.' He invited Derwin into the kitchen.

'Could you take something to Teletos?' Derwin asked when they were sitting round the table.

'No problem. We've been ordered to take a lot of produce there, in case it's besieged. The Specials and Sorcerers are storing food. The ordinary people won't see any, you can be sure of that.'

'I need to get something to the Jeweller's Quarter, but first I must show whoever takes it how it works.'

'Don't look at me! I'm useless with anything more complicated than a water wheel. My eldest son now.... He loves this new-fangled stuff...'

The son was pulled out of bed; Derwin showed him how to use the coconut and he promised to deliver it to Sparkly Diamondcutter the very next day. It was nearly dawn when Derwin left and flew out to sea, and as the sun rose he spotted the troop ships with their escort of warships and whales. Some large seabirds with dreadful vibrations wheeled over the ships - obviously spies. He laughed, because it would help if they reported to the Sorcerers that the troop ships were waiting to invade. Pa Ganoozal, dressed in the uniform of a Daish Shaktay general, was strutting around the deck.

'Good to see you, Derwin,' he began, 'what brings you here?'

Derwin again demonstrated a coconut, this time over a breakfast of fried fish.

'Listen lad,' said Pa Ganoozal after he had called his wife on the Island, to check the nut was working, 'I didn't tell my good lady, but we fully intend to go into Teletos and fight when the time is right. Now we've got the coconut we'll await orders. Who's coordinating operations?'

'Rajay, and I know he needs more troops.'

'I'll talk to him later.'

'Does Lord Jarwhen know about this?'

'Before we left, he said, "Jack, do what you want, as long as it's a collective decision – you're also a guardian." My men have all agreed that if young Conwenna can risk her life for Teletsia so can we.'

That night, Derwin went back to the Island to await developments.

Meanwhile over at Darzeet events were taking an interesting turn. The next day Rajay was in his cabin talking to Coff via the coconuts, Coff being nearby, in his house on the quay. Rajay was chuckling and looking at Hampen, who was trying not to overhear but at the same time longing to. Rajay finished his conversation and cut the contact.

'Did you ever think of getting married?' he asked Hampen.

'Your Majesty, I'm saving up for that, but I want to buy a house first, at Rivers Mouth Port. I'd like to marry someone who comes from a similar level of society as I did, and no naval officer would want his daughter to marry a pauper. Your salary is very generous but I started with nothing when Admiral Zafan saved us from the Mattangan galleys, so it's taking time.'

'My situation was, in a way, similar. I had to win my kingdom first. Having done so, I used the vibrations to ask if Her Majesty and I were right each other, even before I met her. You all know what a success our marriage has been. Feel the vibrations with me on what's in my attention right now.'

'Very cool!' said Hampen.

'Yes, it is. Coff's cousin Amara is a member of their Resistance Group and has given him a wealth of useful information, because her father is the commander of the fort. Recently her parents have been trying to marry her off but she's refused all the young men they've suggested. Coff has been in touch with her and they've had an idea which might enable us to get into the fort. She's told her father that if he can arrange something very old fashioned, a marriage contest, she'll marry one of the contenders. Her father is delighted that for once his daughter is being cooperative and he's even prepared to give a big dowry as an added incentive.

'There's going to be a reception at the fort tomorrow, where she'll meet any prospective bridegrooms, and the next day anyone who's interested has to pass the tests. Those who do so are eligible for her hand, and she'll put a garland on the one she wants as her husband.'

'Sounds like a fairy story! What are the tests?' Hampen could see where this was going. When he signed up for the Daish Shaktay navy he knew he might have to give his life for his adopted country, but he never foresaw this.

'The bridegroom has to hold his own in hand-to-hand combat against one of Commander Cholarta's personal trainers, and then must hit a target with both a pistol and a bow and arrow. The commander doesn't want his daughter marrying a wimp, as he puts it. I can get an invitation for Robin, who'll be posing as Prince Hal of Subersk, and he'll take a number of friends along with him.' They could see the fort from where they were anchored. It was across the large harbour and a park around it covered the rest of the headland. Hampen thought he was off the hook.

'With respect, Your Majesty, might it not become complicated when they discover Robin is only pretending to be the prince? Added to which he's already married.' He had met me, and although he knew I would go a long way for my country, wasn't sure it would include putting up with a co-wife.

'That's not what I had in mind. How about you trying for her hand?' Hampen's original suspicion was correct, he realised.

'But sire, as I explained, I'm not in the league to marry a fort commander's daughter. I'm only a freed slave.'

'The vibrations indicate that she'd be an excellent wife for you. That's what we both asked just now. You'd be well matched if I promote you to admiral, with all the perks, right now,' pleaded Rajay.

'Alright, sire, if you say so, and thank you very, very much for the promotion.'

'You deserve it. We need to get into that fort and this is the way to do it. You're the type of man I like to have working for me. You say yes and get on with the job,' Rajay laughed and slapped Hampen on the back.

'It's a pleasure, Your Majesty.'

'By the way, as a native of Tong I assume you can wrestle? And shoot straight?'

'Yes, wrestling is our national sport and I'm not too bad at shooting. Only Ahren out performs me every time. No one can match him, as I discovered on the Island of Creations.'

Rajay contacted Coff. Amara had been given her awakening and Coff met her at a coffee shop which was a safe house. He did the same as Rajay and asked her to feel the vibrations on what he was thinking. When it was cool he told her he had found her the perfect husband and sang Hampen's praises. She said she would do anything to free Teletsia of the Sorcerers, but didn't expect Hampen to take the marriage seriously.

CHAPTER 6

THE MARRIAGE CONTEST

Rajay was in his cabin with Robin, who now had dyed blond hair and was posing as Prince Hal of Subersk.

'I'm not coming to the fort. I've already been recognised in Darzeet, last time I was here,' began Rajay. 'I've lent Hampen some smart clothes, but I hope they aren't *too* smart!'

'Maybe we'd better swap – his turban jewel is far larger than mine and I'm the one who's supposed to be the prince.'

'Hampen can say he comes from a wealthy family, which is true. He's nervous though - it's a big thing, meeting your intended for the first time. I speak from personal experience!'

'Coff says she's a delightful girl. By the way, do you know why Hampen never went home to Tong?'

'I assumed it was because we offered him a good job in our navy.'

'That's not the whole story. He was ashamed at having been captured and sold as a slave. A question of honour, because the men of Tong fight to the death rather than surrendering or being taken alive.'

'Their loss is our gain. You'd better leave; the launch is waiting.'

At the Coffee Ferry Inn, Fern and her mother were in the front parlour cleaning up and a couple of Sorcerers walked in. The women stood up as they approached.

'We need to search your premises,' demanded one. 'We'll start with your private living area. Take us there,' he pointed at Fern. 'And you,' he nodded at her mother, 'sit down. We want to ask you a few questions.' Fern led the first Sorcerer to the back, praying he would not find anything incriminating. All went well until they came to her room, and on the window sill was her coconut, charging up in the sun. The Sorcerer saw it and picked it up.

'What's this?' he demanded.

'Oh, just an ornament one of the guests gave me.'

'Hmm,' he grunted suspiciously and shook it. 'Very unusual ornament.'

He put it down and went on searching the room. At that moment Ahren contacted Fern.

'Hello, Fern, it's Ahren. Are you there?' he called, and the Sorcerer spun round to see the source of the voice. Fern had to act fast or he might give away vital information. She grabbed the coconut and tapped the bottom to cut the connection.

'Just an ornament, you say? I think I'll have that.' Before he took it Fern managed to tap in the rhythm to raise Ahren again, and he would now hear what was being said.

'Yes, Your Supremacy,' said Fern loudly, close to the nut. 'I'm sure you High Priests will find it very useful, although I can't see how. The young man who gave it to me keeps talking to me through it as if he was still in the room. It's unbelievable because he left last week.' She gave the nut to the Sorcerer, and while he was looking at it she vaulted out of the open window and ran round the corner of the house into the jungle. She could hear the Sorcerer shouting after her. Ahren understood what had happened, gave a bandhan of request and cut the connection from his end.

Fern ran into the caves in the hillside behind the inn. She heard a Special chasing her, ordering her to stop or he would shoot. He found the entrance, but had no light and soon gave up in the pitch darkness. She stood still and silent and mercifully he went away. Fern knew every stone of these caves and soon came out of another entrance further round the hill. She ran to a friend's farm, borrowed a horse and galloped off through the woods and fields to another safe house some distance away.

The Sorcerer decided the strange coconut should be sent to Teletos immediately. He was loathe to touch it and preferred to let the high-ups deal with it.

Mr Coffeeman, Robin and Hampen reached the fort, where the reception to introduce prospective suitors for the hand of Amara was to be held, and everybody who was anybody in Darzeet was there. A number of very different things were going on simultaneously; some Tong traders came over to Hampen and discovered they had some long lost acquaintances in common, and Mr Coffeeman presented Prince Hal (Robin) to Amara, to the delight of her mother and father. What a catch that would be! Their daughter would be a princess, added to which they badly wanted this politically dangerous daughter off their hands.

'The man you must contact is over there,' said Amara under her breath to Robin, between the small talk that they resorted to when anyone else was listening. 'He's a Resistance Group member. He'll take you down to the storerooms. He's talking to that handsome trader from Tong, the tall one with the superb ruby and sapphire turban jewel.' Robin turned and saw Hampen talking to an unremarkable looking young man wearing the uniform of the Teletsian conscript army.

'That's no trader; that's your future husband!' grinned Robin. 'Let's hope he passes the tests and doesn't get knocked out in the combat. He's fine at shooting, but I've not seen him in action otherwise, although I'm told Tongans are generally good at wrestling and the like. I hope to see you on the ship tomorrow evening as the wife of Admiral Hampen. Oh – and tell all your friends they absolutely *must* be outside the fort tomorrow afternoon. You know the plan.' At this point Amara's mother came up, hoping to impress a very desirable possible son-in-law.

'Enchanted to meet your daughter, Lady Cholarta,' Robin put on a foppish air. 'I'm hoping your husband's trainer won't prove an impediment. We don't do much hand-to-hand fighting in my land; we're cavalry men, by and large.'

Amara managed to meet Hampen, introduced by one of the Tong traders. She glanced at him, then shyly looked down.

'I beg you to do your best tomorrow,' she whispered. 'I'll quite understand when you declare the marriage void but I've got to get out of here. The Sorcerers have threatened to send me to a slave farm.'

'My lady Amara, or shall I say I sincerely hope you will soon be my lady, I'll do my best to win you genuinely,' replied Hampen gallantly, hoping he didn't sound gauche in front of this extremely pretty girl who had suddenly come into his life, even if only temporarily.

'I'm honoured,' replied Amara bashfully. She found his attitude charming and noticed once again that he was very good looking. Everything Coff had said about him was true, and more. Was he just being polite when he had given her that answer? She hoped not, because she immediately felt that he was so right for her in every way.

'We'll do our best to get you out of here, but we've got to get *into* here, as you well know.'

'Amara my dear,' interrupted her mother, 'come and meet the new general's son. He's about to be sent to Lahary on top secret business but I'm sure he'll find the time to win you first, if the prince fails.' Amara's mother was incredibly indiscreet and a great drawback to her husband. Amara made a despairing face at Hampen which said it all and complied with her mother's demands.

'I've heard you have an amazing system of storerooms below the fort,' drawled Robin, alias Prince Hal, to Amara's father. 'I'd be grateful of a tour.' The man standing next to Robin, actually a partisan, was asked to take him down there. This would not usually be allowed, but Amara's father was prepared to do almost anything to get his daughter married off. Once alone in the echoing cellars Robin and his accomplice talked strategy.

'I've had a fair amount of experience with explosives,' Robin began. 'Show me the gunpowder.'

'A lot of stuff has been taken up to Coffee Ferry. There's a new rumour going round though. The garrison still here is mostly going to Lahary, including me.'

'If all goes according to plan, no one will be going anywhere much,' replied Robin as they reached the galleries containing the gunpowder. 'Hmm, this will make a fair blast.' He looked at the location of the gunpowder store, well away from the park end of the fort. 'This will blow onto the seaward side of the headland. How do we get out after lighting the fuses?'

'I'll show you the regular exit, but there's also another way out – an opening onto the harbour, high above the water level. The water is very deep down below and goods are hoisted up by pulley from ships to a large opening in the rock. If you're a good diver you could escape that way.' He showed it to Robin, who looked dubious. He was a passable swimmer but no more.

'Do all those in favour of the freedom struggle know what to do?'

'Yes, and the kitchens are at the park end of the fort so the folk working in them should be alright.'

They returned to the reception.

Later in the night, when nearly everyone in Darzeet was sleeping, Roarke arrived in his flyer and silently and skilfully landed it on the deck of the *Spicy Coffee*. It was covered with a tarpaulin to make it look like cargo of some kind. One harbour guard saw it but assumed he was hallucinating. He usually had a small dose of his favourite drug when on night duty and it did give him odd visions, so he did not report what he had seen.

The next morning Robin wore a bandage around his ankle and put on a limp. First there was a buffet lunch in the fort's grounds for the guests and everything was set up for the tests, which would take place in the afternoon. There were a number of contenders and because of this more fighters had been called in, not only the Commander's personal trainer, a vast bull-like man with a shaved head and a neck like a walrus.

Robin, alias Prince Hal, apologised profusely to Lady Cholarta and said he would have to pull out, because he had fallen down the ladder to his cabin the previous night and could not fight. The tests began and Robin absented himself. He limped over to the fort, now deserted except for a few sentries. The gate guards waved him through. He crossed the yard and waited for his accomplice. He could hear the crowd in the park roaring as some poor contender was pummelled into jelly by the professional fighter ranged against him. Robin walked onto the nearby terrace, looked out over the water and saw Dan's rundown traders, some of the disguised Daish Shaktay navy, entering the harbour.

In the park, Hampen discovered to his dismay that the man he was fighting knew most of the Tong tricks – he must have learnt them from the coffee traders. After three rounds they were both still evenly matched. There were no rules so Hampen tried some moves from other systems of fighting. Regrettably, his opponent knew what he was doing. Then he remembered what Rajay had said – put your attention on top of your head and say, 'All pervading power, you are the doer, I am a mere instrument'. In a split second it came to him that he should simply knock this man out with a hefty punch on the jaw with his left hand. Hampen was left handed so it was a mighty blow. To his amazement the veritable gorilla opposing him dropped like a stone, not expecting this simple frontal attack. Hampen stood there dazed while the crowd roared – 'Hampen, Hampen,' in unison.

Robin heard this and smiled; that was one obstacle overcome. His accomplice approached him and pulled him out of his reverie: 'It's all ready down below. I just need you to set the fuses and light them.'

A little later, five other contenders for Amara's hand had come through the combat stage of the tests and now all six were in front of the archery targets. Hampen could see Amara sitting on the dais looking radiant. Momentarily, he was overcome by nerves, because he so wanted this pretty, plucky girl to be his wife. He shot first, but his arrow only made the outer edge of the target – and certainly not the central part, which was required. His heart dropped. Now what? Had he lost her? How could he miss such an easy target? Blessedly his rivals did even worse because a gusty wind suddenly got up. He glanced at Amara, who was saying something to her father.

'Another round,' shouted the herald, and they all shot again. This time Hampen's arrow flew true. The others did well enough but were not as accurate as him. He regained confidence and after a short rest it was time for the pistol shooting. He noticed the partisans getting ready under the trees, and taking his time to pace out the distance to the target aimed carefully.

Dan was about to disembark from what appeared to be the leader of a rundown fleet of ships come to buy coffee and the fever medicine bark. Namoh was ready to go ashore and lead the soldiers to attack the town. Merien, also on a ship, waved at Rajay and Roarke, and they soon met on the quay. Some partisans brought horses for the three guardians and their bodyguard of thirty trusted soldiers, and they set off in the direction of the Sorcerers' Headquarters at a smart pace.

Robin and his accomplice were in the gunpowder store of the castle setting the fuses when disaster struck. A Sorcerer saw Robin going down to the lower levels and was suspicious because he couldn't read Robin's mind, and also, Robin had put on a bandhan to hide his golden aura. That, paradoxically, was the giveaway, because the Sorcerer had heard that Prince Hal was a powerful spiritual personality. If this was so why did he not have a shining aura? Something didn't add up. The Sorcerer followed him at a safe distance and came upon Robin as he was about to light the fuses. He walked silently up and Robin felt his bad vibrations, and turned. The Sorcerer, standing nearby, his back to some barrels of gunpowder, began to chant the spell for annihilation. Robin realised what was about to happen.

'Run, get out of here, fast!' he shouted to his accomplice, who expected to be reduced to ashes at any moment. They sprinted to the opening in the wall and hesitated, looking at the sea far below.

'It's so far!' cried the terrified man.

'Jump or we're finished!' yelled Robin, grabbed his arm and they both jumped down, down, down into the water. As they sank under the surface they heard the most almighty explosion up above. The Sorcerer, in endeavouring to annihilate Robin, had not only himself exploded due to the rebound of the curse when aimed at a guardian, but had also set off the gunpowder more effectively than any fuses could ever have done. Explosion after explosion rocked the fort as more and more stacks of gunpowder ignited. Robin and his accomplice surfaced, breathless and spluttering. 'Hurry,' gasped Robin, and they swam their fastest across the harbour towards the *Spicy Coffee*, praying no rocks from the explosion would fall on them while mayhem was let loose above.

In the park everyone turned to see the blast. People ran screaming in every direction as other explosions followed. Amara jumped off the dais and towards Hampen, who held her protectively and noticed that over her arm she still had the garland of red roses she was to put on her chosen fiancé by way of a marriage.

'Do you really want to marry me?' asked Amara, between the screams and explosions.

'Most definitely! I've found you, I've won you and I'm not going to lose you now. Forget that garland, we'll have a proper wedding later. Alright?'

'Yes, very much so,' She smiled - a moment of calm in the hurricane all round them.

'Let's get you out of here!' Hampen cried, grabbed her and together they careered down the slope to *The Spicy Coffee's* launch.

Amidst the chaos there was order. The partisans ran forward and gave out weapons to those of the conscripts who were members of the Resistance Groups, and while the women and children hastened out of danger a full scale battle was starting. Some of the conscripts who were not committed to either side ran away and some tried to defend what was left of the fort. Coff Coffeeman appeared, cast off his herb seller's cloak and held up his four petalled key to give his followers confidence. Some Sorcerers tried to reduce people to ashes, but nothing happened and the partisans, all of whom had received their awakening and were well protected with bandhans, fearlessly attacked them as they would any other enemy. Soon a number of them lay dead on the ground.

The Specials got out their never-miss guns and the first one was aimed at Coff. This was a blessing, because with the key he was invulnerable to that speciality of the Sorcerers' Teletsia and the bullet rebounded on the man who had fired it. Many people saw that, so the Specials stopped using them and took to conventional weapons, which did work. The never-miss guns would have too, if the partisans lost their faith in their bandhans, but luckily the Specials didn't know this.

Meanwhile Rajay, Roarke and Merien, guided by the partisans, clattered through the streets to the mansion which was the Sorcerers' Headquarters, cutting down anyone who challenged them. They eventually reached it, in the most sought-after suburb, and hammered on the gatehouse door. They pushed past the Specials who refused to let them pass and entered the courtyard. Roarke had a Sasrar key on loan from Lord Jarwhen and put his hand in it, ready to let it fly as a fiery discus if he saw any Specials or guards attacking them, but they fled. The guards had heard, and seen, the explosion at the fort on the headland above and decided leave the defence of their overlords to Their Holinesses' psychic powers.

'We have a letter of surrender for you,' shouted Roarke, as he could see some Sorcerers looking out of the open windows. 'Sign it and you'll be spared.' There was a cynical laugh and he saw the Sorcerers waving their staffs around in the gestures of annihilation. The guardians' bodyguards prepared to attack them.

'Hold your fire! Stand away from the walls,' Roarke cried.

Roarke, Merien and Rajay - a powerful combination. Almost immediately the whole building exploded, much as the fort had done. This was the counter curse for trying to annihilate the three guardians, which was why they had undertaken this particular mission. As at the fort the greatest danger was from falling rocks. A small one hit a bodyguard, knocking him senseless, and the others had to carry him back to the medics unconscious.

On the quayside the Daish Shaktay army and marines had disembarked and Namoh led them to attack the Port Authority. It was a pushover because the Specials on duty had just woken up from their siesta and the last thing they expected were the elite troops of Daish Shaktay demanding surrender or death. There were no Sorcerers around to goad them into action, so they unanimously chose surrender, and Namoh left some soldiers to lock the Specials in their own Port Detention Centre for Undesirable Immigrants.

Meanwhile the Daish Shaktay ships in the harbour ran out their guns. Their first target was the Special Secret Police Headquarters for Western Teletsia, a large building conveniently situated on the waterfront, and soon the facade had been reduced to rubble. The surviving Specials came out holding white cloths of surrender tied to brooms. Again, it was accepted and the Specials were marched into the lockup on the quay.

'Up the hill!' Namoh shouted. 'Support the partisans in the park!' but this wasn't easy as they met strong opposition, and had to fight their way from street to street. Namoh led them fearlessly, so slowly and doggedly they reached their objective and eventually the now ruined fort fell to the combined forces of Daish Shaktay and Free Teletsia.

By late afternoon Namoh's men, helped by Coff and his Resistance Groups, had mopped up any pockets of Sorcerers and Specials still holding out. The whole town was rejoicing, the invaders were being welcomed as liberators and anyone who had formerly supported the Sorcerers now quickly changed their allegiance. However, there was to be no holiday for Rajay and the other leaders. They met on *The Prince Enithar,* moored in front of the Coffeeman's waterfront mansion next to *The Spicy Coffee.* Before they got down to business, Hampen and his fiancée were introduced to everyone.

'When do you want to get married?' asked Rajay.

'As soon as possible,' said Hampen 'Could we have a quick wedding – right now? Traditionally the captain of the ship can marry people on the high seas, so could Dan perform a simple ceremony for us?' Dan looked at Rajay.

'We'll prepare everything in the courtyard of the Coffeeman's mansion and we'll have the wedding later,' Rajay suggested. 'At midnight. Can you manage that?'

'Most definitely, Your Majesty!' said Hampen. Rajay summoned some officers who were not too shattered from the day's fighting and told them to organise the wedding and feast.

'You've got a whole army and navy of admiring men and a whole town full of liberated citizens to help you. If you need money go to my paymaster. Right, get to it!'

'His Majesty is renowned for not wasting time,' Hampen said to Amara as they left together.

'Namoh, I must see the casualty list. Which ship are we using as a hospital?' Rajay asked.

'The *Queen Jansy.* You won't believe it, although we've got over a hundred and fifty wounded we've not lost a single life, and we may be able to save nearly all of them, too.'

'That's the best news I've heard today.'

CHAPTER 7

THE SPUR-OF-THE-MOMENT CAVALRY

Rajay visited the wounded and the guardians gave vibrations. Five were on the critical list and four more in a serious condition, and Rajay gave his attention to them, because they all loved and trusted him, and faith was so important in situations like this.

After some time they returned to the *Prince Enithar* and made plans, both with those on the ship and elsewhere via the coconuts. Fern could not be reached but Rajay had too much going on to worry about a small thing like that. Erin was leaving the jungles and would need some days to reach the Panvale area. He was suspicious of vultures which would come and hover overhead and then fly away purposefully. He suspected they were spy-birds.

Ahren and Saman were in the centre of the country. They had ambushed a number of Specials and Sorcerers manning roadblocks. After the first two or three operations they had come up with a plan which worked, and had made it appear that they were small groups of local partisans doing the damage, in case any Specials escaped to tell the tale.

The roadblocks were invariably in concealed places such as bends in the road, gullies and woods, and Ahren always had someone with him who knew where the Specials would be likely to be waiting. A number of partisans would creep close, but out of sight, and completely surround the road block. Ahren would then approach the roadblock openly. When asked who he was, he would say, 'I'm Ahren Dairyman, one of the escaped rebels.' Either the Specials would think he was playing a joke or they would set about arresting him, because Ahren knew the word was out to capture the seven of them and send them to Teletos. Then he would tell the Specials to surrender or die and at this point they would get angry. The ambush would take place and if there was a Sorcerer present he would get reduced to ashes if he tried to annihilate Ahren. Rajay contacted him and the story of Fern, as far Ahren knew it, came out.

'I'm sure she got away,' he said.

'Have you given awakening to all your partisans?' asked Rajay.

'Yes, and we've also been teaching them how to free people who've been treated and mesmerised by the Sorcerers.'

'Excellent. This war won't only to be won with weapons, as you well know. Have you got a map handy?'

'Yes, it's in front of me now.'

'OK, you've got to try to capture the Specials Posts and the Sorcerers in these places......'

The most serious news was from Derwin, back at the Island of Creations. Wale Fisher's wife lived in a house a little way down the canal from the Restorers' former home. She had heard that Drusilla had one of the rebels a prisoner up in her flat. She wondered if it was Lee or Derwin and was determined to find out, so she crept in when Drusilla was not at home, because Mrs Fisher had formerly been in charge of the pass keys of the Restorers' flats.

She had found Raynor chained up in a dark room full of sinister symbols and there was a treated slave in there too, a pathetic creature huddled in the corner. Drusilla needed him for something and had called him up from the sheds in the yard, then locked him in the room with Raynor. He and the slave were desperately hungry and thirsty, so she gave them food and water. Raynor rallied quickly, but had an intuition that Mrs Fisher should leave. She just managed to slip out of the flat without being seen, by hiding behind a curtain in the hallway, when Drusilla returned unexpectedly. This had been the day before and Wale's wife got a message to Sparkly Diamondcutter, who had been given a coconut and thus managed to spread the news.

Back at the Island we decided to tell Tandi and Raynor's parents about his capture. The parents were sad but resigned, having assumed him dead for five years already. In front of the others Tandi took the news stoically. I told her that maybe there was a good reason why he had allowed himself to be captured, but I didn't sound very convincing and when alone with me she burst into tears of despair. I felt the vibrations and it was cool that he would eventually be all right, so I suggested she asked the same question. She did so and also felt cool, which cheered her up a little. Stellamar called us to say Garma Nalanda had arrived at the Pearl Lords so Tandi spoke to him about Raynor, but I felt very sorry for her. Garma also spoke to Rajay.

'It seems hopeless, but let's be positive,' Rajay advised. 'Look what Conwenna achieved when she was captured. The best thing *you* can do is to take a coconut and rejoin the Teletsian army.'

'I was thinking the same thing,' agreed Garma, 'to have a spy in the Plimpet regiment would be useful.' Plimpet was the port in Teletsia nearly opposite the Island.

'Call me if you have any information.'

Garma reported to the headquarters of this regiment. He said he had some confidential information from his commanding officer, General Woodenton. Once in front of the general, a malicious looking individual with atrocious vibrations, Garma divulged the unfortunate facts that firstly any High Priests who tried to annihilate the enemy would themselves finish up a heap of ashes, and secondly large numbers of Special Secret Police were becoming vegetable-like when they attacked the rebels.

'Captain Nalanda, this information is not new,' replied the general, drumming his fingers on the table in front of him, 'however, officially we do not believe it. Go and join your fellow officers and do not speak about this. We have had orders from the top that before we start any engagement we should put one or two of our conscripts in front of the troops. If they show any lack of patriotism they are to be shot, to show the others we mean business. If I hear any mention of what you told me, you'll be out in front.'

In Darzeet harbour on *The Prince Enithar*, the leaders were talking together in the early evening.

'Roarke, I want you to take me back to the Island in the flyer,' Robin asked.

'Doesn't Rajay need you here?' he replied.

'I want to try and rescue Raynor from Drusilla.' The guardians looked at each other.

'Namoh,' said Rajay, 'we need to get our forces into the centre of the country fast. By tomorrow morning we must know how many of our troops should guard this town to make sure there's no counter-attack and how many horses we can get hold of at short notice. Go now, and report back to me by coconut.'

'Will do.' Namoh took a deep breath and pushed his tired body into action. Rajay sent everyone except Robin, Roarke and Merien out of his cabin.

'Close the door, Robin,' asked Merien.

'You may be able to kill her,' said Roarke, 'but she may kill you too, and the conflict of you two, a guardian and an ex-guardian, will create a serious imbalance on the subtle levels that might have a chain reaction. It won't be simply a question of going in as a partisan and taking out an undesirable, like we've all done many a time. It's vital to destroy the Queen Wasp, but is it worth giving your life for?'

'How many times have you given *your* lives for Navi Septa?' Robin looked intently at them.

'I prefer not to recall my past lifetimes – except for the technological knowledge and the music,' Roarke continued. 'But yes, it has happened to me.'

'I've died in battle here more than once,' admitted Rajay.

'I've been lucky so far, but I've had a number of close calls,' added Merien.

'Maybe this time it's my turn,' insisted Robin, 'but - look after Asha for me if it comes to that.'

'Of course we would. We're your brothers, closer than brothers,' Rajay assured him.

'It's my duty, as a new guardian.'

'Lighten up a bit, Robin!' said Roarke. 'You'll probably survive – you have so far.'

'You should both stay for the wedding,' Rajay went on. 'It'll give Hampen and the girl such pleasure to have us all there.'

Roarke said if anyone could find some instruments he would lead the music and mentioned that some jolly sailors' dances would also go down well. He went to arrange the wedding, Merien and Robin went to help Namoh and Rajay stayed behind. So far so good, he thought, apart from this horrendous business with Raynor and the problem with Fern Innkeeper. He knew what Robin would try to do, but he also knew Drusilla would be vicious, devious and abominably cruel. He contacted Erin again.

'I want to talk to you about those spy vultures. You've got to counter them using subtle power.'

'We'll try, Your Majesty, but we're not very experienced in that direction,' said Erin.

'Can you feel the vibrations?'

'Yes, well enough.'

'Can you write down these words of power I'll tell you?'

'Yes, but give me time to kindle a light and find some writing materials. We're camping at the edge of the jungle.' Rajay cut the connection and soon Erin came back to him.

'Ready and waiting,' he said, and Rajay dictated a number of phrases in the classic language.

'You must have someone surveying the skies at every moment and also someone feeling the vibrations of whatever is up there. It isn't difficult, merely a question of attention. If they feel heat and tingling, especially on the left thumb and fourth finger, get to work.'

'With respect, Your Majesty, how?'

'You know the bandhan of request?'

'Yes, indeed.'

'Once you feel something is wrong, write, "Please protect us from the spy-vulture", or something like that, on your left hand, and circle above it with your right hand. Go on until you feel vibrations flowing on your hands. When you do this bandhan, put your attention on the bird and say the words of power. That should help. Contact me tomorrow and tell me if it does, and if it doesn't, try to shoot them down with conventional weapons.'

'The trouble is they fly so high, we'd be very lucky to hit them.'

'You're right. Anyway, if what I suggested doesn't work, come back to me and I'll think of something else. Go well - go safely.'

Rajay contacted Ahren and Saman once more and told them to watch out for spy birds, and how to take action against them if they spotted any. It was a good thing Erin had mentioned them. Rajay was looking forward to meeting him, a man after his own heart with a determination to free his country from its oppressors, who understood the Mother Earth, her creatures and moods, and even to a certain extent her people, both good and bad.

The wedding went off well considering how quickly it had been arranged, and the guests danced and sang through the night. It was a great way to celebrate the first military victory against the Sorcerers' Teletsia. Hampen got just the wife he wanted: an officer's daughter who was also a courageous and beautiful Resistance Group member. He had been through so much in his short life and was delighted to have a wife who matched him in every way. Roarke and Robin left before the end of the party, along with Merien, who was not feeling at all well. Roarke put Merien's new flyer on automatic so it followed his, and Merien did not have to do anything. Marimba had called from the Island to say that she needed the flyer to deliver messages and nuts, and Merien needed to rest before he could again go on active duty.

Namoh and his men managed to get hold of about fifteen hundred horses by the following day. Some were from the defeated Teletsian armed forces, about five hundred requisitioned from Specials and the rest were bought privately. Although not trained war horses, they could all carry a man, his weapons and his kit. The town's biggest mule dealer sold Namoh his entire stock of riding mules so they were able to send another two hundred mounted soldiers and use the others as baggage animals.

Then the unexpected happened yet again. In the afternoon a force of partisans arrived hidden in some rubber exporters' ships, from the Rubber River. Rajay greeted the four freed and resold slaves, Munnir, Euclip, Chariss and Rollo, who were with them. They had given awakening to thousands of people in Western Teletsia and had started their own guerrilla war; the previous week they had moved on Rubber River Port with the force of partisans and had burnt many of the Sorcerers' and Specials' buildings to the ground. It was a centre of support for the Sorcerers, and as the partisans had first captured all the fire engines and tipped them in the sea over the quayside, the buildings burnt fast and furiously, because they were built largely of wood from the nearby forests.

They also reported that when the Sorcerers tried to reduce them to ashes it hadn't worked, so their lords and masters were themselves reduced to being helpless men who did a lot of silly chanting. Also a number of Specials had been afflicted with a strange problem when they tried to attack any of the boys who had four petalled keys – they became witless and could no longer speak. The attack had been an overwhelming success mainly because it had been so unexpected, although unavoidably a few partisans had been killed or wounded.

'Do you tell people about the power of the awakened Tree of Life?' asked Rajay.

'Oh yes, Your Majesty, all the time,' said Euclip. 'So many people have been convinced that the Sorcerers hardly have any authority in Western Teletsia any more. Folks aren't frightened of them and their power is in fear. Without the Sorcerers, the Specials are like headless chickens with no one to tell them what to do, so they aren't nearly so scary either. We can't thank you enough for what you showed us.'

'Maybe we should put you boys in charge of the Teletsian freedom struggle!' Rajay encouraged them.

Euclip went on to say that they had brought nearly three hundred armed and enthusiastic partisans with them and because of this not so many Daish Shaktay men had to stay behind to keep control of Darzeet.

Rajay visited the hospital ship again and discovered that seven of the nine who were in very poor shape the day before had improved dramatically since he had given them vibrations. The other two had unfortunately passed away peacefully in the night.

'Good luck, Your Majesty!' and 'May the Goddess of Daish Shaktay be with you!' said a chorus of voices as he bid his men goodbye. The navy left for the Island later that day with the wounded men and any soldiers not with the cavalry.

Before setting off inland Rajay insisted that the leaders of the invasion did a fire ceremony in the courtyard of the Coffeeman's mansion, to pray that somehow they could either avoid, evade or overcome the regiments of Teletsian troops stationed around the country while they made their way to the Temple of Support, the seat of the subtle power that ruled Teletsia. It was the temple rather than the capital city they were making for.

There would be at least one moon up throughout the night and Namoh, in charge of the cavalry, prepared to set off at nightfall. With him was Tom Dyeman the farmer's son, Coff Coffeeman and a number of men who knew the area. Rajay, with three coconuts in his saddle bags, was to ride in among the troops. There were a number of grumbles from those who had mules, because they were wilful and stubborn, so Rajay and his bodyguards took some as an example. However, Coff's father then gave him a magnificent gold coloured stallion with a silver-white mane and tail, ready saddled, and he had

to accept it, but with such a spectacular horse it was difficult to remain anonymous. His bodyguards kept their mules.

They left town by the southbound road to Coffee River Ferry and it was made public knowledge that they were going to attack the regiment there. However once in the countryside they turned off the highway into the small lanes. Namoh and the leaders met and utterly destroyed a couple of roadblocks they came across. The surviving Specials, as usual, became witless and unable to speak, so the invaders did not bother to take them prisoner, although they did take their steam cars, weapons and uniforms. They passed through a town and some local Resistance Group members in the cavalry force pointed out the Specials' Station. It was in a large compound and included houses for the Specials and their families. These were quickly captured and their inhabitants given the choice of surrendering or dying. They had been taken completely unawares and in the middle of the night, so they unanimously chose to surrender.

A strong group of armed partisans was left in charge of the Specials' Station and the Specials were imprisoned in their own lockup. The light signalling station was also taken over by the forces of Free Teletsia, who could now send some interesting misinformation. All in all, it was a good night's work. The following message was sent to Teletos: *A small invasion force has been repelled. Disregard messages that say anything else. The situation in Darzeet has been brought under control.* Similar messages were being relayed from other Specials' Posts in the area – the work of Ahren and Saman's men.

The invaders made for a village known to be entirely supportive of the resistance movement some way south east of Darzeet, and it was a fair ride for one night. They reached it on exhausted horses and mules soon after the sun rose and Rajay told Namoh to have his men look for spy-birds once it was light. Namoh, at the head of the column, saw one, took the necessary precautions, and sure enough it wheeled, dipped and fell dizzily into a ploughed field. His men went closer and as it rose up once again they shot it with an arrow, and it flopped back to the earth dead. After this a rota of soldiers who could feel the vibrations well were put on 'vulture observation duty' at all times and quite a few others were brought down.

The soldiers and their horses hid in the barns and farm buildings of the village, while Rajay, Namoh, his officers and aides stayed in the manor house. Soon coconut contacts started coming in with reports of the whereabouts of the enemy. Rajay asked for a map and began making crosses on it as he spoke to Ahren nearing Lahary, Erin in the jungles and Dan on the high seas. Namoh, by Rajay's side, made a suggestion.

'We need some way of spying on the enemy like they're spying on us - from the air.'

'You're right,' replied Rajay. 'We've got three flyers and eight flying horses.' He picked up another coconut and wearily went back to work.

'Your Majesty,' put in Tom Dyeman, who was also in the room, 'being as you won the naval battle with the help of the sea creatures, why don't we ask for the help of the animals here on land?'

'What have you got in mind?'

'I don't know, but we heard the stories – how you and Asha were helped by our ferocious Teletsian tigers and the Woodcutter family were saved by some elephants. Anyone who looks at that map can see we're desperately outnumbered. Our forces are all small, while each Teletsian barracks or regiment has about four thousand soldiers, and we can't assume half of them won't fight.'

Rajay agreed, thanked Tom, and asked to be left alone with the coconuts. He made a number of calls, slept a bit and was woken by Namoh, who came in quietly. Rajay was a light sleeper – years of having to be alert at every moment when he had been fighting for his own country's freedom.

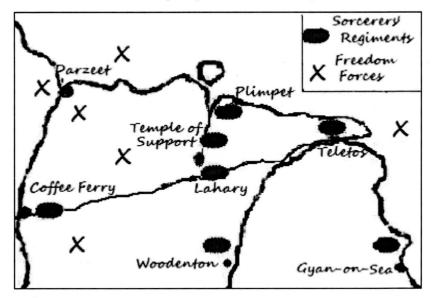

'Rajay,' said Namoh, 'I don't know if it's a dangerously reckless idea but the local people here want us to do a music awakening programme before we leave. Our plan for tonight is to go to the next safe village by the small lanes through the fields, so as to avoid the roads, in the moons' light. If we leave in the late evening we should reach there before daylight. What do you say?'

'Yes, we could do a programme. You round up the musicians and lead it. Part of the cavalry should leave now and the rest of us will follow. I only hope we don't come across a Teletsian regiment when we're split up. I don't think we will because our scouts report they're nowhere near here. Nevertheless, set a strong guard round the village.'

'Another thing. I want you to change horses with me from now on. The one I rode last night was comfortable, sensible and inconspicuous, so you take it tonight. The last thing Valya said to me was, "Keep Rajay safe, if you can," and no one in Daish Shaktay would forgive me if I didn't. I'll ride that gold and silver stallion. A large number of people saw you leave Darzeet on it, and if anyone wants to take you out, they'll go for someone on that horse. Added to which we do look fairly similar.'

'You don't change, do you, my friend?'

'No, in some ways I don't. I want to see Teletsia free as much as you do, but my priority is to make sure our country still has you as its leader after all this is finished.'

'Alright, if you insist. That stallion is a beautiful horse, but he's quite a handful, and if I'm using the coconuts while I'm riding, it's easier to be on something less demanding.'

During the programme Rajay walked down the lane in the direction of the road, some way away. He stopped and talked to a troop of guards, but while doing so heard the ominous chugging of a steam car.

'Get out of sight behind the hedge,' he ordered. 'I'll try to ward them off peacefully. If I can't, attack them and be sure none escape, because they mustn't know we're here and most definitely mustn't see the awakening programme.' The steam car approached and stopped in front of Rajay, who was tottering down the middle of the road. The Specials got out and Rajay could see a Sorcerer in the car. The singing at the awakening programme could be heard in the distance.

'You there,' shouted one of the Specials, seeing Rajay by the moons' light, 'move out of the way or we'll run you down!'

'Grand party going on up there!' chortled Rajay, staggering tipsily and doing a passable job of imitating the Teletsian accent. 'It's a wedding, one of the farmer's daughters - why don't you go and join in? They won't mind a few more guests!'

'We heard a report of a large troop of men on horses. Are they there too?'

'Sorry sir, you've got the wrong place. The only men on horses tonight were the bridegroom and his friends arriving,' Rajay took a swig of water from the bottle he was carrying in case he got thirsty when walking in the warm night. 'There were about twenty of them so I reckon someone can't count. Must be the effect of this wine, making them see double or triple. This stuff is very strong! I can't help you there. Would if I could but I can't.' He took another swig and did a little pirouette in the road.

'What do you reckon?' said one Special to the other.

'Drunk as a lord, no, drunker, drunk as a king. This alcohol is becoming popular since our lads brought the habit back from Chussan. We're wasting our time; let's go and look elsewhere for these horsemen. I think it was a false report from those wretched Resistance people, to give us a lot of unnecessary driving around in the night.'

'Maybe it was the wedding party.'

They got back in the steam car, where the Sorcerer was having a mild seizure, and groaning and twitching. They turned their car round and left.

'With respect, Your Majesty, what would you have done if they'd captured you or insisted on going up to the farm?' asked the leader of the guards, coming out from behind the hedge.

'I gave you your instructions and knew you'd be able to get me out of trouble,' said Rajay briskly, but with a smile. 'Come on, it's time we left.'

'I understand now how our king won Daish Shaktay,' whispered one soldier.

'It was quite something to watch!' agreed another.

'He was enjoying himself, far more than when he has to sit on his throne and dole out justice,' added a third. Rajay overheard this, turned towards the speakers, and the young men were initially scared.

'And when we get back home, don't let anyone tell my wife I've been having a bit of fun!' he laughed. 'That's an order, OK?'

'We wouldn't dream of saying anything, Your Majesty,' replied the leader.

CHAPTER 8

CHECK AND COUNTER CHECK

I, Malvog, scribe to the most illustrious Lords of Teletsia, do hereby record a Council of War.

'Darzeet has fallen to the rebels, and someone closely resembling Rajay Ghiry was seen there,' began the Head of the Intelligence Network.

'So much for respecting our independence,' put in the Head of the Special Police Force. 'The dreaded Mountain Mouse! That's all we need. Not content to destroy our allies in Mattanga, he now comes to make trouble here.'

'There are reports saying the Panvale and Lahary regiments are about to surrender,' said the Head of Psychic Research.

'I received others that everything is fine. Some people can't read the signals,' insisted His Supreme Lordship.

'We have had worrying reports from Rubber River Port,' continued the Head of the Intelligence Network.

'Today I received information that everything is back to normal there too. No one can stand against our subtle power for long,' countered His Lordship.

'I have received a number of signals in the new code assuring us that all is alright again at Darzeet too. Only our most trusted operatives know this one, so the signals have to be genuine,' said the Chief Priest for War and Weaponry. 'Let me show you a map with the whereabouts of our troops. The circles with numbers inside are our regiments and the conscripts are quite able to fight now. The knots are our enemies, based on the latest intelligence reports.'

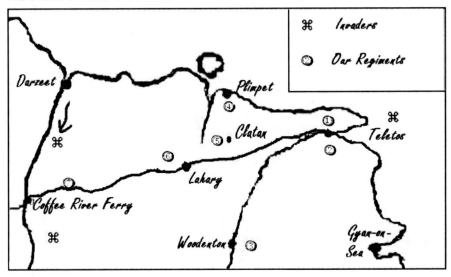

*The location of the invader's forces, flower shaped knots, and
the Teletsian regiments, numbered in circles*

'How do we know the conscripts will actually fight?' asked the Head
of Psychic Research. 'They weren't much good at the Clatan stone
circle, what our enemies call the Temple of Support.'

'We've decided to shoot a few slackers in front of the others, to show
them what happens to people who won't defend the fatherland,' said
the Head of the Special Secret Police Force.

'Good plan,' agreed His Supreme Lordship.

'Our spies who escaped from Darzeet report that a force of cavalry is
moving towards Coffee River Ferry, southwards down the main road.
I am expecting a spy vulture back any time now with further
information concerning their whereabouts,' said the Chief Priest for
War and Weaponry. 'Our Seventh Regiment has left Coffee Ferry for
the centre of the country to link up with regiments Five and Six, but if
it turns around the soldiers can catch the enemy in the hilly, wooded
country near the ferry, where the horses of their cavalry will not help
them.'

'I recently received a report that the enemy cavalry has disappeared.
How can we possibly lose track of an entire force?' objected the Head
of the Intelligence Network.

'We have also received reports that the small army from Castle Mount *is in the jungle south and east of Coffee River Ferry, presumably hoping to meet the invaders coming from Darzeet. We assume the enemy are making for the Clatan stone circle and we will send some of our regiments to the area to stop them,' continued the Chief Priest for War and Weaponry.*

'We must keep a close watch on those enemy troop ships off the coast of Teletos,' added the High Priest of Ports, Naval Matters and Shipping.

'Regiments One and Two, stationed near there, will deal with them. Their guns on the estuary banks will destroy the troop ships if they try to sail towards Teletos.'

At this moment an exhausted messenger entered.

'Your Lordships, I am from the rural areas south east of Darzeet. Partisan forces are taking over the Specials' Posts and are sending misinformation to you. They know the new light signalling codes. I managed to escape and came here as fast as possible. I suspect our entire light signalling and flag code network has been infiltrated by the enemy.'

Imprisoned in Drusilla's flat, Raynor couldn't figure out what was going on. Initially he thought she was insane, but nevertheless really was protecting him, even though her vibrations were abysmal. Then he was shackled hand and foot and at that point he decided she was trying to kill him of hunger and thirst. She nearly managed it, but then Mrs Fisher appeared and gave him water and food, and left a water bottle and some biscuits, which he hid under a loose floorboard, to eat and drink when he became desperate.

That same night, Raynor was alone with the mesmerised slave boy who had been put in the same room. Moons' light filtered through the window and Raynor, who was chained in a corner, beckoned to him. He had just enough wits to come closer so Raynor could give him vibrations, and said words of power to him almost all night. As dawn was breaking and the healing rays of the morning sun shone in through the window, the boy finally threw off the effects of the Sorcerers' 'treatment'. Raynor had no keys – they had been taken from him, no lemons and chillies to help him with the exorcism, and he was locked in a room devoted to black magic. But he had something else – compassion and a gentle heart, and it this enabled the all-pervading power to work through him and heal the boy.

'By the Mother Earth!' he cried, suddenly normal again. 'Wherever am I?'

'Sh!' Raynor whispered.

The boy had been a pupil at the same school as Conwenna used to go to, but had been caught and treated when it was found he was 'subversive'. Raynor showed him how to act as if he was still mesmerised but told him to watch out for an opportunity to escape and then to go to Mrs Wale Fisher's place, or Sparkly Diamondcutter's safe house, because Mrs Fisher had told Raynor about Sparkly. That morning the boy was taken downstairs.

Later still the shackles were removed and Raynor was again given food and water. He spent his time in meditation, made a lot of bandhans and sang some songs to himself. Although outwardly everything was dreadful, inwardly he felt fine. Then Drusilla came to him again.

'It's time to have a little talk. Did you have any visitations in the night, or bad dreams?'

'No,' Raynor replied. He knew she had been trying to scare him witless with the unspeakable rites she sometimes did in the room but he was not affected and found it all rather boring. Drusilla on the other hand found it completely incomprehensible, because she assumed that once she had taken his keys he would be powerless. She sent a Sorcerer to deal with him but he complained that he could do nothing with this young man who refused to be mesmerized and dazzled him with his blinding golden aura. Added to which Drusilla could not understand why Raynor had neither died of thirst nor fainted from hunger.

'I have your keys,' she continued, 'and also one a friend of yours left here. None of you realised it, but I am the power behind the High Priests of Teletsia. I'm making some more keys, which will make the wearer all powerful and able to control great masses of people even more successfully than I've done up until now. I'm going to give you a chance to save yourself and your family. Your friends have very stupidly landed in Teletsia and we've captured them, and also your parents. Come to the window and I'll show them to you.'

She ordered the guards with her to take Raynor to a window and opened the shutter. It was night and in the yard were some cloaked figures also under heavy guard, who did look remarkably like his family members and us in the dim light of the crescent Moon of Compassion. For a moment his heart nearly stopped, but then he felt their vibrations and they were so bad he knew she was trying to trick him.

'I'm disappointed in my High Priests,' she went on. 'I'm going to get rid of all of them and start again. This time I'll rule Teletsia much better and I want you to be my new head High Priest. If you do that your family and friends will be released. You'll have enormous power and together we'll rule Teletsia.'

'And if I refuse?'

'First your family and friends will die and then I'll kill you. Nevertheless, I'll give you some more time. It would be much more sensible if we could be allies. I was a guardian, one of the most senior in fact, but the others got jealous of me and schemed to have me expelled from their little club. I've been ruling Teletsia for generations through these useless High Priests, Sorcerers, as you call them, but it's evident that you and your friends are not going to give up easily, so as the saying goes, 'If you can't beat 'em, join 'em.''

Raynor was silent and was taken back to the sorcery room, his prison. He decided that Drusilla was completely insane but had some sinister power, but he did not believe most of what she had said. The next day she came to see him again because her plan to show him people she hoped he would mistake for his family and us had failed, for some reason unknown to her. Drusilla still had high hopes of using him to rule Teletsia, and like all arrogant, egotistical people it did not occur to her that she was chasing a rainbow, ever elusive, ever out of reach.

'Someone gave me this today,' she said, and showed Raynor Fern's contact coconut, which had been brought to her. 'I think you know what it is.'

'I have absolutely no idea.' Raynor was completely baffled by it.

'Maybe you do. It might be easier for you if I had the truth about this. Disembodied voices come through it. We think it might be some sort of communication tool. I'll leave it with you, and I want you to contact your people and tell them I'd like to meet your leader.'

Drusilla left with her guards, locking the door behind her.

Ahren's force put large numbers of the Sorcerers and Specials at roadblocks out of action. Some had been killed and others had reduced themselves to heaps of ashes, or witless creatures behaving like their own treated victims. Because of this, they could not escape to report on the partisans, but Ahren was disturbed at seeing his enemies like this – it was even worse than leaving dead bodies.

He, Saman and his partisans collected a whole convoy of steam cars, because Specials sometimes travelled to their roadblocks in them. The drawback was that with the steam cars at least some of the partisans now had to travel by road. They had also stolen a number of Specials' uniforms from their now docile or dead owners, but the vibrations of these clothes were appalling to the extent of being painful. The partisans washed them in streams and put them to dry in the sun to neutralise the bad feeling coming from them but it didn't help much. Nevertheless, when they were wearing them they did look convincingly like a convoy of Specials - and they drove towards the centre of the country. They told any real Specials they met that they were on a secret mission for the war and couldn't stop to explain anything, so were allowed to pass.

After dropping Robin at the Island Roarke turned around and made for Western Teletsia, flying high so as not to be too noticeable from the ground. By the middle of the night he was in the Coffee Ferry area. Roarke had a spyglass and was looking for the troops Fern said were making their way eastwards along the main road to Teletos. If Rajay knew where they were he could plot his strategy better. Derwin was also up in the air between Panvale, Lahary and the Temple of Support. He noticed a large number of troops nearing it from both Lahary and Clatan, and alerted Rajay via his coconut.

'We gathered that from the reports we intercepted,' said Rajay. 'The vibrations up there near the temple will do them good.'

Marimba, accompanied by Conwenna, was in the new flyer and they made for the troop ships lying off the Teletos estuary. Their job was to report on the Teletos area. Conwenna also had Marimba's powerful spy glass and they were high up and out of range of even the largest cannon, had they been spotted.

Meanwhile Rajay warned all the groups to keep a watch for spy birds, both by looking for them and by checking their vibrations. The birds had a horrible feeling coming from them which revealed their whereabouts to anyone who was sensitive.

'Rajay, it's Roarke,' he said on the coconut in the early morning, when Rajay and the rest of the cavalry were nearing their destination, a safe village in the hilly, wooded area northwest of Panvale. They would soon meet up with Ahren's group if all went according to plan. Rajay heard Roarke, handed his horse's lead rein to the bodyguard riding next to him and took his coconut out of his saddle bag.

'What's new?' asked Rajay.

'I've spotted the Teletsian troops' camp, not too far from Coffee Ferry.'

'How many of them are there?'

'Masses - they're in tents and I can see their camp fires.'

After finishing the call to Rajay, Roarke landed in a secluded valley in the jungle some way south of the road, put his sleeping mat on the ground and lay down. Later he woke up and after meditating for some time, got his stringed instrument from the back of the flyer and played it, assuming he was alone. As always the strains of his music were hauntingly, ecstatically beautiful, and he was lost in delight. He looked up and saw he was surrounded by jungle creatures: standing, sitting or coiled some distance away. They had felt his vibrations, been entranced by his music and had come to welcome him to their land. There were elephants, outsize deer with fearsome antlers, large wild cattle with long pointed horns, something that was a cross between a rhino and a giant boar, an animal like a large tiger, some very large snakes and other creatures of various shapes and sizes, all at peace with each other and Roarke. He got out his four petalled key, held it up and the animals sensed its benevolent power. He smiled at them, bowed and greeted them courteously, and got into the flyer.

He returned to the air high above the army camp and discovered that they were moving out, but strangely, back in the direction of Coffee River Ferry. He called Rajay, who was relieved that the odds against the allies were now less daunting, as this meant at least one Teletsian regiment was going to be avoided for the time being. Roarke told Rajay about the animals that had come to pay their respects to him.

'That reminds me of something young Tom Dyeman suggested,' said Rajay. 'They might fight for us if we could communicate with them.'

'The tigers are your friends. That option goes with your fourth centre key. Is there any chance of your making contact with them?'

'No, but the flying horses understand human speech and can communicate with other animals…'

'I'll ask Robin to bring them here immediately,' interrupted Roarke.

Back on the Island Robin was fretting. He wanted to try to rescue Raynor but the vibrations were not flowing when he, Lord Jarwhen and Lady Mercola asked if he should. Then the call came from Roarke about using the flying horses to communicate with the wild animals.

'Do you think it would work?' I asked Robin.

'Yes, most probably, and I'll take all of them.'

'It's a pity I can't come with you.'

'No way!'

In the last few days I discovered that I was expecting a baby. We had been married nearly two years and I was beginning to wonder if I would ever have one. But now here I was, grounded when I would have most liked to do something heroic.

'Contact Lord Coban and ask him if he could come with me, because he knows the country well,' Robin said. 'The list of people's personal tunes is on that piece of paper by the coconut on the window ledge.' I looked at the names and somehow got muddled up. I wasn't feeling my best that morning when I tapped the rhythm in.

'Lord Coban, are you there?' I asked. There was silence and I asked again. Imagine my surprise when I heard Raynor's voice.

'Asha, is that really you? How can I hear your voice coming from this nut?'

'It's a device of Prince Roarke's father. How come you've got one?'

'I'm a prisoner of Drusilla Prospector. She gave it to me. She's pure evil. The Sorcerers got me and brought me here to Teletos. I'm in the Restorer's old palace but these days it's full of Sorcerers – and Drusilla, who's even worse than we realised. She wants to break me and make me her new Head Sorcerer. She's behind all of them.'

'We know that ….'

'Someone's coming in. Stop talking….' I looked again at the piece of paper. I now realised I had made a mistake and tapped Fern Innkeeper's code. How her nut had finished up with Raynor I had no idea, but it was the best mistake I ever made. The only problem was I could hear from the way Raynor was fading in and out that Fern's coconut was almost out of power and I hadn't been able to tell him how to charge it up or how to get back to us. Nevertheless we now knew he was alive and where he was.

CHAPTER 9

THE FOREST LEGION

Robin contacted Lord Coban, Stellamar's father, and he and his brother Lord Olon both wanted to go on the flying horses. When Robin spoke to Lord Jarwhen about these new developments the vibrations changed and were now very cool for him to go into Teletsia. With the help of a major storm to conceal the fact that Robin was riding one, and accompanying six other flying horses to the mainland in broad daylight, he was soon with Lords Coban and Olon, explaining what they should do. They set off at nightfall for Western Teletsia with all the flying horses except Robin's noble and powerful Yamun. Robin had another destination and instructed Yamun to fly in a zigzag line to avoid places where Specials might be scanning the skies, because he was not as good at raising storms as some of the others.

At nightfall Roarke landed his flyer near where his map indicated a safe house, east of Coffee Ferry. He walked towards it and noticed a number of people in uniform, so concealed himself, hoping to hear something of interest. He crept up to some bushes at the side of the house and realised this farm had been taken over by the Teletsian army. He could overhear some men talking as they sat outside on a veranda.

'When do you think this enemy cavalry will turn up?' said one voice.

'I don't think they will. Going back to Coffee Ferry is a waste of time,' said a second. Roarke heard steps approaching.

'Hello, Daitya, what news?' continued the first voice.

'The scouts have returned and the enemy cavalry are nowhere on the road between here and Darzeet. They've completely disappeared, and no spy vultures have given any information as to their whereabouts, but the army from Castle Mount has been located at the edge of the jungle,' said a third voice, presumably Daitya.

'So?' asked the second voice.

'The enemy cavalry must have cut across country, in which case it's not our business to go after them. Some other regiment will be called in. A smallish advance force will creep up on the Castle Mount rebels, lure them into the open, and then the rest of us will appear and finish them off. Shouldn't be difficult because there aren't many of them,' answered Daitya.

'Sounds fine by me,' said the second voice, 'as long as I'm not in the advance force!'

Roarke crept back to his flyer hidden in the woodland, where he had left his coconut.

'Erin, it's Roarke, I have to wake you.'

'That's all right, Your Highness, I was on the watch.'

'Call me Roarke. Listen carefully......' and he warned Erin of his danger.

Next Roarke contacted the Pearl Lords, just leaving their home on the flying horses, and told them what he had heard. Lord Coban had been in touch with Derwin, who was rallying groups of partisans in the Clatan area. The partisans in all areas had been asked to attack Specials Posts, free slaves on slave farms and heal them of their 'treatments' if they knew how. Derwin met up with the flying horses in the middle of the night, near the Herders. He hid his flying ship and Zoey disguised it as a hayrick. Derwin vaulted onto Narmad, his own horse. The horses preferred to have riders when on missions – left to themselves they tended to behave like ordinary horses. The power of positive destruction still worked through them but with riders it was more focused.

With Lord Coban was Ahren's horse Zamba. Lord Coban had made a coconut-contact with Ahren, near Panvale, and asked him to make the bandhan to call the horses. Zamba would then respond to the vibrations of the key and be able to find his master. By dawn Lord Coban met Ahren with his partisans, hiding at the bottom of a deep gully in some thick woodland. The flying horse team was complete.

After his spying mission Roarke took his flyer back to the same jungle clearing as before, some way south. He had some food and slept. In the morning he woke and meditated, and when he opened his eyes he had another large audience of admiring animals. He got out his coconut.

'Where are you, Lord Coban?' he asked.

'We're resting near Panvale with Ahren and his partisans. We'll be in the air again soon, and should reach you by dawn tomorrow.'

'I've got even more animals round me this morning. I wish I could tell them what we want of them.'

'One more day,' said Lord Coban. Roarke gave a bandhan of request for as many forest creatures to come near him as possible. He sat in blissful meditation and each time he opened his eyes the crowd around him had grown. He again began playing and singing, and after some time the trees were full of birds too. A hermit walked up and sat among the animals. Roarke was something of an enigma; he was wearing the earth coloured loose cotton overshirt and simple baggy trousers which were typical of ordinary Teletsians, but visible behind him was his sleek grey metal flyer. Also he was playing a beautifully crafted instrument which was inlaid with gold – fit for the prince he was.

'You're a great musician, young man,' the hermit complimented him. He had a long beard and straggly white hair, his clothing was made of skins and his body was wiry and strong.

'I hope it gave you pleasure,' Roarke replied after greeting him respectfully. 'How did you know I was here?'

'The birds told me.'

'You can speak to them?'

'Oh yes. I've been living in this jungle for over fifty years now and I have learnt something of my neighbours' ways.'

'What's your attitude to the Sorcerers?'

'I don't involve myself in the affairs of Teletsia.'

'Could you ask the animals to help us fight them?'

'Maybe. The birds and beasts dislike them intensely because they take some creatures and do terrible experiments on them and force the innocent animals to do their filthy work.'

'I'm expecting some flying horses to arrive soon to help us, so maybe you and they could get together. We need as large an animal army as possible.'

'Flying horses? Who are you?'

'Roarke of Vittalia.'

'I haven't heard of you but I can feel your subtle power. Who are you, really?'

'I'm a guardian, a soul from elsewhere who has taken birth on this world to guide people, if I can.'

'One of the few people I *will* help.'

The hermit called some large gorillas and eagles, and soon sent out messages for anything that could crawl, fly, run or slither to come and help Prince Roarke, his friends and the flying horses. Roarke explained to the hermit about Erin, and also what he had learnt from his spying.

After nightfall he again risked going to the safe house turned enemy headquarters. It was fairly dark with only the Moon of Good Fortune a wafer thin crescent and the half full Moon of Wisdom in the sky. There were sentries walking round the house but it wasn't difficult to avoid them. He hid in the same bushes and soon heard the same voices.

'No holiday!' complained the first.

'When are we pulling out?' asked the second.

'Tomorrow night. The enemy cavalry gave us the slip because they're travelling by night, so we'll do the same. We're going east along the high road to finish off this Castle Mount mob. After that we're to join up with the boys from Lahary. There are reports of a large force of partisans near Panvale who've killed a lot of Specials and High Priests. Some of the partisans can reduce the High Priests to ashes and make the Specials witless,' continued the first.

'This is no ordinary enemy. Why don't the High Priests surrender while they're still alive to do so?' added the second.

'Whose side are you on?' the third went on.

'My own. I want to live, and live in peace,' declared the second.

Roarke gave a bandhan of request that any people like this might eventually get their awakening and become part of the new Teletsia. He returned to the hermit's cave and via the coconut the hermit advised Erin what to do, based on his knowledge of the area. The hermit was mightily puzzled by the coconut but had a surprising grasp of guerrilla strategy.

'If you don't mind my asking,' said Roarke, 'what did you do before you became a hermit?'

'I wanted to start a revolution and destroy the Sorcerers but they captured me. They tried to 'treat' me. I pretended they'd succeeded, behaved like a moronic slave for a week or two, then escaped, and I've lived here ever since.'

'You must have been very strong to have resisted their treatment, their hypnosis.'

'I don't know – maybe I was lucky. When I was young I knew the people who were the Teletsian guardians at that time – maybe they made me stronger. My father worked for one of them.'

The flying horses arrived soon after midnight. Roarke had gone to the hermit's cave to spend the night and heard Ahren calling outside; he had been guided to it by Roarke's directions. Within a short time they had exchanged the necessary news, laid their plans and gone to sleep, the people in the cave and the horses under the stars and moons.

The next day was spent collecting together as many members of the new army as possible and getting them into position. The hermit suggested the perfect spot for an ambush, where the road wound down the side of a valley, crossed a large tributary of the Coffee River and then went up the further hill. The area was wooded, as was much of the land around here, and the river was deep and quite wide. Roarke and the hermit were in contact with Erin. He and his men made their way stealthily to the valley, were ready to fight at moment's notice and hid in the trees near where the ambush was planned. Roarke told Erin about the jungle animals who would help them fight the Teletsian regiment.

At dusk the hermit's eagle friends reported that the Teletsian force was leaving their camp. Roarke was in his flyer, high up with his spyglass out, monitoring events. Ahren, Derwin and the two Pearl Lords stood on the bridge, and shortly before midnight, when all three moons were in the sky, the first soldiers arrived. The officers were on horses and were led by a General and a Sorcerer in a steam car, trundling along slowly at the head of the column.

'Out of the way! The Seventh Regiment needs to pass,' shouted the driver.

'Please sir,' pleaded Ahren, 'I need to talk to the High Priest who is with you. I have some lifesaving information for him.'

The Sorcerer laughed.

'Move!' he shouted, standing up in the open car. The four on the bridge stood their ground. 'Get off the bridge!' The four stood stock still. 'Driver, run them down!' The car and troops started to make their way forward, and simultaneously the four on the bridge jumped to the side and let fly their keys.

Roarke had reprogrammed the Pearl Lords' four petalled ones to operate in fiery discus mode, and Derwin and Ahren had Sasrar keys. The first to die were the Sorcerer and the General, but the keys continued their lethal work, as far back as the order had been heard. Thirty men, all officers or Sorcerers, lay dead within seconds. The car careered through the parapet and into the river, and the riderless horses ran amuck.

'Now! Attack!' Roarke ordered Erin via the coconut.

Erin's men, accompanied by the flying horses, appeared from the forest. The Teletsian troops had seen their leaders slaughtered by miraculous weapons and now saw the flying horses, who collected their riders and withdrew into the jungle. From the dark woods came a cacophony of sounds as thousands of animals poured onto the road which twisted up the side of the valley. Elephants charged, monkeys jumped on people and hit them with rocks and wild cattle gored the foot soldiers. Every animal that could do so attacked the soldiers in some way, and the flying horses, with their riders on them, swooped, kicked and then dodged away into the trees while their riders used conventional weapons. The humans also coordinated the jungle animals through the medium of the flying horses, directing them to where the soldiers were most confused and least able to fight back. The column which constituted the Seventh Regiment was strung out down the road, and the wild animals were everywhere, darting in and out of the moons' light and the shadows of the trees.

Giant eagles flew down and pecked at eyes and throats, the massive tigerlike animals pounced and the rhino-pigs spitted people with their tusks, but it was not random because the animals spared anyone who had a positive feeling. Many of the forest creatures were killed and wounded, but they were fearless and selfless, and full of desire to revenge their fellows who had been taken by the Sorcerers for sinister purposes. There were so many of them – they kept coming and coming, as if the whole of the Teletsian jungles had been emptied to attack the column of thousands of men, many of them unwilling conscripts.

Between the deafening noises of the animals and the screams and groans of the dying another sound could be heard, that of men and horses running away into the woods. Not everyone in the Teletsian army wanted to fight for the fatherland; many preferred to save their skins and go home. Some who did support the Sorcerers, seeing huge constrictor snakes and yet more animals ready to fight waiting under the trees, jumped into the river and there they were met by crocodiles who had been asked to come and help. Those who surrendered to Erin's men were disarmed and put under the guard of some elderly bull elephants – not much good at lumbering around and killing the enemy, but with their enormous tusks they were quite capable of keeping prisoners under control.

Soon after this some surviving Specials and Sorcerers approached Ahren and his colleagues, now standing on the further end of the bridge among the many bodies. The Specials were holding up a white shirt tied to a stick as a flag of surrender.

'I told your people we wanted to talk,' sighed Ahren, 'but they tried to kill us, and now look what's happened!'

'What are your terms?' asked a Sorcerer.

'You must surrender and send a messenger to your overlords in Teletos to surrender the whole country, or worse will happen in the next few days. I'm Ahren Dairyman, and my friends and I are back, as the prophecy said we would be, to set this country free.'

'You arrogant bumpkin!' the Sorcerer scowled.

'After surrendering, you and all your colleagues are to leave Teletsia and go to the island in the Great Sea that the Emperor is kind enough to offer you.'

At this point the Sorcerer, who for years had controlled thousands of people without a word of opposition, lost his temper and began trying to annihilate the people in front of him, even though the word was getting out that this was suicidal. Not only was he reduced to ashes, but all those with him lost their powers of speech and became like animals, unable to talk and crouching down on all fours. They ran off into the woods where maybe some carnivore got them, or perhaps they made it to their homes. A few Sorcerers and Specials did surrender.

'Disarm them,' Lord Coban ordered Erin's men. 'Take the Sorcerers' staffs and the Specials' weapons, and let them go. It can only help us if they tell their friends of yet another of our victories.'

'You lot,' Ahren demanded to about twenty Sorcerers and eighty Specials, heads hung in shame, 'go back to Darzeet or wherever you come from. We'll let you know when to contact the ships which will take you into exile. It will be very much in your interest to obey us.' He had some of Erin's men escort them in the direction of Coffee Ferry. Ahren sighed and shook his head when they had left.

'The truth of the matter is, what would we do with prisoners?' he said to Erin.

The men who were nearby gave thanks to Mother Earth for the victory in the traditional way.

After some time Derwin called for his flying horse and vaulted onto him. He, and Ahren on his horse Zamba, flew back down the road full of bodies to see if any of the medical staff had survived. The victors and Erin's men needed help with the many wounded, including the animals, and eventually found a number of young men and women, conscripts, hiding at the side of the road where they had climbed the trees for safety. Most of them had been members of Resistance Groups and were overjoyed when they discovered Derwin and Ahren were two of the seven rebels.

Once all the unhurt animals had disappeared, many other young people, all conscripts, climbed down from the trees where they had been hiding. None of the Specials or their sympathisers were in the area any more; most were dead and a few had managed to run away. The conscripts came up to the victors and thanked them profusely. The people being guarded by the old elephants were all allowed to go free too.

'That's the end of your call up,' said Ahren. 'You can go home, unless you want to join Erin Heber and the men from Castle Mount.'

More and more conscripts discovered who Derwin and Ahren were. As their colleagues appeared from the trees they put forward a spokesman, a young man of about Ahren's age and a Resistance Group leader.

'We want to help,' he began. 'Some of us would like to join the mountain men, but others could do something else useful. If your people would let us through, we could pretend we've escaped. We'll not say anything about Duke Heber's force and could tell the officers at Panvale that the Seventh has been destroyed by jungle animals. We'll warn them that you're invincible and it'd be better to surrender.'

'If you tell your overlords that they'll shoot you,' objected Ahren. 'We'll find you some horses, let you through and when you reach the troops, pretend you've escaped from us, but discreetly put the word around to their conscripts that we won't kill anyone who lays down his weapons. If we do have to attack, they should lie on the ground as if dead - or run away, or if they can, they would help us enormously if they can attack the Specials, Sorcerers and their supporters.'

'Fine, we'll try,' continued the conscripts' spokesman.

'How many of you have had your inner awakening?' asked Derwin.

'We've heard about it, and some have, but they didn't get much chance to give it to the rest of us, because we were always being watched,' explained another conscript.

'No problem,' said Ahren. 'Get your people together, and apart from the medical units, who must see to some of the animals that are in a very bad way, all of you go over there,' he pointed to the open valley by the river. 'We'll have a short programme right now.'

So it was that Ahren, Derwin and Roarke gave a rapidly convened mass awakening programme, and showed the conscripts of the decimated Seventh Regiment how to be invulnerable to the black magic of the Sorcerers. Later the medical staff came along and were also given awakening – much needed as they were exhausted. It was a welcome end to the battle, allowing the deepest part of their souls to respond to the inspired music of Roarke.

The flying horses managed to round up a number of their ordinary cousins who had escaped and were in the woodland or wandering around the open country. Ahren told the conscripts to wait until morning and then to set off carefully along the high road on horseback to subvert the regiments encamped at the Temple of Support, and even the one at Woodenton, if they could get that far.

When the medical units and the humans who had led the attack were helping the wounded animals, they could not understand why there were no enemy wounded. They were either dead or had fled. Ahren eventually found the hermit, sitting alone on a hillock in the moons' light, and asked him if he knew the answer.

'Yes. Any of the enemy who were wounded and lying on the ground were finished off by the snakes. I sent them in, because we jungle dwellers don't want them lying around suffering for days on end until they die of their wounds. The ways of the jungle might seem callous to you folks, but it's the best way to deal with them.

'If we're all done here, I'll be off back to my cave. Thank young Roarke for his music; that was a real treat – makes a change from birdsong. I liked the awakening programme; and you play nicely too,' the hermit complimented him, because Ahren had improvised on a drum.

'I'm overwhelmed at the way the animals respect you. I have so much to learn from you. May I visit you some time?'

'I'll look forward to it, my boy.' He said goodbye and disappeared into the woods.

Erin invited the victors to join him at his camp on the further hill. His mountain men had enough to talk about for many a long day and celebrated their victory with the conscripts from the Teletsian army who had joined them.

Roarke contacted Rajay via coconut in the early morning. Rajay was awake, awaiting his call; there was no way he could sleep after the news he had just received. His cavalry had by now met up with Ahren and Saman's partisans and were hiding in a wooded valley some way north west of Panvale.

'Hi, sorry to disturb you,' began Roarke. 'With the help of the hermit, the flying horses, our allies from Castle Mount and thousands of creatures from the jungles, we've defeated and destroyed the Seventh Regiment, some way to the east of Coffee Ferry.'

'Incredible! Superb!' cried Rajay.

'Also, Fern, the girl from the Coffee Ferry Inn, found us,' continued Roarke. 'She'd been hiding at another safe house. Can you contact any groups of our people who are ambushing the main road to Teletos? Some conscripts that we've encouraged to escape will be riding up it to tell the regiments at the Temple of Support, Woodenton and so on, how powerful we are.'

'I wish we were. We've got major problems elsewhere,' replied Rajay with a sigh.

This was the news Rajay had received late the previous day:

'Hello,' a voice had said to him some time before, 'I'm Garma Nalanda. Am I speaking to His Majesty King Rajay?'

'Yes, but let's not emphasise the king part right now. Where are you?'

'In the headquarters of the Fourth Regiment outside Plimpet, but I'm in big trouble.'

'What do you mean?'

'The Sorcerers know a lot of the conscripts don't want to fight so they're going to make an example of some of us, if there's a battle, and as I've just turned up here they've decided I'll do for one. They're going to put some of us out in front, say we've refused to fight, and shoot us shortly before the battle begins. Then they'll put the conscripts in the front of the army, and the regular soldiers and Specials will be behind. If the conscripts don't shoot the enemy the regulars will shoot the conscripts from the back.'

'That doesn't seem to be a very intelligent way of deploying your troops.' Rajay was horrified. 'When is this supposed to happen?'

'Soon. Their spies know some of some of your warships have come back from Darzeet, but they aren't sure where the next part of the invasion will come from. They're going to move the Fourth Regiment to the place at the top of the estuary where the coast road meets the road from Plimpet to Teletos. I don't know where your men are but be warned.'

'They're still on the Island, but that's very helpful information. We'll try to save you – don't despair.'

Rajay cut the contact and next called Lee, who was once more in perfect health and preparing to lead the rest of the troops into Teletsia.

'Where are you, Lee?'

'Oh hello, Rajay. I was about to contact you. We're on the south shore of the Island with every able bodied man we can muster. I've been in touch with Stellamar and she's given two coconuts to the local partisans. Once the moons set the partisans on the mainland will attack the shore batteries. We'll cross into Teletsia by the causeway and over the quicksand, as that part is not so heavily guarded.'

'How will you get over the water?'

'We've got masses of boats – the lifeboats and launches from the ships, and anything small enough not to get damaged by the shoals near the causeway. People with horses will swim them across.'

'What about the quicksand?'

'Merien, me and others with keys will stand on the further side of the bar and the others will have to look at the keys we'll hold up. Also we'll string ropes across and ask people to hold onto them, so if anyone does sink we can pull them out.'

'Lee, you're too optimistic,' cautioned Rajay. 'Not everyone has your faith in the keys. I don't want my men finishing up in a patch of Teletsian quicksand.'

'What do you suggest then?'

'We'll send the fleet towards Plimpet so it looks as if we're about to invade the port. That should draw off some of the Teletsians guarding the shore near you. Land on the beach near the quicksand, where there are no shore batteries, with a few men you are absolutely sure *will* have faith in the keys and cross the quicksand with them. Between these men, and the partisans on the mainland behind the shore batteries, you should be able to overpower the people manning the guns on the beaches. You might be able to creep round and attack them from behind. Then the main part of your force could land.'

'OK, We'll try that.'

In didn't work out as planned. One of the partisans, a man who collected seaweed to sell as fertilizer, knew some paths through the quicksand and led everyone across without being spotted by the Teletsian shore batteries. At the same time as the forces were being led through these paths Merien, the master of storms, raised a violent but local one. Although he did not know it, this one turned into a tornado which twisted its way along the shore and the men manning the gun batteries ran for their lives. The storm also wetted the invading troops but not to the extent of disabling them. The invasion force set off for the bridge and road junction at the top of the estuary via the same route as Stellamar had led Raynor and the others on five years before – through the thin woodland and scrub of the coastal areas.

At Plimpet, some way to the east and across the estuary, most people looked longingly at the warships and hoped they would soon be invaded, because many rumours were going round that these invaders were good people. The Sorcerer's Coast Guards shook with fear.

The Plimpet Regiment was some way inland, waiting for the invaders at the bridge. Their Sorcerer general did not much care about the fate of Plimpet and preferred to wait for the invaders where his troops would have the advantage. He intended to kill a few of the conscripts he knew to be sympathetic to the rebels before the fighting started, to encourage the others, and he also had other plans.

Lee sent scouts ahead to where the Teletsian regiment was waiting. He had partisans with him who knew the country well, and as suspected the Sorcerers' army was divided in two parts, one each side of a narrow valley through which the road to the south ran. The invasion forces were heavily outnumbered and outarmed, but at least they were all faithful to the cause. When the scouts returned, Lee decided to take his force to the west of the valley, and approach one half of the Teletsian army from behind. Then he would only have to face half the troops, because there was a narrow side valley behind the main one and the Teletsians were bunched at the end of this, waiting to catch the invaders as they came up the main valley. He failed to realise that the Teletsians also had scouts following his progress.

CHAPTER 10

BUILDERS

Soon after sunrise Robin persuaded Yamun to land on the deck of the largest Daish Shaktay troopship lying off the coast near Teletos, and he could see a flyer there. On the horizon was an island – the same one as Roarke had taken Lee to when they had escaped from Gyan-on-Sea. He told Yamun to go there until he called him with his key. Robin was soon in the captain's cabin, sitting with Pa Ganoozal, Marimba and Conwenna.

'Guess what, Robin, I've learnt how to pilot a flyer!' said Conwenna. 'It's not that difficult, provided your Tree of Life is awakened, and your attention is clear and focused.'

'I prefer Yamun,' Robin replied.

'It's good to see you, but why are you here?' Pa Ganoozal welcomed him.

'Drusilla Prospector has got Raynor and I'm going to see if I can do a deal with her.'

'I heard about Raynor,' Pa Ganoozal looked sad.

'How are you going to get to Drusilla?' asked Marimba.

'I have some ideas, but would welcome yours,' said Robin.

'Derwin told me Sparkly Diamondcutter has got a coconut now. Let's contact him,' Conwenna suggested.

Robin spoke to Sparkly, who told him the city was very empty, because with the Daish Shaktay troopships at the bottom of the estuary and Teletsian regiments near Teletos, many people had fled to the country. He said he could send his grandson Borry with a boat to the island where they had done the fire ceremony if that would be any help.

'Robin, I'll drive the flyer and we'll go together,' Conwenna said. 'I've got a Sasrar key to protect me and so have you, and you're a great fighter. Drusilla would be only too happy if I walked in her door.'

'You don't know what's at stake here,' objected Robin.

'I do. We've got to get to Raynor before she kills him. It's that simple. Let's feel the vibrations. Ask this: will it help Raynor and Teletsia, if we try to go and see my horrible aunt?'

'There's some coolness but also some tingles. We'll leave it until this evening and try again,' Robin declared.

Later, Robin and Marimba were walking alone on the deck together.

'Marimba, as a guardian, you recognise another one, don't you?'

'Yes, Roarke told me you're keeping it secret.'

'That's what the other guardians advised, except from Asha – they felt it was alright to tell her. There's more to this than rescuing Raynor, although that's also vital. It's going to be extremely dangerous and I don't want Conwenna coming too.'

'I don't see how you're going to get to Drusilla without her. I'll take you both.'

Robin deferred to Marimba as she was a more senior guardian. As a result Conwenna spent the day using her artistic talents, busy at the long table in the captain's cabin forging travel passes and other documents, while Robin was below decks having his hair dyed black and his skin tinted brown again.

'I hope when we're through with these wars we can all look as Mother Nature created us!' observed Robin as he looked at himself in a mirror.

That night Marimba, Robin and Conwenna did their best to raise a fog or storm, but they could only manage a thin, patchy cloud cover. They set off with documents, weapons and keys, and Conwenna insisted on a bag of meaty bones and tasty scraps.

'You and your dog food!' teased Robin.

They flew to the east of Teletos and approached the island where Namoh had done the fire ceremony. They hovered in the clouds up above, checked on vibrations it was safe to land, Marimba deposited them and left. Neither of them had been here before but Sparkly Diamondcutter had told them to wait in the clearing in the centre of the islet. After some time they heard footsteps approaching and hid in the trees.

'I definitely saw a flying ship near here,' said one voice.

'Lucky the Weathermaster made sure the skies were fairly clear, so we could see it,' added the other. 'I don't like this place. They did some rituals here and you know what happened when they did that stuff at the Clatan stone circle.'

Robin indicated for Conwenna to have her key ready so it could transform into fiery discus mode. He had more conventional weapons at hand.

'I'll unleash the dog when he picks up a scent,' went on the first. 'That'll flush them out. Meanwhile let's look for this flying ship. I don't believe they take off into another dimension.'

They heard the baying of a dog crashing towards them through the undergrowth. Suddenly it was in front of them – large and heavy, with vast jowls and fanglike teeth. Conwenna gave it the bones; it took them greedily and sat at her feet, happily tucking into this unexpected feast. The Specials didn't feed their dogs very much; they reasoned they would be more vicious if they were hungry. She gave it some vibrations, to which it responded remarkably well and even wagged its tail at her. If only humans were that easy, she thought.

'Quick, follow me!' whispered Robin. They edged round the side of the clearing and made their way towards the riverside. There was a path which led to where the Specials had left their boat, moored to an overhanging tree branch. Robin and Conwenna could hear that the two Specials had come upon the dog and it was snarling ferociously. Robin indicated to Conwenna to jump in the Specials' boat. They cast off and rowed furiously downstream.

'That was a close one!' said Conwenna, when they were well away.

'I'll never laugh at your dog bones idea again. We can't risk waiting for Sparkly's grandson. We'll have to take this boat to Teletos. If we put on those cloaks and hats lying there we'll look like Specials.' Soon they reached the estuary and almost rowed into Borry Diamondcutter, coming upstream. He panicked, assuming they were Specials.

'Borry, it's us,' cried Conwenna. 'Come with us and we'll get past the harbour guards more easily.' He left his own boat tied up under some trees when they were well way from the scene of their crime and nearing Teletos, and together sailed and rowed back to the city. In a Specials' boat, hooded and cloaked in the night, they were not challenged, and some time later Borry dropped them at Sparkly Diamondcutter's water gate, then took the Specials' boat to where he had left his, picked up his own and returned some time later.

Sparkly gave them a warm welcome and introduced them to a lad of about Derwin's age. This was the treated slave that Raynor had freed of his hypnosis and who had managed to escape a couple of nights before. Because these slaves were usually completely witless they were not guarded as closely as might have been expected, and this young man had pretended to be especially docile. He had been returned to the old stables at the back of the Restorer's former property and had simply gone out for a walk in the walled garden late at night, vaulted over the wall onto the canal-side path and run for his life to Mrs Fisher's place. She punted him to the Diamondcutters before anyone noticed he had escaped.

'Drusilla has got Raynor in her flat at the moment but she'll take him down to the cellars soon. That's where they really torture people,' said the boy. 'You must be quick, because she's beginning to realise he isn't ever going to dance to her tune. She'll torment him brutally and kill him when she's got what she can out of him. I overheard that from the Specials.'

It was nearly dawn when Sparkly hid them in their secret room, more like a big cupboard behind the diamond safe and left them to sleep for some time, but first Robin called Rajay.

'We're at the Diamondcutter's,' Robin began.

'How's it going?' replied Rajay, from central Teletsia.

'We nearly got caught on the island.'

'You must move fast or the chances of saving Raynor will be nil. His heart centre is getting weaker; I can feel it when I put my attention on him. If he loses his confidence and becomes frightened he won't be able to withstand Drusilla's sorcery.'

'We'll try today. Wish us luck!'

That afternoon a builder's boat punted across Teletos, over the open water in the centre of the city where the Forbidden Quarter had been before it was sunk by the earthquake, to the area of the Restorers' palace, now the Sorcerers' Headquarters. In the boat was a boy slave, a strong workman who didn't look like a local, and Borry. First they went to the house of Mrs Fisher, on the banks of the same canal that the Restorers' house backed onto.

'Hello Ma Fisher,' said the slave.

'My, how you've grown! It's been over five years!' Mrs Fisher embraced Conwenna, who was in disguise.

'Have you got your pass key?' Robin, the workman, asked Mrs Fisher.

'Yes, and I'll tell the guard on the back gate I have to collect some things I left there, before the Sorcerers took the place over. I've done it before. He's not like the others and he doesn't mind.'

'Conwenna, you and I must put on the special bandhans to hide our golden auras,' said Robin as they did so. 'Off we go, then,' he went on brightly, trying to downplay the mortal danger of calmly walking into the Sorcerers' lair.

The guard on the back gate heard Mrs Fisher knocking, opened it and let them in. She introduced him to the maintenance men, who were carrying a small ladder and their bags of building tools. She explained they were the ones who always did this work and were expected, and they walked purposefully across the back yard, through the archway, into the central courtyard and towards the stairs.

'That sentry at the bottom of the stairs might recognise me,' she said. 'I'll have to leave you because he's a very unpleasant character. Conwenna, you know the way, don't you?'

'Yes,' she replied as Mrs Fisher faded into the shadows. This sentry waved them on when they said they were going to fix the leaking roof in Miss Drusilla's flat.

'At last, I thought they'd never send anyone,' he said.

'Lucky the real builders didn't make it first, but you can count on workmen never turning up when they say they will,' whispered Robin, and Conwenna directed them to her former home. As they passed the first floor they could hear a meeting of the Head Sorcerers in progress. It sounded heated, angry and desperate.

'...And none of our spy vultures have returned for days now, so we've completely lost track of the invaders,' said one voice.

'How can hundreds, maybe thousands of soldiers just disappear?'

'There are reports that the Seventh Regiment has been destroyed.'

'Those hillmen from Castle Mount couldn't possibly defeat our much larger and better equipped forces.'

'The Great One will soon break the leader of the rebels…'

No one took any notice of the workmen, who reached the second floor, nodding respectfully to the various sentries on duty. Once in the upstairs passage outside Drusilla's flat, Conwenna showed the others the right door and then hid out of sight. Borry knocked and after some time a Special opened it, yawning because they had disturbed his siesta.

'Who are you?' he asked.

'Maintenance men,' said Borry confidently. 'We were told to look at the roof, if you don't mind us coming in.'

'You'd better. There's a bad damp stain on the living room ceiling.'

'Is Miss Prospector here?'

'No, she's down in the cellars.'

'I think we should have a word with her,' said Robin. 'We know the way down,' he turned to go.

'Eh – she won't want to be disturbed,' the Special called, but they had already left.

'We've got to look at the drains first,' explained Borry as he again passed the sentry at the bottom of the main stairs. Conwenna directed them to the back cellar steps and here they were stopped once more.

'No one goes down there today,' ordered another sentry.

'With respect sir, we were told to, by Miss Prospector herself,' Borry insisted. 'We often work for her and she was adamant that we came today – don't know why, but orders are orders.'

The sentry nodded and let them pass. Anyone who even knew Miss Prospector's name had to be important in some way. Maybe they were actually torturers, because he knew the prisoner was soon to be dealt with in that way, and then disposed of permanently. They went down to the extensive cellars guided by Conwenna, whose heart was thumping like a drum. Once she had been locked in down there for a whole day, by mistake, when a small child. They looked around and saw a light at the end of a passage with a sentry standing outside a closed door.

'We need to look at the drains in there,' Robin pointed at a door.

'No admittance,' said the sentry. 'What are you doing down here? It's forbidden.'

'Not to us,' Robin continued, and within seconds, with the help of Borry, he had the man pinned to the ground, a knife at his neck. 'Is Drusilla Prospector in there with a young man?'

'Yes, she's doing rituals. Don't go in or she'll kill us all.' He was passive to begin with, but then made a lunge at Robin and tried to escape from his knife, so Robin had no choice but to drive it home. Robin knew how to kill people quickly and silently, if he had to. He was only too aware that a large number of people, including this sentry, might die soon, in any event.

Borry stayed in the passage to keep guard while Robin opened the door and went in. There was a mind-numbing stench, Drusilla was chanting and Raynor was lying chained on a stone slab. Water was dripping from a pipe onto his forehead. He looked pale, exhausted and very thin. Conwenna followed Robin into the room and Drusilla looked round, furious at being disturbed.

'Hello Aunt Drusilla. We meet again,' smiled Conwenna. 'We've come to make you an offer.'

Drusilla assessed the situation. She assumed her sentry was outside, but for some extraordinary reason had let these visitors in. Above her were a lot of Sorcerers, and everywhere in the building were more sentries. This might be her chance to finally capture Conwenna and be done with her, and this other man might prove useful as well.

'You? Do a deal with me? Do you know who I am?' she laughed cruelly and there was a blinding flash. 'I am pure power. But I can use you, Conwenna, because Raynor is not responding and I need a new instrument to work through.'

'Madam,' Robin began, 'I am the Prime Minister of Chussan and I come on a last diplomatic mission.'

'Prime Minister? I'd have thought Albion would at least have chosen someone with some subtle power. You don't even have a shining aura, although you wouldn't know about that,' sneered Drusilla. 'Yes, we could have a few words.'

'Leave us, Borry,' demanded Robin, walking out of the door and into the passage. 'Take my shoulder bag.' His coconut was in his bag and he didn't want anyone calling him at that time. 'Go back to our boat, right now. I'll catch up with you later. And you too Conwenna, I absolutely insist.'

'But...' she objected.

'Leave me with your aunt and don't argue.'

Robin went back into the cellar, lit only by candles. The water continued to drip on Raynor's forehead and Robin turned to Drusilla.

'Madam, I would appreciate it if while we're talking, you could remove that water pipe from Raynor's forehead. It disturbs me to see him suffer.' Drusilla did nothing so Robin did it for her. He saw anger on her face but she did not say anything. 'Miss Prospector, the forces of the Teletsian freedom struggle are closing in on the capital and it's only a matter of time before we take it. If you release my friend, on behalf of the leaders of Free Teletsia, King Rajay of Daish Shaktay, myself, and.....'

'I know who you are. I found your ultimatum.'

'.....we will offer you amnesty and a safe passage to the island in the Great Sea that the Emperor is donating to those who must leave Teletsia. If you refuse you might get killed.'

'I don't want amnesty. I've made some new keys. They're much more powerful than yours, and with them my people and I can destroy you all.'

'You will release Raynor or I will.'

'I am the power behind Teletsia and you will *not* order me around.'

'I will not kill you, because I will never harm a woman.' Robin continued forcibly and strode over to the wall, where there were a number of large iron keys, 'but you will tell me which is the key to his shackles, now!' In answer Drusilla called for the sentry but there was no answer. Conwenna heard this from outside the door, where she and Borry were still waiting.

'Borry, take my shoulder bag too – it's got my coconut in it and I don't want to be disturbed – and get out of here as Robin told you to. I'm going to try something, but you *must* get away quickly and raise the alarm - now.'

Borry decided it was time to obey Robin and Conwenna, and made off smartly up the corridor and out, grabbing the ladder as he left. Conwenna re-entered the room.

'The sentry is dead. We're at war, Aunt Drusilla. Either you free Raynor or I will kill you,' and she took a vicious dagger out from under her clothing. 'You destroyed my father. I'm strong these days and not bound by an oath of chivalry like Robin. You also murdered my mother and now it's your turn.'

'Conwenna no! I told you to get out of here. Where's Borry?' demanded Robin.

'He left.' Conwenna advanced towards Drusilla in an aggressive manner. 'I know who you are, Queen Wasp. I've killed before and I'll do so again.' She had no idea how to kill anyone, no intention of doing so and no idea how to use a sharp knife except for chopping vegetables, but it sounded good and had the desired effect.

Drusilla clutched an iron key hanging from a chain around her throat, pointed it at Robin and Conwenna, and said some ugly words in a dark language. There was another blinding flash and she looked terrified. She ran out into the passage but there was a mighty explosion and the whole building shook and collapsed, and anyone in it would most probably be killed.

Drusilla's body was crushed and her spirit left Teletsia, and Navi Septa, for ever, because she had tried to kill another guardian.

Borry was by this time in the yard. He looked round in horror and felt a localised earthquake which caused the building to come crashing down until it was a heap of stones, broken roof tiles, smashed beams and crushed glass. He dropped his ladder, ran to the wall around the property and vaulted over it, found his boat and paddled down the canal for all he was worth. He did not stop until he was nearly back at the Diamondcutter's. He realised he was carrying Robin and Conwenna's shoulder bags with their coconuts. He knew how to use them and called Rajay.

Rajay told Borry not to contact anyone else for the time being. He had long suspected Robin would try to goad Drusilla into killing him, because Robin was the one guardian who could do this and hope for results, being as she did not know he was a guardian. She would then destroy herself, but in the process possibly sacrifice those around her as well. Nevertheless, Rajay was stunned when he heard what had happened and more so when Borry told him Conwenna had been there too.

The noise of the collapsing building died down. Robin and Conwenna were crouching on the floor of the cellar room with their hands over their heads, but Raynor was still chained on top of the stone slab.

'Are we all OK?' asked Robin, cautiously.

'Just about,' croaked Raynor, 'It's great to see you. Give me water – I'm desperate.' Conwenna hurriedly let the pipe drip into his mouth rather than on his forehead. 'Get me out of these chains. It's the big key on the ring over there, on the wall.'

'Don't move,' said Conwenna as she carefully unlocked his leg irons. She noticed grazes and cuts where they had dug into his flesh.

'She put that awful drip on my forehead for two days, but wouldn't give me any water to drink,' gasped Raynor, drinking thirstily.

Robin tried the door but outside was solid fallen masonry. The cellar, miraculously, was undamaged. 'Collect the water in that bucket,' he ordered. 'We may need it later.'

'Have you got any food? I'm starving,' Raynor went on.

'You're lucky, I put a stale chicken roll in my pocket to give to any ferocious dogs. It's something I do these days,' Conwenna took a squashed packet out of her pocket and Raynor wolfed it down. 'Sorry I don't have any more,' she looked piteously.

'Blow out all the candles except one,' said Robin. 'We may also need those later.'

'What did that scorpion of a woman do to you?' asked Conwenna

'I don't want to talk about it. It's fantastic to be free! What's happened?' Raynor sat upright and rubbed his arms and legs. He was weak and wobbly.

'My Aunt Drusilla has destroyed herself,' Conwenna didn't sound remotely upset.

'Trouble is, she may have done the same for us,' added Robin. 'She's brought the whole building down. I realised that might happen, which was why I told you to leave and save yourself, Conwenna.'

'How come?'

'If a guardian tries to destroy another guardian, a great deal of negativity will also be destroyed. Above us, in the main reception room the Sorcerers were having a Council of War, so the forces of nature finished them off too. Remember what happened when Rajay heard the news about Danard's death, how it tore him and Daish Shaktay apart? Danard wasn't a guardian but his death had a serious effect on Rajay, which in turn had a powerful effect on the whole country,' explained Robin.

'So, big brother Robin's best kept secret comes out!' said Conwenna. 'I suspected it years ago, when you first showed us your sixth centre key.'

'If you knew I was a guardian, why in heaven's name didn't you take my advice to get out? We may be entombed.'

'Drusilla most probably killed my parents. She gave me a horrible childhood and I wasn't going to let her kill Raynor as well. Plus I've figured out how to make these types destroy themselves. Anyhow, don't let's give up hope. Let's all give a bandhan of request that we're going to get out of here.'

'It's cool,' Robin declared, even before they started doing it. 'I hope we aren't half dead by then.'

'Meantime, could you give me some healing vibrations?' murmured Raynor. 'I'm feeling dreadful.'

'Yes, you should have said,' Robin apologised. 'You must have gone through hell.'

'Could have been better, but at least Drusilla didn't do conventional torture on me, only that dripping water and her hideous rituals, which I found incredibly boring.'

Conwenna and Robin sat behind Raynor and after giving him vibrations for some time he perked up enormously.

CHAPTER 11

SMOKE

'Asha, is that you?' Rajay called me early next morning. He sounded worried.

'Yes, any news of Robin?'

'Feel his vibrations.'

'He seems all right. Is there some problem?'

'Yes....' He related what Borry had told him via a coconut.

'I think they might be trapped in those cellars. Yes, that feels cool on my hands. We must rescue them while there's still time. I'm not going to give up hope, and I'll tell Tandi that they're in hiding for the time being.'

'Let's hope you're right.'

'Roarke, are you there?' asked Rajay that evening, having called Roarke and the others briefly in the morning to tell them Borry's news.

'Yes, I'm flying towards where you are. I'll be with you shortly. I've got Derwin with me, and Ahren and the Pearl Lords will be coming with the horses later. I'll drop Derwin off at the Herders so he can pick up his flyer. We got a bit delayed because we kept finding more and more conscripts who'd run away into the woods, and they all want to help us.'

'What did you tell them?'

'We advised them to go to their homes and give awakening to as many people as they could, or join Erin's troop, or form themselves into partisan bands and attack the Specials and Sorcerers. They've had a bit of military training now and they've got plenty of weapons. If any Specials surrender, I said they should give them the option of the island in the Sea of Illusion, and meanwhile imprison them in their own jails. I also gave out a few coconuts, so if you get calls from people you've never heard of, that's who they are.'

'That's fine, but there's a change of plan. Can you fly over the Temple of Support and find out what those Teletsian forces there are doing? That's an absolute priority. We're going to attack Teletos, because we have to try and get to Robin and company. Asha and I are convinced they're still alive, but if they're trapped somewhere we must rescue them soon.'

'Can't the resistance people in Teletos do that?'

'No, because the Sorcerers may be doing their best to get to them too, and in any case, sooner or later we must take the capital. There are bound to be forces guarding the city but at least it won't be their whole army, if the Sorcerers' regiments from Clatan and Lahary are waiting for us near the Temple of Support. It's a good place for them, because the vibrations are so strong there they'll either get much better or much worse. And if it's worse they'll only be a problem to themselves.'

'We've all seen that!'

'I want you to confirm that they're actually up there, though. Then I need you to come here and I'll also need Derwin and his flyer. We must meet Lee and his men near the port of Plimpet this morning and you must pick me up in your flyer. The troops here can leave for Teletos now and we'll follow later.'

In the early morning Lee, over two thousand Daish Shaktay men and about four hundred local partisans crept through the scrubland on the western side of the estuary near Plimpet. Merien had met up with Derwin during the night.

'Merien,' said Lee on the coconut, 'where are you?'

'We're in Derwin's flyer, above you, trying to hide above the few clouds. We'll await your orders.'

'Roarke, are you somewhere around, in your flyer?' Lee also called him.

'Yes, I can see Derwin and I'll wait for your instructions.'

Lee and his forces advanced down a side valley towards the main one, to where the first bridge over the estuary was situated and where they had been told the Teletsians were waiting for them. About twenty Sorcerers – almost all that remained in the Plimpet area, could be seen on a hill at the side of the armed forces, preparing to wave their staffs around and chant the gestures of annihilation. Below them, also on the hill at the side of the main valley, were the soldiers – conscripts, regular soldiers and Specials, but in front of these were a number of conscripts in chains, including Garma.

'I know one of those conscripts,' said Freddi the failed assassin, looking through a spyglass and standing beside Lee, in the valley.

'Another one is Garma Nalanda,' observed Lee, having also taken the spyglass.

'What are the Sorcerers' men going to do?'

'Shoot them.' Lee got out his coconut and made a call, 'Derwin, now – quickly or it will be too late.' Then he made another one: 'Roarke, now.'

The two flyers appeared from behind clouds and made for the area above where the chained conscripts were standing. From each flyer many large grey baglike shapes were thrown out and as they hit the ground they exploded in a mass of flames and smoke – mostly smoke. The flyers landed in the chaos, a man got out of each and with large metal cutters freed the prisoners.

'Run for it,' shouted Merien, having cut free one conscript, 'our people won't hurt you.'

'Get in the flyer, Garma,' demanded Rajay, wielding the other cutter.

'Excuse me, but your voice sounds like King Rajay,' said Garma. 'Please give me the cutters and you get in the flyer.'

'Get in, that's an order,' repeated Rajay sharply, already freeing another hostage. Garma did as he was told.

Merien was not so lucky. While he was cutting the bonds of another of the conscripts who was about to be shot, a Special guarding this one wounded Merien, who was holding the metal cutter so could not get to his own weapons. The Special advanced to finish him off. Luckily Derwin appeared out of the smoke and prepared to let fly his Sasrar key. The Special had not threatened him, but had tried to kill Merien. The key left Derwin's hand and beheaded the Special. Derwin cut free the last conscript, picked up his key and helped Merien back into the flyer hovering nearby. They took off through the smoke.

'I'm not too bad,' whispered Merien bravely from the back seat. He was lying down and his neck and shoulder were bleeding profusely.

'I'll take you straight back to the Island.'

Derwin didn't talk as he flew back to the Island and Merien, behind him in the passenger's seat, didn't say anything either. Derwin assumed it was because Merien knew that flying fast took absolutely perfect attention. Some time later they landed in the yard of Lord Jarwhen's mansion. He turned round and saw Merien slumped on the seat unconscious and blood everywhere. Lord Jarwhen and some men were ready with a stretcher.

'Oh no, this isn't possible! Not again!' he cried as he saw his grandson. 'Quick, get him inside! Make sure the surgeon is ready!'

Roarke's flyer took off through the smoke and Rajay looked out onto the troops below. With his practised eyes he noticed something. Lee's scouts had reported that the Teletsian troops were on either side of a valley through which the road ran, but he only saw troops on the west side, where Lee would attack when he arrived. Rajay took Roarke's spyglass and asked him to hover high over the area while he scanned it.

The first thing he noticed was that the group of Sorcerers standing on the hill overlooking the valley were not making any attempt to annihilate the invaders. Obviously the Sorcerers knew it was suicidal and a waste of time to even try. Lee's troops could be seen on the further hill in the scrubby bushes and trees. He realised that the Teletsians must have discovered where Lee and his men were coming from, and although the troops to the west of the valley were still there as reported, the ones which were previously on the east side had been moved, and were now hiding in the scrubland behind where Lee's force would come, so his men would be caught between the two parts of the Teletsian army.

'Lee, abort the mission – now,' Rajay commanded via his coconut. 'Return to the Island as quickly as you can. The Teletsians have laid a trap for you and I don't want my men massacred.'

'But..' Lee replied, astounded.

'Just do it. Trust me - we can still win this war. Make for the estuary with the men, to that place with a stream and what looks like a boathouse from up here.'

'That's where we met Stellamar, when we were escaping before. I'm sure I can find it.'

'Lord Coban's fishing boats will be there to pick you up. Take some partisans to guide you and send the rest on southwards, but only if they can hide themselves in the scrubland, in order to get past the Teletsian army. They should take guns with them. Do any of them have horses?'

'Yes, most of them.'

'Only send the ones with horses, so they can make a quick getaway. Make sure their leader has a coconut, because I may need to contact him.'

'Will do.'

Lee followed Rajay's instructions and had most of his men turn round, abandon their baggage, and run as quickly as they could back the way they had come. The brave Daish Shaktay soldiers did not want to do this to start with, but Lee said the order came from Rajay, so they relented. The partisans meanwhile forced their horses through the rough scrubland and by a roundabout route reached the road some way south, where it ran over a wooded hilltop. Once there, Rajay told the leader, by coconut, to stop and make ready their guns, as many as they could. They had handguns and some small cannon with them, loaded on packhorses.

He called Lord Coban and told him they needed to evacuate his men fast. They had planned this in case anything went wrong with the invasion, and soon a flotilla of pearl fishers' craft and other boats made their way from where they had been hidden on the estuary banks under trees, to the boathouse. The Teletsian Sorcerers' troops were still waiting in the same place, and Rajay assumed they would start to chase Lee and his now rapidly retreating forces, but after some time nothing had happened. The Teletsians were still in the same positions as before.

'Armies like ours don't usually take the trouble to invade, then run away just before they meet the defenders, the Sorcerers' troops,' observed Roarke. 'Plus the word is out that you're directing operations, Rajay, and you've got quite a reputation for being clever and devious. Maybe these chaps think we are playing a trick on them – that Lee has ordered his troops to run away to make them chase his soldiers.'

'You may be right,' replied Rajay, looking through the spyglass. He called the leader of the partisans on the wooded hilltop to the south of the Teletsians.

'Don't open fire yet, and try not to let the Teletsians see you,' Rajay ordered.

He watched carefully, and had Roarke fly north to where Lee's troops were approaching the boathouse. There were still no signs of pursuit from the

Sorcerers' army. Rajay noticed a large number of fishing boats and Lee's troops starting to scramble aboard and make off up the estuary to safety. He asked Roarke to fly back so as to be above the Teletsian Sorcerers' army, and as he did he noticed a small contingent of mounted Teletsian troops galloping up the road in the direction of the boathouse. He called Lee to warn him, and Lee said virtually everyone was by now on a fishing boat. He was waiting until last before boarding, to make sure no one was left behind. Rajay called the leader of the partisans again.

'Now, fire all your guns as violently as you can, as if you're beginning a major attack. Try and make them think you're the whole force. Then, before they can get close to you, jump on your horses and gallop south. Abandon the cannon, because we have plenty more and the main thing is to get everyone out alive. We have to keep the Teletsians away from my men as long as possible. They're on the boats now, but those little craft don't move very fast so we need to buy time for them.'

'Sometimes one has to run away from the field of battle to win the war,' Roarke commented as he held the flyer motionless, far above the Teletsian ground troops. 'The Plimpet regiment will no doubt stay in this area in case our people invade again.'

'That's something – one less Teletsian regiment to deal with. By the way, I apologise for being short with you,' Rajay said to Garma, sitting quietly in the back of Roarke's flyer. 'We have to attack Teletsia, and need people who know their way around the town to guide us.'

'Your Highness, I've only been there once, for a short visit when I was a boy.'

'For some reason we need you. It was very cool on vibrations,' Roarke explained, from the driving seat. 'How are you, by the way?'

'Fine, thanks to Your Highnesses.'

'Call me Roarke – or Dr Tarl if you prefer!'

Lee, at the boathouse, asked a fishing boat to wait for him hidden in the long reeds, while he made sure everyone was safely away. He left most of his gear, including his coconut, on the boat. He went back to the roadside and could not see any of his soldiers, but round the corner came three armed Teletsian horsemen - scouts. They had not seen him as he was behind a tree. He quietly took off his jacket, the uniform of the Daish Shaktay army, and his sword, so he could now pass for an ordinary Teletsian, with luck. His other weapons were concealed under his long, loose overshirt.

'Check out that boathouse, you two. I'll wait on the road,' ordered the leader.

Unfortunately at this moment the leader's horse noticed Lee, and so did its rider, who rode towards where he stood. The other two were looking at the many tracks of the departed soldiers on the ground, going towards the boathouse.

'Looks like they all left on boats,' shouted one scout, from the direction of the boathouse.

'Where are the rest of your lot?' demanded the one who was coming closer to Lee.

'I don't know what you mean, sir. I live up yonder and heard a great noise, so came to see what was going on, but when I got here the place was deserted.'

'I need to ask you a few questions.'

'Sir, I'll be happy to tell you what I know, which isn't much.' Lee was standing a little way back from the road and the other two scouts could not see him.

'Look at this, sir,' Lee pointed to his uniform jacket and sword, which he had put on the ground. 'Seems like some soldier left his stuff behind.' The scout dismounted to inspect Lee's discarded belongings, Lee grabbed him in a wrench he had learnt from Witten the Tong, hit him hard and temporarily stunned him. Lee was strong, skilful and an experienced fighter, and before the man had fully realised what had happened, Lee vaulted on his horse and urged it up the path by the stream where Stellamar had led them five years before.

It was over in a moment but now he had to escape. The other horsemen were soon after him and as they galloped they unsheathed their swords. Lee could now use his key in fiery discus mode, which he did as his pursuers closed the gap, because the horse he was riding was slow and stumbled frequently in this treacherous open woodland. He let fly the key, the Teletsian scouts were beheaded, then he jumped off his stolen horse to retrieve it, hoping its owner would not appear while he was on the ground. He remounted and galloped on, making for the bar of quicksand and praying it would not be guarded.

In the early afternoon he heard the welcome boom of the surf, smelled salt in the wind and saw the coastal dunes in the distance through the sparse trees. He took off the horse's army saddlecloth and most of its giveaway military harness, so he was left with a basic saddle and simple bridle, and rode towards the road. It was deserted but he did not recognise it. He checked on the vibrations and it came out coolest to go right, which he did. He cautiously trotted up the road and after some time saw the track he had come in by that morning, but as he turned into it, around the corner further along the road he saw two steam cars approaching. He urged his horse on and hoped he would not be followed up the narrow sandy track through the dunes.

He reached the flat expanse of quicksand and his horse stopped, snorted and tried to turn around. He held up his Sasrar key, put his full attention on it and urged the horse on. No way would it do so; it reared up and Lee nearly fell off, so he abandoned it and continued on foot. He made a bandhan of protection over himself and ran on. The sand held his weight, but before he was across some soldiers, who had followed him in the steam car, saw him and opened fire. Luckily they missed, as they were quite far away, and soon Lee disappeared into the dunes on the further side of the quicksand.

Ahead was the beach and beyond it the causeway to the Island of Creations. The tide was high and his pursuers would doubtless drive their steam car round the quicksand, then up the beach after him. He prayed to Father Sea to save him and waded into the surf. Soon he was out of his depth and had to swim, and the cross current dragged him away from the causeway. Now and again there were rocks either just above or just below the surface of the sea, which he had to be careful to avoid. So far there was no sign of the Teletsian soldiers, who would not follow him in the water but could still kill him with their guns. The distance was much greater than he remembered from the early morning, when the tide had been low and he had been in a boat. He swam on exhausted, desperately trying to get out of range of the soldiers who were now shooting at him when they could see him in the waves. His breath was rasping, his limbs exhausted and eventually he could do little more than let himself float, praying the currents would deposit him on the Island not the mainland, where he would no doubt be picked up by the Teletsian Coast Guards.

Before all this happened Rajay had called Lee on his coconut but no one answered, because the fisherman with whom Lee had left it did not hear Rajay, and would not have known how to respond even if he had. He waited for some time, hidden in the reeds, but when Lee did not return he made his getaway, because he heard the Teletsian scouts and assumed Lee had been caught or killed.

'Lee isn't answering for some reason; maybe his nut needs recharging. There's not much more we can do here,' said Roarke. 'What now, Rajay?'

'We have to join up with Ahren and Erin, and make for Teletos.' Rajay took out his coconut. 'Erin, where are you?'

'Hello, Your Majesty,' Erin replied. 'We're hiding in woodland to the south of the road between Panvale and Lahary.'

'How about the spy vultures?'

'We've brought down twelve so far. I don't think any have escaped us but I can't be sure.'

'Excellent. Could you move eastwards? We've got to attack Teletos.'

In the late afternoon the man on guard at the lighthouse at the Island of Creations end of the causeway sent his peacocks out on a routine flight to check the beaches. They returned very agitated and the guard followed where they led, to a figure slumped on the sand. The guard ran towards him, praying that whoever it was still lived. Lee felt someone touching him and opened his eyes to see a number of peacocks standing around him and the guard peering at him.

'Whatever are you doing here?' the guard asked, as he knew Lee. 'I thought you were invading Teletsia.'

'We were, but – I'll explain later. Give me a hand to get up, I'm dead beat.' Lee vomited some sea water and collapsed again.

The surgeon did his best with Merien, and Lord Jarwhen and Lady Mercola gave him vibrations. He regained consciousness in the evening and even though he was not at all well asked to see me, alone.

'Come, sit with me,' he began quietly. 'I didn't have time to make a bandhan of protection before we went in. I was about to, but we had to move fast to save those hostages.'

'You've made it this far, surely you'll pull through,' I replied.

'I may not. We guardians knew that soon some people would be born who would make the journey to Sasrar, and then everything would start to change and our work here would be done. That's more or less happened now.'

'You can't talk like that.'

'Yes, I can. We've all had good times together and it's best if you remember those.'

I sat with him and he drifted into a peaceful sleep. Some time later I realised I could not hear his breathing any more. He had slipped away, gently, unobtrusively and with a smile on his face, but I cried and cried the whole night long. Suddenly everything was unravelling in a way which was more unpleasant than I could have ever imagined.

CHAPTER 12

AN UNDERGROUND OPERATION

In their underground prison at the ruined mansion in Teletos, Robin discovered that some other rooms leading off the cellar they were in were also intact, but search as he might he couldn't find a way out. Supper consisted of water and some sweets that Conwenna had in her other pocket. Robin had his fire-box with him to rekindle flame, so they blew out the candle and slept for a while, very uncomfortably, on the floor.

It felt like morning and Robin woke up, expecting to open his eyes to utter darkness, but there was a faint glow coming from both him and Conwenna, just below their throats, on the chest. He took his Sasrar key from under his clothing and a warm light radiated all around. He had forgotten this power of the seventh centre key, which only manifested when needed. He was delighted; now they didn't have to rely on the candles for light. He closed his eyes once more and lay on the damp floor. It was a long day with nothing to do and nothing to eat. In what they assumed was the evening they slept, and woke later, unsure of the time.

Conwenna got up and explored again, after which she sat down in the next cellar for a while. She heard a faint tapping and noticed it was coming from under a trapdoor in the floor, hidden by some fallen beams. She called Robin and meanwhile tried the door of a cupboard in the room. It swung open to reveal a round cheese and some crockery pots with lids.

'Food!' cried Conwenna with delight, taking the tops off the pots.

'Yes, but let's find out about this knocking first,' said Robin, coming in behind her, even though he was as hungry as she was. They had not noticed the trapdoor before because of the beams. Robin moved them, opened it, went down some steps, and below in a room like a dungeon, blinking in the light of the key was a haggard looking middle aged man lying in a corner with a leg-iron chaining him to the wall. He was wearing the uniform of a Teletsian officer.

'Water!' he rasped weakly, and Robin hurried back up to the other cellar to fetch some. Conwenna spied the key to the leg iron hanging on the wall the other side of the cave-like room, and freed him.

'May the Mother Earth be praised,' he got up and staggered out of his prison. 'What happened? Who are you?'

'My name is Conwenna and I used to live here, but right now we're trapped.'

'Not *the* Conwenna, the one who….?'

'Yes.'

'By the Mother Earth! I'm Woodenton, General commanding the Second Regiment, or was. I was summoned to talk strategy, but the High Priests, Sorcerers you would call them, accused me of collaborating with the rebels and threw me down here. They gave me food and water, but not since that terrible explosion.' Robin and Raynor joined them and General Woodenton's face lit up. 'Norray, I mean Raynor! They got you too?'

Raynor greeted the general, gave him some water and they helped him up to the cellar, because he was very weak. Conwenna brought the food from the cupboard and they had quite a picnic – cheese, biscuits and some dried fruit and nuts.

'So now there are four of us,' said Robin as they ate hungrily, 'but we've still got to get out of here and we're no nearer that.'

'Oh, but we are,' the general disagreed. 'On the further side of that dungeon is a sewer. I could hear water running in it before the building collapsed and there's an iron grill gate into it. I'm sure it will lead to the canal.'

'Conwenna, do you know about this?' Robin asked.

'I know the end which goes out into the canal but not this part.'

The grill was latched but not locked, and they opened it easily. Robin went first to see if the tunnel was still open. Conwenna was shaking with fear and he or Raynor held her hand at all times. This was the worst part of all for her. In places the tunnel had been narrowed by falling masonry, but they managed to move the stones and squeeze past, and some time later, having crawled through the now dry sewer, the four of them stood on the path at the side of the canal in the early morning. A lot of people were in the ruins of the main house but no one was interested in four tattered and dirty people walking in the other direction. General Woodenton had taken off his army shirt so was in his vest, and Robin and Raynor were unshaven and looked like vagrants, of which Teletos had many these days. They made their way towards Mrs Fisher's house and after banging on the door were welcomed in – very warmly. They sat in the living room while she gave them more food and drink.

'Raynor, I'm asking for the amnesty you promised,' said General Woodenton. 'I am no longer a supporter of the Sorcerers' Teletsia.'

'I should think not, sir, after what they did to you! Yes, of course my pledge will be honoured, but maybe you should return to your regiment as if nothing has happened. In that way you might be able to help us a lot.'

'It's now stationed to the south west of Teletos,' explained Robin.

'When I arrived, the Sorcerers put me straight in the cellar, and it's possible that no one in the army knows I was imprisoned there. Get me to our family townhouse. I'll pick up a clean uniform and my personal steam car, and we'll see what can be done. Trust me and I'll help you end this war very soon.'

'I can take you all wherever you want to go in the boat,' Mrs Fisher offered. 'You'll have to row though, because I'm not as strong as I used to be.'

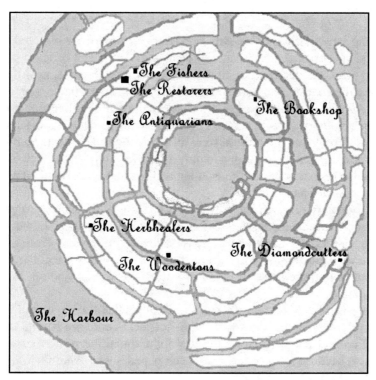

Teletos after the earthquake

She went to the wholesale fish market and bought some baskets of fish, so as to make the fugitives look like fishermen delivering their catch. Robin and Conwenna helped Mrs Fisher punt; Conwenna because she knew how to, and Robin, because although he wasn't very skilful, was strong. Raynor and the general were still weak from their imprisonment so couldn't help much.

Teletos was in chaos because there were now three small groups of Sorcerers trying to take control of the city. General Woodenton was dropped off at the water gate of his town mansion, and once safely indoors he had a much needed bath and changed his clothes. The others punted on to the Jewellers' Quarter, to the house of Sparkly Diamondcutter, where they found Sparkly and Borry sitting in the kitchen, in despair. Borry jumped up when he saw them.

'May the Mother Earth be praised!' he cried. 'How did you get out of the ruins?'

'By her grace! The Great Mother looks after her own,' replied Robin with a smile. 'Have you got our coconuts?'

'Yes, over there,' he pointed to their shoulder bags, hanging in the corner of the room. Robin contacted me, then Rajay, and finally Raynor gave Tandi an abbreviated version of the truth. I don't know which of us was the most relieved.

In the late afternoon General Woodenton set off from his opulent town house in his personal steam car, complete with driver and official flag on the roof, to meet his aide Raynor, alias Captain Norray Nalanda, near the bridge carrying the road to southern Teletsia. By then Raynor had a very valuable document with him that Sparkly and Conwenna spent the afternoon preparing. Sparkly's second job was forging documents for resistance workers. Those who had imprisoned the general were all dead, and to all intents and purposes he was a senior general returning to duty after a few days leave. He and Raynor reached his regiment late in the evening and he immediately called a meeting of his senior officers.

'I fortunately received most of my instructions and managed to get out of the High Priests' Headquarters before the fateful explosion,' he began. 'We have been ordered to surrender. Here is the charter from Their Holinesses. I'm not sure who I'm supposed to surrender to, because they were going to tell me later, but were regrettably all killed. No doubt we'll soon find out from some other source.'

The general held up Sparkly and Conwenna's handiwork, complete with a forged official seal of Teletsia, so all his officers could see it. The news was flashed around the country by the few light signalling posts that were still operative, because most of them had been wiped out by Ahren's troop, Erin's army or the Resistance Groups.

CHAPTER 13

THE TEMPLE OF SUPPORT REVISITED

The partisans who had diverted the attention of the Plimpet regiment when Lee was organising the retreat all either disappeared back to wherever they came from or joined Namoh's force. The Daish Shaktay soldiers who had escaped on the fishing boats returned to the Island of Creations and were told to set up camp on the beach facing Teletsia, and to look as if they were about to invade again. Numerous small craft bobbed about in the sea near the shore. The Plimpet regiment marched to the Teletsian shore, and the two forces faced each other across the strait, because as yet the order to surrender had not reached the Teletsians, or if it had it had not been accepted.

The regiments in the area of the Temple of Support did not get the surrender message either because there were no signalling posts up there and the posts in Lahary, Clatan and Panvale were out of action. Once the soldiers from these places had left to defend the Temple there was not much to stop Rajay, with Namoh's force, and Ahren and the other partisans moving in. That afternoon Derwin, doing a routine inspection in his flyer, noticed the regiments still around the Temple. He contacted Rajay, busy at the Lahary Slave Farm healing slaves, capturing Specials and Sorcerers, and generally cleaning the place up with the help of his men, now they no longer had to march on Teletos - thanks to General Woodenton, Raynor, Robin and Conwenna.

'Either they don't know about the surrender at the Temple of Support, or they don't want to know,' said Rajay. 'I'll call General Woodenton and see what we can do.'

Rajay called him and he said a messenger should be sent. Rajay contacted Garma, who was with Namoh, guarding the main road from the west of the country to Teletos, with some of the cavalry.

The next morning Garma rode up the track to the Temple of Support dressed as an officer of the Teletsian army. He had a coconut in his saddle bag.

'Halt! Password!' demanded a group of soldiers as he neared the temple. In the distance Garma could see one of the regiments – a good two thousand strong.

'I don't know it,' replied Garma. 'I'm from General Woodenton, Gyan-on-Sea Regiment. I have a very important message to deliver to your commanding officer.'

'Then you should know the travelling password. You don't go any further unless you give it,' ordered an officious young conscript who appeared to be in charge. Garma felt his vibrations. They were appalling; he was probably a trainee Sorcerer. Garma rode back down the track until he was out of sight of the watch post, got his coconut out and called General Woodenton, who soon gave Garma the necessary information, after which he returned to the checkpoint.

'The travelling password for this week is "doomsday".'

'How come you suddenly know it?' asked the self-important conscript.

'I consulted General Woodenton. Now please let me through.' He was allowed to proceed because the conscript was extremely stupid, did not think Garma's remark unusual and only obeyed orders. Garma was escorted to the tent of General Ironcore, who was in charge of one of the regiments.

'So, you've got news from Woodenton?' he began. His vibrations, although not good, could have been much worse.

'Yes, sir. I gather you're not aware that the High Priests have surrendered.'

'I most certainly am not, and I can't possibly accept this on a verbal instruction from someone I've never met before,' replied the general. 'Who are you, anyway?'

'I'm one of the general's aides. We've been in contact with our conquerors and they've lent me a means whereby you can talk to General Woodenton yourself.' Garma took his coconut out of his pack. He tapped in the code for Raynor.

'Captain Norray Nalanda?' said Garma to Raynor, maintaining military formality. 'I'm with General Ironcore near the Clatan stone circle.' The general was flabbergasted by this strange nut and when he heard the voice of General Woodenton was even more wary.

'This is Woodenton,' he began. 'I'm near Teletos.'

'How do I know this isn't some sorcery of our enemies?' replied General Ironcore. 'It's impossible for a man to fit inside a coconut, so there can't be a voice coming out of it.'

'Our conquerors are far superior to us technologically. Call it sorcery if you like, but it works. Listen Ironcore, does the name Drusilla Prospector mean anything to you?'

'We don't mention her in public.'

'Meaning you know she's behind the High Priests. She's dead, done for, and she won't be back, ever. How are you all feeling near the stone circle?'

'I'm fine, but many of the Specials and regulars are suffering from shaking attacks, and all the High Priests are desperately sick.'

'Exactly. There's no way we can oppose the people who have defeated us, because the very forces of nature are on their side. Garma, I know you're listening. My aide tells me you must give the great gift with your attention while I speak.

'General Ironcore, the High Priests and any in league with them are doomed. If we attack these invaders we will be destroyed, because their sorcery is far stronger than ours. I have here a document from the governing body of High Priests ordering us to surrender, and if you need to see it I can get it to you tomorrow.' Garma was standing behind General Ironcore, awakening his Tree of Life. Suddenly Garma felt coolness on his hands.

'I must admit what you say about surrendering makes a lot of sense,' said Ironcore in an unexpected about turn, 'but the other two generals here won't see it that way.'

'The leading High Priests have again been destroyed when the entire building they were using as a headquarters caved in on top of them. This is well known in Teletos,' continued Woodenton. 'But now for the part most people *don't* know. Underneath it all was Drusilla Prospector. Our conquerors refer to her as the Queen Wasp, and that being so the swarm of High Priests now has no queen, so it is finished. Our conquerors are our liberators and I suggest you accept that, because otherwise you'll find yourself going the same way as Drusilla, the Specials and the High Priests.'

'Alright, I believe you. There's definitely something going on we simply cannot oppose. What's the next step?'

'Allow your conscripts to go home. Give your regular soldiers that option too. Any Specials or High Priests have one sensible alternative: surrender. If they do they'll be escorted to an island in the Great Sea. If they don't they'll be killed.'

'Most will fight to the death,' objected Ironcore. 'The regulars and Specials are completely hypnotised by the High Priests, and not only that, they'll kill me for suggesting surrender.'

'May I share an idea?' interrupted Garma.

'Of course, Nalanda, that's what you're there for,' said Woodenton, pretending to be somewhat sharp with him, via the coconut.

'Maybe General Ironcore could tell the other generals that the order is to return to the fort at Lahary immediately. Meanwhile we'll put the word around for the conscripts to desert.'

'Ironcore,' interrupted Woodenton. 'Do yourself a favour and follow my aide's advice. If you do you'll live to enjoy a much more peaceful, free and happy Teletsia, and I guarantee you won't be killed or banished.'

'I'll try.'

The plan didn't materialise. General Ironcore's superior, General Steck, overruled him and ordered the troops to prepare for battle the following morning, as scouts had reported a force approaching from the south-west. Garma returned to Namoh's cavalry, now between the temple and Lahary. This was the force General Steck's scouts had seen. Garma gave Namoh information about the Teletsian troops: how many, where they were and so on. Up at the Temple of Support the conscripts knew by now who they could trust with the information about the surrender and many of them slipped away under cover of darkness. General Ironcore also disappeared.

That evening Lakriman Woodseller, who had been given a coconut by Derwin, contacted Rajay. He reported that a large contingent of regular soldiers, Sorcerers and Specials from the now defunct Woodenton regiment was on the road to Lahary Fort. Rajay raised Erin Heber on the coconut.

'Erin, it's Rajay again.'

'What's new, Your Majesty?'

'We need your help. Where are you?'

'South of Lahary. We ambushed a few groups of Specials and Sorcerers and have taken over some Specials Posts. We're making our way towards Teletos, as you asked.'

'I'm going to have to ask you to change your plans yet again,' and Rajay explained the message from Lakriman.

'How do we deal with them this time?'

'The Sorcerers? The same way as you did the vultures, with your subtle weapons, or if that doesn't work brute force. The Sorcerers can't hurt you. Their power is getting weaker by the moment now Drusilla is gone and they can't stand against the bandhan or the keys. As for the Specials – their never-miss guns won't work if you all do your bandhans. Plus there are over a thousand of you and only about five hundred of them.'

Erin, on the road between Lahary and Woodenton, soon saw Roarke's flyer approaching, bringing Garma, still wearing the uniform of a captain in the Teletsian army. Roarke left Garma and flew off to do some reconnaissance work. Later he returned to say the enemy was approaching over the next hill, then took off for Rajay's encampment, where he was needed. Erin had a horse, which he lent to Garma, who rode it towards the approaching force of regulars, Sorcerers and Specials. Erin's men were hidden in the fields of tall maize at the sides of the road.

'Hello,' began Garma, 'are you from the Woodenton Regiment?'

'That's us. Loyal to the fatherland,' said the leading Sorcerer.

'I'm from the Lahary Regiment,' lied Garma. He was getting good at this. 'If you march quickly you can make it to Lahary Fort before the invaders.'

'Alright, but you must come with us,' replied the Sorcerer.

'That is not possible, because I've got to warn the Panvale contingent.'

'You come with us,' repeated the Sorcerer.

'I've told you, I have another mission,' reiterated Garma.

'I can't read his mind,' complained the second Sorcerer.

'Nor can I,' said the first one. 'He's a traitor, and with the enemy!' He started to try and annihilate Garma, but because Garma was wearing a four petalled key the Sorcerer himself began smouldering. Erin's men poured out from the maize fields and the Sorcerers tried some annihilating but were cut down by Erin's men before they even had time to destroy themselves. The Specials had not had time to prime their never-miss guns and were outnumbered by Erin's tough troop. Soon the surviving regulars, Specials and Sorcerers surrendered.

'Give us your weapons, including the Sorcerers' staffs,' ordered Erin. 'Then we'll escort you to the fort at Lahary.' They had no option but to agree. Erin called Rajay on his coconut.

'Your Majesty, I'm sending you some rats to put in the Lahary trap.'

'We'll use the fort as a holding jail for any Specials and Sorcerers who surrender, until we can send them to the time warp island. Your men can guard it.'

At that moment a young Sorcerer of about Garma's age emerged from the maize field where he had been hiding, having run into it when the skirmish began. Garma went over to him, thinking it odd he should reveal himself when he could have stayed hidden.

'You too,' ordered Garma, 'put your staff on the ground and your hands on the top of your head.'

'Sir,' he replied, 'you may not believe me but I was a friend of Raynor Antiquarian at the academy when we were both there. I knew that place was all wrong, but unlike him I didn't have the courage to run away, and finished up becoming a High Priest, or as you would say, a Sorcerer. I've never done anything evil or murderous, I promise you. Is there any chance I might be forgiven?'

'I don't know. Wait a moment.' Garma told the rest of the group to start marching towards Lahary, which they did, and when this was well under way he called Rajay with his coconut. 'Your Majesty, I've got a young Sorcerer here who says he was a friend of Raynor's and wants to mend his ways. I don't know what to do with him.'

'How are his vibrations?' Rajay asked.

'Not as bad as you'd expect.'

'Try giving him awakening. It might work.'

So Garma got off his horse, tied it to a tree and sat down on the side of the road with the young Sorcerer, who soon felt a cool breeze on his hands, indicating his Tree of Life had awakened and the darkness in his soul was starting to lift. Of all the Sorcerers in Teletsia, he was the only one to come right.

The next morning what was left of the Teletsian armed forces faithful to the Sorcerers arrayed themselves between the invaders and the Temple of Support. Some were shaking, some were having mild epileptic fits and some were very scared because of dreadful reputation of the place, but they stood their ground. A few Sorcerers stood to one side in a huddle, on a knoll near the temple, unsure as to whether to try to annihilate the opposing army or whether not to bother with what they now knew to be a hopeless exercise.

A cavalry force could be seen approaching from the southwest and the Teletsians loaded their cannon. Then the main force of the invaders unexpectedly appeared from the other side of the temple. This was because Roarke, up above with his spyglass, had warned Namoh the whereabouts of the powerful cannon and which way they were pointing. Namoh had led his men round the back of the temple in the night and as the sun rose, he appeared from the south east at the head of his cavalry.

He gave the order to charge and the ground shook as nearly a thousand horses galloped over the rise. They knew they had to wait until the enemy showed aggression before they could use *their* powerful weapons, which were only for defence, not attack. Namoh was in the front, galloping flat out, closely followed by everyone else. He was having trouble controlling the gold and silver stallion he had exchanged with Rajay, and suddenly he and his horse crashed to the ground. The Teletsians saw Namoh fall and discharged their weapons, assuming the invaders were in range, that some sniper had brought down their leader and that most of them had not heard the order to fire. But the invaders were *not* in range, so the bullets from the Teletsians fell short. They could not aim their bigger guns through the stones of the temple, so none of the freedom forces were hurt.

Now they had been attacked, the invaders let fly their keys – many four petalled ones, which had been upgraded by Roarke to operate in fiery discus mode, and a whole cloud of them flew like a meteor shower towards the Sorcerers' Teletsians surrounding the Temple of Support. The keys selectively beheaded most of those whose hearts were rotten. Very soon it was over and the survivors surrendered.

Rajay, who had been riding among the troops, reached Namoh, lying on the ground after the rest of the cavalry charged on. Two men had dismounted to see to him. He was lying on his face and not moving. Blood was seeping from his right side. Rajay jumped off his horse and made to turn him over.

'Sire, we'd best not touch him until the medics arrive; even if he's alive, his back may be broken,' said one of the men. Rajay knelt down, devastated. Not only had he lost Merien, a friend of many lifetimes, and Zafan and Bonor, so dear to him in this one, but now yet another of his faithful companions was in deep trouble, possibly dead. He cautiously felt for a pulse and was relieved to find one, although it was weak. Namoh's other arm was under his body at a very unnatural angle. Rajay stood up, got his coconut from his saddle bag and called Roarke, flying high overhead.

'Come quickly, Namoh's been hurt.'

'How badly?' asked Roarke.

'I don't know, but he's unconscious.'

'That's tragic. We've won the battle; I can see from up here.'

'I'm aware of that, but I hope we've not lost Namoh. His brother gave his life for Daish Shaktay - it would be too much if Namoh gives his for Teletsia.' Soon the medical team arrived and the doctor slowly turned Namoh. He opened his eyes and looked dazed.

'Rajay! Where am I?' he gasped painfully. Rajay could see his arm was badly crushed, and possibly his chest, ribs and lungs as well.

'My prayer is answered - you're conscious!'

'I was floating high above the earth, but when you came, somehow I returned. The pain….. let me go.'

'No! I'm not losing you too! You *will* get better. Roarke and I are going to take you to Stellamar and her father. They saved you last time.' Namoh closed his eyes, struggling for breath.

'Asha told me,' he whispered weakly. 'Danard has come back… I can too. It's been wonderful to be with you… but…' it seemed he was going.

'Namoh! Stellamar wants to marry you. You must live! Do you want to break her heart as well as mine?' Namoh opened his eyes and tried to focus them.

'Are you serious? Isn't she – too far above me?'

'You're absolutely right for each other.'

Namoh closed his eyes and passed out, but his breathing was easier. His horse had stumbled into an animal's hole and fallen heavily on him, but having done so, got up and galloped off with the rest of the cavalry. Rajay helped lift his friend into Roarke's flyer and went with him. Rajay was silent; his full attention was on giving Namoh vibrations as he lay, half on his knee.

Roarke did not speak either, he was trying to get as much speed as possible out of his machine. Together they took Namoh to the house of the Pearl Lords. As they landed, Stellamar and her father were waiting with stretcher bearers, and for the second time he arrived there nearly dead.

'I'm here for you, Namoh,' said Stellamar softly, as he was put on a stretcher. He smiled feebly.

Roarke followed them into the surgery and had his high powered spyglass in his hand. The nurse laid Namoh out and carefully removed his clothing, while the doctor put the bottle of liquid under his nose that would make him lose consciousness completely when he inhaled the fumes coming from its contents. Roarke was standing behind, adjusting some knobs on his spyglass.

'Look through this, doctor,' he suggested, 'and you'll be able to see inside Namoh's body, where the bones are broken.'

'Is this another of your inventions, Your Highness?'

'Yes, more or less. You can also look at the soft tissues,' Roarke demonstrated.

'This is incredible!' cried the doctor after looking at Namoh's arm, shoulder, rib cage and abdomen, 'I can see exactly where I need to operate. It's serious – I don't know if I can save him.'

'Hurry, we don't have much time,' urged Stellamar. She could feel Namoh's life force fading, even though he was surrounded by those he loved and who loved him dearly. Together they tended his wounds, the surgeon with his skill, Roarke with his advanced technology, and Rajay and Stellamar with their vibrations, the highest form of love. All the guardians gave him vibrations, one taking over from the other throughout the rest of the day, that night and the next day and night too. At times he seemed to be dying, but then his iron will to live returned, and he survived this critical period, breathing with difficulty on account of his badly crushed ribs. Like all of Rajay's friends he had a phenomenal inner resilience.

Back at the Temple of Support any Specials and the few Sorcerers who had survived the keys and surrendered were escorted back to Lahary Fort. All the keys had finished up in the middle of the temple, in between the four great menhirs. Everyone knelt in gratitude to the Mother Earth and thanked her for this final victory which enabled Teletsia to be free of the accursed Sorcerers and their regime of fear.

There were no casualties at all on the side of the invaders, apart from Namoh. When the Teletsian troops saw him fall and discharged their weapons at the invaders, they were still out of range, but because the Teletsians had shown aggression our forces were justified in letting go their keys in fiery discus mode.

Only the Plimpet regiment still had to be dealt with, so Roarke picked up Garma and flew with him to General Woodenton, with his regiment outside Teletos. They landed the flyer in front of the General's headquarters, a large tent in the middle of the camp.

'Now that's a grand way to come and see your commanding officer!' laughed the general as Garma hurried towards him. 'Good to see you, Garma. And who is your pilot?'

'May I introduce Prince Roarke of Vittalia?'

'What an honour, and how can I help you both?' The general greeted Roarke respectfully.

'Sir, we need your help,' Garma went on. 'The Plimpet regiment has not surrendered and is on the shore, stopping the rest of the Daish Shaktay soldiers invading again. If you have the surrender document, and could take it to the general in command and show it to him, maybe he would see sense. We do not want to have another battle, because if we do, we may not be as lucky as we were at the Temple of Support. We'll take you to the Plimpet regiment in the flyer.'

'You're absolutely correct. We mustn't risk losing any more of our soldiers' lives. Anything to get a chance to go in your flyer! But they may shoot us out of the sky when we approach them.'

'They wouldn't manage that,' Roarke assured him, 'the flyer is protected by an invisible shield. But they might destroy us when we get out of it.'

'I'll fetch the document, and then we'll figure out how to show it to the Plimpet general without getting killed in the process. It's General Sparkus, isn't it?'

'Yes, that's him,' added Garma.

'We've met on occasions, although I can't say I found him very pleasant.'

General Woodenton went back to his tent, a luxurious affair with flags on the corners and sentries guarding the entrance, to fetch the precious forged charter that was saving so many lives. When he reappeared he had Raynor with him, wearing the uniform of a Teletsian officer. He still looked rather thin and pale but his face lit up when he saw Roarke and Garma.

'I've called some of our partisans who are in the Plimpet area and when we get there they'll lend you horses, so you can turn up to see General Sparkus with the sort of transport the Teletsian army will expect,' grinned Roarke. 'Now let's go. Raynor, you squeeze in too. You mustn't talk to me while we're flying or we might fall out of the sky, because I'll hold the flyer up with my attention as much as anything else, but it would be better if both of you come with General Woodenton. It'll look more genuine if you have two officers with you.' General Woodenton looked understandably nervous.

'Sir,' Raynor set his mind at rest, 'Prince Roarke designs these flyers, and he knows more about what he can do with them than anyone. Don't worry, we'll get there safely.'

'If you say so,' he replied apologetically. 'I can see the new Teletsia is going to be very different from the one I'm used to. OK, let's not waste any more time.'

General Woodenton again played his part to perfection, and the last Teletsian regiment surrendered on the beach between the quicksand and the causeway.

Small bands of Sorcerers and Specials kept arriving at Lahary, begging to be let in, because it was known that no one inside the fort would be harmed by the conquerors. Erin and his men were quite happy to undertake the guarding of the fort and were welcomed by the people of Lahary. Rajay returned to the troops as soon as Namoh was out of danger, so Erin finally met him. The mountain men, under their much loved duke, were disappointed that they had not done more fighting.

'Think yourselves lucky,' Rajay told a group of Erin's officers, 'my freedom struggle lost me many good men and some of my closest friends. Fighting may sound glorious and valiant, but in reality it's a vicious, bloody and heart-rending business. You saw enough to know that. Having you there as backup was a great help to us.'

Ahren's partisans, the Daish Shaktay cavalry, and Lee with the rest of the Daish Shaktay force, entered Teletos after spending a few days at the slave farms on the way there. Gwant and Mabron hurried to Clatan, where they discovered to their horror that their parents had been arrested and mesmerised. They were almost the last people in the country to have suffered in this way.

They were still in the lockup of the Special's Office in Clatan and the twins tried to free their parents of their mesmerism. Mrs Riverside responded but not their father. Later Ahren and many others went to help them but Mr Riverside never fully recovered – he completely lost his dogged determination to become rich and respected, became almost childlike and was unable to make any decisions at all. Because of this his sons took over the running of the farm.

Robin and Conwenna stayed in Teletos with Sparkly Diamondcutter. Robin coordinated the different Urban Resistance Groups and made sure calm and order prevailed during the surrender and changeover of power. As soon as it was safe and we were sure the other regiment near Teletos had accepted the surrender, and Rajay and the rest were satisfied that there were no more Specials or Sorcerers lurking nearby, Tandi, her children, Lord Jarwhen and Lady Mercola, Marimba, our parents, me and some other people from the Island were brought to Teletos in the *Prince Enithar*. The Daish Shaktay navy sailed up the estuary as our escort and it was a grand way to return home.

There was an official reception for all seven of us - how different from the day we had left nearly six years before! As we walked through the town flower petals were thrown from upstairs windows carpeting the streets, and music played on every corner. Children gave us garlands and bunches of flowers, and crowds cheered us everywhere.

Lotus and Daisy, Tandi and Raynor's twins, had the best day of their young lives as onlookers showered them with sweets, dolls and other toys. It was a long walk through the city I remembered so well from my childhood and soon the twins' little feet started to hurt, so Raynor, Robin and the others took turns to carry them on their shoulders. Conwenna and Derwin collected their presents in large baskets donated for the purpose. Tandi also soon became tired, because of her pregnancy, as did I, and just as we were about to drop out of the procession a man with a mule cab appeared and offered us a lift.

'You'll be fine with him,' Conwenna gave him a smile and a wave of her hand. 'It's Mr Angel, who helped save me from the Sorcerers.'

The reception was in a large square – usually a market place - and the guardians of Teletsia, Stellamar and her family, presented us seven with the keys of the city. An enormous crowd had gathered, there were speeches of gratitude for us 'rebels' and the many others who had helped to free our country, and bonds of eternal friendship were formally made between the new Teletsia and the King of Daish Shaktay, the Crown Prince of Vittalia and the Prime Minister of Chussan, in other words our friends Rajay and Roarke, and Robin, who was standing alongside the other guardians, now revealed as the spiritual advisors of our world. Lord Coban, the elder guardian of Teletsia, called Conwenna over.

'Young lady, please accept this token of our gratitude,' and he put a diadem with four petalled flowers made of gold and coral on her head.

'Today, you must look like a queen,' he said loudly, so at least some of the onlookers could hear. 'Teletsia is to be a democracy from now on, but your extraordinary bravery deserves special recognition.'

Conwenna looked extremely embarrassed.

'You should have this, not me,' she said to Stellamar, who took the diadem off, unhooked the jewels from the gold frame which made them into a crown, and it turned into a necklace.

'This is for you,' she said, giving Conwenna a hug and putting it round her neck. 'It looks lovely and you truly deserve it.' The crowd roared in applause because they knew the stories about us.

Lord Jarwhen invited Rajay to say a few words, and called for quiet, so he could be heard by the crowd.

'The freeing of Teletsia has been a group effort, and many of us have been involved, like a swarm of bees, all working in harmony,' Rajay began. 'My army and navy no doubt helped, and little could have been achieved without the numerous partisans and Resistance Groups all over the country. But nothing would have changed permanently unless two things had happened. Firstly, the one known as the Queen Wasp, who was behind the Sorcerers, had to be disposed of, and secondly, many of you had to have your inner awakening, which changed the level of awareness in the country and enabled everything to work out, seemingly effortlessly and spontaneously. For both these happenings you must thank the seven young people who fled to the north, and also the husband of one of them, Robin Markand.'

Rajay asked Robin and the rest of us to stand forth, and there was another roar of applause.

As we were all leaving, a poor man with two boys, dressed in clean but simple clothes, came up to Conwenna. She recognised him as the rubbish collector who had helped her escape from the Sorcerers' palace, and

he introduced his children, now both going to school thanks to her gift of golden bangles. The celebrations finished with a grand open air meal in the Antiquarian's back garden, for those of us who had come to know each other so well over the years, and Raynor showed everyone the seat by the fish pond where we had first read the prophecy.

Lord Coban and Lord Jarwhen took charge of setting up the new government. Initially there was a Council of Elders, which included the senior guardians of Teletsia and a number of responsible citizens such as Professor Nalanda, Erin Heber - no longer a duke, Hograr Dyeman the farmer, Pat Foodman from Gyan-in-Sea, Lakriman Woodseller and Raynor's father, Kitab Antiquarian. Raynor, Lee and Ahren, along with Stellamar and some young people who had been leaders of the Resistance Groups, such as Coff Coffeeman, and Saray and Garma Nalanda, took an active part in reorganising the entire country. General Woodenton became the head of the army and the new police force, and he made sure they were much more friendly than the dreaded Specials. The Nalanda family were reunited when their mother was found in a slave farm near Darzeet, and freed of her mesmerism by Lee and Ahren.

CHAPTER 14

THE SWARM OF BEES

In one way that is the end of the story, but stories don't ever really end. The night Merien died all the guardians felt his passing, as they were very close on a subtle level, and we were all devastated.

They spoke about him often as everyone missed him so much.

'He had the right name,' observed Robin some days later, when we had got over the initial shock. 'He was so joyful, he breezed through life, so detached and so at ease in any situation.'

'But we guardians also make mistakes, and regrettably, failing to put on the bandhan of protection probably cost him his life,' continued Roarke.

'I should have been more alert and saved him,' added Rajay.

'You couldn't be everywhere,' Lord Jarwhen tried to ease Rajay's conscience, 'but it's tragic that he had to give his life for Teletsia.'

The surviving Sorcerers, who had lost virtually all their sinister power, and any remaining Specials, most of whom now behaved like witless animals - and no one could do anything about this - were duly shipped off to the time warp island in the sea and never seen again. When Lee and his parents went to see the ruins of their home, they discovered many stacks of documents in a locked outhouse in the yard, which had apparently belonged to Drusilla Prospector. They were the records of the meetings of the leading Sorcerers. When we read these we realized how close they had been to destroying us, right back to when Raynor's brother Mardhang had been spying for them, when we escaped from Teletsia. It made Raynor feel better, because he had always felt bad about his brother's sorry end.

Some days after our victory celebration we were back on the Island of Creations, Robin and I were talking with Rajay under our favourite tree, and

Namoh was with us. He was now well enough to sit in the garden and Stellamar was beside him. His right arm would never allow him to wield a sword or gun again, although he would be able to use it for anything not requiring strength, and at least he would walk.

'I should never have let you take that stallion, and then you would have been alright. As you're well aware, some horses look where they are going, and some don't, and he was too headstrong,' began Rajay.

'It could have happened to anyone, on any horse,' insisted Namoh.

'I doubt it. It's noble of you to take that attitude.'

'Do you want me to go home quickly in Roarke's big flying ship, or with the navy?' Namoh pointedly changed the subject.

'You've got some unfinished business here, haven't you?'

'What do you mean?'

'Your wedding! I can always find people to help me look after Daish Shaktay. You'll have to stay in Teletsia because Stellamar is needed here. You can be very useful, what with all your experience.'

'If you say so,' he and Stellamar smiled at each other.

'And where wives are concerned, you have the edge on me - Zulani saved my life once before we married but Stellamar has saved yours twice.'

'Let's just say it was a joint effort, and it's a blessing that Namoh has survived,' said Stellamar modestly.

For some months Ahren and Lee, travelling around on their flying horses, did a great job of coordinating the Freedom Bands, bands of Daish Shaktay soldiers and other people trained to dissolve the remaining slave farms and heal the slaves. There were a number of slaves who had already escaped but were still mesmerised, so the Freedom Bands visited them too and gave relief of many heartbroken families. Ahren was presented with the Clatan Slave Farm by the people of his area and after it had been cleared of its dire vibrations with the help of a number of fire ceremonies it became his lifelong home.

Raynor did not want to be involved in government because he was far more interested in reforming the way young people studied. He, Tandi and the children went to live at Gyan-on-Sea, where he was immediately given a Professorship in the Wisdom of the Tree of Life, and later became the Vice-Chancellor of the University.

Lee announced his intention to marry Coral Aydriss as soon as our land was free. She came down to Teletsia shortly after Rajay returned home and quickly won the hearts of the Teletsians by helping Lee clear the slave farms and give awakening throughout the country. After some years democratic elections were held and Lee became the Prime Minister. As the old hermit on the island suggested, Lee did occasionally pay him visits, but he has never allowed his head to become too big for his shoulders and is always approachable and friendly towards any of the people of Teletsia who need his help, added to which his children tease him, very respectfully, when their now comfortably plump father takes himself too seriously. He has been re-elected so many times it looks as if he is in the job for life, and his surname, Restorer, has turned out to be right, except he didn't restore old buildings like his father; he helped restore the whole country to sanity and happiness.

Derwin settled permanently in Vittalia. He and Roarke continue to work together and their technological developments have transformed all our lives. We of the countries of the Tree of Life have moved forward three hundred years in two decades, because Roarke and the other guardians feel it is safe for them to share the technological knowledge they brought from the other planet, locked up deep in the memory banks of their subtle systems.

Some years later Derwin visited the Melitsian Isles, the powerful kingdom in the Eastern Ocean, to demonstrate a flyer to King Zarko, who we met on our great journey at Mazdan and Master Theon's school. Derwin was asked to lead an awakening programme for the members of the court and one of Zarko's sisters and her mother noticed him, renowned as one of the children of the Teletsian prophecy. Soon after he returned home to Vittalia, an official marriage proposal arrived, and on vibrations he accepted because it was very cool to do so. When Derwin eventually met Princess Kaya he discovered his graceful, ebony-skinned fiancée was one of the most beautiful women on Navi Septa. They married, and as they got to know each other he found that her personality was as pleasing as her looks.

Roarke surprised us all by marrying Saray Nalanda, the daughter of the professor. She may have been temporarily attracted to Lee when he and Roarke first visited them, but Roarke, in his cool and discerning way, noticed her. Roarke, Saray and Garma provided the music at Lee's wedding, and he made his intentions clear soon after, with the full approval of both sets of parents. They have recently become King and Queen of Vittalia, and their concerts are famous - when they visit any of us they treat us to their beautiful compositions.

Rajay and Zulani went to Lee's wedding, although I could not, as my baby's arrival was imminent at that time. I was concerned about Conwenna, who never felt at ease in Teletsia, and I spoke to Zulani about her on our coconut. Zulani met her at the wedding celebrations, and invited her to Malak Citadel, because she had seen Conwenna's artwork and needed good designers to help start industries producing porcelain, tapestries and furniture. Conwenna was such a success that she stayed and stayed, and she, Zulani and others created the businesses that make these beautiful things for which Daish Shaktay is so renowned. Although our technology is now very advanced, so our lives are comfortable, we like anything close to us to have good vibrations, and anything beautiful and hand made by people who are awakened souls does have good vibrations.

Conwenna married a successful businessman who became one of Rajay's ministers. She met him in the course of her work and they live near Rajay and Zulani's gracious palace, since the capital moved back to Santara. Sadly, she has never had any children of her own but adopted two and because Conwenna was well known, it became fashionable to adopt, so there are virtually no orphans in the whole country.

It took Rajay some years to offload the day to day administration of Daish Shaktay so he could spend his time developing the subtler side of his citizens, in other words their awakened Trees of Life. To begin with he would sit in the council meetings of his ministers, listening to suggestions from his former companions and others, again and again telling them to collectively check their ideas and decisions on the vibrations. This is how all our countries are administered.

Ahren went to live on the farm he had been given near Clatan and some months later a groom arrived with a horse. Namoh had been going through the Pearl Lords' stables and discovered it had come with Ahren, so he sent it back. It was the one Ahren had exchanged when he escaped from the slave farm, so he decided to return it and rode over to the farm, leading it with him. He entered the farmyard, saw two girls pulling a handcart full of rose blooms and the elder one came over and patted the horse.

'It's my Brownboy!' she cried, delighted. 'You must be from the famous Ahren Dairyman, because we heard the stories and worked out he must have needed my horse for the freedom struggle. I was so happy we could help in some little way.' Ahren was taken aback.

'Um, yes,' he looked at her. She was a healthy girl, with regular features, of medium height and build, with lovely twinkling eyes and a radiant smile. There was no anger, no recrimination, only open hearted gratitude towards him.

'Could you tell Mr Dairyman how much we all want to thank him and his brave friends for giving us a new country? My family and I decided that if we ever did see the horse again we'd give it to him. Are you his groom?'

'No, I'm Ahren. I wanted to return him myself, and beg apologies.'

'Don't even mention it! Come and meet my parents. What a tremendous honour! My name is Churi.'

The family, who grew flowers for scented oils, were thrilled to have a visit from one of the country's liberators. They invited him into the front parlour and treated him with great respect, and not at all as a repentant thief. They had had their awakening some time before and Ahren showed them how to use the vibrations to improve the yield of their flowers, by vibrating some water and then putting it in the irrigation system and the well. He also showed them how to vibrate seeds and cuttings before planting them. They were fascinated and invited him to stay for a day or two. When he got home to Clatan he told his parents about Churi and how impressed he was that she wasn't at all bothered about his theft. He spoke about her for longer and more enthusiastically than might have been expected.

'You're a hero these days,' said Ahren's father, 'but it's time we found you a wife and you settled down after all this gadding around, especially now you've got that big farm to look after.'

'You'd better marry this girl,' Ahren's mother continued. 'Your father and I would much prefer you to choose someone from a similar background as us, even though we wouldn't be surprised if one day you brought home some exotic young lady suggested by your friend King Rajay.'

Ahren went out into his parent's garden, so as to be alone, and called Namoh on his coconut to tell him what his parents had said. Namoh answered, and Ahren asked to speak to Lord Coban, because he would not go ahead with something as important as marriage without the approval of one of the Teletsia guardians.

'He's not here at the moment but would Stellamar do? She's standing next to me laughing,' said Namoh.

'Yes, give her to me.'

'Hi Ahren,' Stellamar took the nut. 'What's going on? The vibrations on whatever you're talking about are tremendous.'

'I think I just met my wife.'

'I do too. Go for it. Can we come to the wedding?'

'Most definitely, as long as she accepts my proposal. I haven't asked her yet.'

Of course Churi was delighted to become Ahren's wife, having lost her heart to him when they first met. They have a daughter and two sons and live on their beautiful farm in the rich countryside north of Clatan, with fields of flowers stretching down to the river and a famous herd of dairy cows. Apart from Robin's and my flying horses, the others stayed in Teletsia and live there most of the time. They have had a number of foals and are now quite a herd.

Derwin flew me up to Chussan from Vittalia after I had been taken there in Roarke's big flyer. When Robin arrived some time later on his flying horse, my Tama was not with him and he said he hoped I didn't mind but he had left her in Daish Shaktay with Rajay. I was pleased and had had the same idea, as I rarely rode her, but never said anything as I didn't want to hurt Robin's feelings; he had taken so much trouble to train her for me. She and Rajay are the best of friends and she has been very useful to him, because although nowadays he has a flyer he prefers using Tama for short distances.

Robin immediately took up his office as Prime Minister, and very successful and popular he was too. I did not have to be the First Lady of Chussan because before we returned Albion married a girl from the mountains. Robin and I moved to Chussan City, to our little house in the garden of Albion's palace. Nog, who lived to a great age for a dog, and Kootie, Derwin's sheepdog, came to live with us because their masters had both gone south. Nog's role in helping us to get to Sasrar made him something of a celebrity.

Robin has given up politics now, and shortly before he did, Derwin came to visit and casually mentioned he had bought us a large farm some distance from Chussan City, in the foothills of the mountain range. Derwin has become so wealthy, as Roarke's chief designer, that we did not feel bad at accepting it and these days we have an agricultural college where Robin teaches the students how to farm our Mother Earth successfully but without abusing her. When we returned home after freeing Teletsia my daughter was born in due course and we have had three more children, two boys and another girl. The younger ones are at Valya's junior school in Daish Shaktay, and my elder daughter, Lark, is at Mazdan's school on the island, where he keeps a strict eye on her, because she takes after her unpredictable mother more than her reliable father.

We of the countries of the Tree of Life have a strong political alliance under the leadership of the Emperor of the Sea of Illusion. Our lands are peaceful, well defended and secure - our armies, navies and flying forces are powerful and so far no one has dared give us any trouble. Between helping to take care of our countries, raising our families and other important concerns, those of us in this story have an essential and lifelong job – we go all over the world giving the subtle knowledge to people on the other four continents and share with the vast family of Navi Septa the great joy, peace and creativity of the all-pervading divine power, which radiates through our awakened Trees of Life.

However, there was more in store. Some years later, one day I was feeding the chickens, ducks and geese on our farm, collecting the eggs and putting the birds in their huts for the night. Having done so I sat down to rest on the low wall outside the hen run, as our birds are a lively lot and one often has to chase after them to get them into their little houses. I looked out over the broad valley which spreads into flatter country in front of our house and farm buildings, and we can see the river stretching into the distance. It is so beautiful and always takes me to a deep level of blissful peace when I sit and contemplate it, but on that day something happened which went far beyond anything I had ever known before.

First I felt an inner stillness and ecstasy, and a coolness emanating from all my subtle centres, starting from the lowest one and soon enveloping my whole being. Then as this sensation rose up, like a column of golden light, to the uppermost centre, the thousand petalled flower on the top of my head, the flower seemed to open. My consciousness expanded into the skies above me and I became somehow hollow and a part of infinity. The world of matter dissolved into a world of love, of intoxicating joy, and I was suddenly aware of so many dear friends, relations and other awakened souls of Navi Septa, some unknown to me personally but known in the depths of my spiritual heart, all in some way a part of me and me of them. I felt honoured to be part of such a company and this oneness of bliss was the supreme reality.

I noticed a vast swarm of bees winging their way out to the plains, which at that time of year were a massed carpet of flowers that attracted many insects. Just as each bee made up a part of one entity – the swarm, so the individual part of me was one of those cells in the collective being which was our growing family of awakened souls on Navi Septa. There was no separate Asha any more but just oneness, and this supreme, serene oneness was paramount - any individuality was like watching a drama.

I was, in essence, an endless, eternal, infinite part of that whole, still bliss that is way beyond time and space. I was a part of and at one with that Great One, from whom all universes, all life, all that ever was, is and will be, comes from, and it was as if I was waking up after a long slumber, and now again knew who I really was. The feeling of deep love, profound gratitude and utter devotional holiness flowing out of my heart for everything, everybody and most of all for our creator cannot be put into words. It completely dominated my being in silent rapture.

I sat in wonder and some time later, as the light was fading Robin came back from the hills where he had been seeing to our flock of sheep. He came and sat beside me and saw my shining face. He understood. Somehow, he was no longer only my much loved husband, but also a spark of infinite and eternal joy, a part of the cosmic swarm of bees of which we were all a cell.

'You felt it too? It's great, isn't it?' he said.

'You can say that again!' I replied.

'That's only the start of the next stage.'

'You mean you already know about this?'

'It's been a part of me for lifetimes. Our whole planet, what is called 'the Earth' is like that now, and everyone there lives this. This is why we wanted to come and share it with you.'

'Thank you, Robin. Thank all of you guardians.'

'The ecstasy gets deeper as more worlds and their inhabitants join the oneness, and there are many inhabited worlds throughout the millions of galaxies in the universe. We are deeply honoured to be instruments of this, the whole purpose of creation.' Robin paused and looked out over the plain, then went on, 'Not only that, if I hadn't come here, I wouldn't have met you, and that's been quite an experience. By the way, what's for supper?'

'Grilled trout. The children have been fishing and they've also cooked them. It's supposed to be a surprise for you,' I explained, because being holiday time they were all at home.

'OK, I won't spoil it. Let's go and eat.'

That evening I called Conwenna in Daish Shaktay with my coconut and she told me they had had a big fire ceremony in the garden of Rajay's palace in Santara at exactly the time I had experienced my extraordinary inner revelation, and she, and all the people there had undergone the same transformation of awareness.

'Today was the equinox, and it was exactly twenty-one years ago that we set off on our quest,' she reminded me. 'Rajay thought we should remember it with a fire ceremony. They did a big one in Teletsia, didn't Lee call you?'

'No, but I forgot to charge our nut yesterday so it wasn't working.'

The next day I called Lee, Tandi and Raynor, Ahren and my brother Derwin, and we had all experienced the same thing at the same moment. Derwin had been at his drawing board with Roarke in Vittalia, designing yet another amazing flying ship, and the others had been at the Temple of Support in Teletsia, doing a fire ceremony. This golden net of shared love, which reaches from heart to heart, is starting to cover the whole earth. By the grace of the Great Mother of all creation, who manifests through the Tree of Life within each one of us and in so many other ways, our world is being transformed into a terrestrial paradise.

Because of this our gratitude to Her could never be fully expressed, but these stories are an attempt to do so.

APPENDIX
A FEW EXTRACTS FROM THE PROPHECY

These are from the version presently in the astrologers' house in North Chussan.

This book is a warning, a salvation, a key, or a portent of doom, depending on who reads it. Teletsia is a very important country, because it is here that the root of the Tree of Life has its seat. It is from here that the awakening of the whole planet must start. Only then will the fulfilment of this world be achieved, the reason for which it was moulded from the dust of the stars, over billions of years, by the great Mother of Creation. She places the kernel of life within each suitable planet, and it will grow, slowly and steadily, and the souls she creates, first as tiny one celled creatures, will slowly rise through all the levels of life until they reach humanity. Humans must allow themselves to be elevated even further, to become a conscious part of the great cosmic being. When we become one with it, then we will know that unlimited joy which vibrates through the whole creation. We must rise to the flower, which will open on the top of the tree. That is where we will find inner peace and joy.

There will also come souls from elsewhere, the guardians, who will try to guide the people of this world, but the growth has to come from those of this planet, whose name is Navi Septa, meaning the new seven awakened inner subtle centres. The guardians cannot awaken the seeking within the inhabitants of this world; they can only guide, give advice and set an example. The seeking for inner awakening and fulfilment will come when the time is right, in the place that is right.

Man's outer side - his mind, emotions, physical body et cetera - are a reflection of his inner nature, his soul. This is the inner `Tree of Life' and it has shining flowers, like jewels, and the trunk is like a golden thread, and is a reflection of the whole universe. All the different powers of creation are reflected within us. The human soul and body are like a miniature blueprint of creation, and are connected with every aspect of it. For example, the abdomen area corresponds to the sea, over which humans need a guide. Consequently this area is the subtle seat of the power which guides man - the teacher or master. However, men who set themselves up as guides for mankind and are in fact the opposite would damage the lives of the people in the countries where they are found. On the level of the Mother Earth, which also has a 'Tree of

Life' or soul, the sea principle would be disturbed by these evil men and could eventually rise up and engulf the them and their land. It is therefore vitally important to be in tune with the universe as a whole.

There may come a time when Teletsia will be ruled by black magicians, sorcerers who pretend to be priests, and who unleash many dangerous psychic forces. They will use these forces to confuse, dominate and destroy people. When these sorcerers have almost total power a group of young people will arise, like lotuses out of a muddy pond, who will save the day when the outlook is beginning to look hopeless. These sorcerers will have certain powers of hypnotism, and will rule by fear and their ability to control the minds of their subjects, but their power can be overcome by innocence and sincerity, selfless bravery and faith in the power of righteousness.

The young people who are to be the catalysts for change must make a long journey, both inward and outward, to the far north, where the answers will be revealed. In that land they will come to understand their true potential, that inner power which exists within every individual. They will come to be at one with the force of creation, and if they can grow to spiritual maturity this vibrant awareness will flow through them and help them to be powerful instruments for benevolent change. There will be signs of this in the stars, because the hopes of the stars in the heavens are reflected in the minds and hearts of people on earth. Everything in creation is connected, and if one is in harmony with that, then the signs are there to show the way. But people are free to make mistakes, and nothing is fixed, nothing is certain. Humans have the gift of free will, and have the ability to rise to the heavens, or sink to the depths.

The first band of young travellers, or innocent ones, must start their journey from the Temple of Support. Out of this a stream flows which becomes a river and eventually reaches the sea. The temple is made of vast, roughly quarried rocks with a vague impression of an elephant's head hewn into the side of each one. There are four large menhirs making a square in the centre and many smaller ones which twist around these in a spiral. Near the end of the spiral are seven springs, in a small valley at the north of the temple. There is a hidden power in this temple and it would be foolish to abuse it.

There are seven jewelled keys to match the seven jewels of the soul, and the first one is intimately connected with this temple. The subtle centres of the inner Tree of Life correspond to these keys, which are effective in certain areas of the world. The travellers can open the inner doors of the soul with these keys, and also use these magical jewels to travel safely across the world. Without both these blessings, physical and spiritual, the difficult journey is unlikely to be accomplished successfully. The keys must not be handled by the unworthy. The people to whom they are lent or presented must give them up should the need arise, or should the custodians of the jewels need them. The keys are, among other uses, to help the seekers on their journey, and are not to be hoarded, and the travellers must be prepared to part with them when the time is right. Anyone who hoards them for their value as jewellery, or who fails to sacrifice them for the good of his or her soul, or if the keys fall into the hands of evil men, will see how they inflict destruction if used wrongly.

The agents of the forces of evil will try to stop the travellers from making their journey, because once the trees are in bloom the doom of these harmful people is at hand. The tulsi herb will nullify the destructive energies of negative beings, or even destructive spirits, and can be used by the seekers of truth to protect themselves. There will be people who actively oppose the natural course of evolution, because where there is light there is also darkness, but out of the two comes growth. When the time for the great leap of consciousness is approaching, the evil forces will manifest.

When the swarm of bees has evolved and known the nectar from the flower on the top of the tree, it will be time to cleanse Teletsia. By this time the visitors from afar will be with the members of the swarm, and will help them in every way. These visitors from the blue and green planet of the star called Sol will come many times, but not all will remain true to their path. One may go sour and become a Queen Wasp. Until she is destroyed, the other wasps will regenerate, time after time. She will seek to create others like her, who only want to steal, control and dominate. They may become very powerful, but their power is dependent on the forces of darkness, and darkness can always be dissolved by light.

It came to me, the potter, the writer of this work, that in the ancient records it was written that once upon a time the world was nearly destroyed by a terrible devil who had a boon: he couldn't be killed by anything on two legs or four. So the creator made a special swarm of bees, who, as they were insects all had six legs, and the creator told them to go and sting this devil. They did as asked and the devil died. The bees did too, but they were reborn again and again, evolving through all the levels of creation, until they became people who would search for and find some higher spiritual knowledge. Like bees, who are collectively aware of their queen and operate almost like one organism, they would have a common desire – to put the world right when the outlook again looked bad.

When the jewel children have journeyed to the top of the tree and have gained some of the fruits of wisdom from there they must return to the root, for it is here that the agents of darkness will congregate in large numbers. These agents will try to prevent the flowers on the Trees of Life from opening, because if enough trees are in bloom, the power of the evil ones will be diminished. The trees which can bloom easily will be found all over Teletsia, but especially in the country districts near the Temple of Support and in the mountains to the south, beyond the great jungles. When a flame haired girl and a young man, barely more than a boy, come to Castle Mount on a flying bird, then doom is at hand for the Sorcerers. These two will have and share the great gift from the far north, and at that time the people of that mountain area in the south of Teletsia should mobilise and make their way to the plains for the final battles. It would be very foolish to tamper with the Temple of Support at this time, and evil people should not even go there, because the earth Herself might rise up and fight back.

The cosmic being of transformed humanity, the evolved swarm of bees, will emerge soon after. Nothing can stop this. Those who refuse to recognise the truth I have set out here, or who deny the existence or importance of the Tree of Life, will be given time to understand, develop and change, but if they absolutely cannot grow into the new consciousness, they will be thrown off into oblivion, because that which cannot evolve must be discarded. That is the way of Mother Nature.

This does not have to happen. Initially, all we need do is to allow the Tree of Life to be awakened within us. Then instead of being cast down into an abyss of deep water, we can gently enter this ocean of eternity and infinity, and float sweetly and gently, surrendering to the quietly rocking motion of the waves of time, and will be washed to the shores of that new land of beauty and wonder. The Great Mother of Creation will see to this, if we surrender to her love, wisdom and power, and her ability to bring all things to fulfilment.

All who heed this prophecy will be safe and saved, and will awake, like an animal that has been hibernating through the cold dark winter, to a sunny spring morning, to explore this new divine existence. There will be many, from all the nations and peoples, who will share this experience and it will be very soon, once the lands of the Tree of Life are free and enough people from these countries have their Trees of Life awakened, and are eternally grateful to the Great Mother who has made this possible.

Lightning Source UK Ltd.
Milton Keynes UK
UKOW021032221011

180760UK00001B/24/P